MW00574812

SALT-GLAZE CERAMICS

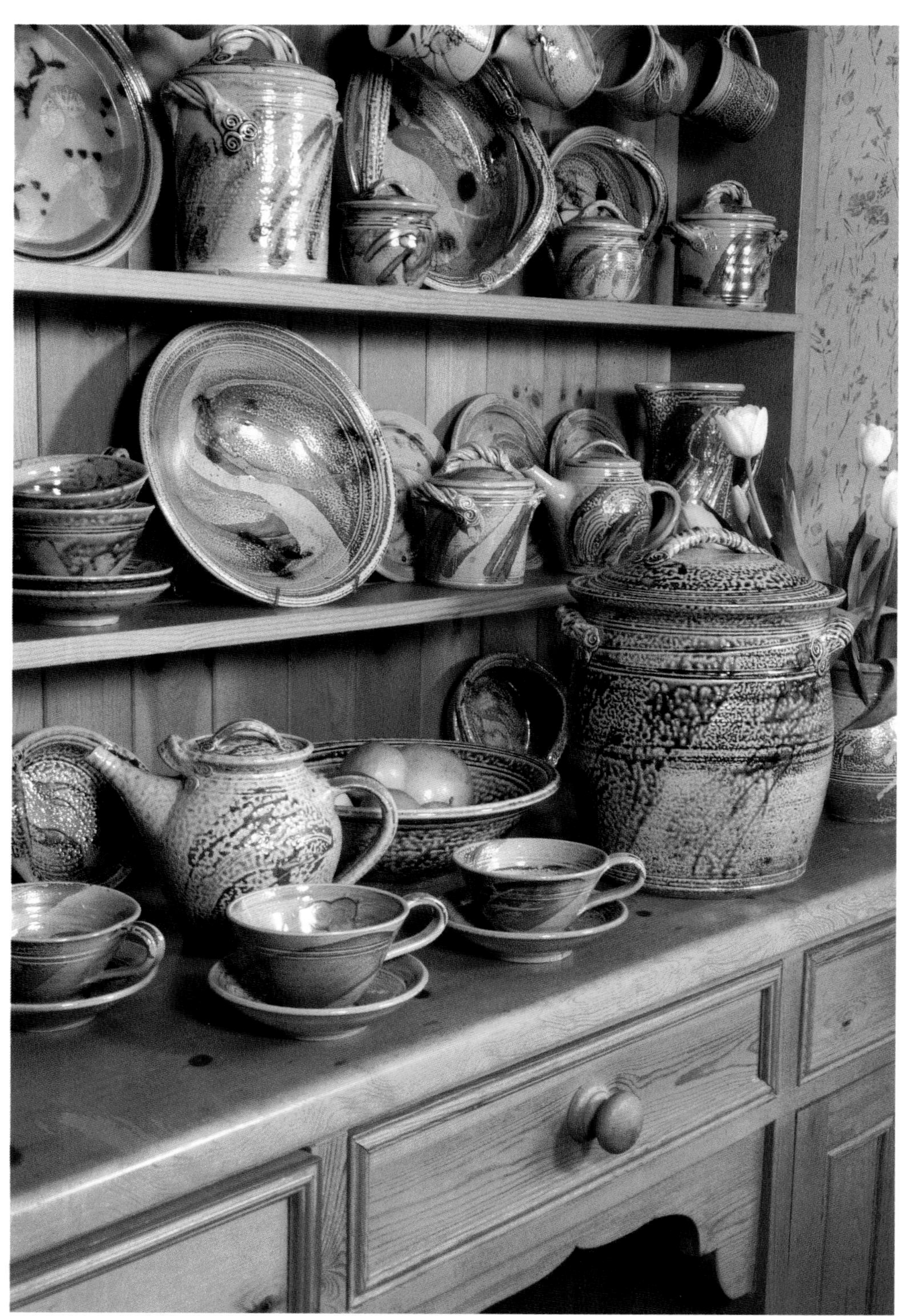

Salt-Glaze Ceramics

Rosemary Cochrane

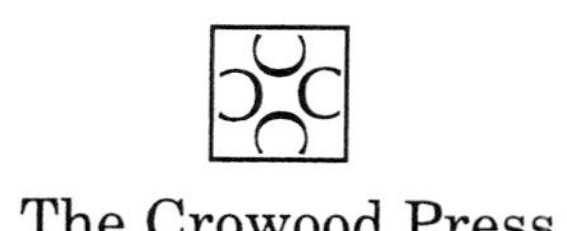

The Crowood Press

First published in 2001 by
The Crowood Press Ltd
Ramsbury, Marlborough
Wiltshire SN8 2HR

British Library Cataloguing-in-Publication Data
A catalogue record for this book is available from the British Library.

ISBN 1 86126 435 6

Photograph previous page: Dresser display of functional salt glaze by Rosemary Cochrane.

Photographic Acknowledgements
Photographs in this book were taken by the author, the artists themselves and by the following photographers: Paul Adair, Ole Akhoj, Martin Avery, Nic Broomhead, John Churchill, John Coles, University of Derby CEDM Photo and Video Library, Andrew Fielding, Erol Forbes, Rod Forss, S. Goodbody, Robert Greetham, Jordi Guerrero, Peter Harper, Carrie Herbert, Jonathan Horne, D. Joyce, Hans-Dieter Kellner, Peter Keverne, Artiem Kyriacon, John Lascelles, Simon Laycock, Peter Major, D. McNeill, Graham Murrell, Gerry Noble, Jaap Olof, Sue Packer, Ravi Pasricha, Al Pelowski, James Robson, Didier Rochefort, Clive Rowat, Johan Sandborg, Claude Simon, Harvey Smith, Pierre Soissons, Clive Streeter, Bill Thomas, Nick Tipton, M. Weller, Howard Williams, Stephen Yates.

Photographs were also supplied by the following: the University of Wales Aberystwyth, the National Museums and Galleries of Wales, Chesterfield Museum and Art Gallery, the Museum of London, Nottingham City Museums and Galleries, the Hexham Courant, and the Lion Salt Works Trust.

Typeset by Florence Production Ltd, Stoodleigh, Devon
Printed and bound in Malaysia by Times Offset (M) Sdn. Bhd.

Dedication
For the alchemists of clay, salt and fire; salt-glaze potters of the past, present and future.

Acknowledgements
I should like to thank all the salt-glaze potters who have so generously and freely shared their own knowledge and experience of the salt-glaze process. The response to the survey that I conducted between the end of 1999 and early 2000 was tremendous. I was able to trace almost all the potters seriously involved with salt glaze in Britain since the 1950s, and to compile the account of the successful revival of salt glaze in Britain today. Particular thanks must be given to those potters I interviewed, and for all the information and images sent by individual salt-glaze potters, including material from those who are not mentioned individually. All of it was invaluable in helping to produce the book. Thanks also to the international potters who all willingly sent their contributions.

Grateful thanks also to the following individuals who assisted in a variety of ways: Clive Cochrane, Jo Connell, Michael Evans, Hazel Forsyth, Janet Hamer, Frank Hamer, the late W. A. Ismay, Anne-Marie Knowles, Alex McErlain, Lolly Torbensen, Josie Walter, Andrew Watts, Pamela Wood.

Thanks to the following institutions, too: the University of Wales Aberystwyth, the National Museum and Gallery of Wales in Cardiff, the Museum of London, Chesterfield Museum and Art Gallery, Derby Museum and Art Gallery, Erewash Museum Services, Jewry Wall Museum in Leicester, Nottingham City Museums and Galleries (Nottingham Castle Museum).

Finally, thanks to Rachel Allen at The Crowood Press for her encouragement and patience.

Contents

Foreword by Jane Hamlyn 7
Introduction 8

Part One: Salt Glaze in Context 9

1 The European Tradition of Salt Glaze 9
2 Salt Glaze in Britain 23
3 Industrialization and Studio Art Pottery 31
4 The Revival of Salt Glaze 44
5 Contemporary British Salt Glaze 57

Part Two: Salt Glaze in Practice **71**

6 The Science of Salt and Soda 71
7 Making for High-Fired Salt Glaze 79
8 Kilns 101
9 Packing, Firing and Salting 115
10 Alternatives 132

Part Three: Inspirations for the Future **145**

11 Vapour Glaze in the Twenty-First Century 145
12 The International Scene 152

Bibliography and Further Reading 165
Useful Addresses 168
Museums and Collections 170

Index 170

Foreword

Once upon a time not long ago in the history of ceramics, salt glazing was at the forefront of technology, and was the height of sophistication. The new salt-glaze stonewares imported to England from Germany in the early 1600s must have seemed vastly superior to the rough peasant earthenwares commonly in use at the time, and their popularity led to a rich period for European salt-glaze manufacturers. During the eighteenth century, as the Industrial Revolution progressed, attempts to produce pale, refined salt-glaze ware for the growing middle class were superseded by the more successful development of cream-ware and bone china. And while nineteenth-century salt glazing produced a wealth of simple, utilitarian pots and kitchenware as well as the Art Pottery of Doultons and the Martin Brothers, by the early twentieth century it was regarded as a crude technique largely relegated to the industrial production of chimney pots and sewage pipes. Thus the salt-glaze story so far had been one of riches to rags.

Meanwhile Bernard Leach, somewhat dismissive of salt glazing, focused the attention of studio potters towards glazed stonewares in the Anglo-oriental tradition, and it was not until the 1950s that interest in salt glazing began to revive among studio potters. This revival was initiated by a number of factors: a desire for more individual expression; a re-evaluation of the beauty of past examples; an interest in the vagaries of chance that salt glazing presents; and a reaction against hackneyed glaze effects, plus the potential for new discovery that salt glazing offers to studio potters, whose aspirations for the technique may be far different from those of industry. Salt glazing is a demanding discipline, labour intensive and risky, but the beauty of its effects and the talents of its practitioners have won an appreciative audience in recent years. *Salt-glaze Ceramics* by Janet Mansfield was published in 1991, and gave an international perspective of the process, with the emphasis on the influences and motivation of the ceramic artists.

Potters wishing to learn the ways of salt had recourse previously to only two books, both published in 1977 and now out of print: *Salt Glazed Ceramics* by Jack Troy, and *Salt Glaze* by Peter Starkey (the latter often referred to as 'the salt-glazer's bible'!). Now, however, Rosemary Cochrane, herself an accomplished practitioner, has written a thoroughly researched, up-to-date sequel, a well balanced resource guide that clearly sets out the history, principles and practices of salt glazing, and offers fascinating insights into the working methods of individual artist-potters. Publication is particularly well timed since many of the environmental concerns regarding salt and soda glazing have been allayed by recent scientific research. This is a book about the skill and technique as well as the art of the salt-glaze potter, whose story continues to be written.

Jane Hamlyn

Introduction

The Alchemy of Clay, Salt and Fire

There is a real magic about the transformation of two materials into a surface so visually exciting and seductively tactile as salt glaze. It can vary from a light, smooth sheen to a thick coating of clear glaze that has the texture of orange peel. It is a seemingly simple process, brought about by the reaction of common salt on clay. Salt glaze is unique in the way that it is an integral part of the clay body. When salt is introduced into the kiln it bursts into a cloud of vapour that swirls around the clay pots and transforms their surfaces. The glassy surface is formed as the sodium oxide in the salt reacts with the alumina and the silica in the clay, to produce sodium alumino-silicate: the glaze. The rich and varied effects that salt vapour can produce are the subject of this book.

Detail of bowl by Rosemary Cochrane.

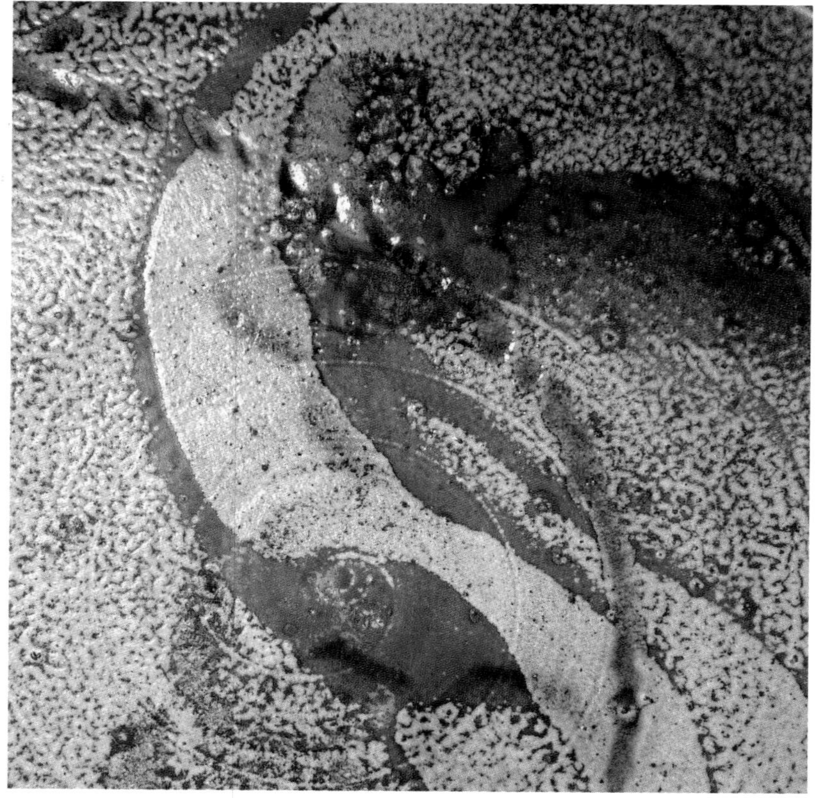

Salt is not the only sodium agent that is now used to produce a glaze, and the results from soda firings are hard to distinguish from salt glaze. Together they can be called 'vapour glaze', and that term, as well as 'salt glaze' and 'soda glaze', are used throughout the book. In many cases the words 'salt' and 'soda' are interchangeable, but where the reference is to one agent in particular it is made quite clear.

In Part One, the story of salt glaze in Britain is traced from the importation of German wares through to the contemporary salt glaze produced by individual studio potters. Part Two continues by covering all the practical aspects of the process. The final section celebrates the work of the most recent generation of salt- and soda-glaze potters in Britain at the beginning of the twenty-first century. It concludes with a gallery view of the fascinating work of international potters, with particular reference to the latest work in the continuing salt-glaze tradition in Europe.

Salt glaze generates much interest from potters, collectors, and those who come across a piece of pottery in either a museum, contemporary craft gallery, or in someone else's home. Understanding something of the process can add to the pleasure of using a functional salt-glaze pot, or it can lead to a passion to become involved in making salt glaze. The fascinating, tactile nature of salt-glaze surfaces are the product of the alchemy of salt, clay and fire, and are to be enjoyed.

I
Salt Glaze in Context

1 The European Tradition of Salt Glaze

The tradition of salt glaze is exclusively a European one that followed on from the development of high temperature firings and stoneware pottery in Germany. It has been used to produce functional glazed stoneware for over six hundred years. From the earliest manufacture in small family-run potteries that supplied local rural communities with utilitarian pots, to the profitable, industrial mass-production of pipes, salt glaze has endured as a functional and hard-wearing surface.

The earliest European experiments to produce a hard, non-porous pot began in Germany as early as the seventh century, and the first true stoneware was manufactured around 1300. The first pots that were clearly identified as salt-glaze were produced around the end of the fifteenth, early sixteenth century. Germany played the leading role in the development of European salt glaze, exporting wares far and wide, long before it was made in Britain or elsewhere. The vast number of imports of the robust salt-glaze bottles and tavern wares from Germany gave the British entrepreneurs a powerful incentive to produce stoneware and compete in the market.

It was the German immigrant potters who undoubtedly brought some of their knowledge of the salt-glaze process to Britain. The first salt glaze to be developed in Britain in the mid-seventeenth century was styled on German imported wares, although it was not long before British salt glaze found its own directions. Early salt-glaze potteries were based in London, but the manufacture of salt-glaze stoneware soon expanded into thriving industries in Staffordshire, Nottinghamshire and Derbyshire, with smaller centres in Bristol, Liverpool and Scotland.

Early German Stoneware

The Rhineland was a focus for the pottery industry and for salt-glaze stoneware in particular. Pottery towns grew up around the rich deposits of suitable clays that were low in fluxing materials. These clays could be fired to high temperatures and would fuse and vitrify at 1,200°C or more to produce a stoneware body. Unlike the easily chipped and porous earthenware pots, stoneware is hard and impervious. It was ideal for general storage, transporting and storing liquid, and for decanting and drinking it too.

Earthware and Stoneware

Earthenware and stoneware are the two simple classifications of pottery. Both the firing temperature and the clay will determine the type.
Earthenware pottery is porous or semi-porous. It is not fired over 1,200°C. Any clay can be used to make earthenware pots, but earthenware clay itself contains materials that make it unable to withstand high firing temperatures.
Stoneware pottery is strong, hard and dense, with low porosity. It is usually fired over 1200°C. Stoneware clays can be fired to high temperatures without deforming.

Early Stoneware Glazes

Occasionally a glaze is found on fourteenth-century pots from the Rhineland: these earliest glazed stoneware pots are coated with a thin sheen caused by light deposits of wood ash. The kilns were fired with wood, which was in plentiful supply, and during a firing the wood ash from the burning fuel would be carried by the flames through the kiln, and form a glaze as it settled on the pots and interacted with the clay. Gradually, during the sixteenth century, the glaze developed into salt glaze.

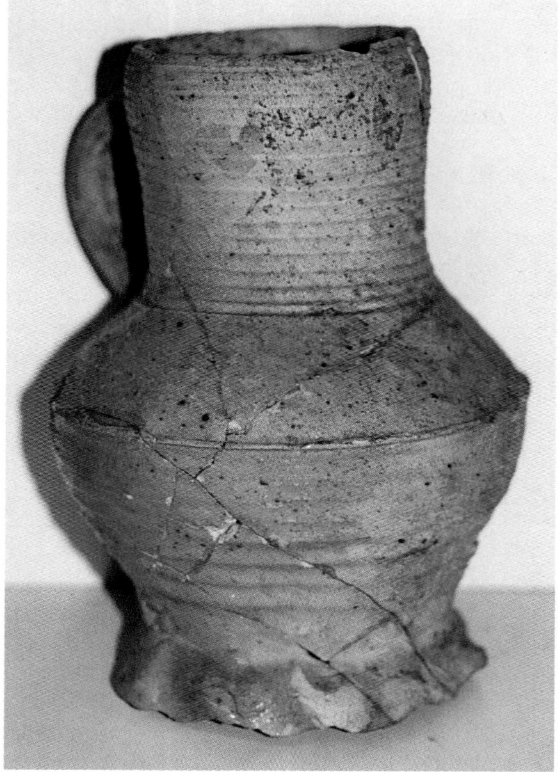

Mug. German, possibly late sixteenth century. Unglazed stoneware with light patchy iron wash over pale grey body. (Jewry Wall Museum, Leicester)

An analysis of the early Rhenish glazes is published in David Gaimster's book, *German Stoneware 1200–1900*, in an appendix entitled 'The Technology of German Stoneware Glazes'. This work was undertaken in 1991, and analyses the chemical composition of the glazes. The results show how the chemistry of the glazes changes from a potash-rich, pure wood-ash glaze, to a soda-rich salt glaze. The formation of an ash glaze has already been described. True salt glaze occurs when salt is thrown into the kiln towards the end of the firing. It vaporizes, and the sodium oxide reacts with the silica in the clay to form a clear, glassy coating on the surface of the pots.

It is still uncertain how it was discovered that salt could be used as the primary glaze component. It is possible that salt-impregnated timber from barrels of salted herrings may have been used to fuel the kilns, and that the salt was recognized as the source of the extra sheen on the pots. Alternatively, it is known that in the past, salt was thrown onto the embers of a fire because the resulting force of the vapour would help to clear the chimney of a build-up of soot. If the flues of the wood-fired kilns were ever cleared in this way, it is possible that some residual salt in the fireboxes could have contributed to forming a glaze during the next firing. Whether this did ever happen will remain a matter of conjecture. Nevertheless, somehow the link between salt and a glaze was made.

Kilns and Firings

The design of the kiln plays a critical part in the efficient use of the fuel, and in the potential for a maximum temperature. The European potters of medieval times were producing earthenware pottery from vertical updraught kilns, but these could not reach the higher temperatures that were essential for stoneware. However, horizontal kilns, with a stoking pit below the stacking chamber, meant that the firings could be hotter and better controlled. These changes in kiln design evolved gradually, but as the higher temperatures were achieved, the true stoneware pots began to appear.

To produce salt-glazed stoneware, the potters also needed to find effective ways of introducing the salt into the kiln. Perhaps to begin with, salt was loaded onto the wood before being placed in the firebox. In due course, however, they evolved the method of shovelling the salt through openings in the roof and sides of the kiln. With the process of salt glazing, it was important that the kilns were packed so that the pieces would be protected from the direct flame and ash-laden fumes, and not be contaminated. Stacking the kilns would have taken time and expertise, as the wares were balanced on top of one another, rim to rim and base to base, with discs and rolls of clay used as spacers. It is often possible to determine the position of a pot in the kiln by examining the direction of the glaze flow. Stacking scars were common, but do not appear to have affected the export value of the bottles and tavern wares.

The kiln atmosphere is an important factor in determining the final appearance and colour of salt-glazed pots. There are two extremes, oxidation and reduction, with a neutral state in between. For oxidation, the vents in the kiln would remain open to allow a good intake and circulation of clean air in the kiln. For reduction, in order to starve the kiln atmosphere of air, any vents would be kept closed. Using wood as the fuel naturally produces a reduced atmosphere, as the wood takes air from the kiln to ignite and burn each time it is stoked. A reduced atmosphere in the kiln was maintained by sealing up the vents and fireboxes at the end of a firing. In the case of the pale-coloured, low iron-bearing clay, the final result was grey, and any patches of brown on these pots are the result of partial re-oxidation.

To produce very different final colours, the German potters coated the clays with an iron-rich slip or wash, hiding the light grey, firing clay body. Drip marks can be seen on the sides of many pots. By opening the vents and introducing air into the kiln at the end of the firing, an oxidizing atmosphere was created during the early part of the cooling stage. This caused the surface colour of the iron slip to be drawn out, to produce a range of browns. The typical mottled or 'orange peel' texture of salt glaze is the result of the combination of a sandy coarse-grained clay body, and a fast cooling without a 'soak'. 'Soaking' the kiln – that is, holding the kiln at the top temperature for a long time – will result in a smoother glaze finish even on a coarse clay body.

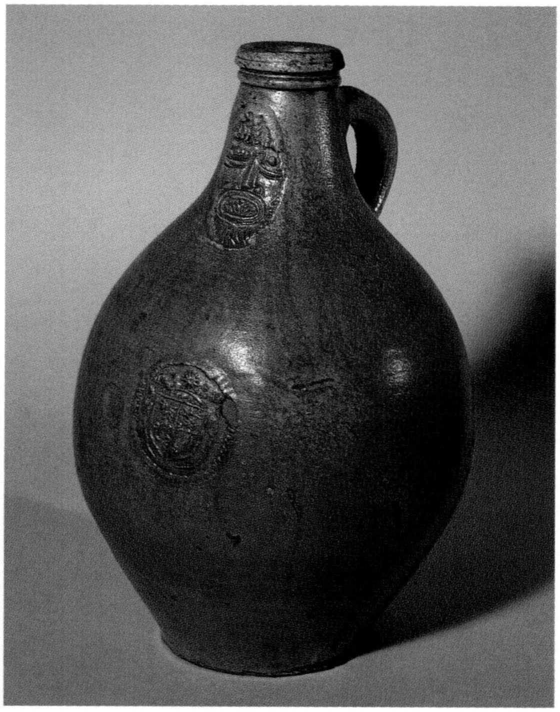

Bottle. German, seventeenth century. Bearded face mask and coat of arms. Kiln scarred with drips of iron wash. (Manchester Metropolitan University.)

German Salt-Glaze Exports

There are many hundreds of examples of German salt-glaze pots displayed in museums throughout Britain, just as elsewhere in Europe. The earliest are imported, some over 400 years old: some of these are finds from excavations, others have survived constant use over many years before being discarded or put away on shelves. The remainder are from collections of the late eighteenth and nineteenth centuries, commissioned or purchased in Germany by British merchants and the middle classes to grace their tables and drinking sessions.

German pots led the European tradition of stoneware and salt glaze that was to change the face of British pottery production. In Britain, it was the qualities of those pots that speeded up the race to discover the secret of stoneware production and of salt glaze – and in the

Stoneware salt-glaze 'schnelle' or tankard with pewter cover, Siegburg, Germany. Workshop of Hans Hilgers, about 1580. Cordons around the neck and base. Panels on three sides, applied moulded low-relief depicting Samson and Delilah. (National Museums and Galleries of Wales)

twenty-first century their form, decoration, texture and colour still hold a fascination. The German tradition of salt firing survived longer than in Britain, and the firing techniques have been handed down through generations of family-owned potteries. By understanding the process by which those colours and surface qualities were achieved, we can appreciate how to control our own salt kilns to produce certain effects.

The Principal German Wares

German salt-glaze wares are generally categorized according to the area in which they were made. The interaction of the different local clays, the specific firing conditions, and the amount of salt vapour reaching the wares, all contribute to the characteristics of the individual styles of each region. In addition, the potters often developed distinctive forms and decoration for their pots. The principal sites of stoneware production in the Rhineland included Siegburg, Langerwehe, Cologne, Frechen, Raeren, and in the Westerwald at Koblenz, Hohr and Grenzhausen. There was also an important centre in Saxony at Waldenburg.

Siegburg

Siegburg had one of the longest and most productive traditions in making pottery and in the development of stoneware. It was made using fine-grained, iron-free clay that fired to a light yellow to whitish body in a lightly reducing or neutral kiln atmosphere. The salt glaze is very thin and barely distinguishable on the earlier pieces, but from the mid-sixteenth century it appears more definitely on the various jug forms.

The most distinctive are the tall wine beakers and jugs, ribbed and grooved top and bottom, and the '*Schnelle*', a cylindrical tapering tankard. Usually the sides are sectioned into three panels of applied decoration, the fine clay being particularly suited to producing detail. Inspired by woodcuts and engravings, the scenes are biblical, mythological, armorial or rustic. Later pieces have a heavier coating of salt glaze, and reached a point of technical excellence in the first part of the seventeenth century. However,

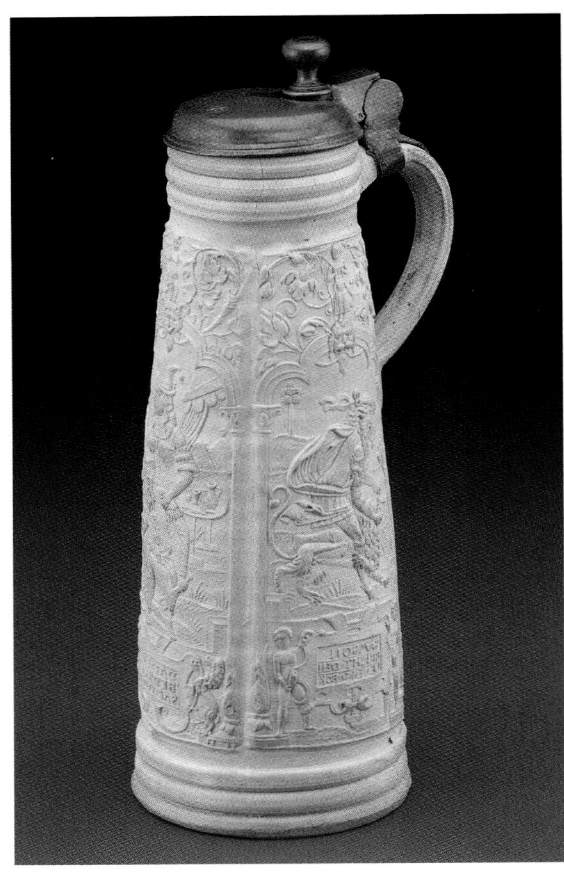

a large number of workshops in Siegburg were destroyed during wars in the 1580s, and many potters had already migrated to the Westerwald region when, fifty years later, the town was completely destroyed by Swedish troops.

Langerwehe

Langerwehe lies between Aachen and Cologne, close to deposits of high firing clays. It was a major centre for stoneware pottery from the fourteenth to sixteenth centuries, when the focus of production was on undecorated utilitarian wares. Early examples of Langerwehe brown salt-glaze wares are very similar to those from Raeren. Large water jugs, some of which were for export to Britain, had applied medallions representing the potter, dealer or customer, and were a particular item of the late sixteenth century. Salt-glaze manufacture continued into the nineteenth century, but the large, barrel-shaped jars used for the preservation of food, which became a significant part of the Langerwehe production, were not required by the British market.

Cologne

The city of Cologne was a major producer of German salt-glaze ware during the first half of the sixteenth century. The local clay fired grey in the reducing atmosphere of the kiln, but typically this would be covered with an iron slip or wash by dipping or pouring. By re-oxidizing the surface of the pots in the early stages of cooling, the familiar warm brown, reddish-brown or speckled-brown fired surface colours were produced. The fine sandy clay, when salted and then 'soaked' at the top temperatures, resulted in a smooth sheen. The Cologne potters learned to control the kiln atmosphere well, in order to achieve the desired effects with their clays and slips.

The greybeard or 'Bartmann' jugs and bottles are now amongst the most popular pieces on display from Cologne, and it seems likely that they were intended for the luxury end of the market. They were skilfully made, and the applied relief ornament is especially striking. The bearded face of a man or mask is applied to the throat or neck of the bulbous jugs, and moulded and sprigged intertwined oak leaves and acorns, or rose briars and flowers, adorn the body of the vessels. The applied decoration was made from moulds, and the figurative or botanical friezes, portrait roundels and plant ornaments were copied from pattern books. From around 1500 these pieces have turned bases, and many are seen with pewter lids.

The decline in Cologne's production of salt glaze was rapid. Resented by the earthenware potters, and meeting hostility to their firings because of the problems caused by the smoke and pollution from the kilns, the stoneware potters were driven out of their workshops in the city centre. Following legal proceedings in 1544, the bailiffs were sent by the City Fathers to knock down the kilns. Salt-glaze production ended within the city of Cologne, with a total ban in 1556. Many skilled potters migrated to Frechen or Raeren, and took with them their designs and techniques.

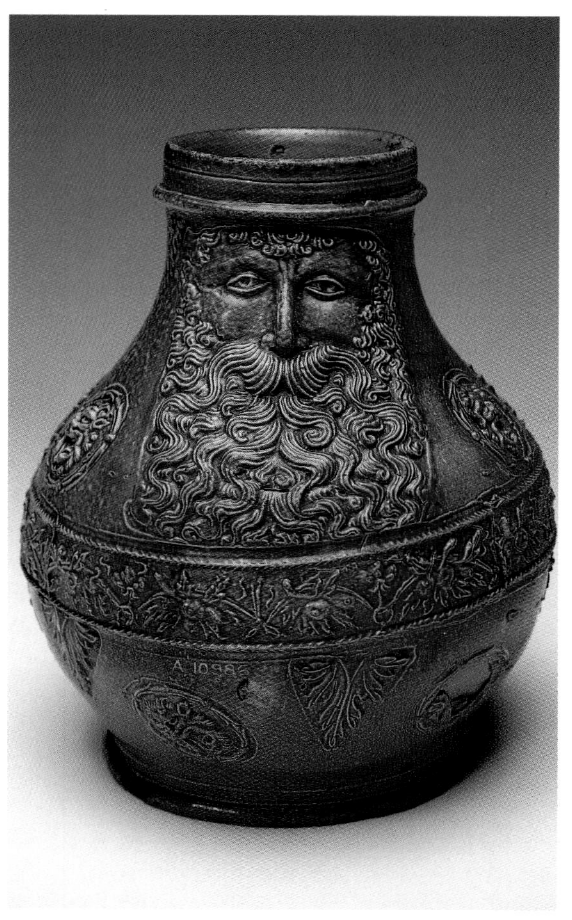

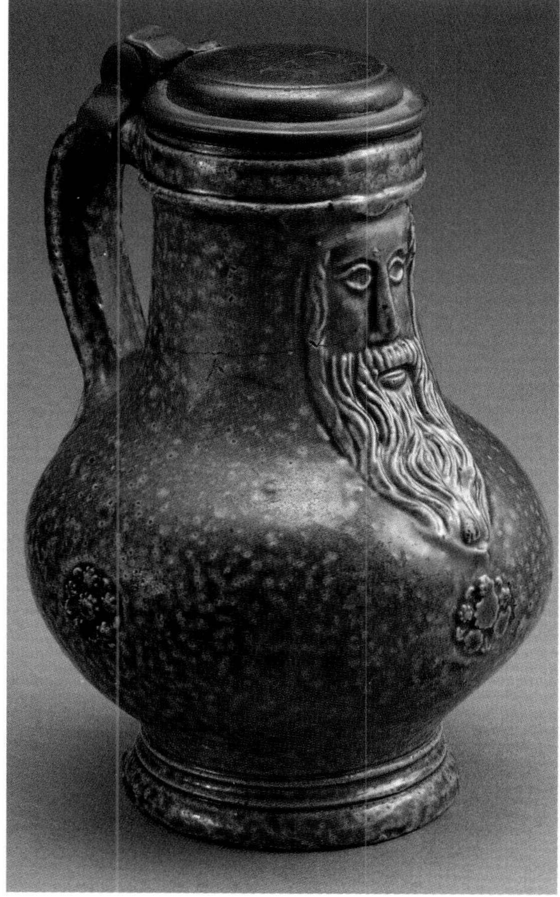

(LEFT) 'Bartmann' jug with pewter lid. Stoneware salt-glaze German Rhineland, late sixteenth century. (National Museums and Galleries of Wales)

(FAR LEFT) 'Bartmann' jug from Cologne, 1525–50. Dark grey clay body with patchy brown surface under a lustrous speckled salt glaze. Decorated with a rectangular bearded face mask, foliage, fruit and blossoms and lion mask roundels. Found in London. (Museum of London)

Undecorated flagon with handle. Salt glaze. Likely German seventeenth century. Found Humberside. Grey clay body, iron-washed under richly textured 'Tiger' glaze. (Jewry Wall Museum, Leicester)

Bellarmine Jugs and Bottles

There is a fascination about the bearded face that decorates the neck of so many of the brown salt-glaze bottles and jugs from the Rhineland. Originally this was called 'Bartmaske', and the face takes on a variety of expressions, from benevolent and smiling to a fearsome frown. The earlier ones from between 1500 and 1575 are likely to have kinder faces and be more finely moulded than the cruder, more jovial or devilish expressions which came later and were mainly from Frechen. It is most likely that they were modelled in the likeness of the mythical 'Wild Man' of North European folklore.

The 'Bartmann' jugs and bottles from the Rhineland were exported to London in large quantities during the sixteenth and seventeenth centuries. In Britain they were a very popular import, and by the late seventeenth century had become known as 'Bellarmines'. This name alluded to a certain Cardinal Roberto Bellarmine, a cleric of the Pope and who had died in 1621. Bellarmine was despised by the Protestants for his criticism of James I who, after the failure of the Gunpowder Plot of 1605, had legislated against the Catholics. The connection between the Cardinal and the frowning bearded face on tavern bottles came about as a joke and in contempt of the Cardinal. The first salt-glaze potters in Britain made bottles decorated with stylized copies of the bearded face for a short time around 1675.

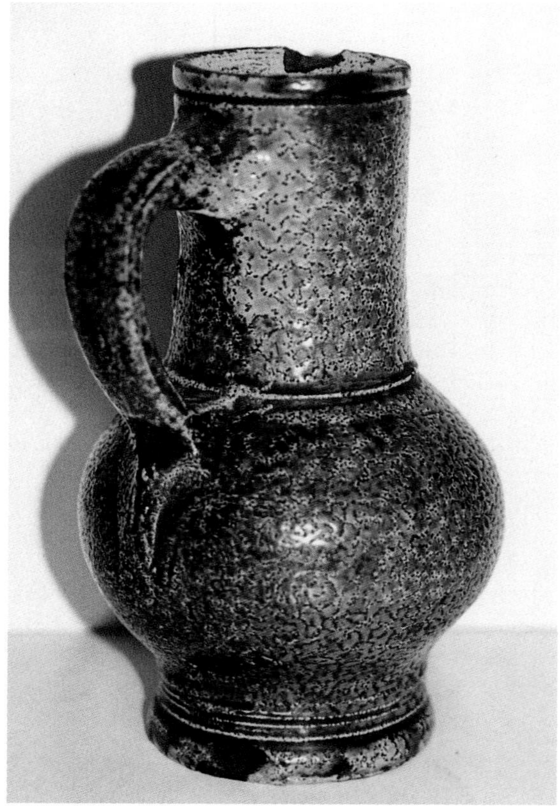

Frechen

Frechen lies south of Cologne and shared the same clay deposits. The chief salt-glaze products from Frechen were the glazed pitchers or 'Bartmannkrug'. These were made in a range of sizes, and many have decoration applied to the belly of the pot. The bearded mask was originally more stylized than those of the Cologne wares. Although the same buff-grey clay was used, the so-called 'Tiger' glaze on some Frechen pottery has a distinctive pitted surface, unlike the smooth glaze of Cologne ware.

It is possible that sand was added to the clay: using a coarser clay body, with a variety of sizes of silica particles, would encourage the salting to produce an uneven glaze on the surface of the pot. Iron oxide in the slip or wash that covers the clay, migrates to these parts. Without 'soaking' at the top temperature the glaze will not smooth out and so, in theory, remains immature. It is also likely that the kilns were cooled rapidly. A period of oxidation at the end of the firing or in the early part of the cooling would have encouraged the brown colours.

The mottled surface may originally have been unintentional, but many a happy accident can lead to fortune. The Frechen potters soon realized that the effect was seen as a quality and should be produced deliberately, as it was in great demand by foreign markets. Many of these 'getigerten', or 'Tiger-ware', bottles and jugs were given additional value by being embellished with silver mountings when they were imported into England. After the sixteenth century it is hard to distinguish Frechen wares from those of Cologne, no doubt partly due to the fact that many of the potters had migrated from that city to work in Frechen, and took with them their own ways of preparing the clay and firing.

Raeren

Raeren, now in present-day Belgium, lies close to Aachen. Between the fifteenth and seventeenth centuries the production of stoneware

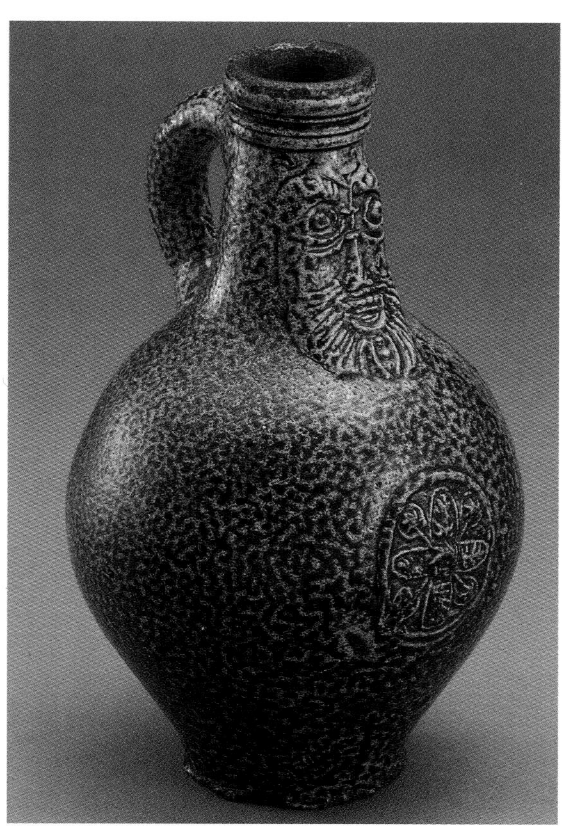

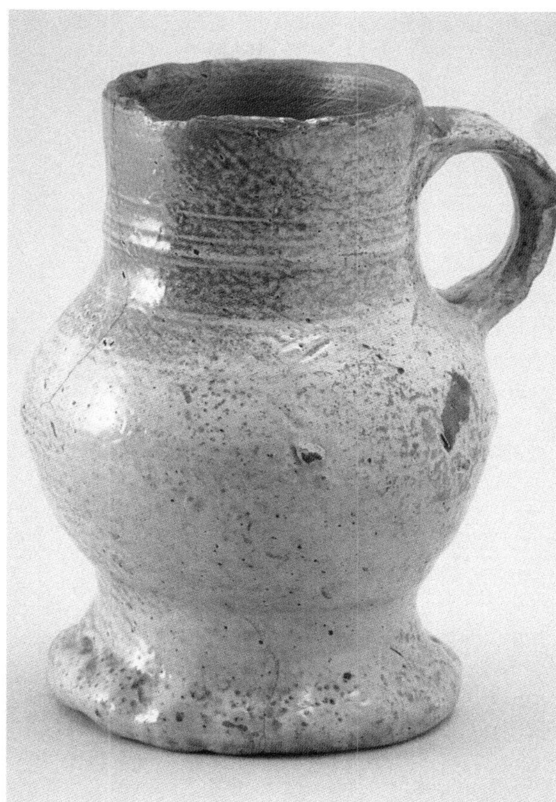

(FAR LEFT) 'Bartmann' bottle. Stoneware salt glaze. German seventeenth century, likely Frechen. Bearded face mask applied to neck, oval medallion on body. Iron wash under coarse-speckled salt glaze, 'Tiger' ware. (National Museums and Galleries of Wales)

(LEFT) Mug. Salt-glaze stoneware. German, Raeren, sixteenth century. (Nottingham City Museums and Galleries)

was a thriving industry, with its height in the second half of the sixteenth century. Many pieces were imported into Britain. The stoneware clays are fine grained and high in iron, and they fire to a dark grey in a reduced atmosphere. Earlier pots followed the styles of Cologne – bulbous bottles with tapering necks – and of Siegburg, with thumbed bases. They are often depicted in the paintings of Pieter Bruegel. The work was given an iron wash, dipped and coated in an iron slip and, in the oxidizing atmosphere at the end of a firing, produced a wonderful lustrous brown sheen under the salt glaze.

The Raeren potters became highly skilled, and their later work is distinguished by precision and elaborate decoration. Cylindrical tankards, or '*schnellen*', gave way to the new, shaped baluster jugs with turned bases and moulded ornamentation. A typical feature was the crisp horizontal profiling or rilling, achieved with the use of wooden templates. Friezes of applied relief ornamentation, medallions and friezes of strapwork inspired or copied from woodcuts and engravings, were mass-produced in moulds and appear on the tankards, goblets, pitchers and jugs. Many have pewter or silver mounts.

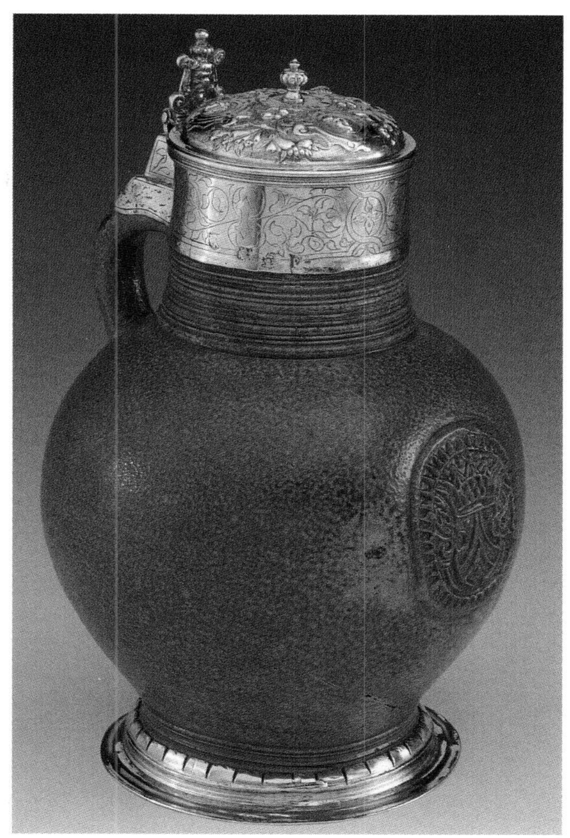

Alepot. Stoneware salt glaze. German, mid-sixteenth century. With silver mounts, London 1562–63. (National Museums and Galleries of Wales)

An innovation that eventually eclipsed the production of brown wares of this area was the production of grey stoneware, with areas of cobalt blue highlighting the decoration. It was a distinctly different approach that began around 1540 with the development of a lighter, finer clay body. A thin sheen of salt glaze covered the reduction-fired grey stoneware body. The grey contrasted with the blue colour that was used to flood around, or wash over the intricate mouldings. By the late sixteenth century these fine elaborate pieces were examples of the very best craftsmanship. They would have been exported to Britain in relatively small quantities, with a high commercial and social value.

Westerwald

A major salt-glaze stoneware industry was not established in the Westerwald until the 1590s, when potters migrated there from Raeren. Extensive deposits of clays in the region are especially suitable for salt glaze, with a low iron and high silica content; the towns of Hohr, Grenzau and Grenzhausen are just some of the places with reputations built around the salt-glaze industry. Today these form the one township of Hohr-Grenzhausen where, until the 1990s, an unbroken tradition of salt-glaze kilns had lasted for 500 years.

The potters from Raeren brought with them their skills and styles of production. Potters from Siegburg had also taken refuge in Westerwald, and at the end of the sixteenth century pottery production in this area had become an eclectic mix of salt-glaze and stoneware skills. By the 1620s, a more distinctive, heavily salted range of ware appeared. Baroque-styled baluster jugs and mugs were covered with applied ornamentation and motifs, with cobalt blue and manganese purple painted under the glaze. When fired, the colours appeared against a light grey background. The grey body was achieved by firing in a heavily reduced atmosphere, with no re-oxidation during cooling.

Common household objects in the blue-grey salt-glaze stoneware travelled with emigrant potters world-wide, and some of the earliest North American salt-glaze stoneware of the eighteenth century imitates those Westerwald pieces. In Britain some very early trials to copy the style were abandoned. A small production of light grey monochrome tea services, press-moulded and modelled ornaments and also table items appeared in the Westerwald in the eighteenth century. It is interesting to compare these with the early white Staffordshire pieces that were produced around the same time, and exported to Europe.

The production of utilitarian wares for the kitchen and tavern continued into the eighteenth and nineteenth centuries; Sauerbrunnen and

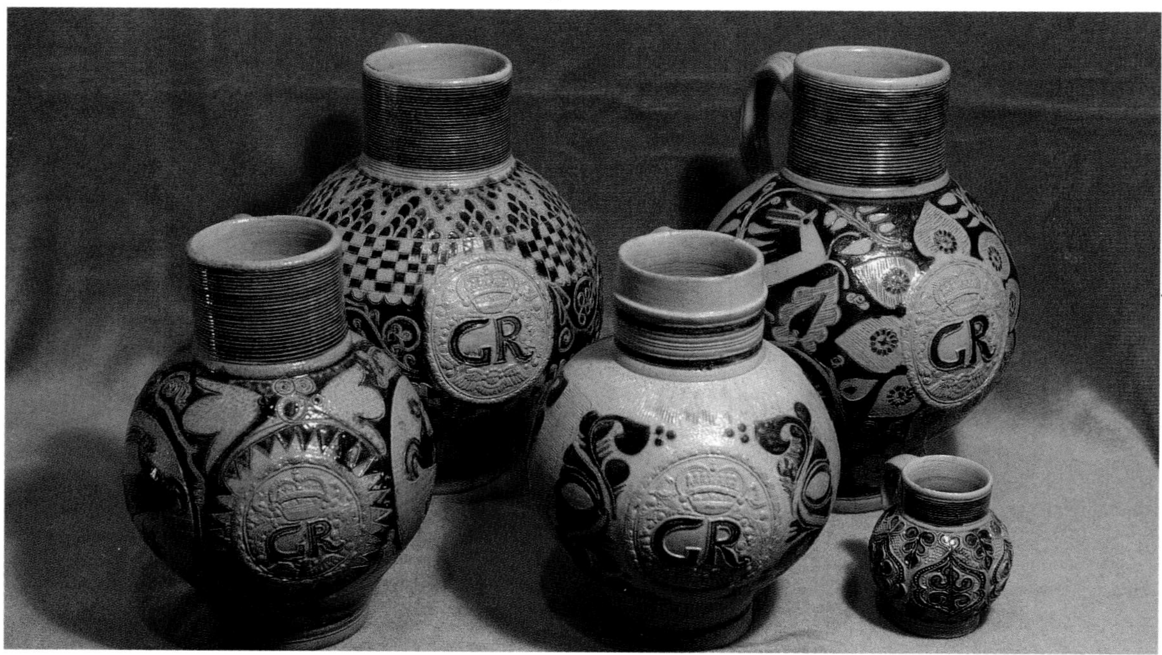

Group of Westerwald 'gorges' or mugs. Early eighteenth century. With applied and incised decoration and cobalt-blue painted under salt glaze. (Private collection)

Branntwein (mineral water) bottles were a typical product. These crocks and water jugs were made from cheap, impure clays that were fired under reduction, but cooled under oxidation, producing yellowish to orange-brown colours. Decorated wares were in decline, although modelling was reintroduced at the turn of the nineteenth century, and simple domestic blue-grey wares are still made.

Saxony

To the east of the Rhineland, the town of Waldenburg was one of several that produced salt-glaze stoneware with many of the characteristics of the Rhenish pieces. The earlier manufacture of dark brown wares gave way to a simple grey and blue style, which is still produced in the region of Saxony.

Cobalt

The use of cobalt had begun in the early 1500s in several of the regions, firstly only on brown ware, but later on the grey wares. It was applied in two ways: in the first it was painted directly onto the pots as 'smalt', powdered ore mixed with sand and an alkali flux such as potash. In the second technique, known as 'Smaltebewurf', the cobalt ore was mixed with the salt to vaporize as it was thrown into the kiln towards the end of a firing, so the pots were completely covered with a blue glaze. This was the method adopted at some potteries in Saxony, where the cobalt deposits were located and it was therefore cheaper and could be used less sparingly.

Exports from Rhineland

The production of salt-glaze stoneware in Germany was well established throughout the Rhineland by the time it was flooding into Britain. It was immensely successful in supplying the whole beer- and wine-drinking scene with a robust range of mass-produced wares. The majority of the imports were the 'Bartmann' jugs and bottles from Frechen, near Cologne. Here was an opportunity to compete with similar products in the obviously lucrative market for tavern ware. There were many itinerant potters working in Britain, bringing with them their knowledge and skills from Europe. So it is hardly surprising that the earliest British salt glaze copied the German forms and, in the beginning, sought the same surface qualities.

Imports to Britain

The first salt-glaze pots seen in Britain were those imported from Germany as early as the mid-fourteenth century. The majority of the brown stoneware bottles from the Rhineland

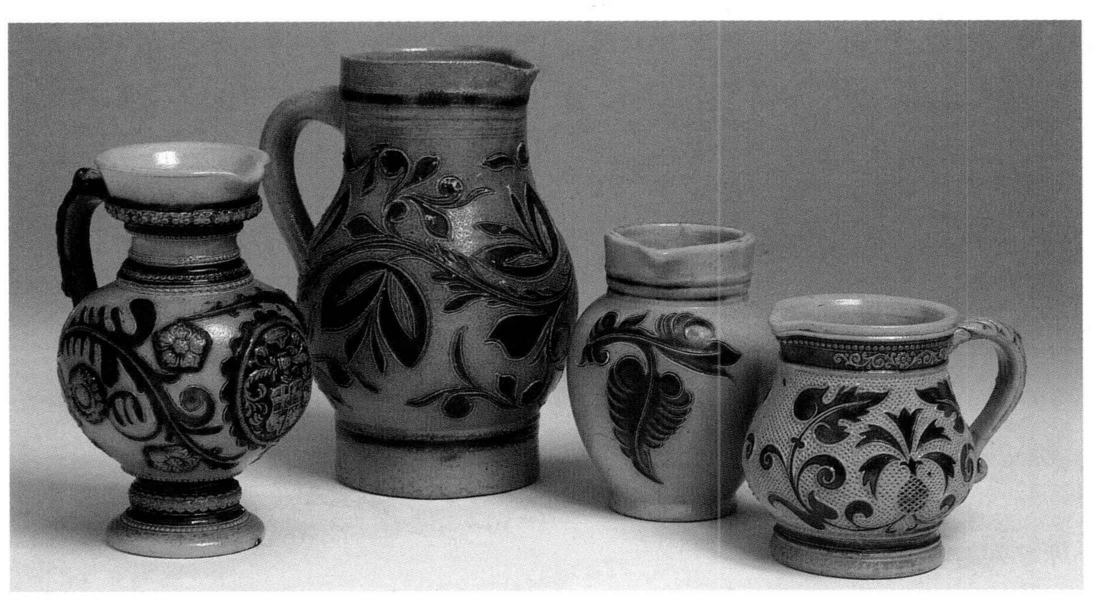

Group of nineteenth- and twentieth-century Westerwald grey and blue salt glaze. (Private collection.)

Salt-glaze stoneware 'bellarmine', medallion showing a man holding a cup and staff. Height 21cm. Mid-seventeenth century. Woolwich. This bottle represents the earliest salt-glaze stoneware made in England, and with one other came out of the sea, probably off Folkestone, Kent. The Museum of London has the only other extant example known. (Jonathan Horne)

were shipped to London from the Low Countries, together with the wine and beer that was decanted from the casks into the vessels. 'Bartmann', as we have seen, were fat-bellied jugs and bottles that came to be nicknamed 'greybeards' or Bellarmines; they were a very common article, and hundreds have been found in London and elsewhere. During the second half of the sixteenth century, London became a redistribution centre for the imported Rhenish stoneware.

The goods would be re-exported to all the other British ports, around East Anglia as far north as Newcastle on the east coast, and right round the southern ports, into Bristol in the west and some as far north as Scotland. The vast trade in Rhenish stoneware, supplied from various centres, reached a high point during the seventeenth century. In the first half of that century alone, it is estimated that over twenty million of these mass-produced stoneware vessels were imported to London. It is hardly surprising that the British potters had an interest in developing their own robust high-fired pottery. The taverns of England were filled with German salt-glazed mugs, tankards and bottles and English drinkers. To supply such a demand would be to gain a place in an obviously lucrative market.

The Competitive Search

The story of British salt glaze, or certainly the intention to learn the secret of its manufacture, begins as early as 1593 in the reign of Queen Elizabeth I, when a courtier Henry Noell was granted a patent 'to provide and buy in . . . all manner of stone pottes . . .'. Twenty-one years later, in 1614, Thomas Browne and others were granted a twenty-one year patent to make 'all manner of stone pots, jugs, and bottles not usually made in the realm' – although it is almost certain that he never manufactured any. Then in 1626 two merchants, Thomas Rous and Abraham Cullen, were granted another fourteen-year patent to manufacture stoneware pots, jugs and bottles, and although they planned to bring a potter from Frechen to work in England, again there is no evidence to suggest that this happened. A patent brought out in 1636 for a high temperature kiln shows that the search for the secret of stoneware was still ongoing and urgent.

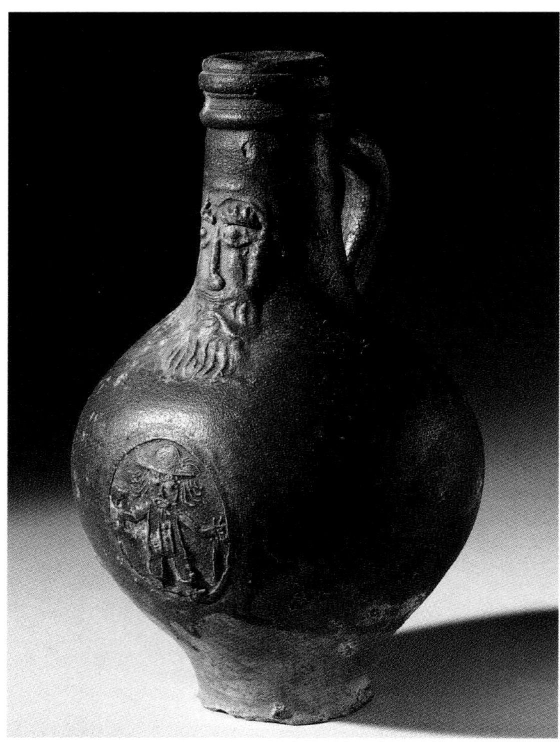

The Secret Discovered

Real evidence of the very earliest salt-glaze stoneware made in Britain are the few mugs and bottles that came from a kiln near the Woolwich Ferry. The excavated pieces have been dated between 1640–50, and were made from Frechen clay by immigrant potters. By the 1660s, a potter from the Rhineland, Symon Wooltus, was working in Southampton and had produced stoneware pottery. It appears that both he and his son worked for a Captain Killigrew, who had made an application for a patent to make 'stone bottles and blew canns' on 30 April 1672. A certain John Dwight of Fulham beat him to the race by seven days.

John Dwight and Salt Glaze

John Dwight's name is now synonymous with that of the first commercially successful manufacturer of English salt-glaze stoneware. Dwight's first patent, granted on 23 April 1672, was for various ceramic bodies, including chinaware and '. . . the stone ware vulgarly called Cologne ware'. John Dwight first experimented

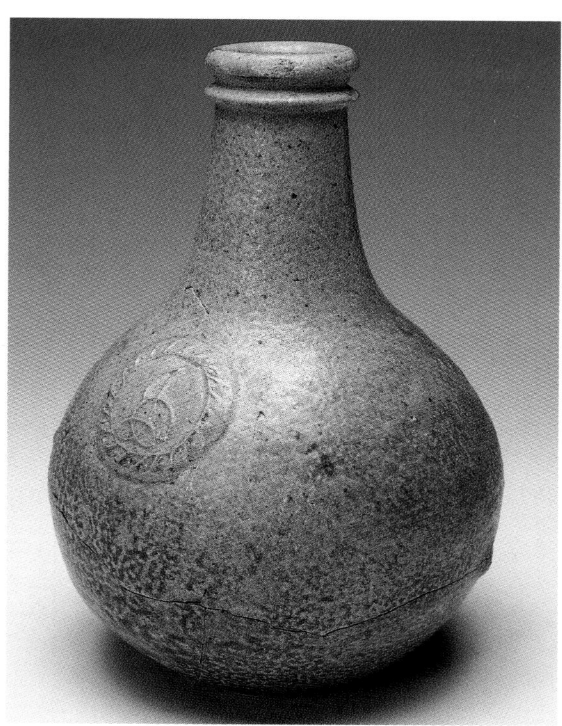

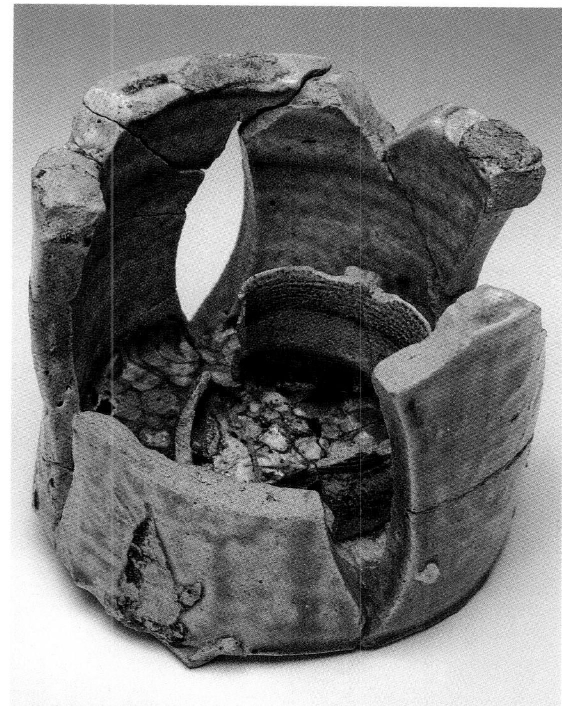

(FAR LEFT) Bottle, 1675–85. Incomplete, with cordoned rim and applied medallion with JD monogram. Possibly made for John Dwight's personal use. Made from a pale clay body with a reddish-brown slip. (Museum of London)

(LEFT) Saggar, c.1680. Incomplete, with four knife-cut marquise-shaped apertures and v-shaped notches in the rim. The notches enabled the fused stacks to be separated with a small crowbar or similar tool. This form of saggar is particularly common after 1680, and they are usually found with gorges inside, as this example. The gorge sits on a pad of refractory clay. (Museum of London)

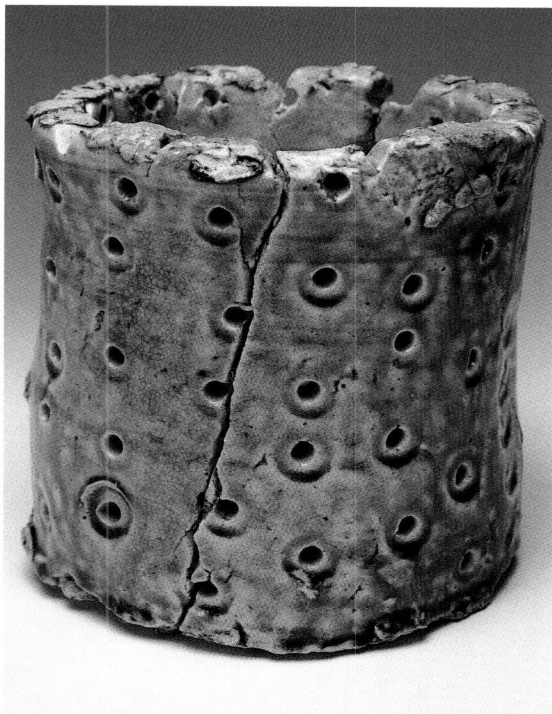

(LEFT) Saggar, c.1683–85. A cylindrical saggar with several rows of small perforations, made from an ordinary stoneware body with more or less quartz sand added. The saggar is thickly coated with a greeny-brown salt glaze. Only 5 per cent of the Fulham saggars are of this form, and the very restricted access they allow to the kiln atmosphere points unequivocally to fine-ware production. (Museum of London)

with making stoneware in Wigan, before he moved to establish a pottery at Fulham in London.

The Fulham Pottery

The pottery was well located, and all the raw materials could be brought close to it by barge: large quantities of wood, Dorset 'ball' clay, Isle of White sand, and the essential salt, which at that time was imported from Spain and Portugal. Dwight employed Southwark potters to develop a way to fire a kiln that would reliably reach the high temperatures required for stoneware. He clearly knew something about the way German salt glaze was produced, but the archaeological finds from trial kilns prove that he certainly had technical problems in setting up its manufacture. In time the major faults of distortion cracking and melting were resolved, and later the use of saggars helped to protect the thinly potted wares from the full force of the flames.

Initially the production of decanters, jugs, bottles and drinking mugs was for the tavern trade. Imported German wares influenced these early products, and brown salted 'Bartmann' bottles copied the applied decoration of masks and seals. Some early white pieces were decorated with cobalt and manganese slips, imitating Westerwald wares. By 1675 the worst of the firing and glazing problems had been overcome. The bottles of the early days of the Fulham Pottery were well crafted, with forms more elegant than the first copies of the German

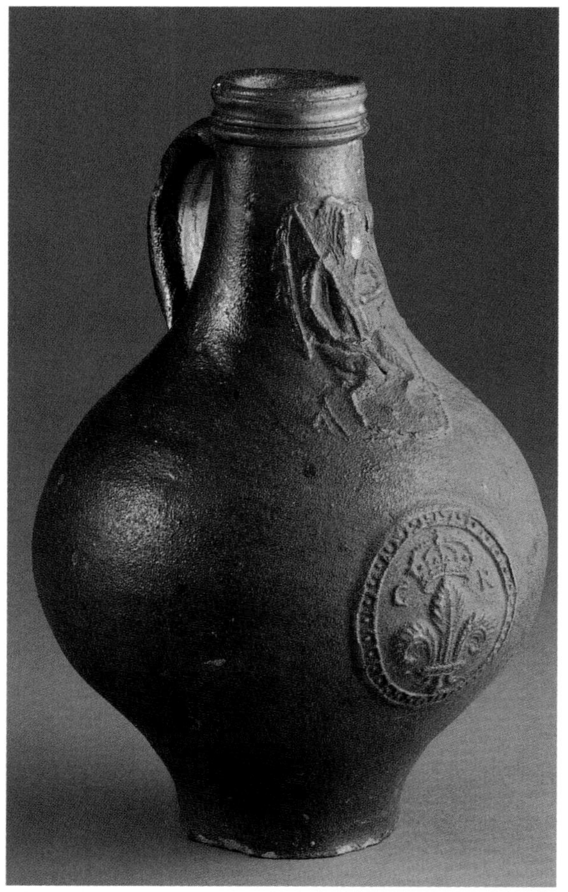

Bottle with rectangular medallion of the figure of Pan. Attributed to John Dwight, Fulham; c.1675–1700. (National Museums and Galleries of Wales)

pieces. Mugs and gorges, a bulbous form of mug, were light and thinly turned on the lathe.

During the next two years, confident in his ability to supply Cologne ware in large quantities, Dwight made various agreements with the Glass Sellers Company of London to take the whole of his production at a fixed price in return for the monopoly to supply for four years. Iron-dipped brown stoneware, though of excellent quality, became largely undecorated, as speed was all-important when it came to mass production.

Dwight's experiments were not restricted to salt glaze, and his abiding hope was to discover the way to make porcelain; with it the salt glaze took a new direction. While developing a refined white clay in the early 1680s, he produced a range of superbly thin, salt-glaze 'finewares' as the pioneer of utensils for tea and coffee drinking. In addition he introduced some marbled stoneware. There are a number of magnificently modelled busts and figures, considered to be some of the finest pieces of their kind. They are enhanced with the thinnest coating of salt glaze that picks out every detail of the excellent craftsmanship. Dwight himself is unlikely to have done the carving, which more probably can be attributed to other artists.

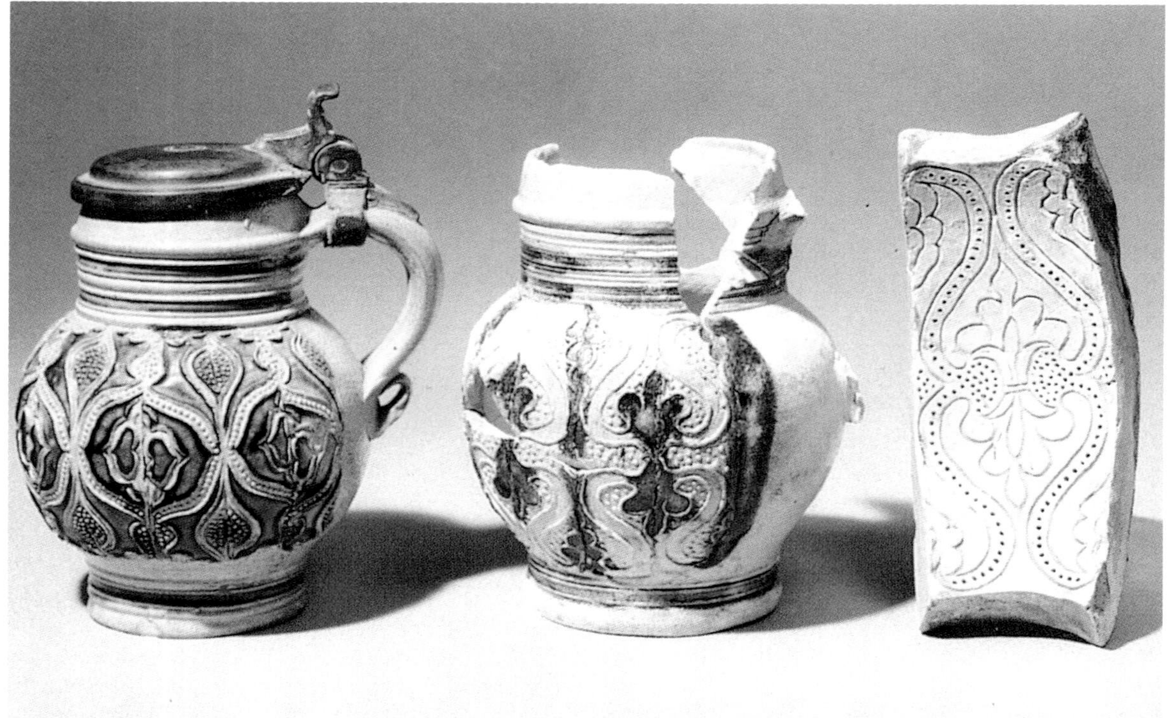

A Rhineland Westerwald lidded tankard compared with a remarkably similar pot and mould recovered from Dwight's Fulham factory; c.1675. 12cm high. (Jonathan Horne and the Museum of London)

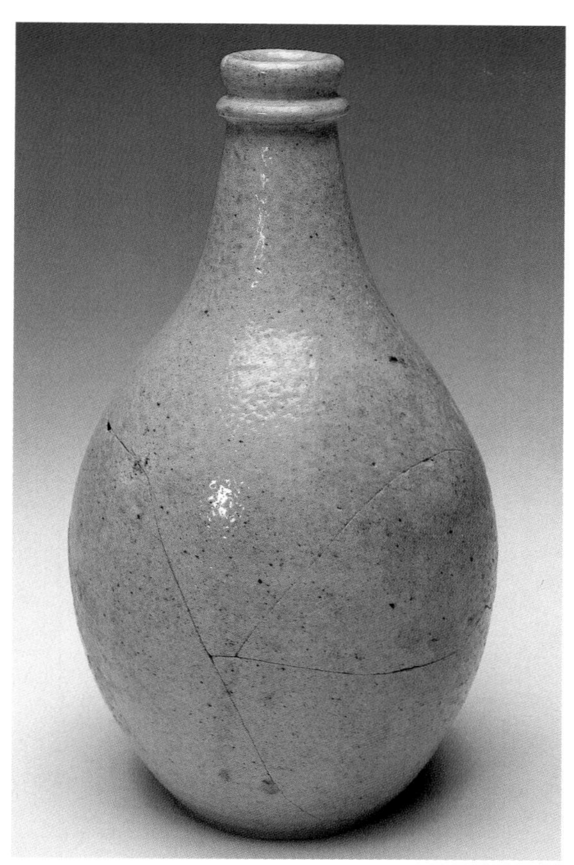

Bottle, c.1685–95. A pale grey, natural salt glaze, iron-dipped bottle or flask with rim cordon. Otherwise plain. A unique vessel form found in the disused cellar which lay behind John Dwight's first house in Fulham, later the Golden Lion. (Museum of London)

Kilns

The early stoneware kilns at Fulham were updraught and woodfired. They were built to the same design as kilns used for lower fired, tin-glazed earthenware, but the potters learned to coax them to reach stoneware temperatures. They were rectangular, with a vaulted load floor above the hearth, and an arched roof. Major repair work was needed frequently, as the salt badly deteriorated the brickwork. This type of kiln was used in London until the 1780s. The circular-shaped bottle-kiln, used throughout the eighteenth century in the Staffordshire salt-glaze industry and in Liverpool, did not appear widely in London until the nineteenth century.

The Spread of Production

Dwight's second patent of 1684 renewed his monopoly on the manufacture of salt glaze, and

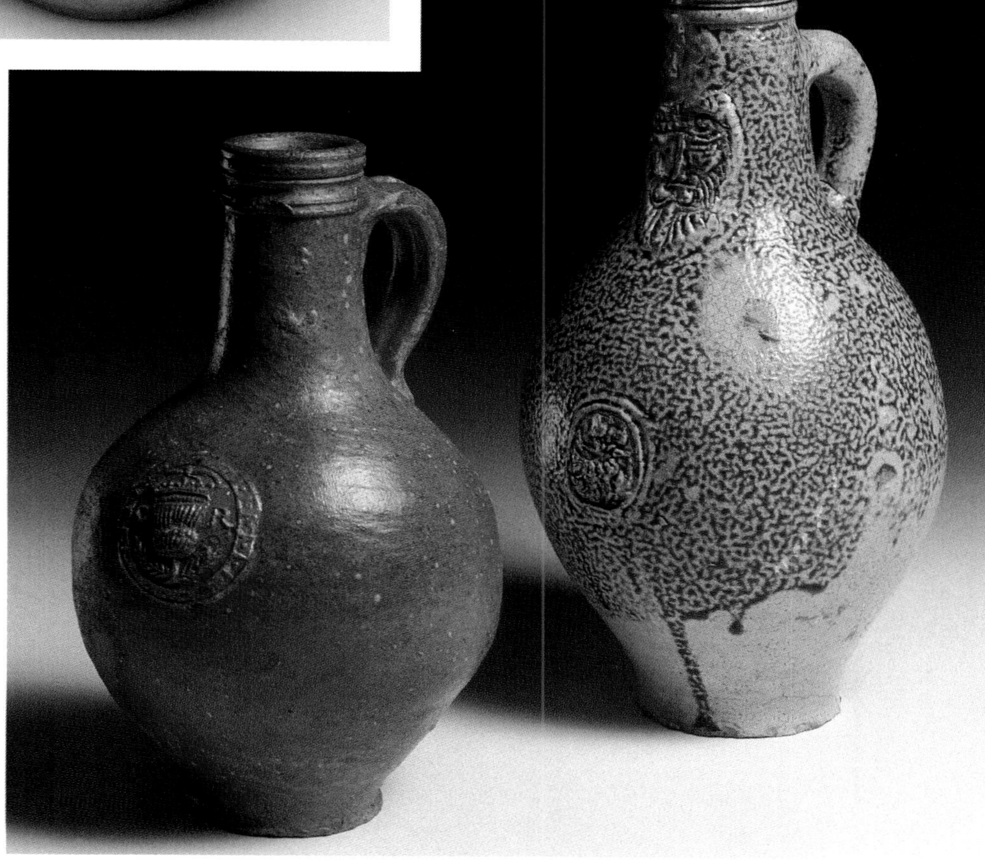

Left: A rare stoneware salt-glaze bottle bearing the insignia of the crown and thistle and the initials 'CR' (Charles II). Height 21.1cm. 1675–85. Right: A tall 'bellarmine', still containing the remnants of a charm against witchcraft. Height 26cm; c.1685. Probably London. The unusual proportions of this bellarmine together with the crude mask and rudimentary seal suggest that this bottle is not of continental origin. Witches' bottles were commonly used during the seventeenth century and were usually buried under the hearth or threshold as protection against witchcraft. (Jonathan Horne)

he continued to protect fiercely his control of the manufacture of salt glaze, selling as many bottles as the Fulham Pottery could produce. But the process was no longer a secret, and many other potters were experimenting with it; indeed it has been easy to identify the areas where these experiments were going on, from the many infringements of his patent, and from the ensuing lawsuits. Other London potteries, Derbyshire, Nottinghamshire, Staffordshire and Bristol began to develop and market their own brand of salt-glaze wares as soon as the patent expired in 1698. By that time Dwight's health was failing and he took no further action to prosecute other potters who had infringed his patents. When Dwight died in 1703, stoneware manufacture was well established in all those places.

The production of British salt glaze quickly expanded. London potteries were able to benefit from being close to the facilities of the port, and were able to use the export market. On the other hand, regional potteries had the advantage of cheaper local raw materials. Nottinghamshire, Derbyshire and Staffordshire were to become serious competitors in the market, for they too were soon producing well made and distinctive salt-glaze stoneware.

2 Salt Glaze in Britain

Once the London potters had begun their challenge of Dwight's monopoly of the production of salt-glaze wares in Britain, it became evident that potters in other regions of the country were equally determined to progress their own knowledge of stoneware. By his initial success, and because of his determination to control the commercial gains of his production of salt glaze, Dwight had led the transformation of a domestic industry into one of massively increased production. As well as the home market, the trade pattern too was revolutionized, as the mass production of English brown stoneware eventually turned the flood of imported stoneware from Germany: by the late seventeenth century much salt-glaze stoneware was being exported from England to Germany. Over the next two centuries the manufacture of salt glaze flourished, producing massive quantities of common articles used in daily life.

London, Nottinghamshire, Derbyshire, Staffordshire, and to a lesser extent Bristol and Glasgow, became major centres of salt-glaze production in the eighteenth century. Liverpool was a busy trading port, and the salt glaze that was produced there was most likely all for export. Elsewhere salt-glaze stoneware manufactured by local potteries was for domestic use, and an infinite variety of brown stoneware pieces have survived to the present day, a testimony to their durability. They represent the huge output of utilitarian wares that included ale mugs, jugs, cooking and storage vessels. In addition to the cheaper items, the full range of brown salt-glaze stoneware includes commemorative pieces and more refined tableware, and tea and coffee pots. By the second half of the eighteenth century the production of brown salt glaze in Staffordshire was of little importance. Instead the 'Potteries' were concentrating on the manufacture of the increasingly desirable white salt-glaze tableware, for which they gained a special reputation. One or two Scottish potteries also produce some fine white salt-glaze tableware between 1730 and 1770.

The Regional Centres

The characteristics of any pot are derived from the local clays, the firing effects and the particular methods of manufacture. A wonderful variety of the most attractive and brilliant qualities of salt glaze can be found by looking at past pieces of the salt-glaze wares of the regional centres. Interwoven with the history of the development of salt-glaze manufacture is the expertise and hard labour of the craftsmen. For the most part they remain anonymous, but their skills have conspired to leave us as a legacy a fascinating array of traditional salt-glaze pieces.

'Nottingham Ware'

Nottingham began its history as a pottery town as early as the tenth century, and from the mid-twelfth century the local wares were commonly glazed and unglazed earthenware. Although in the late fourteenth century a very early type of stoneware was in limited production, it was the local earthenware pottery industry in the Nottingham area that was well established, when the tough German-made salt-glaze bottles began to be imported for use in the taverns. The Morley family had long been connected with pot-making, and James Morley of Nottingham was one of those named for infringing Dwight's patent in the lawsuits of 1693, when he

(BELOW) Posset pot, 1700. Height 10½ in. Light brown, salt-glaze stoneware made in Nottingham. Inscribed on the reverse 'Samuel Watkinson Mayor and Sarah, his wife Mayoress of Nottingham 1700'. The base is double-walled with a cutout design of a spray of flowers. (Nottingham City Museums and Galleries)

(BELOW RIGHT) Mug, 1781. Lustrous brown salt-glaze stoneware made in Nottingham. Incised flowers and inscription 'T & G Holland of Nottingham Made at Nottm Feb 16th 1781'. (Nottingham City Museums and Galleries)

admitted to selling 'brown' mugs. From the 1690s, Morley's firm led the production of Nottingham salt glaze for nearly one hundred years, making great profits from the sale of the cheap, hard-wearing mugs to the ale houses.

Although the majority of salt-glaze pots made in Nottingham must have been ordinary tableware and simple drinking vessels, it is the more special pieces that have been carefully preserved, and which therefore survive in comparative quantity. Posset pots, loving cups, pierced mugs, jugs, punch bowls, teapots and tea caddies are just some of the array of pieces still to be found in collections.

The very best of true Nottingham wares are finely potted. The simple shapes are thin-sectioned and were precisely turned on a lathe. The surfaces of the pots have a rich, lustrous sheen, and the salt glaze itself provides the thinnest of coatings. Nottingham pots in particular show how salt glaze will pick out every detail on the surface of the clay, and a great variety of decorative techniques were used to embellish the pieces and fully exploit this quality. It is these decorative qualities that have inspired the work of several contemporary makers of salt glaze.

Some of the early Nottingham pots carry carved designs: these are double-walled vessels, where the pattern is carved through the outer wall leaving the inner wall untouched. Many of the Nottingham pieces were decorated with the incised designs of the outline of flowers drawn on the surface, while on others the embellishment was impressed or stamped. Pots were refined on the lathe, and this tool provided the opportunity to produce precise incisions turned in bands around the profiles. Rouletting wheels were used to impress bands of pattern around the forms, complementing the skilful lathe work. Names and dates were often incised on pieces, and combinations of all the techniques were used on the more elaborate and special commemorative wares.

The 'sprig' designs were made in moulds and applied to the surface of the pots. The sides of thicker-walled pots were facetted, and the linear pattern and texture is particularly effective when salt glazed. The overall texturing of a surface was sometimes combined with bands of grogged slip, and this 'breadcrumb' type of decoration is especially associated with Nottingham bear jugs, when it is used in a crude representation of the animals' fur. Press moulds with detailed designs enhanced by the salt glaze were used to produce a range of table and fancy items.

To be able to appreciate fully the refinement and lightness of the Nottingham pieces, they have to be handled: only then can the workmanship and skill of the eighteenth-century potters be truly admired. In comparison, later pieces from the next century are considerably heavier, as hand finishing had given way to moulded decoration in the drive to speed up production and satisfy an expanding market.

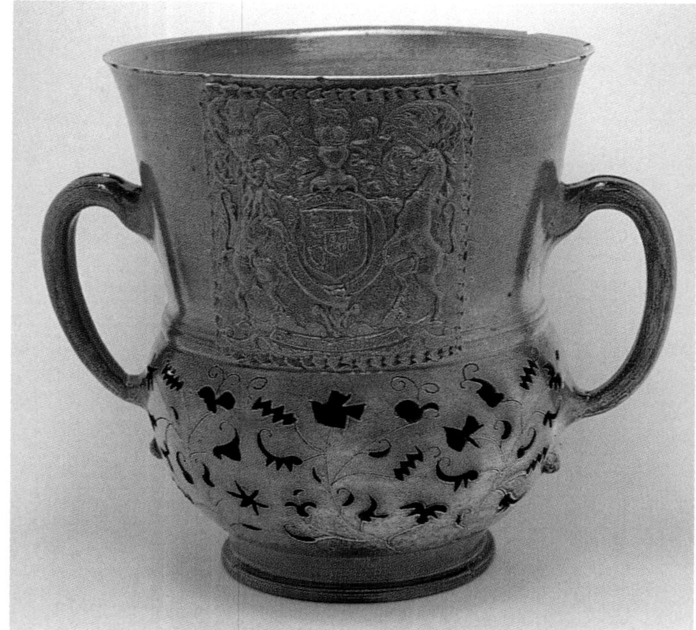

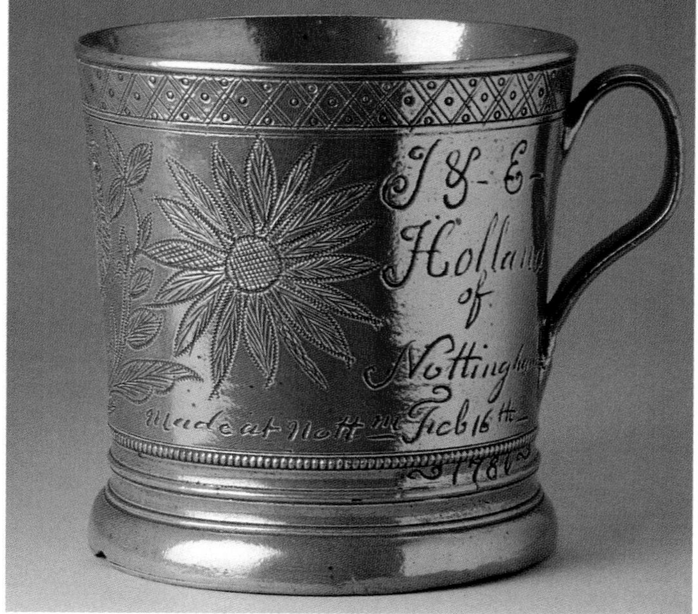

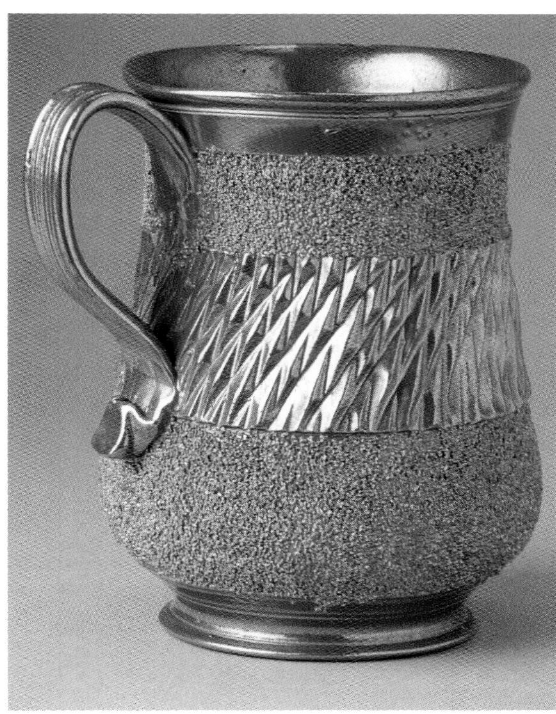

Mug, c.1750. Salt-glaze stoneware made in Nottingham. Breadcrumb and cut decoration. (Nottingham City Museums and Galleries)

It is thought that the kilns of the Nottingham area were square. Very few saggars have been found amongst the other kiln furniture, and it is probable that kiln shelves were used to protect the wares, which show little of the effect of being directly touched by the flames of the fire. The colours of Nottingham wares range from a dark metallic treacle-brown through to orange, and result from the use of different clays and the vessel's position in the kiln. The smooth, dark, metallic surface was achieved either from the high iron content of the clay body, or from the application of a very thin, high-iron slip. The iron-rich surface tended to produce a lustrous sheen at high temperatures. Clay was brought from Derbyshire, and it is not surprising that some of the early, lighter-coloured salt-glaze pieces, particularly from the Derbyshire factory at Crich, are difficult to distinguish from those made in Nottingham.

Derbyshire

The Crich pottery began salt-glaze production at the same time as Morley's in Nottingham, and made very similar pieces. By the mid-eighteenth century other Derbyshire potteries had taken to manufacturing utilitarian, brown salt-glaze stoneware, and it continued to be produced at several potteries in Derbyshire for a further two hundred years until the 1940s. In particular ink, blacking and furniture-paste bottles, along with bottles and jars for every other purpose, became the mainstay of production. Kitchenware certainly remained a most important part of production for firms such as Bourne's at Denby and Pearson's near Chesterfield.

The potteries close to Chesterfield, at Whittington Moor and Brampton, produced an array of pots for the home and kitchen. Their wares became generally known as 'Brampton ware', and are typified by the durable kitchen-

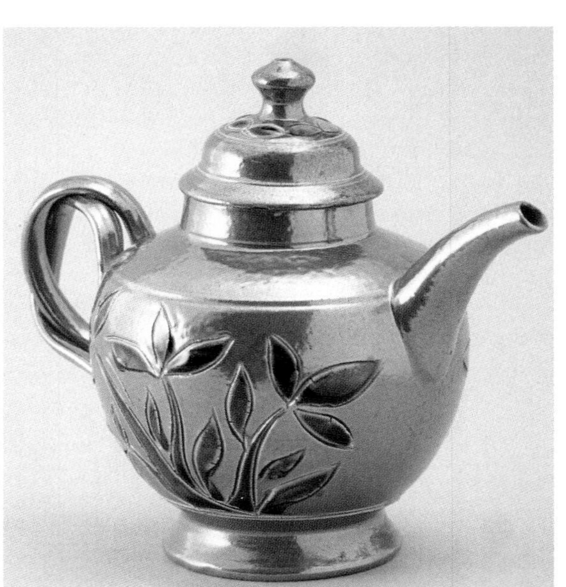

(FAR LEFT) Teapot, c.1775–1800. Nottingham salt-glaze stoneware. A delightful piece, lustrous brown, with a crossed strap handle and decorated with incised flowers filled with high-iron slip. (Nottingham City Museum and Galleries)

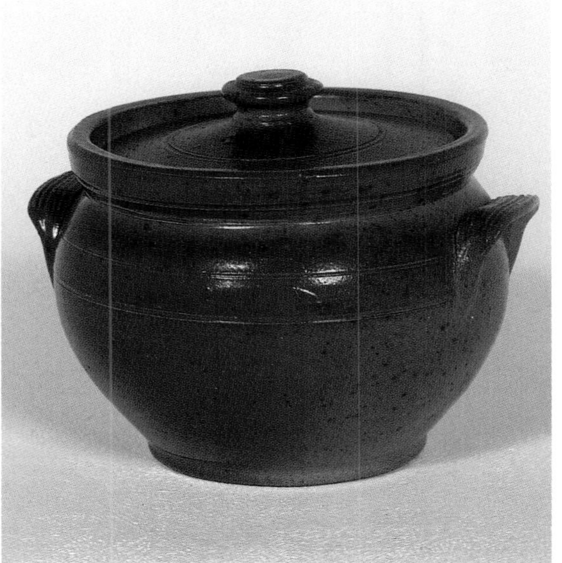

(LEFT) Hash pot, nineteenth century. Brampton, salt-glaze stoneware. The domestic wares, stewpots and storage jars were undecorated apart from the occasional rouletting. As practical pots, never intended to have a decorative role, their considerable aesthetic value has been largely overlooked. (Chesterfield Museum and Art Gallery. Photo University of Derby CEDM, Photo and Video Library)

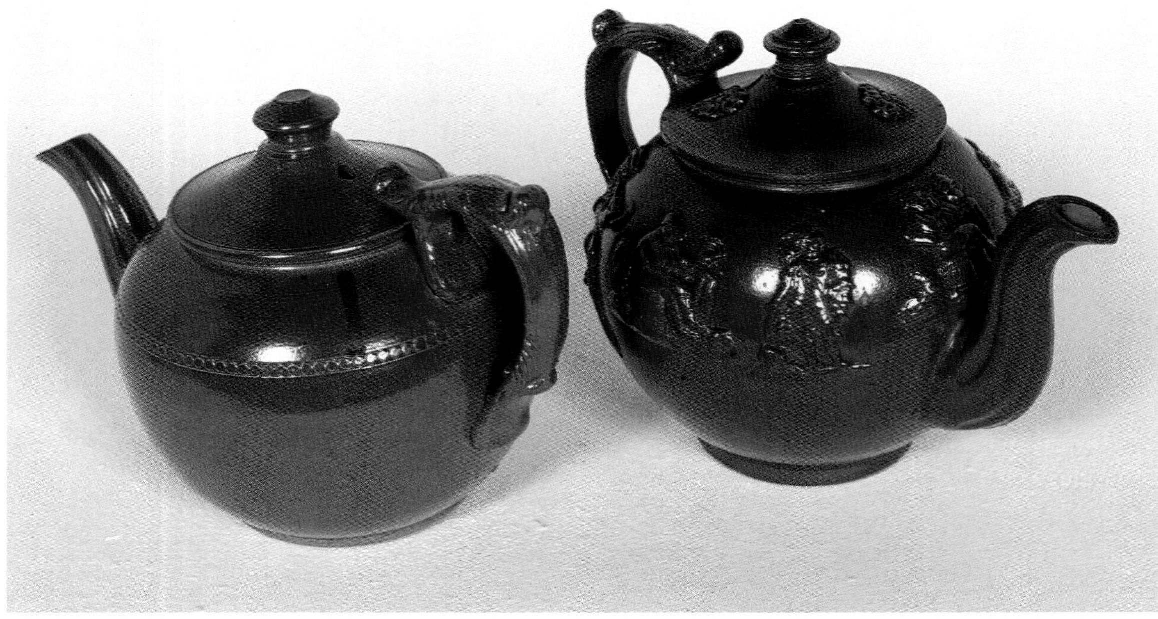

Two teapots, nineteenth century. Brampton, salt-glaze stoneware. Left: Dark/ mid-brown, plain apart from simple rouletting. Right: Lustrous dark brown with applied sprigs of figures. Greenish glaze inside. (Chesterfield Museum and Art Gallery. Photo University of Derby CEDM, Photo and Video Library)

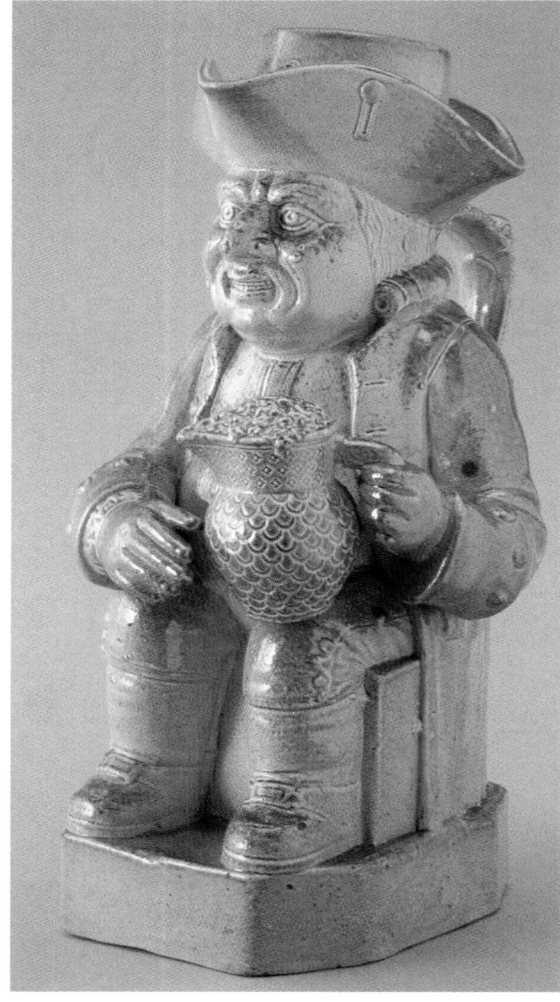

Toby Jug, c.1840. Brampton, Derbyshire, salt-glaze stoneware. These pieces often have a decorative role as well as a practical one. Made from an almost white clay, giving a light honey colour under the salt glaze. (Nottingham City Museums and Galleries)

ware made in the brown salt-glaze stoneware: stew and souse pots, bread bakers, store jars, dishes, bowls, pudding moulds and colanders are just some of the items that were made for particular use in the kitchen and illustrated in the factory catalogues. Much of the plainer Brampton ware is dark brown, and today it is the simplicity of these functional forms that are an inspiration to potters making domestic wares. For the salt-glaze potter in particular, they stand as examples of the way that the salt-glaze form, with only a touch of simple decoration and coated with the thinnest sheen of glaze, can be a pure delight.

Some of the more decorative and ornate Brampton-ware pieces – such as tea and coffee pots carrying sprig decoration, and moulded Toby jugs – were made from both the dark clay, and a pale clay that fired a light honey-coloured salt glaze. However, the fancy ware was only a minor aspect of production, and the vast majority of the Chesterfield wares were mass-produced bottles and jars, mostly for commercial mineral water manufacturers and fruit processors, also for cooking and storage pots, and to a lesser extent, water filter manufacture.

Staffordshire Salt Glaze

In contrast to the brown kitchen pots of Nottinghamshire and Derbyshire, Staffordshire pottery manufacturers became best known for the production of wonderfully fine salt-glaze white wares. Great importance and prestige had been attached to the discovery of the techniques of salt glaze, and tradition holds that Staffordshire has made its own claim to the invention of salt glaze. Simeon Shaw set out to record the pottery industry in the *History of Staffordshire Potteries*, that he compiled from contemporary reports and published in 1829. He recounts this story, which today reads as an amusing anecdote:

> At Stanley Farm (a short mile from the small pottery of Mr Palmer, at Bagnall five miles east of Burslem) the servant of Mr Joseph Yates, was boiling, in an earthen vessel, a strong lixivium of common salt, to be used some way in curring pork; but during her temporary absence, the liquor effervesced, and some ran over the sides of the vessel, quickly causing them to become red hot: the muriatic acid decomposed the surface, and when cold, the sides were partly glazed. Mr Palmer availed himself of the hint thus obtained, and commenced in making a fresh sort – the common Brown Ware of our day . . .

The 'Potteries' Early Salt Manufacture

The Staffordshire towns around and including Stoke-on-Trent are known generally as 'The Potteries'. The concentration of the pottery industry had developed and thrived with the benefits of local clay deposits, local supplies of coal to fire the kilns, and a good central position for communication and trading. Undoubtedly North Staffordshire potters had begun to experiment with salt glaze in the late seventeenth century, and a Thomas Miles made the earliest that is recorded there. He produced a crude kind of white stoneware in 1685, as well as a brown stoneware.

The salt-glaze process was obviously no longer a secret, but Dwight's patents of 1672 and 1684 meant that any potter firing stoneware and salt glaze would be wise to do so secretly. Between 1693 and 1698 at least six Staffordshire potters were cited in Dwight's lawsuits: Joshua Astbury, three Wedgwood brothers, Cornelius Hammersley and Moses Middleton. When the patent finally expired in 1699, several potteries were ready to produce salt-glaze stoneware: Robert Astbury, Thomas Wedgwood and Joshua Twyford are amongst the most distinguished who became major producers of the full range of Staffordshire salt-glaze ware. Aaron Wood, Enoch Booth and Thomas Whieldon were also producing salt glaze from the mid-eighteenth century.

Some mystery surrounds the part that the Elers brothers played in the early years of Staffordshire salt glaze. John and David Elers came as silversmiths from Holland to London; however, they became interested in ceramics, and were assistants to Dwight from 1690 to 1693, before setting up their own small pothouse in Vauxhall. Having lived in Cologne they most certainly would know the way salt glaze was made, and had admitted to making 'Browne Muggs' when named in one of Dwight's lawsuits. They came to work at Bradwell Hall in North Staffordshire for about seven years, returning to London in 1698.

In a letter written much later, in 1777, Josiah Wedgwood attributes the Elers with 'improvements' in the pottery manufactory, amongst which is included 'glazing our common clays with salt which produce Pot d'Grey or stoneware'. Simeon Shaw describes in his book the kiln that the Elers used at Bradwell, and implies that it was not of the kind for salt glazing. The evidence is contradictory, however, as he also records that when the Elers fired their salt kiln 'their oven cast forth such tremendous volumes of smoke and flame . . . as were terrific to the inhabitants of Burslem . . .'. At the time, like many other potters, they would have been exceedingly secretive about manufacturing methods. However, no salt-glaze shards have been found amongst the many fragments of the red unglazed stoneware teapots for which the Elers are most famous.

Staffordshire Clays, Kilns and Firings

The local Staffordshire clays would withstand the stoneware temperatures, although the whitest clays, used for slips and in the development of the fine wares, were eventually imported from the West Country. Salt was easily obtained, from mines in nearby Cheshire where the exploitation of rock salt dates back to the 1670s. But as elsewhere, the development of the design of the kiln was an all-important requirement for the Staffordshire potters, before they

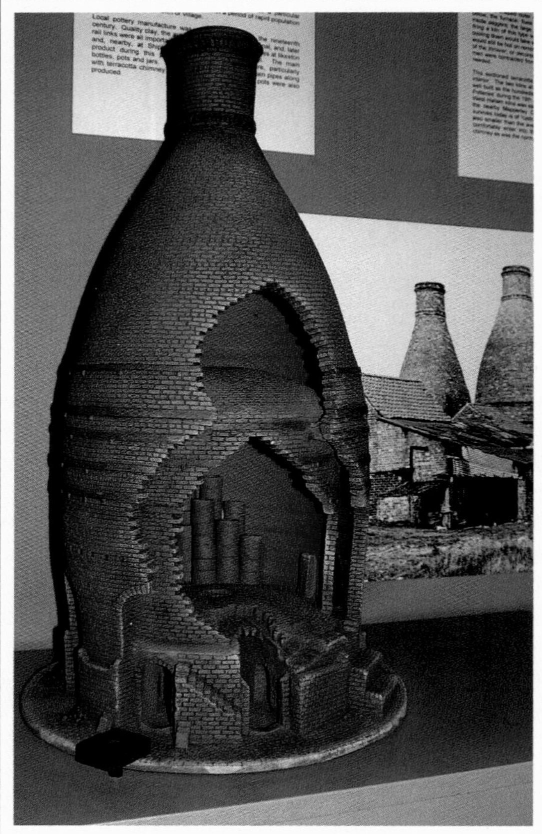

(RIGHT) Bottle kiln, c.1900. Model showing the structure of the basic kiln design. A salt kiln would have had adaptations: a wide space between the inner and outer walls, to make room for the scaffolding, and salt ports in the dome. (Erewash Museum Service)

The Bottle Kiln

There are two main parts to a bottle oven. The outer, bottle-shaped structure is the hovel: this acts as the chimney, and as protection from the weather. Inside, the circular oven has a domed roof. Around its base are the fire mouths, from which flues and bags carry the heat to the centre of the kiln. Heat rises through the stacked wares out through the top. In the early twentieth century a down-draught version of the bottle kiln was developed, to use the heat more efficiently.

could succeed in reaching the higher temperatures of stoneware firings.

Bottle kilns, already used in Staffordshire, proved to be a good design for stoneware, with some slight adaptations for the salt firings. In the dome of the oven there would be a series of holes positioned over the flues of the fire mouths below. Scaffolding would be erected around the kiln, so the workers could climb up to the different levels of the dome at the time of salting. They would tip the salt off iron spoons into each hole, and plug the holes to hold the vapours in; they would then move on to the next, repeatedly circling the kiln in a process that would take up to five hours.

Wares were protected from the direct flame and from the full attack of the salt by the use of 'saggars', cylindrical containers into which the pots were placed; they varied in size according to the shape and number of pots to be placed in each. Wares were placed in the saggars with none of the pieces touching, supported with small pieces of the refractory clay from which the saggars themselves were made. The walls of the saggars were pierced with several holes, each about 5cm (2in) in diameter, so that the salt fumes could enter the space and surround the pots with the glaze vapour. The saggars also served to stack the wares in the kilns, with pads of clay supporting and separating each one from the other. A conical clay cover, protecting the wares, covered the top one. They would be arranged one on top of the other to form a 'bung', and each bung would be lined up under one of the holes through which the salt would enter the kiln.

Crouch Ware

There are several clearly defined stages and types of salt glaze produced in Staffordshire. The earliest was possibly produced in 1690 at Burslem, and was known as Crouch ware, made from local clays mixed with sand. Before firing, the pots were dipped in an iron-stained wash, and the finished pieces are plain light brown. Because local, less pure clay was used, this type of ware was inexpensive and continued to be made for many years, along with darker brown salt-glaze wares. The pieces are of a high quality and extremely light and thin walled, as the clay body could be turned on a lathe. Incised and rouletted decoration is common.

Drab Ware

Drab ware was produced in the 1720s and 1730s, and offered a new type of elegant tableware for the market. The pieces were made on the wheel using the local grey and light grey-brown firing clays. Applied relief decoration in white clay was made by impressing the clay into a metal die and used to delicately embellish the pieces. White clay would also sometimes be

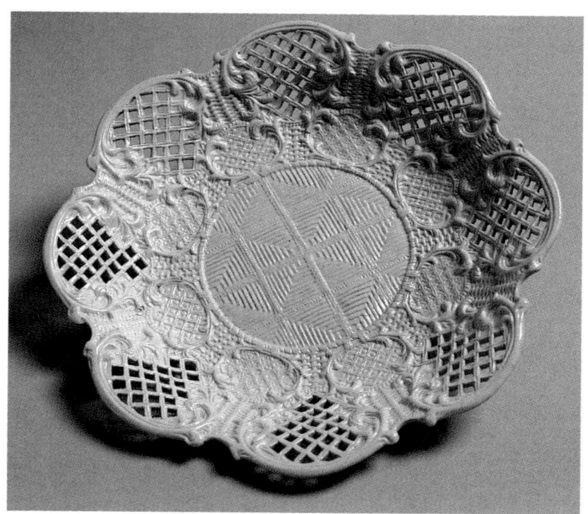

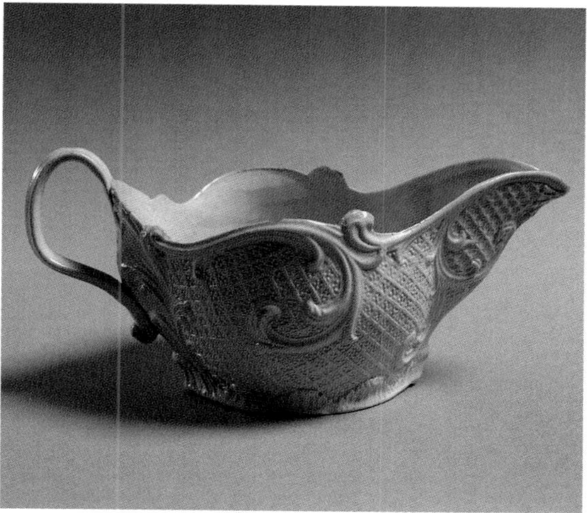

(FAR LEFT) Staffordshire white salt-glaze stoneware, c.1760. Fine press-moulded dish with scroll and basket-work in relief. Panels of pierced trelliswork around the rim. These patterns were also used in porcelain and lead-glazed earthenware. (Private collection)

(LEFT) Staffordshire white salt-glaze stoneware c.1750. Sauce boat, possibly Thomas and John Wedgwood. This type of ware was made by both the cast- and press-moulded methods. (Private collection)

used for press moulding the handle and spouts of the jugs and pots.

White wares

Although brown salt-glaze stoneware was produced in Staffordshire, the most distinguished salt glaze from the Potteries is the white ware. Mass produced by the industry, and originally using the metal moulds discarded by London silversmiths, it reached a high degree of perfection and established a high standard for future ceramic manufacture. White wares are first seen in the early plain pieces made from the lightest burning clays, covered with a white slip made from Staffordshire pipe clay.

Around 1720 the white Devon clays were being imported; these were at first used as a slip, and by adding calcined flint an even whiter effect could be obtained. Later this mix was also used to make a new white firing clay body, developed in response to the demand for white wares from London, and to emulate the white porcelain from China. White on white, the pieces were thrown, and moulded decoration was applied to the wide range of shapes of the tableware. The salt glaze lightly covers the pieces, picking out the relief details of the surfaces that have the appearance of lace.

The manufacture of salt glaze in the eighteenth century was widespread throughout the six pottery towns. These were the very early days of industrialization. The factories were still small and generally family-run concerns, and the craftsmanship in the work of these potters is clearly evident. Wares were both press-moulded and slip cast, and both these methods speeded up production so that an unlimited number of forms of tableware was available to the ever-demanding market. Plates and dishes were pressed over a convex plaster mould, and the single and double tea caddy was a favourite article made in a press-mould. All the press-moulds would have been made from metal, alabaster, bisque-fired clay or plaster.

The process of slip casting began in the 1740s, and all the moulds for slip-cast wares were made from plaster of Paris. Many of the blocks from which the slip-cast moulds were made have survived. These original masters are either alabaster or plaster of Paris; some have been cut directly into clay and then bisque-fired, or in some cases salt-glazed. The skill of the block-cutters was paramount, and the result of the crisp quality and details of their carving can be admired in the salt-glaze pieces. The thinnest coating of glaze picks out the finest detail of the intricate relief decoration on all the white wares. Mass production had arrived, and in the Potteries, as the manufacture of the moulded white wares flourished, that of brown stoneware declined.

Colour

Cobalt was used to bring a colour to contrast with the white clay. The 'scratch-blue' wares appeared between 1740 and 1780. The technique of incising lines on the plain white body of a piece and then filling it with zaffre, an impure form of cobalt, was used to decorate souvenir and personal commemorative wares.

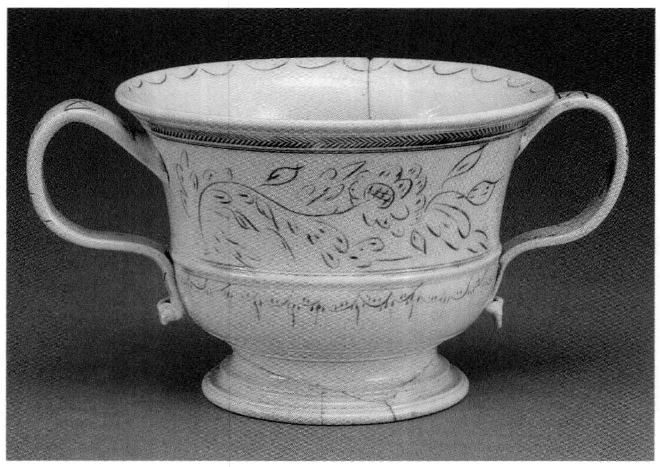

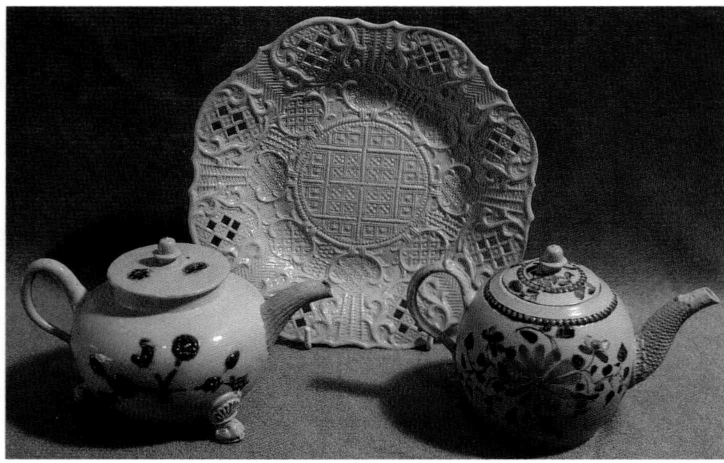

(ABOVE LEFT) Two-handled cup, c.1755. Staffordshire salt-glaze stoneware with 'scratch blue' decoration. Delicately inscribed floral decoration. Shallow band of rouletting below the rim. (National Museums and Galleries of Wales)

(ABOVE RIGHT) Group of Staffordshire salt-glaze stoneware. Plate, c.1760. Press-moulded with scroll and basket-work in high and low relief with pierced trelliswork. Teapot with ornamental handle and spout, decorated with polychrome enamels. Honeysuckle flower, raised and beaded detail. Teapot, c.1740 on moulded tripod feet. Ribbed spout, plain handle. Decorated with applied rose in blue-stained clay. (Private collection)

Much of the Staffordshire salt glaze is difficult to attribute to any one potter in particular, but Enoch Booth signed or initialled many of his scratch-blue pieces. Incised decoration follows the lines of stylized flowers and plants, and filled with blue, they trace their way across the smooth, salted surface of a loving cup or punch-bowl.

The surface of fine white salt glaze was found to be a good base for enamel painting, and by the 1740s several factories were producing skilfully painted wares. The extensive use of coloured enamels on a surface already decorated in relief, produced a cheaper but delightful alternative to the expensive imported Chinese porcelain. Coloured pigments would be painted on plain-fired, salt-glaze stoneware pieces, and re-fired at a much lower temperature. Many of the painted designs were Chinese or European inspired, while others celebrated current affairs. On occasions it seems an excuse for a somewhat gaudy and lavish excess of colour.

The 1760s saw the ultimate flourish of ornamentation. Contemporary silverware was often used as the basis of designs, and basketwork and pierced trellis patterns offered yet another fashion for the adornment of white salt-glaze tableware. Once again the combination of the craftsmen's skills and the lightest coating of glaze on the white surface produced pieces that can make us catch our breath with pleasure.

Changes in Fashion

The price of fuel for the high temperature kilns, and a further salt tax that had been imposed in 1732, made the cost of salt glaze high. By 1775 Staffordshire white salt glaze was in decline. Furthermore the white firing body that was so successful for high-firing stoneware temperatures proved just as good for lower earthenware temperatures, and this led to the development of lead-glazed 'Creamware'. This new fashion was soon to eclipse the popularity of salt glaze, and by 1778 the production of Staffordshire white salt glaze had ceased.

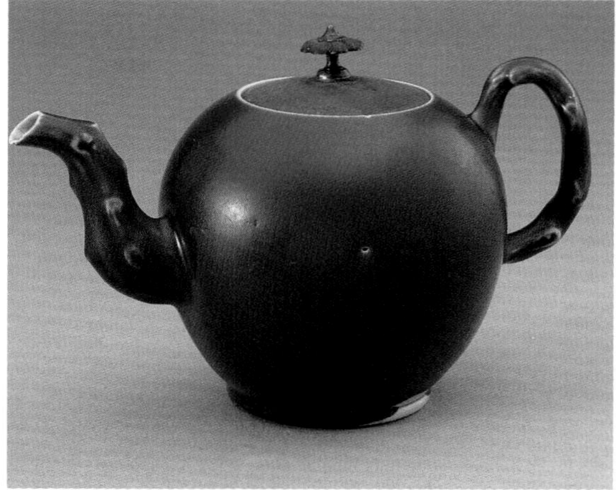

Teapot, c.1760. 'Littler-Wedgwood' blue glaze, salt-glaze stoneware. Cobalt was used in a bold way for striking effect in the 'Littler-Wedgwood blue' wares, manufactured between 1749 and 1763. These wares appear to have been fully dipped and coated in a fusible slip containing cobalt, prior to a salt firing. (National Museums and Galleries of Wales)

3 Industrialization and Studio Art Pottery

After Dwight's patent expired in 1698, those London potters who had already begun to work with salt glaze were quick to go into full production and compete in the market. Several rival pothouses in Southwark and Vauxhall, and other parts of Lambeth, began to make a range of brown salt-glaze stoneware. The most common item was the ale mug, generally straight-sided with incised decoration that was appropriate for the particular inn, or commissioned by the customers. After Dwight's death in 1703, the Fulham Pottery's main output continued to be brown stoneware. But without his entrepreneurial influence the finer wares were to be abandoned, and wares from Fulham Pottery became like that of any of the London pothouses, all with a very similar range of salt-glaze products.

'Fulham Ware'

By the mid-1750s most tankards and jugs had sprigged decoration and were part-dipped in a high iron wash. This fired dark, to contrast with the paler clay body that was sometimes lightened further with a dip in a white slip. Although this type of ware was made at other potteries and copied outside London, it became known generally as 'Fulham ware'.

Different sprigged decoration can be found on jugs, mugs, goblets, loving cups, bowls and commemorative ware. The 'hunting scene' was frequently depicted, showing trees and farms with the hounds and their quarry. The best examples have crisp detail and thoughtfully placed decoration, though some of the later

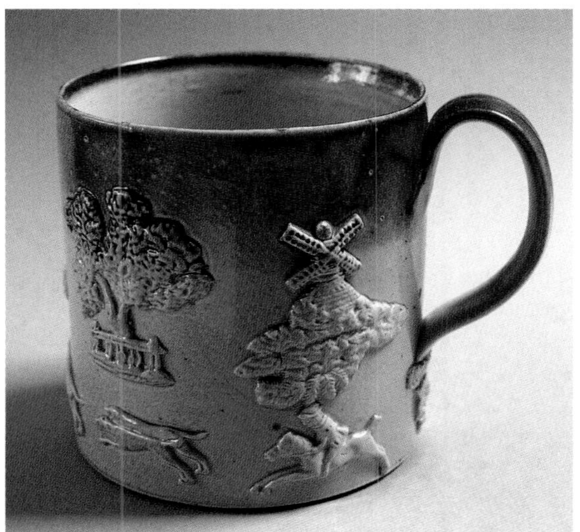

(FAR LEFT) A lathe-turned pint mug. Stoneware salt glaze, c.1710. Fulham. The silver mount has a maker's mark: 'HW'. The mug has been dipped in white slip before the application of an iron-wash. Dwight discovered the essentials of white slip, which included the use of ground flint, but he was quickly copied by the Staffordshire potters.

An extremely rare coffee pot and cover copying a metal shape. Stoneware salt-glaze c.1710. Probably Fulham. The coffee pot has many similarities to the mug, particularly the handle, which is almost identical. (Jonathan Horne)

(LEFT) Hunting Mug, c.1825–50. Possibly J. Bourne, Derbyshire. (Private collection)

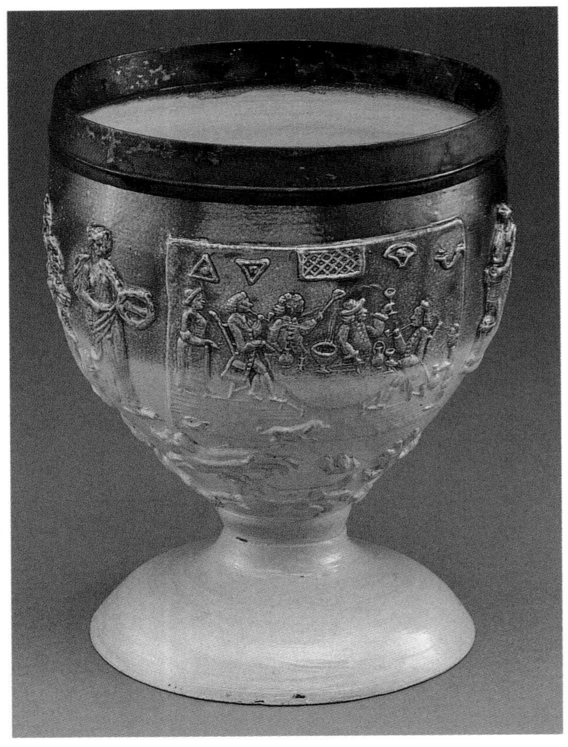

(RIGHT) Goblet, c.1794. Mortlake, London. Salt-glaze stoneware, silver rim, hallmark 1794. Applied panel after Hogarth's painting 'Midnight Modern Conversation'. (National Museums and Galleries of Wales)

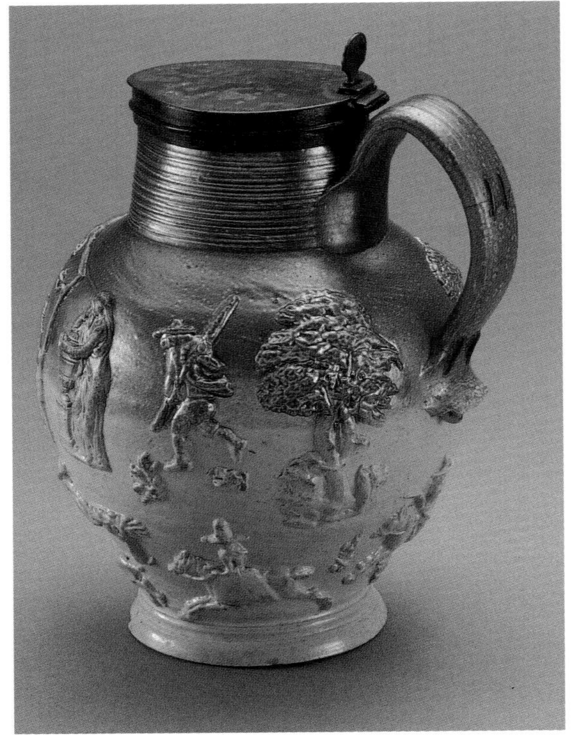

(FAR RIGHT) Hunting Jug with silver lid, c.1800. Mortlake, London. Salt-glaze stoneware. Sprigged country and hunting scenes. Applied panel after Hogarth's 'Midnight Modern Conversation' on reverse. (National Museums and Galleries of Wales)

ones are more clumsily assembled. The firm of Doulton continued to produce this type of ware well into the twentieth century.

The Fulham Pottery itself remained in the Dwight family for over 150 years. After a less productive period its fortunes were revived, and by 1832 Fulham was the second largest stoneware bottle factory in London, and the eighth in Britain. Mechanization increased the levels of production, and by the 1890s a work-force of 200 were making patent bottles and water filters, sanitary wares and architectural stoneware. Salt firings ceased in 1928 when the smoke and fumes from the coal-fired kilns became an intolerable nuisance.

Decline and Fortune

Salt glaze had always been regarded as a cheap way to produce durable pottery, and elsewhere in London other potteries continued to be successful in their salt-glaze production. From the mid-1800s moulded wares and gin flasks in particular, were added to their list of products. Fulham, Lambeth, Vauxhall, Southwark and Mortlake were the focus of the prospering London potteries. Delft ware continued to be

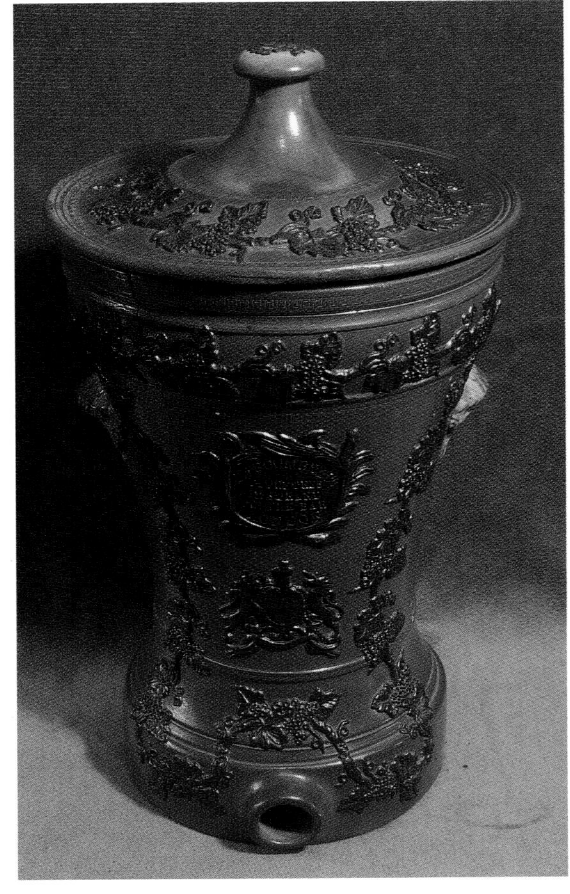

Water Filter, c.1860. Possibly Doulton. Pale clay body with iron-wash and dark lustrous grape-vine sprigs. (Private collection)

produced, sometimes at the same pottery and alongside the production of salt glaze.

Over the second part of the nineteenth century the production of domestic wares in London declined. Ever larger storage bottles, filters and laboratory equipment and sanitary ware, battery cases and telegraph insulators were added to the list of manufactured salt-glaze goods, and drainpipes and containers became the most lucrative of all the products. Bigger manufacturing enterprises, like those of James Stiff, Stephen Green and Doulton, were quick to take over many of the smaller potteries, with the firm of Doulton and Watts occupying almost the whole of the Lambeth riverside by the turn of the century.

The growth and fortunes of the Lambeth pottery of Doulton and Watts eventually came to dominate the production of salt-glaze ceramics, both there and at branches in the regions, although they were by no means the only companies producing salt-glaze stoneware. In 1873, both Doulton and James Stiff and Sons published their first illustrated product and price lists. They show a very similar range of goods, from chemical apparatus and drain pipes to water filters, and all manner of general stoneware bottles and jars, kitchenware and utilitarian products including spitoons and carriage warmers. Additional products made by Doulton were listed elsewhere.

Further Industrialization

Brown salt glaze continued to be manufactured elsewhere, but the nineteenth century saw the balance of production change as the availability of resources, improved transport networks, industrialization and social changes all took their effect. The salt-glaze industry was increasingly taken up with the production of containers and bottles of every size and description. Regional centres were just as productive, if not more so than the London-based potteries. The continuing industrial revolution and the movement to improve the poor social conditions in Victorian cities produced further changes – and with them came an opportunity for huge profits by the owners of salt-glaze factories. Drainpipes, sanitary ware, water filters and electric insulators established the fortunes of the major firms and extended the days of salt-glaze manufacture into the twentieth century.

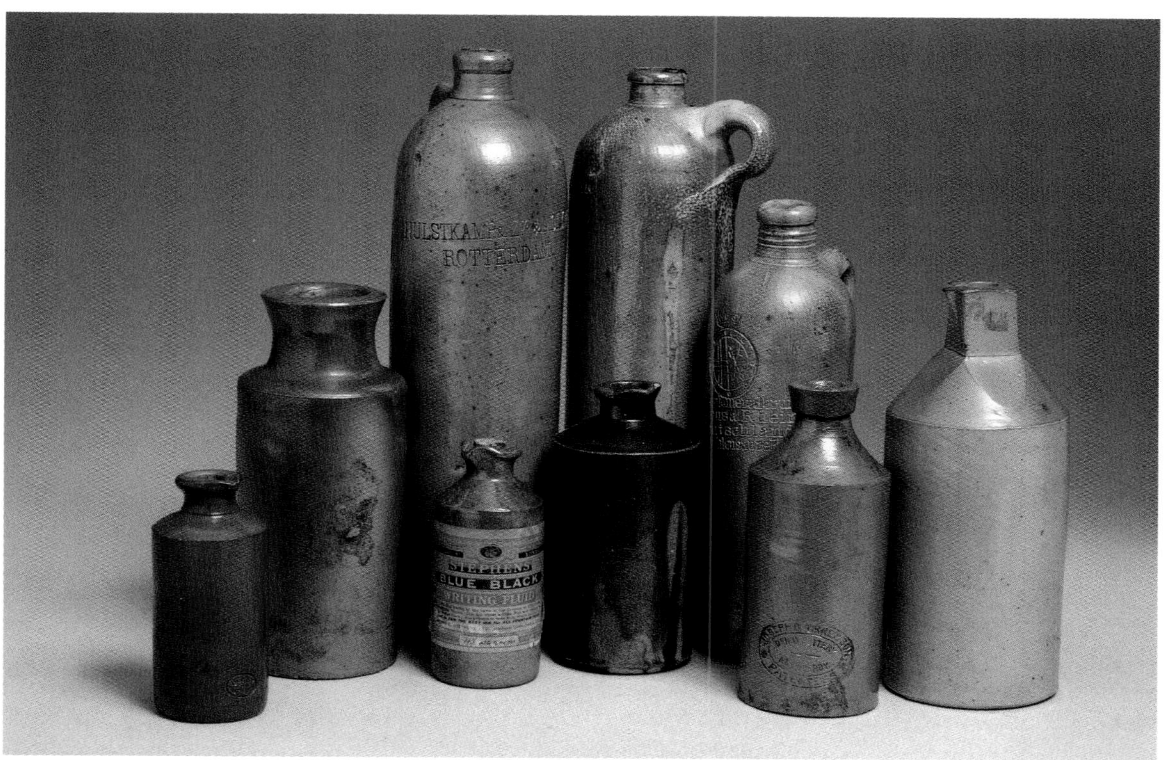

Collection of late nineteenth- and early twentieth-century brown salt-glaze stoneware bottles from Britain and Germany. Back: Westerwald 'Apollinaris', mineral water bottles. Front: various ink and blacking bottles manufactured in England. (Private collection)

Doulton and Salt-Glaze Stoneware

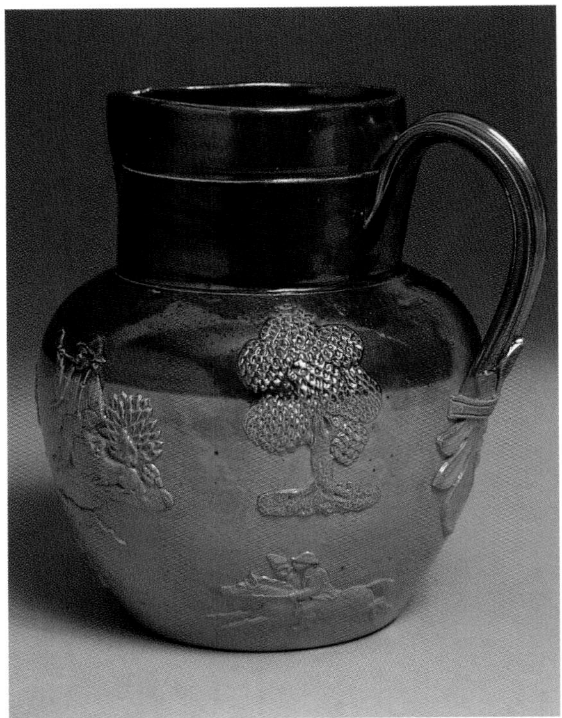

Hunting Jug, c.1900. Marked Doulton Lambeth. Sprigs of a type often copied at Fulham. (Private collection)

The firm of Doulton has always been one of the leading manufacturers of all types of ceramics, including architectural and industrial products, utilitarian and high-class tableware, ornamental and collectable decorative wares. Full ranges of exemplary products have been made in terracotta, earthenware, salt glaze, stoneware and bone china. Doulton came to dominate the production of salt-glaze ceramics in London and at factories in Burslem and elsewhere in the regions, and the whole Doulton story has been well documented. The following account concentrates on tracing Doulton's manufacture of both industrial and decorative salt-glaze wares, at the Lambeth Works in particular. There, the continuous production of salt glaze in Britain was maintained from the eighteenth century right through to the mid-twentieth century.

John Doulton

Born in Fulham in 1793, John Doulton became an apprentice in 1805 at the Fulham Pottery, founded by John Dwight a century before. He stayed there until 1812, throwing on the wheel to produce the range of utilitarian stoneware products. He then moved to a small pothouse on Vauxhall Walk, and in time became part-owner of the firm Jones, Watts and Doulton, which made mainly salt-glaze bottles and jars. The manufacture of cheap mass-produced bottles and domestic ware began at the start of the nineteenth century, and brown salt-glaze stoneware continued to be made throughout the development of all the other products. Hunting jugs and a small range of ornamented products and fancyware items such as the novelty-shaped spirit flasks, remained part of Doulton's production until the eventual closure of the Lambeth Works.

In 1826 the business was moved to an old-established pottery on Lambeth High Street; from here it began trading as Doulton and Watts. In the late 1830s architectural terracotta and garden ornaments were an important line in the Doulton production. Over the next fifty years the works grew, and a series of new and larger kilns were built for both architectural terracotta and the increased production of salt glaze. The expanding chemical industry needed an acid-resisting material for a variety of vessels for processing and storage, and had found that salt-glaze stoneware was ideal. But it was the salt-glaze sanitary ware that launched the fortunes of the company, with the manufacture of drainpipes and heavy industrial products.

Henry Doulton

John was only forty-two when his second son, Henry, chose the pottery as his future career. He was a dedicated and ambitious apprentice, gaining experience in every aspect of the pottery trade, and he was soon taking a principal part in running the business. By the mid-nineteenth century, London and the new industrial cities of the provinces were being sanitized to improve both the health and the living conditions of the crowded populations, and it was going to require vast quantities of drainpipes, conduits and related wares to improve the situation.

Henry saw the potential of the market and established the Pipe Works that became known as Henry Doulton and Co., Drain Pipe Manufacturers, a short distance from the Lambeth Works. He initiated the large-scale production of vitrified salt-glaze stoneware sewers and water pipes, and was ready to supply the market demands when the Public Health Act was passed in 1848. Whilst many other firms competed by producing cheaper, porous earthenware pipes, the salt-glaze pipes were superior. The name of Doulton became synonymous with that of quality, and many of those original pipes are still in use today.

The 1970s saw an end to all industrial salt firings. In the hundred years leading up to that, the firm of Doulton was amongst the world leaders in the production of all heavy clay, salt-glaze products – and during that time the Lambeth Works also became renowned for a very different type of ware.

International Trade

The Great Exhibition of 1851, and subsequent international exhibitions, did much to promote British manufacturers abroad. The Doulton stand at the South Kensington International Exhibition in 1862 exhibited mainly salt-glaze stoneware bottles and containers, a new water filter, pipes, sanitary and chemical ware and electrical insulators. A few of the traditional Lambeth-style jugs and mugs were included in the display. There was also one large salt-glaze stoneware salt-cellar, decorated with applied relief and with incised lines coloured with cobalt in the style of the Rhenish stoneware. It was this piece that heralded the start of a revival of an English form of the Rhineland salt-glaze stoneware.

Doulton Lambeth Studio

Henry Doulton was committed to maintaining and improving the quality of the industrial products for which his salt-glaze stoneware had proved so appropriate. To begin with he had little interest in developing the art of ceramics, and was reluctant to make any investment in it. However, the new art schools of the late nineteenth century were producing well trained designers who looked for employment and experience in industry. It was John Sparkes, principal of Lambeth School of Art, who eventually persuaded Henry Doulton to allow the school to work in association with the factory, and later to employ a few of his students. In the late 1860s a new branch of the industry developed the studio production of decorated salt-glaze art pottery, with the recognition and promotion of the individual artists. This was the key to the future of salt glaze in the revived tradition of decorative stoneware.

The 1871 international exhibition at South Kensington launched this revival. New-style work shown by Doulton was the result of many months of making, and there were many rejects from the firings before good quality pieces emerged from the kilns. Salt-glaze 'Doulton ware' was soon very fashionable, alongside faience and other types of art pottery that were produced in the Lambeth Studio pottery. Demand for Doulton ware grew, and a new building for artist studios and workrooms was built. By 1881 Doulton employed over 200 artists and assistant decorators, many of whom were women. Henry Doulton encouraged and provided the environment for individual expression, and all the pieces were marked with the artists' monogram or initials. These products were a significant part of the Arts and Crafts movement that promoted and supported hand-made artefacts, and it was in this way that salt glaze played an incomparable part in establishing the first recognized definition of studio pottery.

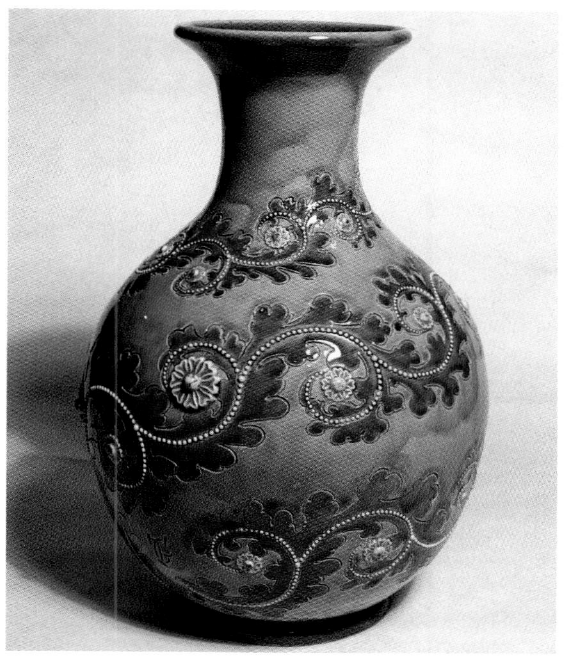

Vase by George Tinworth, 1878. Doulton Lambeth Ware, salt-glaze stoneware. 35cm high. Decorated with beaded runners. (Private collection)

Individual Artists

George Tinworth joined Doulton in 1866. The surfaces of his earliest stoneware jugs and vases were carved into the clay, with added bands of decorative relief. It was these pieces that were shown in Paris in 1867. The 'History of England' vase he made was an extraordinarily intricate piece of modelling, still much influenced by the German style of salt-glaze stoneware, and exhibited at Chicago in 1893 with other work of the Doulton artist potters. His talent set the foundations for the success of the Lambeth Studio, and over the years he decorated many hundreds of pots. He was also particularly skilled at modelling, and produced fine architectural panels, many with a religious theme, in both salt-glaze stoneware and terracotta.

Hannah Barlow came to work in the Lambeth Studio to help prepare the pieces for the 1871 exhibition, and she remained with Doulton for over forty years. Some of her earliest work imitates the Staffordshire technique of 'scratch blue' pieces, and she became well known for her sgraffito designs that incorporated drawings of animals and country settings. Her brother Arthur Barlow joined Doulton at the same time as Hannah, but he died young. Florence Barlow was Hannah's sister and was talented in the portrayal of birds, and a third sister, Lucy, became an assistant to them both.

Students from the Lambeth Art School were taken on in the earliest days of the Lambeth Studio, and the school remained the source of the majority of the Doulton artists. Literally hundreds of artists and assistants have played their part in the success and significant reputation that the Lambeth Studio gained.

Clays

Ball clays from Dorset and Devon were used to make the small brown jugs and similar wares; for larger pieces the clay was mixed with grog. The position of the pots, the atmosphere in the kiln, and the amount of iron in the clay body affected the colour. The clay body that fired a warm light brown was used only occasionally for decorative pieces: for these, either the clay was coated in a white slip, or an iron-free, paler firing body was used to give a better background for the brown, blue and green colour range of the Doulton wares. Various light-coloured bodies were made up with the ball clays and the addition of different proportions of materials such as ground calcined flint, china clay

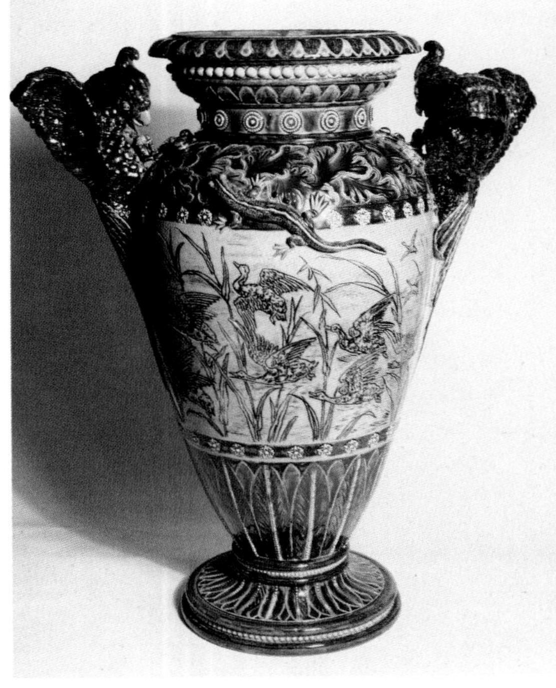

(RIGHT) Large vase by Hannah Barlow, 1876. Doulton Lambeth Ware, salt-glaze stoneware. 59.6cm high. Sgraffito centre frieze of flying geese. Moulded cockatoo handles and applied lizards. (Private collection)

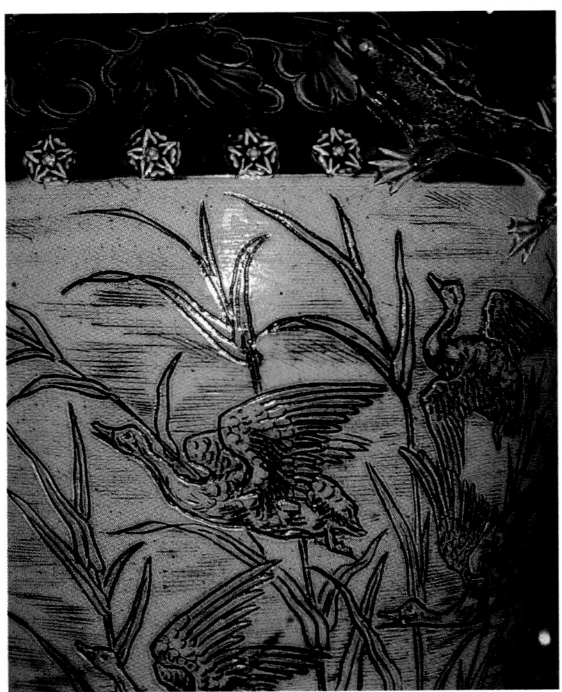

(FAR RIGHT) Detail of flying geese by Hannah Barlow. The sgraffito technique of incising lines either through a slip, or directly on the clay surface, and infilling with a stain.

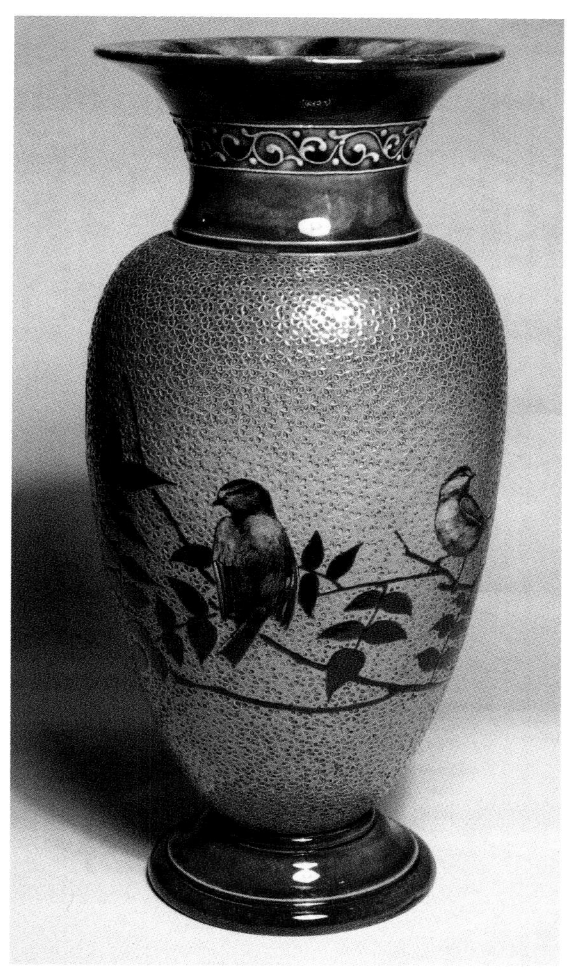

(LEFT) One of a pair of vases by Florence Barlow, c.1891–1902. Doulton Lambeth Ware, salt-glaze stoneware. 35cm high. With 'pate-sur-pate' bird decoration. (Private collection)

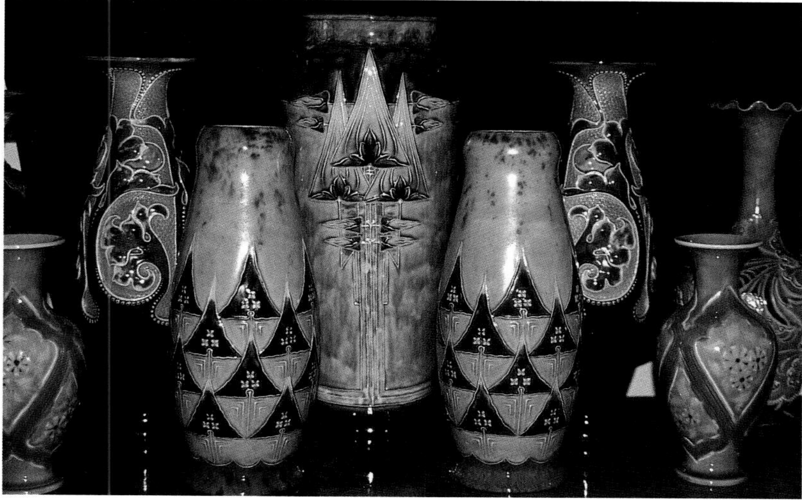

(ABOVE) Doulton Lambeth Ware, salt-glaze stoneware. Tallest piece 35cm high. Superb examples of the craftsmanship, creative design and colour of the period: between 1891–1907. Includes work by artists Frank Butler and Eliza Simmance. Assistants, juniors and students worked on the repetitive parts of the decoration, and several artists may have made a contribution to one piece. Designs were never repeated, except for the intentionally symmetrically styled pairs popular in Victorian times. By 1882 there were over 1,600 shapes. (Private collection)

from Cornwall, Cornish stone and other sources of feldspar, silica sand, and grogs including fine porcelain.

Some pots had a coded reference marked on the base, to identify the clay body. The qualities and effects of each material were noted, and recipes were carefully balanced to produce workable clays with good firing properties. The fine particles of the clays responded well to the salt, and took a high, smooth glaze, and the fluxing materials helped to vitrify and fuse the applied glazes. An excess of china clay was known to repel the salt glaze, and the clay that was prepared for making teapots was known to produce an orange colour when applied as a slip on a darker clay body.

Colours and Decorative Techniques

The earliest decorative styles of Lambeth Studio were briefly inspired by both historic German salt glaze, with modelling and moulded relief and colour from cobalt and manganese oxides, and the early Staffordshire scratch-blue pieces with incised lines.

Before long the more individual designs and interpretations of ornament appeared. At first the colours, painted on as a slip, tended to fade and be burned out in the firing, but in time a range of more stable colours was developed; 'Doulton blue' was a particularly distinct and popular colour. Pigments of metal oxides were mixed with a slip made of the same clay as the body, and were applied onto raw pots.

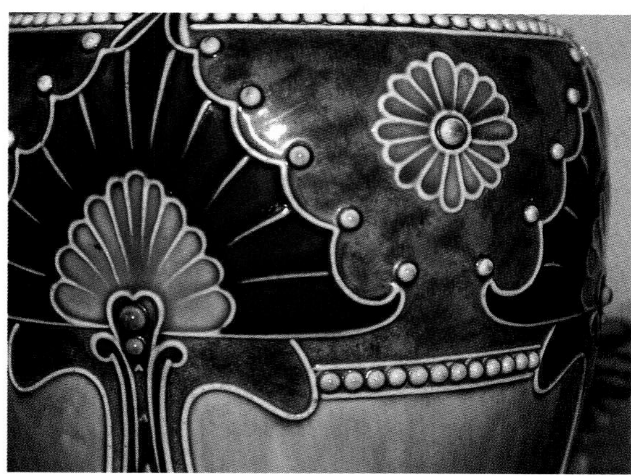

(ABOVE) Detail of a large vase by Frank Butler, 1904. Doulton Lambeth Ware, salt-glaze stoneware. More than one decorative technique was employed to cover the surface of the impressive variety of ornamental pieces. Relief decoration was embroidered with applied dots and borders and flowers, and raised slipped lines were flooded with colour. (Private collection)

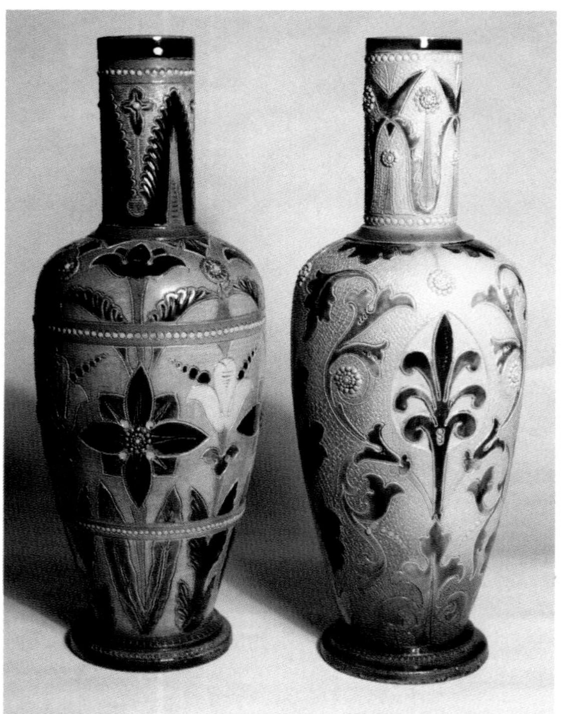

Two vases from the firm of C.J.C. Bailey, c.1880. 42cm high. In London, Stiff and Sons and C.J.C. Bailey were just two of the other potteries in Britain who saw the success of the Lambeth Studios and set up their own art departments, employing artists and producing art pottery. Doulton remained unsurpassed in the use of salt glaze for decorative wares. (Private collection)

The salt-glaze surfaces of Doulton ware are mostly colourful, very glassy and smooth, and evenly glazed, with none of the usual distinctive effects of the salt vapour. There is no hint of an orange-peel texture, except on the early sgraffito work and the earliest pieces of decorated wares that were a warm golden-brown colour. At a glance they might well be overlooked as being salt-glaze. The thin glaze gives brightness and depth, and beautifully subtle effects to the edges of colour. With the exceptionally light covering of glaze, the detail of the modelling and the relief decoration are crisp and well defined. Stoneware glaze technology was still in its early days, but glaze experiments produced a new range of glaze effects, used on other ranges of art pottery by the turn of the century.

Firings

The decorative pieces were salt-fired in the large, 9m (30ft)-diameter kilns amongst the industrial wares. Early experimental pieces were often spoilt, unless they were shielded from the flames and the fiercest attack of the salt by the industrial wares around them. In time kiln designs were modified, and decorated wares were deliberately placed on shelves in positions where they were protected from the flames. Doulton wares were never placed in saggars, and the salt vapour was allowed to play round the surfaces freely.

J.F. Blacker vividly describes the salt-firing of a down-draught bottle kiln at the Lambeth Factory of Doulton in 1922 in his book *The ABC of English Salt-Glaze Stoneware*:

> On arriving at Doulton's, I found the men – stokers and burners – in the midst of their work, the fires of the kiln, seen from the outside through the fire-holes, roaring upwards to the dome-shaped top, then forced downwards so that the smoke, driven to the bottom, escaped beneath the floor through a series of tubes, then by a tall shaft to the open air.

Soon the first part of the salting began:

> The fire holes were successively opened, and, just in the same way that the coal was fed to the flames, the coarse-grained rock-salt was shovelled into what was now really a burning fiery furnace.

This would be the test salting, and it would be a few hours before the trial piece could be drawn from the kiln, and the time for the final salting judged ready. J.F. Blacker describes the dome of the kiln:

> . . . there were some sixty apertures, each loosely covered with a brick. From these issued both flames and fumes, which, however, were not very dense at this stage . . . Round the dome ran an iron platform having a protecting rail outside, whilst facing me was a ladder to give easy access to the top of the kiln, and two wooden boxes filled with salt.

Wearing thick, coarse leather gloves and using long-handled iron ladles, and with their faces covered with handkerchiefs, the stokers and burners began the salting. They worked in pairs, the burners charging their ladles with salt as the stokers removed the bricks, and the salt was then fed into the holes.

> Each stoker ran up to the top hole in the dome, and with his leather gloves removed its covering brick, whilst his burner stood ready on the platform with his ladleful of salt, which was soon hissing in the fiery flame below. Forth

> leaped smoke from the combustion, but the first hole on each side was covered with wonderful celerity . . .

Smoke would escape from the holes so the whole area around the kiln was filled with a dense screen of fumes. This operation continued round the dome, and then the lower holes were also baited with salt. Blacker ends his description: 'The salting was over, the process was ended and we were not tired.' A comment that the stokers and burners surely would not have appreciated.

Industry and Art

It is to his credit that Henry Doulton sustained his commitment to the production of art pottery alongside the development of products of the heavy-clay industry. Although Doulton ware was so successful, the major part of Doulton's commercial production was still utilitarian brown wares and salt-glaze industrial ceramics. Other works had been established at St Helens, Rowley Regis, Smethwick, Burslem and Paisley, and a large and profitable trade grew from the export of salt-glaze stoneware pipes to cities throughout the world. From the turn of the century Doulton was the principal manufacturer of every industrial salt-glaze product, including conduits for electric cables, rail insulators, and all the stoneware required by the chemical industries.

'Martinware' 1873–1914

At the same time that the Lambeth Studio at Doulton was being established, the Martin brothers were setting up their own independent studio pottery. The first of its kind, it was the precursor of the studio potter's workshop of the twentieth century.

Robert Wallace, the eldest of the four brothers, had studied at the Lambeth School of Art in the 1860s, and began stone carving and sculpting there. He worked very briefly as a modeller in the Doulton Studio before choosing pottery for a career, working independently in his own studio and elsewhere. Walter and Edwin followed their brother through the Lambeth School of Art and the Doulton Studio, and then in 1873 the firm of 'Martin Brothers' was founded at Pomona House in Fulham.

At first, the salt kiln at the Fulham Pottery was used to fire work, and the Martins would place their delicate ware amongst the drainpipes and storage jars. But the work's schedule demanded that the kilns were opened whilst they were still very hot, and the smaller, more fragile studio pieces could not survive the thermal shock and losses were high. Later the brothers were able to lease a disused glass-kiln at Shepherd's Bush, but in 1877 the 'Martin Brothers' studio moved to Southall, where they built their own salt kiln. The early years were a struggle as they strove to understand the process of firing a smaller kiln in order to produce the stoneware temperatures for their salt glaze. But eventually Martinware was successfully produced over a period of nearly forty years.

Each of the brothers specialized in a different area of production. Robert Wallace directed all the work of the studio and specialized in modelling. Walter became an excellent thrower and decorator, and was also interested in chemistry; he produced all the colours by grinding and mixing the pigments before they were painted onto the wares, and was also involved in packing and firing the kiln. Edwin was particularly skilled in drawing incised lines on the clay forms, and applying

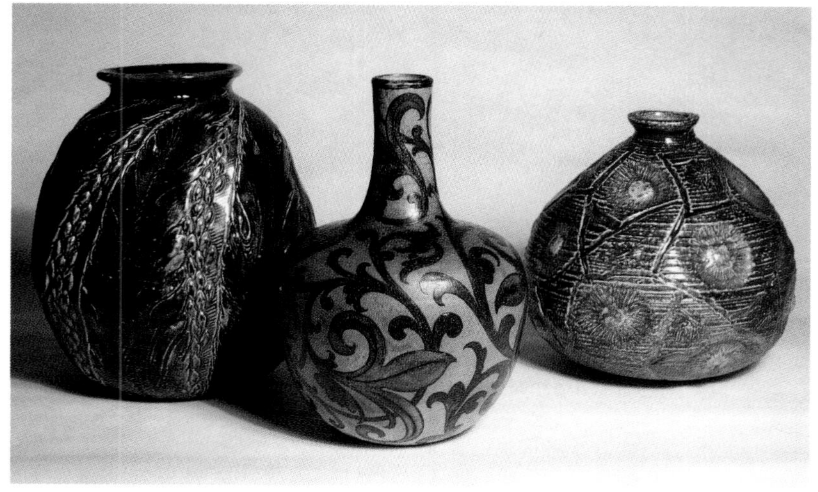

Group of pots by the Martin brothers. Salt glaze.
Left: 23cm high, 1891.
Centre: 23.5cm high, 1889.
Right: 19.5cm high, 1883.
(Private collection)

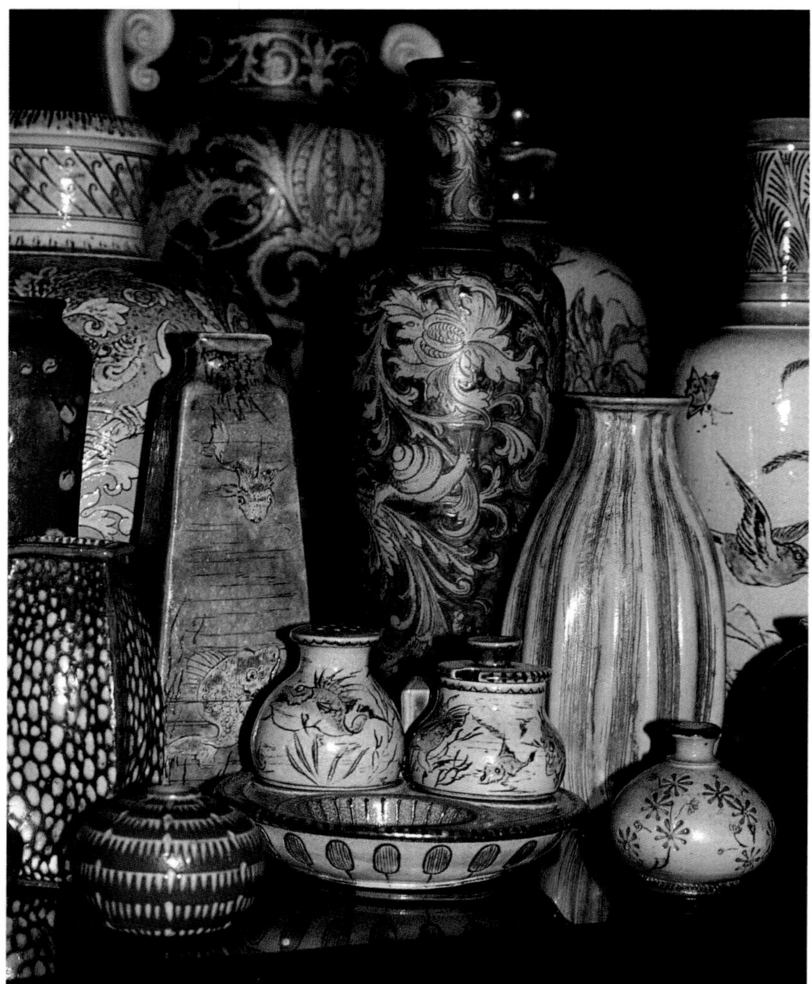

Collection of 'Martinware'. The extraordinary and prolific salt-glaze work of the Martin brothers was produced between 1873 and 1914. Jars, jugs, vases and smaller objects were adorned with floral or geometric designs, birds and animals, fish, frogs and reptiles, carved, etched, embossed, stamped and pierced. Colours range from a lustrous black, through soft blues, greens and all shades of brown. The thin coating of salt glaze, which picked out the lines and detail of the modelled decoration of the designs, enhanced every aspect of 'Martinware'. (Private collection)

raised ornament to his designs; but being the youngest, he was given many of the uncreative, mundane tasks. Charles, the fourth brother to join the firm, eventually took charge of business and sales.

The creations of the Martin brothers are remarkable, covering all kinds of objects, a great variety of forms, and every imaginable technique and decorative style to exploit the qualities of salt glaze. Described as 'eccentric, idiosyncratic and unique', the work is an eclectic mix of the Gothic revival of 1860s, the Renaissance revival of 1880s, Japanese, and anything else in which the Victorians delighted.

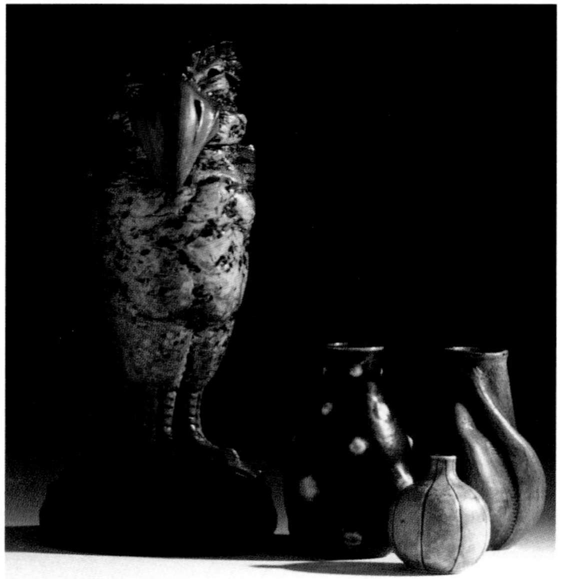

Small vases with 'Wally-bird' lidded tobacco jar. Made by Wallace Martin, the jars express a bizarre and outlandish sense of humour. A pair, made in 1886, was a caricature of Disraeli and Gladstone. (University of Wales.)

Doulton and the Twentieth Century

Much of British industry was in recession at the turn of the century, and the company of Doulton had to seriously rationalize all aspects of its production. Art pottery had never made a profit for Doulton, and as fashion called for brighter colours, so the demand for Lambeth salt-glaze wares declined. At the start of war, in 1914, the Doulton studio at Lambeth closed. All twenty-three coal-fired kilns and the huge rectangular saggar kiln were given over to industrial and utilitarian wares, although production of bottles and smaller articles continued. The Lambeth site had become increasingly unsuitable for the location of nearly thirty coal-fired kilns, many of which were also used for salt firings, and all of which emitted an unacceptable level of pollution. Much of the industry was moving to regional factories.

Architectural and Sculptural Salt Glaze

'Doulton ware' was developed from the clay body that was used for art pottery. It first appeared as coloured, salt-glaze stoneware tiles, but was soon promoted for architectural use as a way of adding colour to further enhance and add decoration to both the exterior and interior of terracotta buildings. The vestibule of Lloyds Bank in Fleet Street in London, built in 1883, was one of the early schemes to use Doulton ware extensively, and it remains a breathtaking example of colour and inventive decoration. The hard, high-fired salt glaze withstood the grime of city air and the effects of the weather, and was used for the façades of public houses and for fountains and monuments.

With further experiments, another salt-glaze product called 'Polychrome Stoneware' was developed in the 1930s: a white slip was painted onto the body of the clay before applying the pigment, and this made the colours brighter. High-fired to 1,250° C and salt-glazed, the material was vitrified and had a hard, shiny surface that was resistant to the acidic, polluted atmosphere of cities. Two Polychrome salt-glaze friezes were designed by Gilbert Bayes in 1939; the largest, 'Pottery Through the Ages', dominated the façade of Doulton House on the Albert Embankment in London until the building was demolished in 1978.

The Last Years of the Lambeth Studio

In 1920 the Lambeth Studio again began to make decorative wares. Some new developments in stoneware glazes had been made, but salt glaze continued to be used to produce interesting pieces, including various colourful architectural reliefs and sculptures made from salt-glaze stoneware. The success of these was due to the hard-wearing properties of salt-glaze stoneware in comparison to the softer majolica ware.

But in 1925 only twenty-five artists were employed. World War II interrupted production, after which the Lambeth Studio was revived for a few years, but on a very small scale, with only four or five artists.

Doulton Artists

AGNETE HOY AND HELEN WALTERS SWAIN

Agnete Hoy, a Danish potter and designer, used to direct a small studio making hard-paste porcelain pieces at the firm of Bullers in Stoke. Following the closure of Bullers in 1952, Doulton offered her a studio in Lambeth to make and design stoneware pieces, many of which were salt glazed.

The kiln that was used to fire the studio department's pieces had an internal dimension of about 0.3sq m (4sq ft), and had been redesigned for salt firings. The results were good, although in the beginning the fireman, whose considerable experience was with the large industrial salt kilns, was dubious that such a relatively small kiln would ever salt satisfactorily. It was fired with coal or coke, and rock salt was introduced directly into the fireboxes. The work was placed in saggars that had no holes in the sides, and salt vapour entered under the lid that was propped up with refractory spacers. Often the artists would be there to watch the packing and unpacking of the pots.

Helen Walters Swain joined Agnete as her senior assistant in 1953. Helen recalls how Agnete would work with the headman of the making-shop to produce the forms for a range of vases, goblets, bowls and lamp-bases. Upstairs the pieces were thrown and then turned on a vertical lathe and burnished. In the studio downstairs, the artists carved the designs into the surface of the clay with a bamboo tool, sometimes incising through a white slip. A

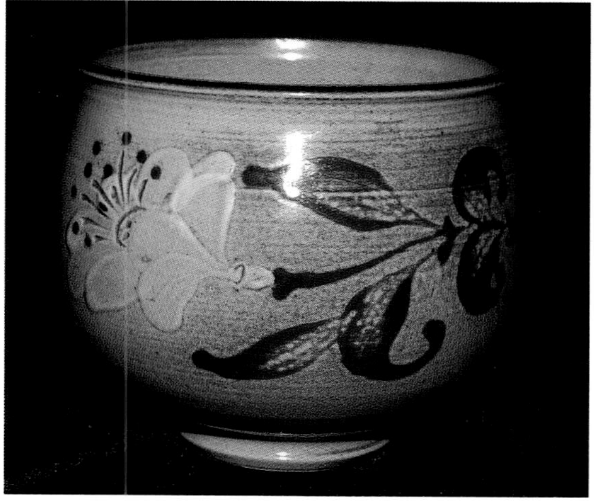

Doulton Lambeth Ware. Small bowl 1952. Prototype, thrown and decorated by Agnete Hoy, with white and green-brown slip on a cream body. Salt glaze. Agnete's brushwork was particularly fine. Her individual designs involved incising and carving as well as slip decoration, under-glaze and relief moulding. (Private collection)

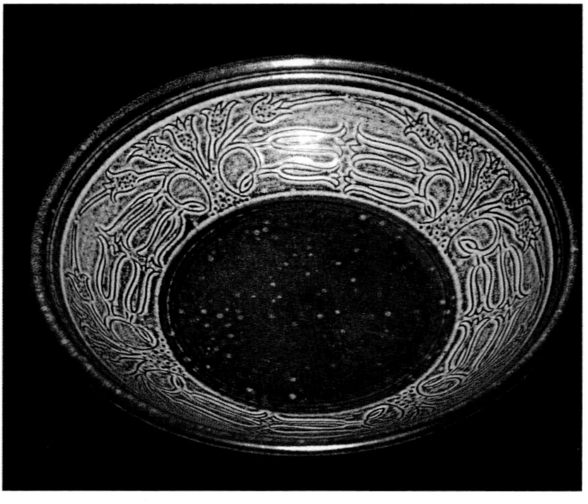

Doulton Lambeth Ware. Small dish 1955. Decoration by Helen Walters Swain. Honeysuckle design carved into band of white slip, then washed with cobalt and iron oxide mix. Iron oxide wash to clay body. Salt glaze. (Private collection)

thicker slip was also used for decorative brushwork. The pot was then placed on a turntable, and selected areas brushed with thin liquid oxides of either cobalt or iron.

Both individual pieces by Agnete, and designs for limited reproduction decorated by her assistants, were produced in these ways. When the Lambeth Studio finally closed down in 1956, both Agnete Hoy and Helen Swain continued their careers in studio ceramics and teaching.

Doulton Ware 'Z' Clay Body Recipe for Salt Glaze

Copied from the notebook of Helen Walters Swain:

10	North Devon Ball Clay
3	China Clay
3	Potash Feldspar

(Very strong and clean burning. Responds well to an iron-bearing slip)

An Inspired Revival

The colourful and decorative Doulton wares have rarely been the inspiration for salt glazing by potters in Britain. Instead it was the orange-peel surfaces of early imported German bottles and Nottingham brown wares, with their high lustrous sheen, that seduced the first modern revivalists. But paradoxically there is a connection between studio potters and the heavy-clay industrial side of salt glaze, in that more than one potter admits that one of the inspirations to build a salt kiln was curiosity about the surface quality of salt-glaze drainpipes, and the appeal of those pitted textures and the range of bright orange colours.

ANDREW OSBORNE AND JENNIE HALE

Only two contemporary studio salt-glaze potters followed in the style of studio art pottery: Andrew Osborne and Jennie Hale were inspired by the work of the Martin brothers and Doulton wares, when they began salt firing in the 1980s. Their production of salt glaze was all too short, and since 1986 they have worked exclusively with raku firings.

They became involved with salt-glaze firings during the mid-1980s, when Jennie was apprentice to Marianne de Trey at Shinners Bridge,

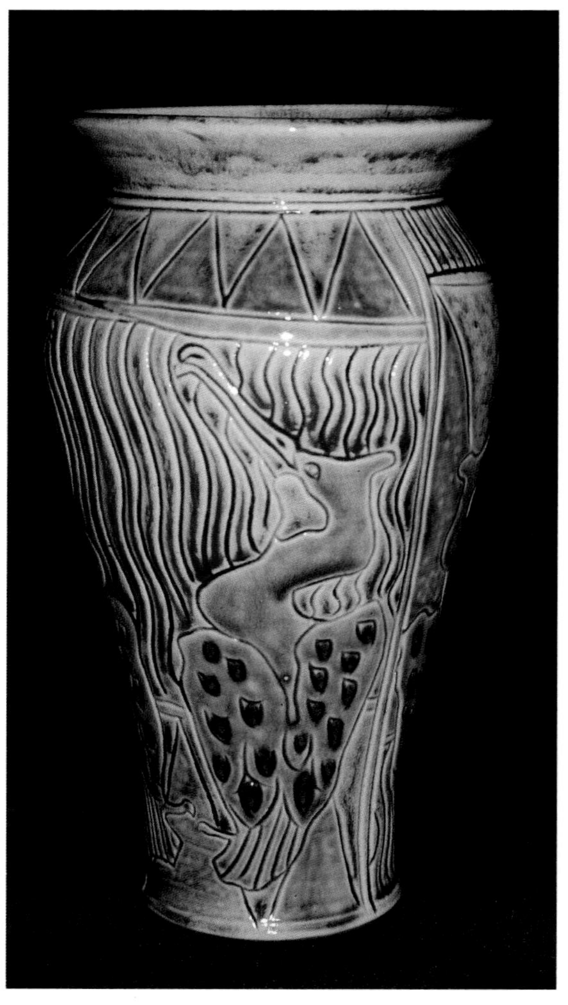

Tall vase by Jennie Hale, 1980s. Salt glaze. The drawings of the animals and birds are clearly observed, and are reminiscent of the work of Hannah and Florence Barlow.

and Andrew worked at the Dartington Pottery Training Workshop in Devon. They became interested in salt glaze and learned to fire the salt kiln there, experimenting and sharing a variety of clay bodies and glaze recipes with the other potters. In 1982 they established their own pottery in Devon, where they built a 17cu m (60cu ft) salt kiln, using heavy firebrick seconds from British Steel. They fired with oil, and used 40kg (90lb) of salt at each firing.

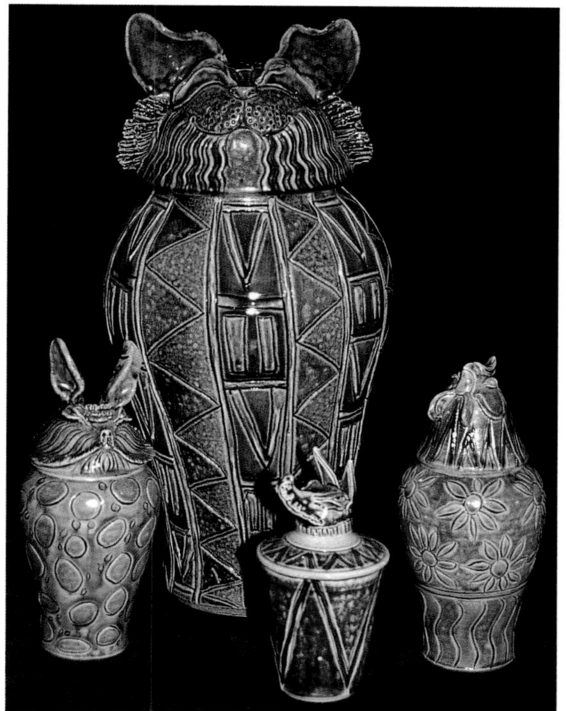

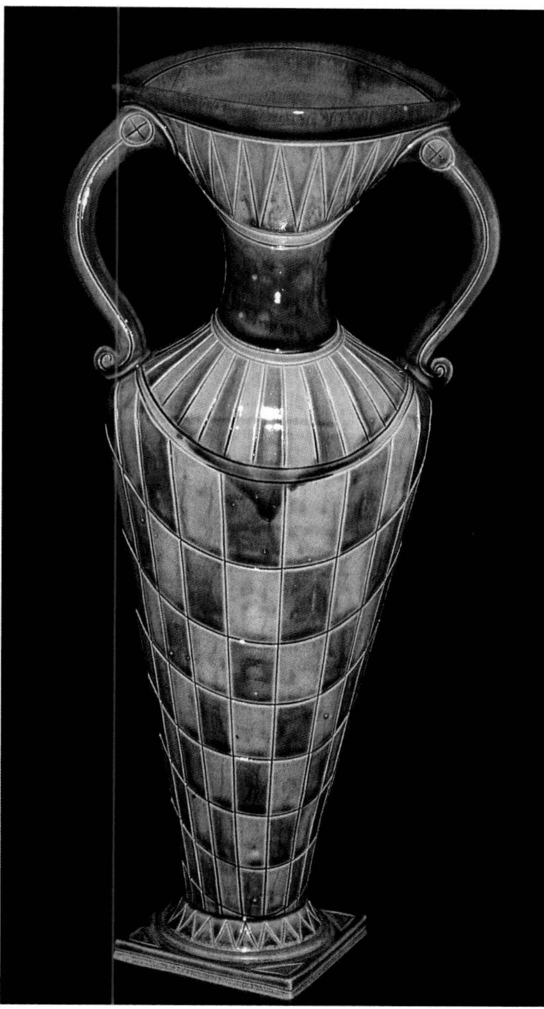

(LEFT) Group of lidded jars by Jennie Hale, 1980s. Jennie was attracted to the work of the Martin brothers. She created amusing and entertaining beasts, some with the appearance of an Egyptian mummified creature. The sgraffito technique works well to pick out the patterns on the hollow thrown and modelled lidded jars.

(RIGHT) Tall vase by Andrew Osborne, 1980s. Salt glaze. Andrew's designs were influenced by his previous work as an architectural draughtsman. His pieces are covered with an abundance of geometric decoration.

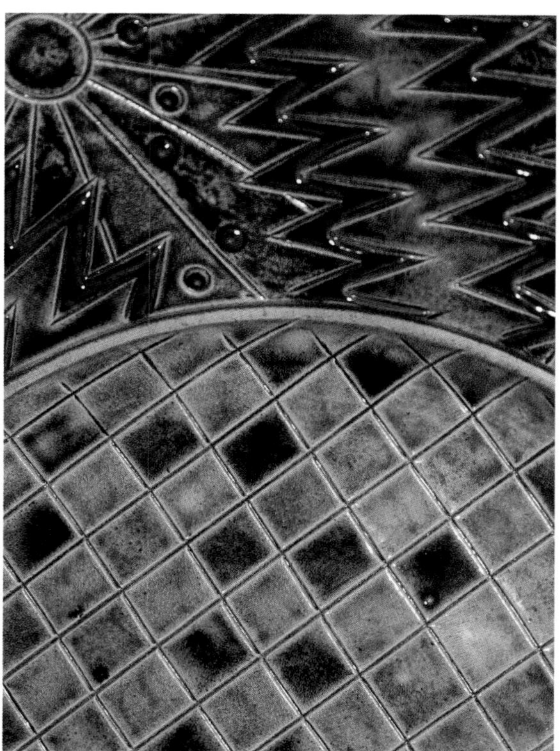

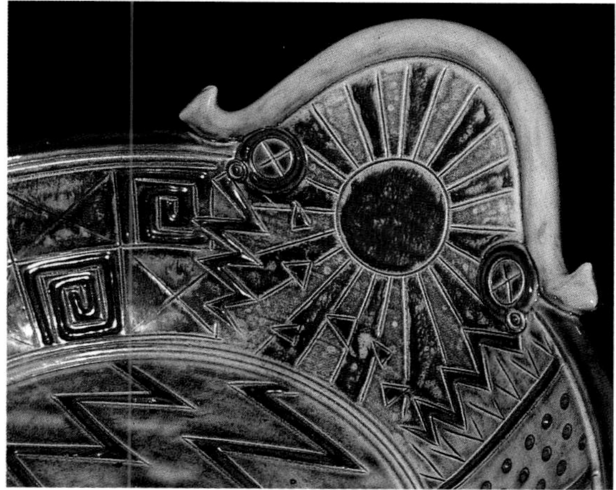

(LEFT) Detail of a large dish by Andrew Osborne, 1980s. Salt glaze. Precisely drawn, incised lines, with trailed lines of raised slip, in-filled with colour. These pieces make the closest connection of any contemporary studio potter's work to the artist designers of the Lambeth studios, and yet, by the boldness of their stylized constructed forms, they hold a clear identity with a later period.

(RIGHT) Detail of plate by Andrew Osborne, 1980s.

4 The Revival of Salt Glaze

Salt Glaze in Studio Potteries

With the exception of the Martin brothers' work, salt glaze had always been seen as an industrial process, and when their studio closed, no other small individual workshops had been established. It is now generally agreed that Bernard Leach was the first studio potter in Britain, following in the workshop traditions of the Far East. On his return from Japan in 1920, with the Japanese potter Shoji Hamada he built his pottery and kilns at St Ives in Cornwall. He took on many students, and his philosophy and workshop methods are described in his book *A Potter's Book*, first published in 1940. In it, salt glaze and the early experimental salt firings at St Ives are mentioned.

Salt Glaze at St Ives

Bernard Leach writes that he admires the qualities of the German bellarmine jug and the orange-peel texture of salt glaze. He considers the orange-skin surface of the glaze unsuitable for table use with cutlery or silver, but 'admirably suited' for many other domestic uses. He wonders why '. . . some potter does not give us salt-glazed jars and vases, fruit and cake bowls' – although it was never to be considered as a production line for the St Ives Pottery. In the book's short section entitled 'Salt-glaze packing and firing', he recounts, 'We have had only two salt-glaze firings, which took place at times when our round three-foot kiln needed rebuilding and we could, therefore, afford to use it for such experiments.' Firing it with wood, and recommending the use of coarse wet rock salt, he thought that any kiln used for salting rendered it useless for any other ware.

David Leach, Bernard's son, returned to St Ives in 1937 after completing the course at Stoke Technical College. He recalls that the round kiln, which was largely fired for slipware production, was used to experiment with salt on several occasions prior to being repaired. When asked about Shoji Hamada's interest in salt glaze, David had no recollection of him ever doing any salt firings in Britain, although he did become involved later. (When Hamada returned to Japan in 1924 he took with him some slipware dishes and old German salt-glaze bellarmine jugs, but it was not until a few years after his first visit to America in 1952 that he started salting. In 1956, at Mashiko, he built a two-chambered salt kiln that held about 200 pots, and salt-glaze pots became a small but essential part of his work.)

Much later, in 1956, Janet Leach married Bernard and joined the pottery, and in the following years made a small amount of salt-glaze work. The salt kiln had been built by young potters working at St Ives, and was ingeniously joined up to the chimney of the large chambered kiln. Trevor Corser has worked at the Leach Pottery since 1966, and recounts that several of the young potters who came to work at St Ives during the late 1960s experimented with salt glaze, but with varying results. The kiln logs and dusty draw-rings from those days are still to be found on the shelves in the workshop. They are evidence of the curiosity about the process of salt glazing that has drawn many potters to try it out for themselves.

The Oxshott Pottery: Denise and Rosemary Wren

Undoubtedly Denise Wren and her daughter Rosemary must be considered the most important pioneers of salt glaze in studio pottery. Denise and Henry Wren founded the Oxshott Pottery in Surrey in 1920, at the same time that the St Ives Pottery was established. Denise is considered to be the first independent woman studio potter, and as well as producing pots she designed and built a series of small coke-fired kilns, the plans of which were always made available and sold to other potters.

Rosemary, their daughter, was born in 1922; and when Henry died in 1947 she was still a student at Guilford, just about to enter the Royal College of Art. In her third year there Rosemary decided she wanted to show salt glaze in her Diploma show. A Martin Brothers' jug, a gift from Archibald Knox, and a small salt-glazed mug picked up by her father on the battlefields in Belgium, were part of Rosemary's home background, and she had discovered more of the richness of the salt-glazed surfaces in the Victoria and Albert Museum, next door to the college. 'I was often ensnared by a high-up row of early German bellarmines, . . . listening to their quiet singing of the fire.' Had it not been for Rosemary's wish to make salt-glazed pots for her college show, Denise might never have discovered the technique that she exploited with such creative vigour over nearly twenty years.

In an article written in 1996, and published in *Ceramics: Art and Perception* in 1997, Rosemary looks back on the years of salt glazing at the Oxshott Pottery. She describes how, in 1950, with the help and encouragement of Denise, she resurrected a small, disused coke-fired kiln for the first firings. The first pots made were tall tankards thrown in a siliceous ball clay from the Dorset firm of Pikes, and decorated with sunflower sprigs. She writes:

> They were based on the fine German 'stein' in the V & A. Although industrial salt glaze was being manufactured at this time, it seemed that no other artist potters had carried the whole process 'through' personally, in their own workshops, since the Martin brothers. There was no one to ask, but the available technical information made the process sound simple; it appeared that one had merely to take the temperature up to the vitrification point of the clay, throw salt onto the flames at the rate of a pound to a cubic foot, and there you were. It would be tedious to describe the many ways that the 'simple' process could go wrong! Our most useful booklet was issued by the company Borax Consolidated: it explained how to avoid the qualities we most liked, so we reversed their advice.
>
> Our tiny kiln was a Bourry type, with a front overnight firebox and a deliberately oversize fire-bed to make sure of reaching temperature. I got cooking salt from the grocer, the bed of red-hot coke was ideal for volatilizing the salt, and the firing was a great success. . . . At the end of the term I made another kiln-full of more delicate sprigged pots based on English eighteenth-century ware.

The Oxshott Pottery coke-fired salt kiln in use by Denise and Rosemary Wren 1958–67. Rosemary packing domestic ware. The extra pipe-work was for gas firing, but it was never used.

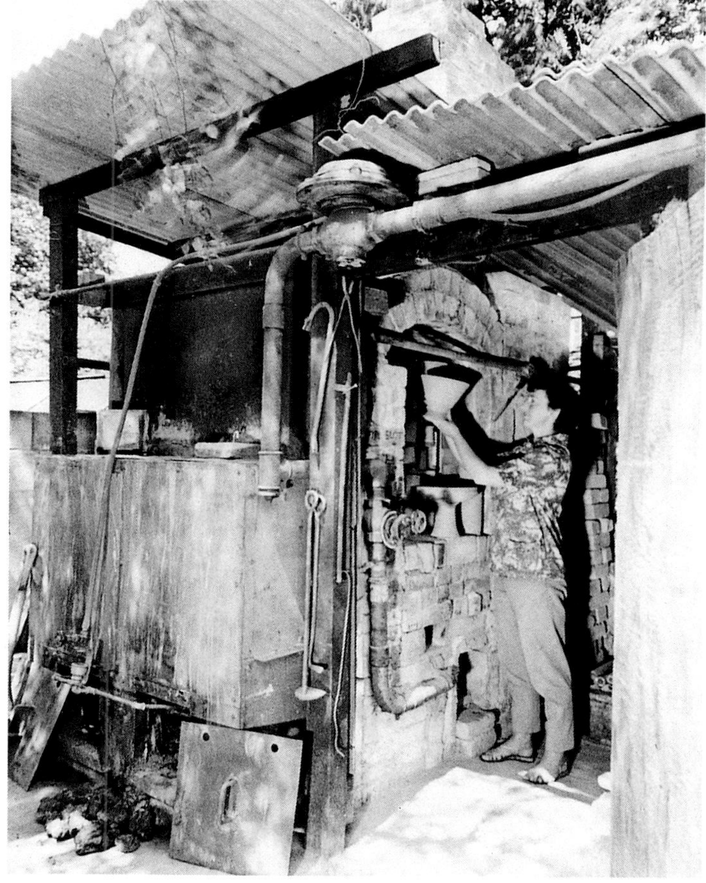

The Coke-Fired Kiln

With the help of the Coke Department of the Gas Board, Denise designed a large coke-fired kiln for salt-glaze stoneware firings with a pot-chamber 0.9m (3ft) deep and wide, and 1.2m (4ft) high. A prototype was built, but later improved when the wall between the furnace/firebox and the pot space collapsed. The kiln was built with Morgan Crucible's MI 28 bricks, the first of a new generation of lightweight insulating and refractory bricks that replaced the traditional set-up of heavy firebricks with Kieselguhr or molar backup. They were washed with a special high alumina jointing material and, although reasonably unaffected by the attack of the salt, the face of these bricks did spall. The levels of industrial pollution were being reduced under legislation, and the Gas Board advisers considered that the flue of the kiln must be fitted with a wet scrubber that collected and neutralized the acidic emissions from the salt fumes. But as the equipment was exceedingly noisy to operate and produced a dense fog, its use was soon discontinued.

The salt was introduced through secondary air holes, onto a ledge above the flame slot. The quantity of salt was divided into three batches, and the damper was closed after each salting. Each lot was flicked in with a tablespoon, with time for the temperature to rise between each batch:

> The salting was always done very late at night as we had near neighbours, but they were appreciative and just closed their upstairs windows. We had over a hundred firings in this kiln between 1958 and 1967, surviving its two major drawbacks – a heavy deposit of iron-bearing ash, which we could no doubt have avoided with saggars had we wished; and the fact that the flames were very hot before they were led from the furnace into the kiln. [This caused a sudden rise in temperature and shattered the larger pots.] After that we biscuit-fired everything, but it rather spoilt the simplicity of once-firing.

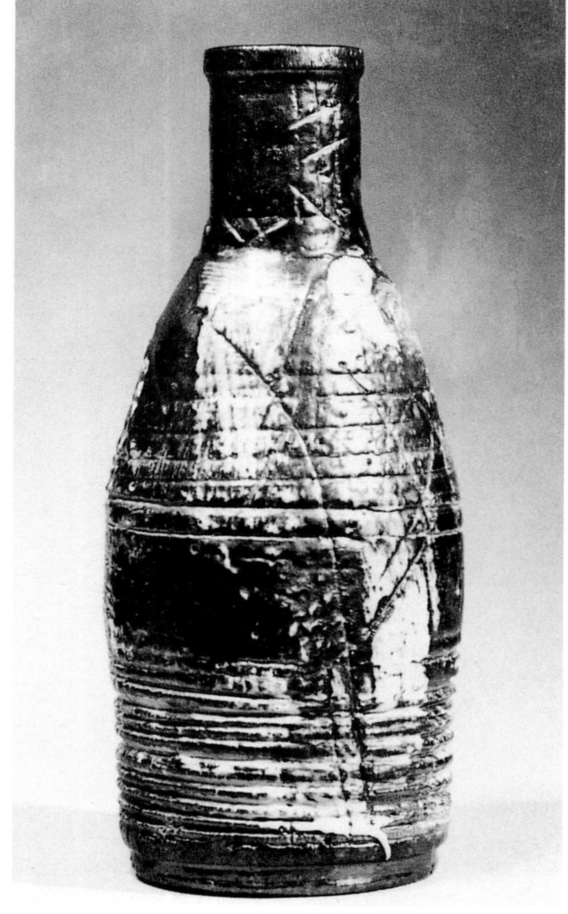

Bottle 8in high, by Denise Wren 1959, salt glaze. Rough clays and decoration over deep throwing rings with wood ash, iron, copper and cobalt ores. Fired to 1,310°C using coke, water and wood.

Early Pieces

Rosemary is modest about those early pieces:

> Our first pots were pretty conventional. We both liked the way a simple scratched pattern develops an emphasis of light and dark just with the salt, and we added very little else at first. Each firing was either hers [her mother's] or mine, as the members of the Oxshott Pottery had always worked as individuals. My mother's pots were mostly for flowers, with some mugs that could be used for drinking.

Inspired by a visit to La Borne in France in the summer of 1950, Rosemary began to make functional domestic ware; however, she gradually abandoned that line of work, and in preference made individual hand-built animals and a few sculptural pieces. These grew in size, and at times one on its own might fill the kiln. Rosemary fired them after a normal salt-glaze firing, 'making use of the sheen produced by the residual vapours given off by the kiln and its furniture'.

Denise's pots had become more and more rugged, and Rosemary recalls how her mother felt about her pots and the firing process:

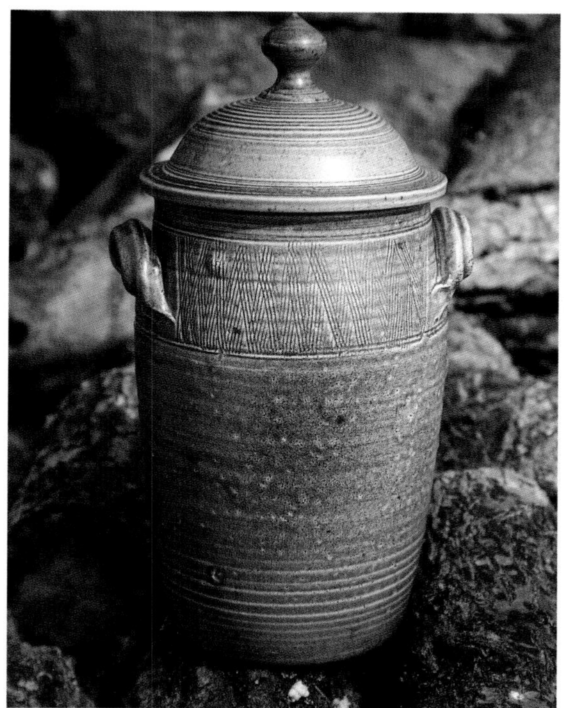

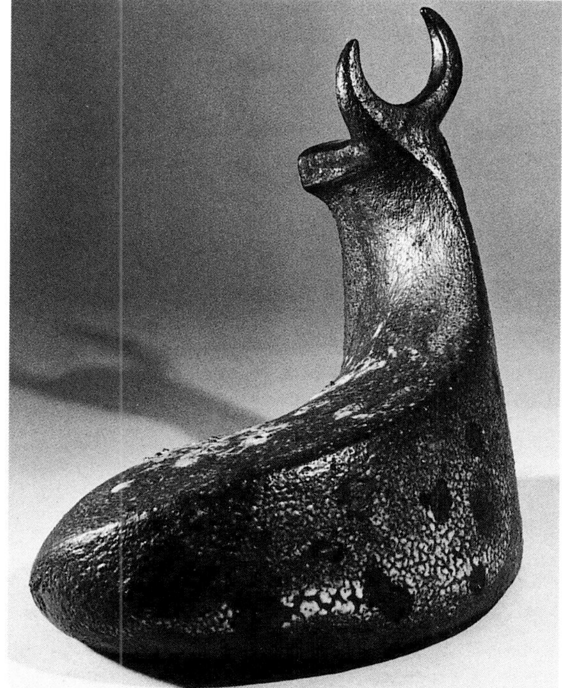

(FAR LEFT) Tall, lidded store jar by Rosemary Wren. Salt-glaze domestic ware, late 1950s. (Private collection)

(LEFT) Alderney Bull, 9in long, by Rosemary Wren, 1963. Stoneware: hollow, hand-built, with some vitrified slip and Alderney seaweed ash. Residual salt firing. (Private collection)

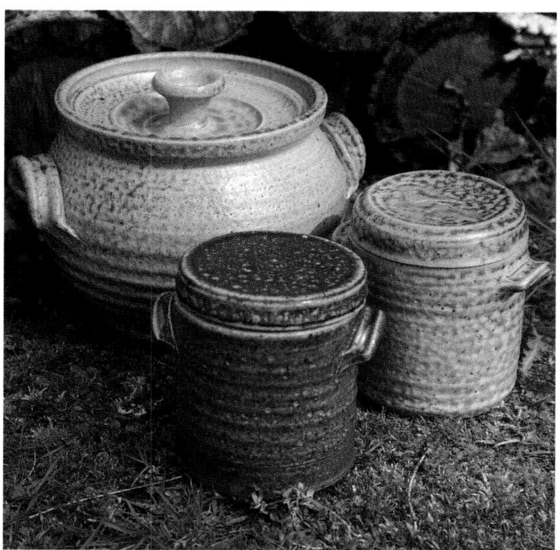

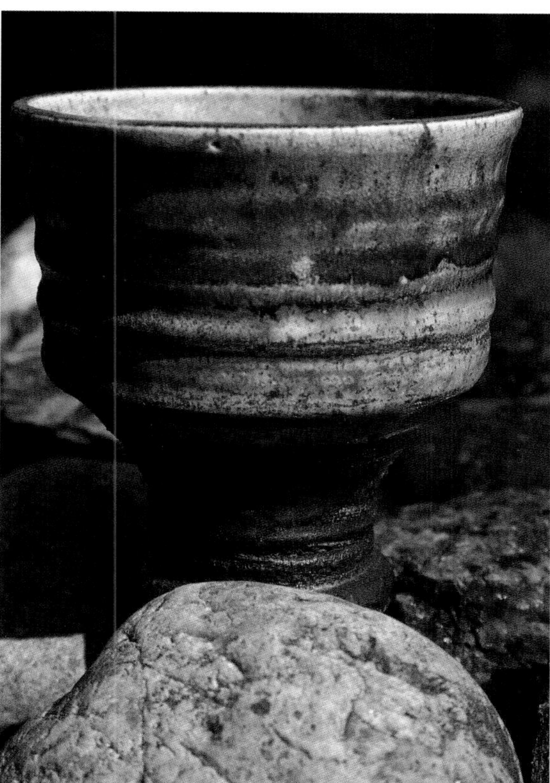

(FAR LEFT) Lidded store jars by Rosemary Wren. Salt-glaze domestic ware, late 1950s. (Private collection)

(LEFT) Small stemmed bowl by Denise Wren, 1960s. Salt glaze. Tawny browns, greens, black and titanium yellows, obtained with unrefined ores and wood ash and fired to 1,310°C. (Private collection)

Salt glaze spoke of the qualities of the clay and the fire, its decorative qualities also arising from the way it was made. Occasionally she rubbed them over with a handful of rough wood-ash, a brushful of vitrified slip or rutile and at one time strewed powdered crude minerals inside the bowls and plates, a daring procedure for those days, which gave some exciting results. She was very methodical and kept careful notes on how each piece was treated; she wanted her pots to be more colourful, but the brown dust from the coke tended to overpower everything.

In a talk given in London by Shoji Hamada, Denise asked him for advice about controlling salt glaze. His philosophical reply was that 'Salt glaze is very good for humility.'

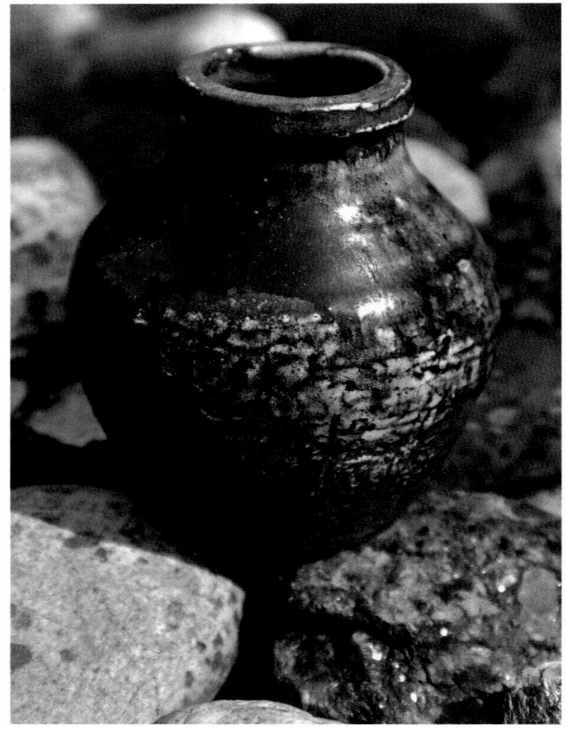

Small vase by Denise Wren, 1960s. Salt glaze with cobalt and wood ash.

First Exhibitions

The first small exhibition of salt-glaze work by Denise and Rosemary was shown in 1959, and other exhibitions followed during the early years of the 1960s. The work sold well at the Craftsmen Potters' Association shop in Fouberts Place in London, where a 0.6m (2ft)-high, salt-glaze lidded jar hung outside in a frame above the doorway, a commissioned piece made by Rosemary for the shop when it was opened in 1960. The shop and sign moved to its present premises in Marshall Street in 1967, and the jar remained there until 1997.

In the early sixties during the salt-firing years at Oxshott, the artist-designer William Gordon came to rent a workshop at the pottery for a short time. He had been experimenting at a small salt-glaze factory at Brampton in Chesterfield, using the industrial technique of slip-casting in porcelain and the industrial kilns. He stayed at Oxshott for ten years, but although he sometimes helped to fill the coke hopper for the big salt kiln and discussed glaze recipes, he never did any salt glaze there. Other potters came to see the coke-fired salt kiln, and would have been able to buy copies of the plans. A smaller gas kiln was also designed by Denise and used by Rosemary, but not for salt glaze.

In 1967 Denise Wren showed some magnificent salt-glaze pieces and a few modelled elephants at the Commonwealth Institute Gallery; but immediately afterwards she was faced with the impasse of no longer being able to fire her big coke-fired salt kiln because the suitable gas coke was no longer available, gas technology having undergone great change. Then aged seventy-eight, Denise felt that the salt glaze was her best work, and had been made at the height of her powers; and so she took the decision to turn to other firings. Rosemary, too, had produced her

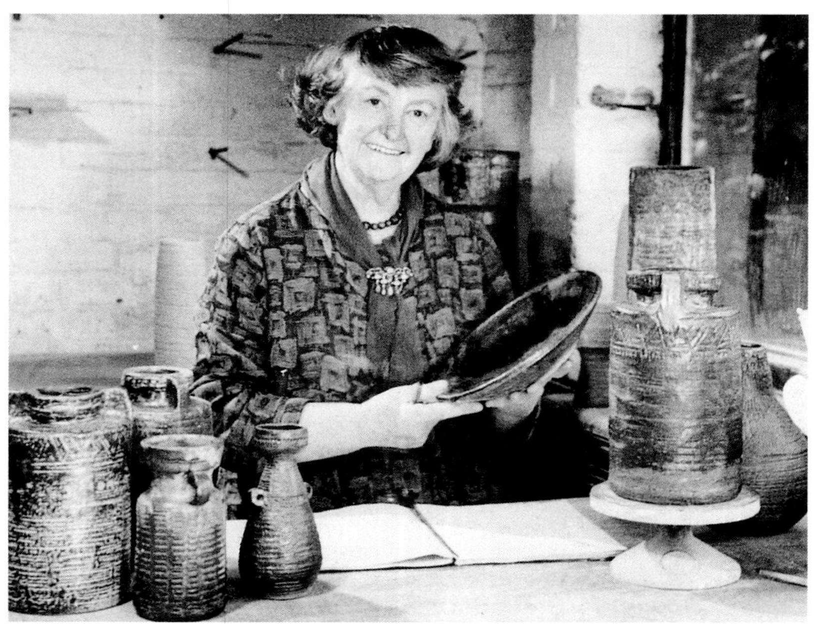

(BELOW LEFT) Denise Wren at Oxshott with salt-glazed pots for the Commonwealth Institute Exhibition, 1967.

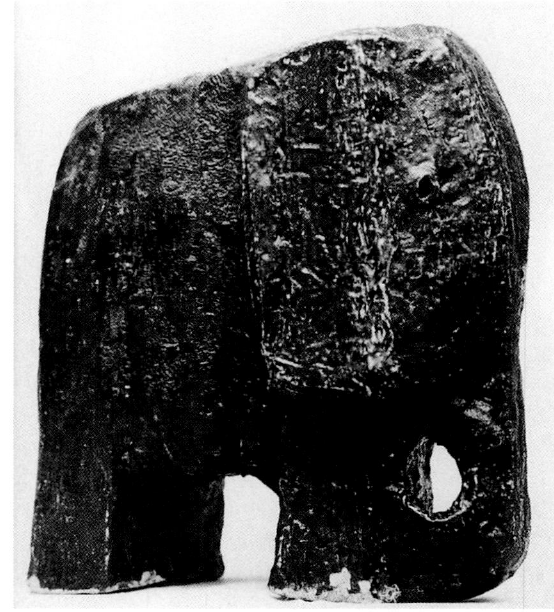

(BELOW RIGHT) Elephant by Denise Wren. Shown at the Commonwealth Institute Exhibition 1966/67.

last large pieces from the residual-salt firings: a giant anteater and a Hoolock gibbon, both now in a private collection.

Increasing Interest

The pioneering development of salt glaze in studio pottery carried out by Denise and Rosemary Wren at the Oxshott Pottery was unparalleled. The number of individual potters who had their own small workshops was still quite limited in the 1950s, and those who did would be working in relative isolation. But there were a few others who were amongst the first potters, after World War II, to take up salt firing.

John Chappell

John Chappell established a pottery at Berkhamstead Common in 1953, where he spent several years developing salt-glaze techniques. He went to study in Japan where his enthusiasm for salt glaze was renewed – but tragically he was killed in a motorbike accident in Australia, en route to an exhibition of his work in New Zealand in 1964.

David Ballantyne

In the late 1950s, David Ballantyne established his own workshop at home whilst continuing to run the ceramics department at Bournemouth College of Art. Firing in a drip-feed oil kiln using waste sump oil, he used a porcelaneous body, and then decorated his pots by impressing and engraving through slips, inspired by the pre-industrial and early nineteenth-century English tradition.

Mary Rich

Mary Rich was one of David Ballantyne's students at Bournemouth in the late 1950s. She recalls:

> Some of the work of older students was fired at the salt-glaze pipe works of Sharpe Jones, which was working in Bournemouth at that time. This was my first introduction to the process, which fired me with enthusiasm. I was fortunate to work for a short time in David's workshop where he made salt glaze. The methods of making were amazing, and the concept of using different bodies, slips, slip-glazes, oxides and colours on a once-fired piece seemed to open up limitless possibilities.

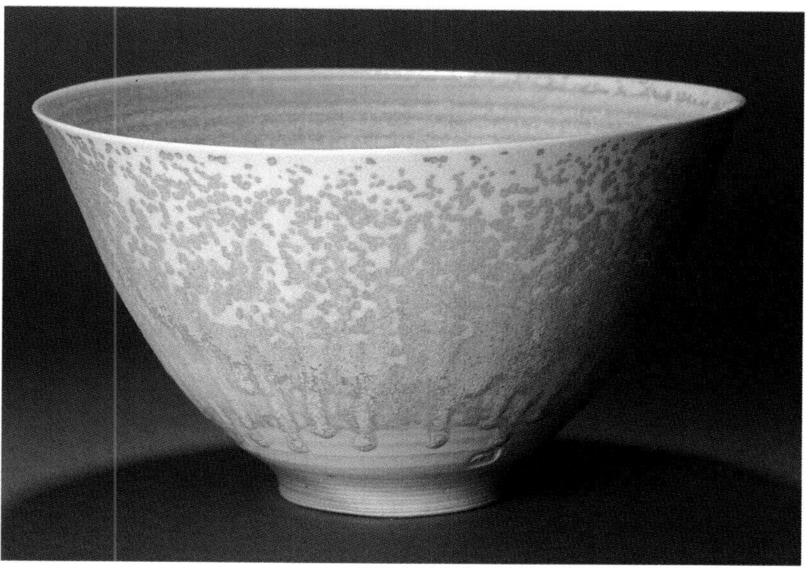

Bowl by Mary Rich, 1977. Salt glaze. Layers of slip and slip glazes. 'I used a buff smooth stoneware clay, reduction St Thomas and White St Thomas stoneware clays, a Crank mixture, a high-firing white earthenware and porcelain.'

In 1962 she set up her studio pottery in Falmouth and, like the Wrens, had help from the Gas Board to design her gas-fired salt kiln. All the pots were raw-glazed and once-fired. The kiln was built of tough refractories, helped with molochite bricks and tiles – but it was still necessary to carry out constant repairs. On moving to her present pottery near Truro in 1970, Mary changed to fire with oil. She rebuilt the salt kiln three times up to 1983, when she was enticed away from the rigours of salt firing by the simplicity of a small propane kiln; now she makes only porcelain pieces.

Guy Sydenham

During the period 1960–88, Guy Sydenham and his son Russell were producing salt-glaze pots, first on Long Island, then on Green Island in Poole Harbour, Dorset. Guy had a long and creative career at Poole Pottery, and was also a lecturer at Poole College of Art. He started his salt glazing by chance. In his autobiography *A Potter's Life*, he describes how he was walking on the south-west shore of Brownsea Island:

> I found that what from a distance looked like beautifully coloured pebbles, were not pebbles at all, but a multitude of pieces of salt-glaze drain pipes. Being lapped wet by the sea and shining in the sun, they were the most beautiful earthy colours that could be wished for. Textures, too, in abundance. Colours from lustrous blue-black, dark satiny browns and warm rich gingerbread browns to leathery tans. Ochre to beige, soft yellows with tinges of green to the cool grey of the Brownsea Island clay itself.

This was his inspiration to try salt glazing on Long Island.

The pots were made using the fine-grained and very plastic Dorset blue-ball clay from a cliff on the island. They were decorated with sgraffito work, through slips prepared from other local clays and giving different colour and texture. The first firing was in a kiln dug into a bank, fired with driftwood. A piece of iron pipe led from an old drum filled with sea-water to the kiln, and the salt water was dripped into the fire mouth. Guy went on to build other top-loading kilns, and continued to drip in the sea-water as that method is kinder to the brick-work and allows the salt glaze to build up slowly. The salt firings at the Green Island Pottery continued until 1988.

Salt-glaze stoneware bottles by Guy and Russell Sydenham. Long Island and Green Island salt glaze, 1960–80. A range of colour and texture was produced from just the few natural local materials. Left: white industrial clay with wood ash and cobalt, 1,300°C. Centre: tan slip, and dark pigment. Right: tan slip and dipped in heavy manganese.

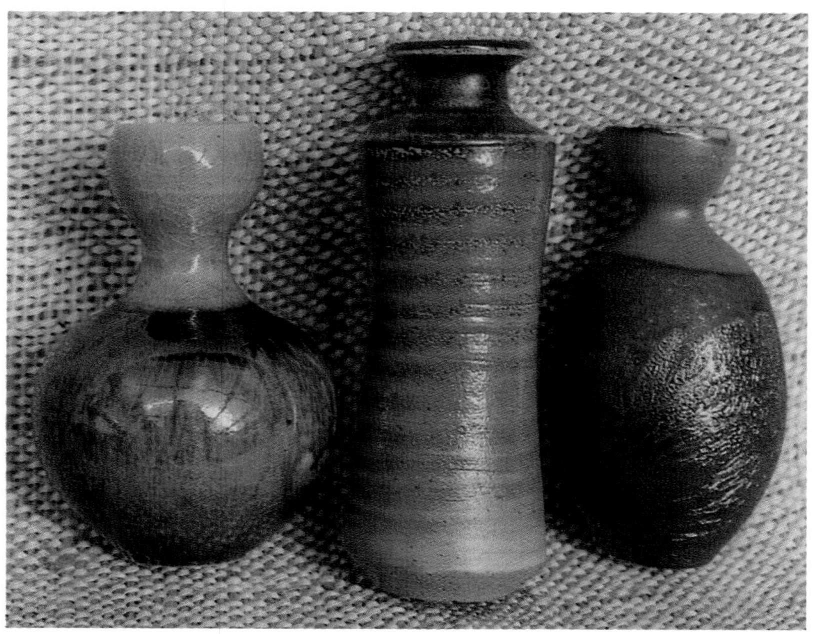

The Spread of Salt Glaze

Craft Potters

The last salt-glaze art pottery from the ceramic industry had been produced at Doulton in 1956. From the 1920s, through to the 1950s and 1960s, a few of the early studio potters used the salt-firing process for their own individual production of ceramics. But most were hardly aware of the work of other studio potters. *Pottery Quarterly*, studio pottery's first magazine, was founded by Murray Fieldhouse in 1954, and began to draw together the potting fraternity. Then the Craftsmen Potters Association was founded in 1957, and gave its members a forum for the exchange of ideas and techniques, as well as providing a retail outlet.

In the 1960s, the craft of the potter began to achieve wider recognition, and the character of ceramic courses at certain of the art colleges began to change. Gradually they opened up to offer a more practical focus on pottery, with clay and glaze technology and opportunities for kiln building. In this atmosphere of change, salt glaze was beginning to interest some of the new wave of young studio potters.

Harrow

In 1963, at the Harrow School of Art, Victor Margrie and Michael Casson together designed the new two-year vocational course in studio pottery, which they then led for ten years. At the time it was unique. Within the framework of workshop practice and a 'hands-on' approach, the students learned production throwing, clay and glaze technology, cultural history and visual studies, also practical knowledge about equipment, and kiln building. This offered the students an opportunity to acquire all the skills that would enable them to earn a viable living in the future.

Students came to attend the Harrow Studio Pottery course from around the world. Many had already qualified elsewhere and held degrees in other subjects, and thus they brought with them a breadth of knowledge and references from other traditions that, combined with their own commitment and enthusiasm, created a remarkable and energetic atmosphere. The course also gave them unparalleled contact with other makers who came to teach, demonstrate and assess the students' work. There is a long list of names of prominent and inspiring tutors, though this account concentrates on those particularly involved in the revival of salt glaze.

The opportunity for kiln building at Harrow was no doubt a key factor that led to this salt-glaze revival in studio pottery. In 1964 Walter Keeler, who had been a student at Harrow Art College and had recently completed a teacher training, was asked to teach one day a week on the new studio pottery course; he was given the brief to add a creative element to what was otherwise a very practical course. At the time he was involved in building his own first salt kiln, and this inspired him to lead the students into designing and building kilns in the yard of the annexe of the art school.

Several small experimental kilns were built from a pile of second-hand bricks, and after successfully reaching stoneware temperatures, the idea came to try salt glaze. A number of students expressed an interest in the process, and before long a bigger kiln was built and fired frequently. In 1969, all moved to a new building with open land for a kiln site. This coincided with the closure of the local gas works, and the decommissioned works meant there was an endless supply of firebricks, mostly unused. Students who were prepared to work on the kiln site enthusiastically started building kilns under Keeler's direction. Much of the equipment and materials was begged, borrowed, improvised or invented. With the students, he explored and encouraged a range of different firings: raku, wood, stoneware and salt.

Those committed students from the early years of the course at Harrow, should be given credit for carrying out a great deal of experimental work on salt glaze, from which following students benefited. A number of now internationally known professional potters trained on the Harrow course in the 1970s, including Jane Hamlyn, Toff Milway, Micki Schloessingk, Peter Starkey and Sarah Walton. Since then, through their connections with colleges, workshops and demonstrations, and in gallery exhibitions in Britain and abroad, they have inspired many others to appreciate the qualities of salt glaze, playing a significant part in the growing number of studio potters taking up salt firing in Britain today. Others from the Harrow course chose to live and work in Europe and elsewhere, or returned to their home countries.

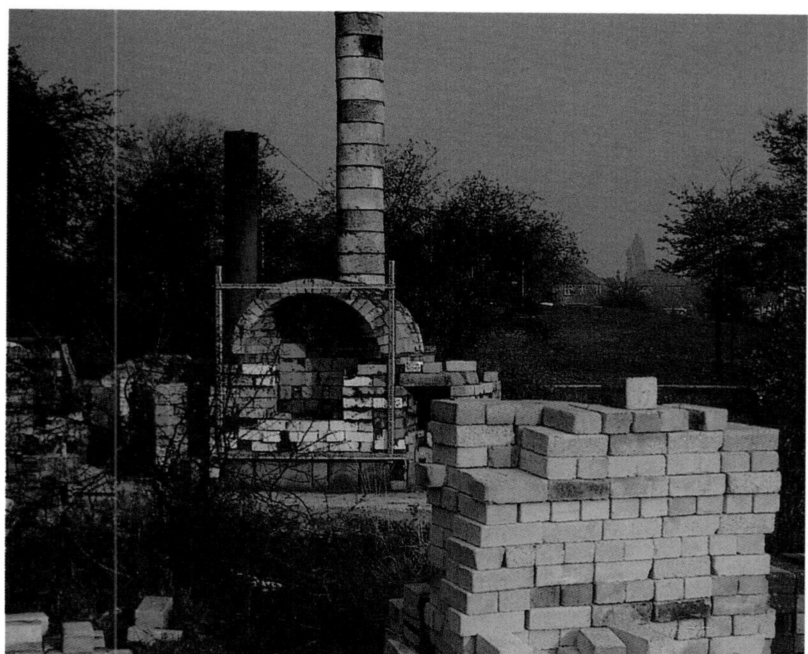

Harrow kiln site, 1972.

Farnham

From the late 1960s the ceramics course at Farnham Art College also produced a number of distinguished salt-glaze potters. Under the direction of Henry Hammond and Paul Barron, his senior lecturer, the three-year diploma course had a strong academic content, in addition to the practical level of making – though in contrast to Harrow, this was taught without any emphasis on vocational training. However, kiln building was an important element of the course and was encouraged. The Canadian potter John Reeve spent some time teaching at Farnham, and played a big part in this aspect. Several students were attracted to salt firing and remained involved with salt glaze for some years after they had left Farnham.

GEOFFREY FULLER

Fuller was a mature student at Farnham from 1966 to 1969. He relates how he became attracted to salt firings there: 'Coming from Chesterfield, a centre for making salt-glaze stoneware from the 1740s through to the 1930s,

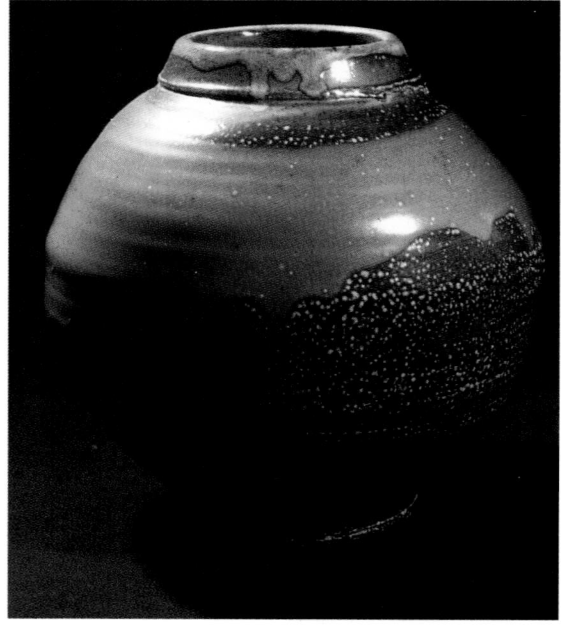

Round jar, by Geoffrey Fuller, 1968–69. Made as a student at Farnham Art College. Clay body, a mix of equal parts Leeds fireclay and SM ball clay. SM ball clay slip.

I was very familiar with the products of the area. The idea of using just clay and fire to produce glazed ware was very appealing, so in 1968 I began to produce pots purely for salt firing.'

Having watched a group of students fail to get results from several salt firings in an oil-fired catenary arch kiln, Fuller was determined to make a success of it by firing it alone:

> The kiln took twenty-six hours to reach 1,300°C, and took 30lb [16kg] of salt thrown in by hand in parcels of 5 to 10lb [2 to 4.5kg] wrapped in newspaper, starting at 1,150°C until 1,250°C. It took thirty hours to cool, but when opened it was full of green 'tiger-ware', top to bottom. By the time I fired the third kiln I had learned to manipulate the atmosphere from heavy reduction to almost oxidizing, and was achieving a wide range of colour and texture in the pots. I had also learned to stack ware-on-ware using alumina wads, and relied totally on draw-rings and the eye for colour in the chamber, since cones, once salted, were useless. With almost no information available on salting in the late sixties, we worked on empiricism, common sense and the hard-won knowledge gained from analysing each firing.

Two dishes by Robert Johnson, 1990s. Rutile blue slip/glaze. Oil-fired kiln to 1,300°C.

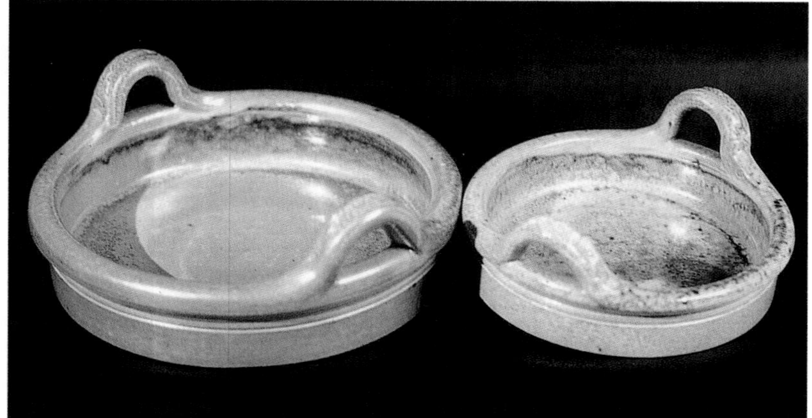

On leaving Farnham, Geoffrey Fuller became absorbed in working with earthenware. Although he put aside the salt-glaze process for his own work, he has never lost his enthusiasm for it. When he taught at Chesterfield College of Art from the mid-seventies to 1987, the students were encouraged in all kiln-building activities, and it was no doubt Fuller's own interest and experience of salt firing that resulted in half the students salt glazing in any given year, during that time.

ROBERT JOHNSON

Robert Johnson was one of Geoffrey Fuller's students at Chesterfield, and started salting there in 1977. He says:

> I saw the salt-glaze pots that Geoff had made while he was a student at Farnham. I was already wanting to wood-fire, but the colours of these pots were a revelation – oyster-shell pinks, tans, bright oranges, chestnut brown, cool greys, and of course the 'tiger-skin' effects. I was smitten at the first sight of these pots, not only because of the wonderful colour palette, but also by the direct, vigorous forms. My tack was set that day for the remainder of my course at Chesterfield.

On leaving college, Robert Johnson set up his own pottery in Scotland.

RICHARD LAUNDER

Richard Launder was a student at Farnham from 1972 to 1976. His early pieces were functional in form, but in the following years his work changed as he became involved in 'exploring and expanding the area between function and sculpture'. He used high temperature salt glaze, but also experimented with firing at much lower temperatures than usual, producing a range of new glazes and textures on the pieces. Now living and working abroad, he still occasionally uses salt, at either end of the temperature range. He tends to favour the lighter side of the spectrum, seeking a patina of colour and nuance of texture, rather than a glaze. He is concerned with working predominantly with conceptual ideas in abstract sculpture, and has exhibited in Britain, Greece, Norway and America.

ANDREW MCGARVA

Andrew McGarva left Farnham in 1979, having gained sound practical experience of kiln building and firing there. He had also travelled and worked in the village of La Borne, in central France, where he was won over by the quality of wood-firings and the rich flashing of ash in combination with a small addition of salt. He wanted to make functional pots and was drawn to the European tradition, and especially the qualities of both English slipware and French country pots. He saw wood-fired salt glaze as the obvious choice for his work, and when he joined the Casson's at Wobage Farm, he shared the building and firing of the wood-fired salt kiln. He sought the subtler but nonetheless dramatic effects of the wood and light salting. In

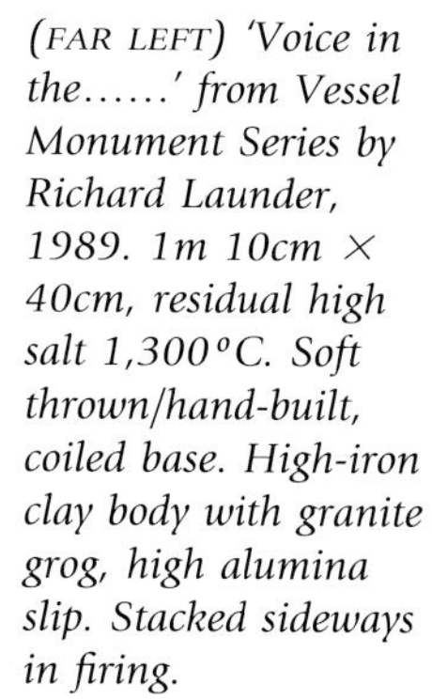

(FAR LEFT) 'Voice in the......' from Vessel Monument Series by Richard Launder, 1989. 1m 10cm × 40cm, residual high salt 1,300°C. Soft thrown/hand-built, coiled base. High-iron clay body with granite grog, high alumina slip. Stacked sideways in firing.

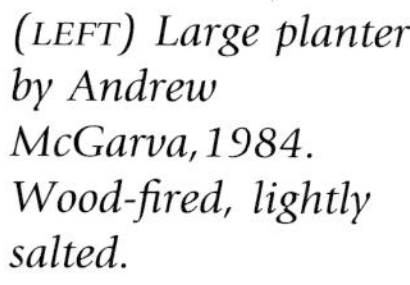

(LEFT) Large planter by Andrew McGarva, 1984. Wood-fired, lightly salted.

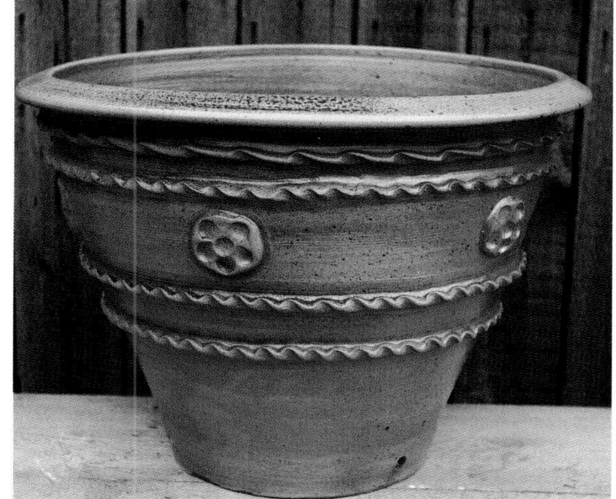

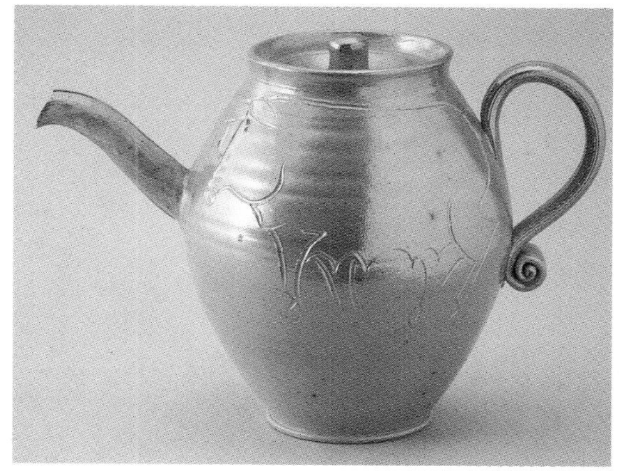

Teapot by Andrew McGarva, 1987. Wood-fired, salt glaze. A contemporary interpretation of the finesse, precision and detail of eighteenth-century white salt glaze. (Nottingham City Museums and Galleries)

the mid-1980s he, like many other potters, was faced with changing market demands, and salt glaze gave way to his painted stoneware techniques.

In 1990 he moved with his family to set up a pottery in Burgundy. After ten years, he is returning to wood-fired, high temperature techniques, and is looking again at the traditional North European wares. Some of the jugs have the characteristics of the early German salt-glaze pots seen in Breughel's paintings and the local pots from Puisaye, in the Nievre region of France where he now lives. It may not be long before the salt glaze reappears on his pots.

Inspiration from France

La Borne

As the interest in hand-made pottery was re-awakened in Britain, students and potters travelled around Europe in search of new opportunities and workshop experience. The traditional wood-fired pots from central France were made for the local communities and regional markets, and although they were exported when production increased, they never came to Britain in any quantity. But La Borne was to become the inspiration for a number of British potters, amongst them some salt-glaze potters.

French country pots displayed at Wobage in the 1980s. (Private collection)

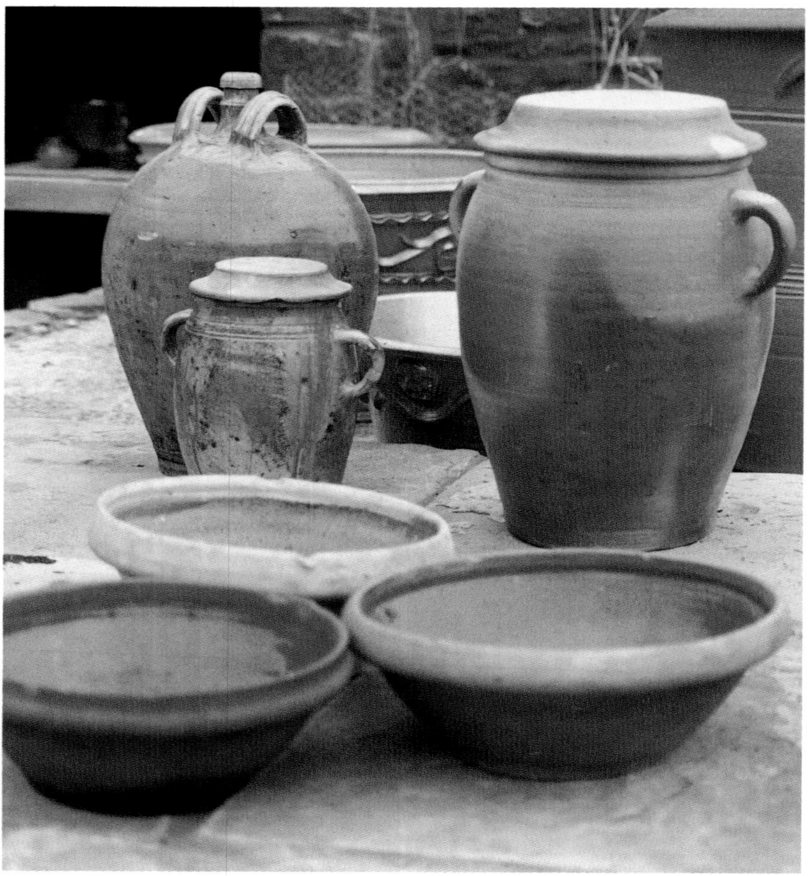

The clay of the region, around La Borne and Saint Amand en Puisaye, is particularly suited for stoneware salt and wood firings, and is capable of withstanding high temperatures. It also contains iron pyrites, which give the fired pots their distinctive warm-coloured, speckled surface. The simply made, robust pots have attractive surfaces, created by the lengthy wood-firings and deposits of fine ash and salt. The flame carries the ash, which forms the natural ash glaze on the surface of the pottery. Wherever it was unlikely to reach, the small pots of salt were placed for local salt glaze effects. Many potters still use this method in La Borne, in both wood and gas kilns; however, true salt firing was never a traditional practice there. La Borne has hosted several gatherings for special community firings of the wood-fire kilns.

Connections with La Borne:

CHRISTINE PEDLEY

Christine Pedley was a student at Harrow Art School from 1964 to 1966, when she heard about La Borne. She went to work as a thrower in La Borne in 1968, where she joined Janet Steadman; then in 1970 she set up her own workshop. She says: 'I began using salt in my own small down-draught wood-fired kiln, according to the La Borne tradition. I call this method "semi-salt" wood firing, the use of salt pots giving a little extra sparkle of local flashing to the wood-fired pots.'

Her first full salt firing was not until 1974, in Mashiko, Japan. For the past sixteen years, circumstances have led her to use a gas kiln, with which she has chosen to go for the full effects of salt, with a true salt firing. She uses the method of blowing dry salt into the kiln, which gives smooth, satiny surfaces throughout.

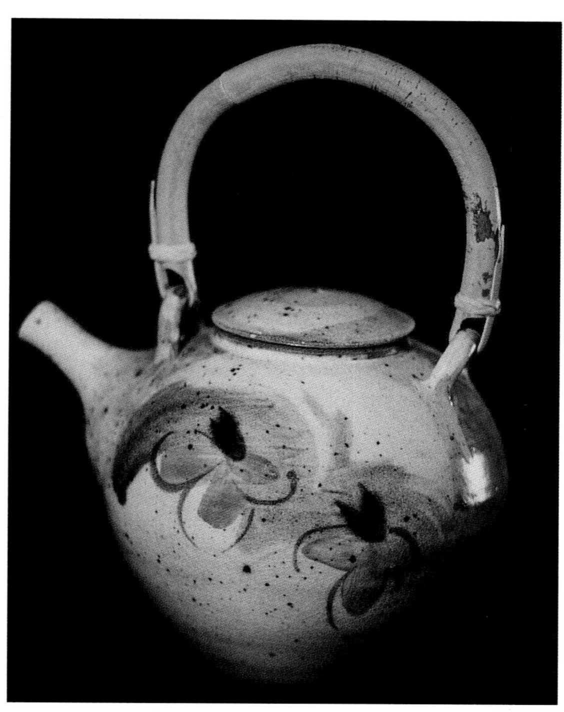

(LEFT) *Large teapot by Christine Pedley, 1990s. White slip decorated with oxides and stains. Salt glaze, gas-fired stoneware.*

Among the seventy potters living in and around La Borne today, there are many using wood-firing kilns. However, she is one of only two doing full salt firings. She intends to experiment with salt and soda in her new hard-brick gas kiln.

GWYN HANSSEN PIGOTT

Gwyn Hanssen Pigott began potting in Australia, and lived and worked in Britain from the mid-1950s. She moved to La Borne in 1966, to build a wood kiln and establish her own pottery. While living in France she also taught at both Harrow and Farnham, inspiring and encouraging the students at the time when the first salt kilns were being built. She now lives and works in Queensland, Australia.

Establishing the Revival

IAN GREGORY

Ian Gregory played a particular part in breaking new ground in the early days of the revived salt firing. He started his salt glazing by chance in the 1970s when he wanted to build a kiln, and the only solid firebricks he could purchase locally came from an old bottle kiln that had been used for firing sewage pipes: 'They had a heavily salted surface, and I knew that they could not be used for any other type of firing.' His first kiln was a 28cu m (100cu ft), two-chambered wood-fired salt kiln. It was the beginning of a passion for both kiln building and salt glaze. He has had exceptional experience of kiln building, and his book *Kiln Building*, first published in 1977, was republished in a second edition in 1995. His book, his teaching, numerous workshops, travels to build kilns and his own making have been inspirations to other potters on their journeys into salt firing.

His early salt-glaze work included a range of domestic tableware and architectural modelled sculptures. As he moved more into hand-building, his interest in salt glaze increased. He saw how the attack of the salt defined the making process, revealing every mark on the clay, helping to develop the fine detail, and highlighting

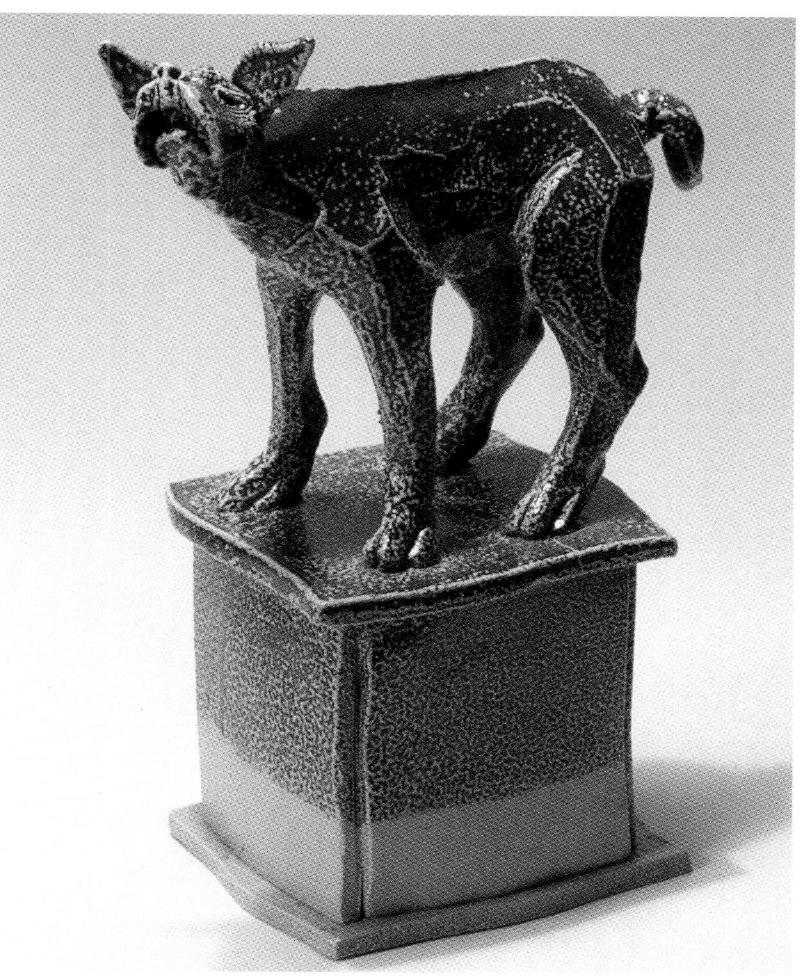

(BELOW) *'Standing dog on base' by Ian Gregory, 2000. Salt glaze, 1,280°C. Tan slip. The clay body includes 15 per cent paper pulp. A crisp definition of orange-peel and flashings from the flame suit these sculptural pieces.*

the surfaces of his sculptural pieces. He writes about the salt-glaze process: '. . . the materials become a battlefield of the elements of earth, fire and water, which only occasionally I am able to control.'

The Exchange of Information

The magazine *Pottery Quarterly*, later renamed *Real Pottery*, was a valuable source of information for potters, and several articles were printed covering the subject of salt firing. When *Ceramic Review*, the magazine of the Craftsmen Potters Association of Great Britain, was first published in 1970, it extended the opportunity for the exchange of ideas, experiences and information in the articles and letters. Issues 33 and 34, which came out in 1975, contained two articles on salt glaze, and in following years there have been many more.

Peter Starkey's book on salt glaze was published in 1977. Inevitably this became the close companion of the burgeoning number of salt-glaze potters in Britain. It outlined his own practical methods and was an inspiring guide for anyone making pots for salt glaze, and building and firing a first salt kiln. In it Starkey writes: 'The obvious reason for salt glazing is, of course, to achieve the particular qualities, and texture and colours and surface, which no other technique can give.' He also encouraged the potter to look beyond the conventional aesthetics of salt glaze.

Only a certain number of colleges could offer facilities for building and firing kilns, but in doing so they were in a position to make a practical contribution to encourage the renewed interest for salt glaze. British salt glaze re-emerged as a process for studio potters. It was seen as a means for individual expression, and by the 1980s there were a number of well established salt-glaze potters in Britain. The salt-glaze process inspires passion and enthusiasm, and it is no wonder that these individual potters infected others with their energy, and a fascination for the surface qualities of their work.

5 Contemporary British Salt Glaze

In the following profiles, six of the most influential and successful British salt-glaze potters describe the different and personal ways in which they have worked with salt glaze. We start with Walter Keeler, who led the kiln building at Harrow, and we end with Peter Starkey who wrote the book for salt-glaze enthusiasts. Together with Jane Hamlyn, Micki Schloessingk, Sarah Walton and Michael Casson, they represent the wide range of salt-glaze ceramics made in Britain today. Their passion for the process is undeniable.

Walter Keeler

Walter Keeler was first fascinated by the tactile surface of salt glaze when, as a boy, he had found pot shards on the banks of the Thames. From 1958–63 he was a student at Harrow Art College, and his interest in salt glaze was rekindled when he saw the work of Rosemary and Denise Wren, although salt firing was not an option for him then. He taught an evening class from 1963 whilst still a student, and by the time he began to teach kiln design on the new Studio Pottery course at Harrow in 1964, he was building his first salt kiln. His involvement with the students' experimental kilns and firings strengthened his commitment to produce salt glaze.

By 1968 Keeler had his first full-time salt kiln. He was also producing oxidized stoneware from an electric kiln. Bored with the results from the latter, he discovered that by firing the stoneware pieces in the salt kiln they came out brighter and with more life. He established a routine of having one or two non-salt firings between each salt firing proper, capitalizing on the effects of the residual salt-flashing by leaving large areas of the outside of the pots unglazed.

Keeler moved to South Wales in 1976. His priority was to make a living, and all the additional chores involved in salt firing made it the least profitable proposition. He continued to make functional stoneware in an oil-fired catenary arch kiln, but at the end of the seventies there was a general collapse in the market for traditional domestic pottery, and he decided to revitalize his work by returning to salt.

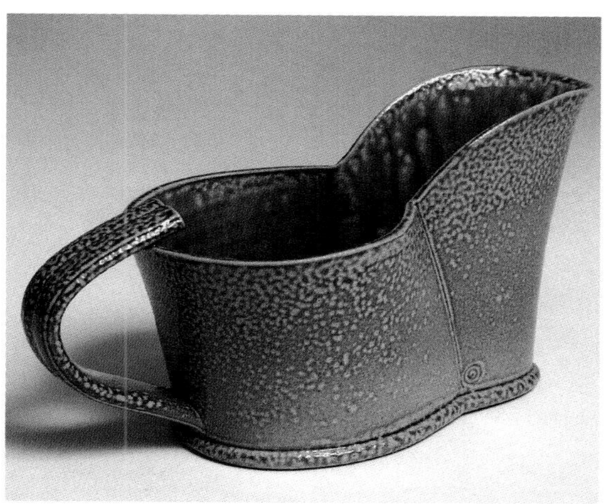

(FAR LEFT) Teapot by Walter Keeler, 1982.

(LEFT) Jug by Walter Keeler, 1983. Thrown and altered with extruded handle.

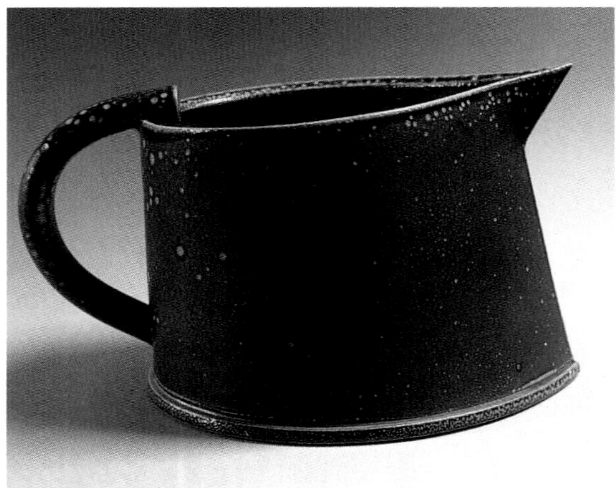

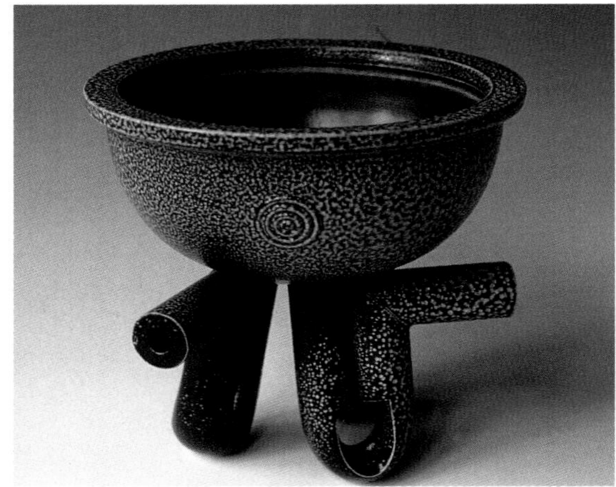

(RIGHT) Jug by Walter Keeler, 1989.

(FAR RIGHT) Tripod bowl by Walter Keeler, 1999.

He recalls how the new work came along, piece by piece, and more lateral in its thinking as regards form and function. He was excited by the idea of functional pots that were one-offs, and his new distinctive pieces, assembled from thrown and altered elements, were received well.

Talking about making for salt glaze, Keeler says:

> I have always worked in anticipation of firings, thinking about how the finished piece will look when I'm working on the wheel. I like the idea of edges and detail and sharpness, because the salt picks up on them in a particular way that is appealing. Initially – in the earliest salt-glaze work – I had looked for the qualities of the nineteenth-century salt-glaze pots, dipping red slip onto the shoulders of the pots and then using a white slip as well, which gave softer, more subtle results. I was never interested in using a lot of different or complicated slips. I wanted the basic qualities that you get from salt glaze.
>
> I liked the orange-peel, but not too much of it – I liked the different intensities of the orange-peel, and the new colours developed from some of the earlier pots of the late 1970s, when I was still making the traditional-looking jugs and dipping the tops in white slip. I began to spray mixtures of oxides on them before they went into the kiln.

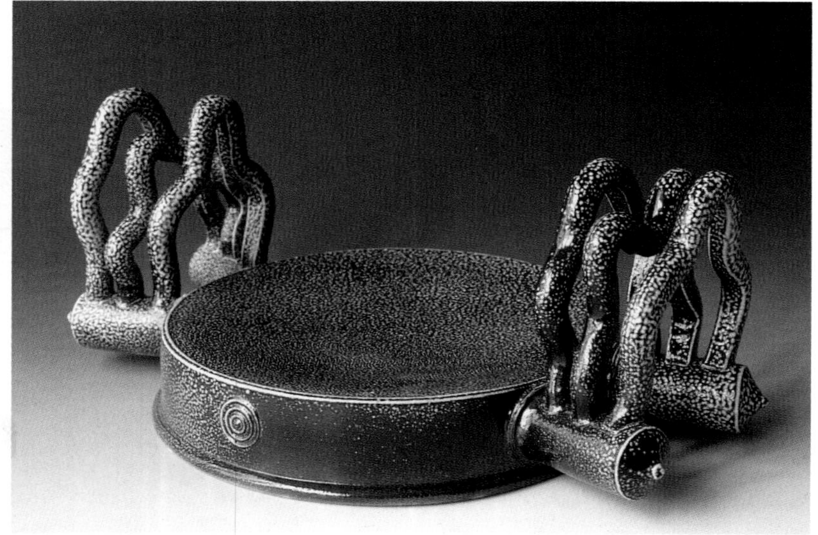

Dish with toast-rack handles by Walter Keeler, 1999.

The more complex shapes would not survive the application of raw glazes and slips, so he turned to biscuit-firing the new work. He took advantage of the biscuit stage to spray on more colour and to manipulate subtle changes of the salt-glaze surface qualities.

Salt glaze gives the pots unique qualities, and Keeler explains its appeal:

> It is very distinctive and can be very flattering to a pot. It moistens the pot, rather like having the pot fresh on the wheel again, gleaming with light on it. The pot goes dead as it dries and is biscuit-fired, and it can be very difficult to bring it back to life again. Salt always seems to touch the pots to bring back that freshness. I get different sorts of qualities around the kiln, but they all fall within a range that I find acceptable. Some pots I feel will carry a heavier salting, whereas another one definitely will not. I choose where I place the pieces accordingly.

Keeler holds a deep respect for the British tradition, and feels a natural sense of belonging to it. It is important for him to make pots that he believes relate to the ceramic tradition. With his own innovative talent and skill he is able to place those historical traditions into the present times. His work is influenced by hard-edged objects, and yet it expresses a sensitivity and gentle humour. While it is function that underlies the starting place for all his work, his fundamental interest is in form. Paying close attention to detail, each piece is made with meticulous precision, and he uses the salt glaze in a very sophisticated way to enhance the forms. Integral with the clay body, the thin salt glaze hides nothing, restores the freshness of the making, and in that way reveals the skill of the craftsman. The salt-firing process bestows a perfect finish on Keeler's pots.

Keeler explains his latest change in direction to glazed earthenware. The inspiration stems from a fascination with eighteenth-century Staffordshire ceramics, and in particular the Creamware and tortoiseshell wares of Thomas Whieldon. It continues to be form that interests him most in pottery, and his salt-glaze work begins to be affected by certain elements related to the new earthenware pieces, such as detached handles and spouts mounted on plinths. He sees that for each piece to succeed it is vital to choose the most fitting medium, whether salt or earthenware, and he says that he recognizes his need for both processes in order to realize his ideas satisfactorily. He is adamant that the salt-glaze work remains important, and has hopes of developing new salt-fired colours and surfaces.

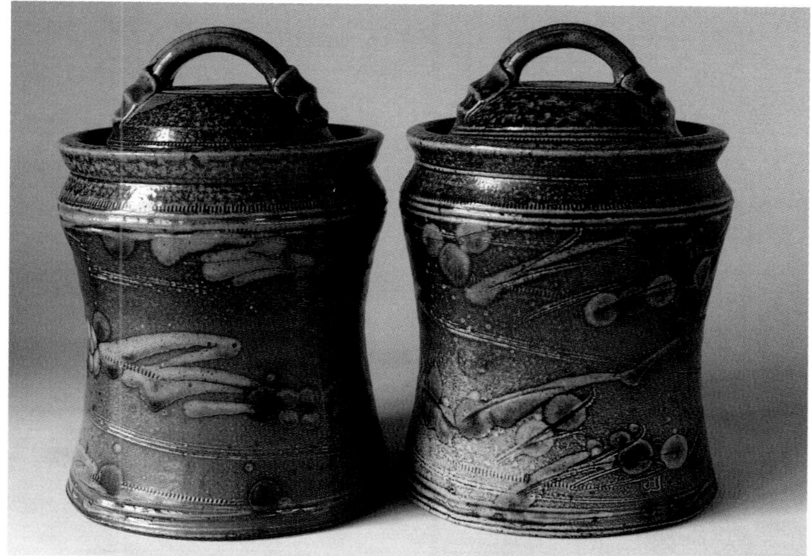

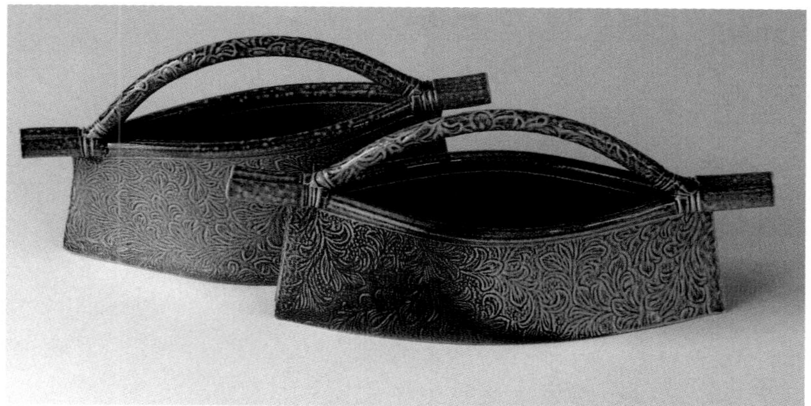

(TOP) Two lidded jars by Jane Hamlyn, early 1980s.

(BOTTOM) Purse pots by Jane Hamlyn, 1987. Embossed slabs with extruded handles.

Jane Hamlyn

When Jane Hamlyn left Harrow College of Art in 1974 with her Studio Pottery Diploma, a lifetime commitment to salt glaze was not her ambition. The production of functional ware was central to the Harrow vocational course, and although she had watched the kiln-building and salting activities of other students, she was primarily determined to earn a living as a potter. It was when she worked with Peter Starkey in Norfolk, in the first months after college, that she became completely entranced by the salt-firing process. In 1975 she moved with her family out of London to build a kiln and set up a workshop in Everton, Nottinghamshire, and there she committed herself unequivocally to salt glazing.

During the next fifteen years she earned a modest living from her salt-glazed pots, while exploring and experimenting with the process. Her husband, the painter Ted Hamlyn, took responsibility for firings and maintaining the kiln, enabling her to concentrate time and energy on making. She discovered new qualities in salt glaze, exploring materials, processes and decorative techniques, which offered the potential for further development. The desire to experiment and develop ideas has meant she has never allowed herself to be restricted by a standard production range, although function has always been a keystone of Hamlyn's work.

In 1986 a new body of work emerged after a Crafts Council bursary and the purchase of a slab roller. Hamlyn had already developed her distinctive textured handles, and by impressing textured wallpaper into soft clay, her

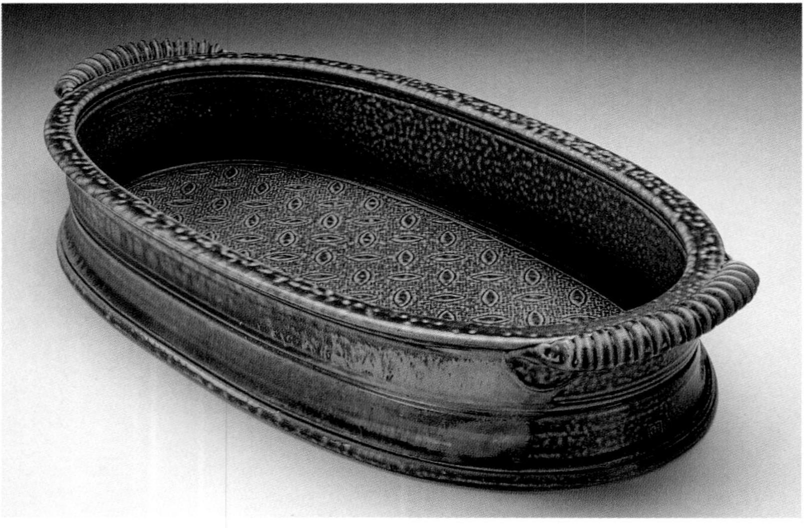

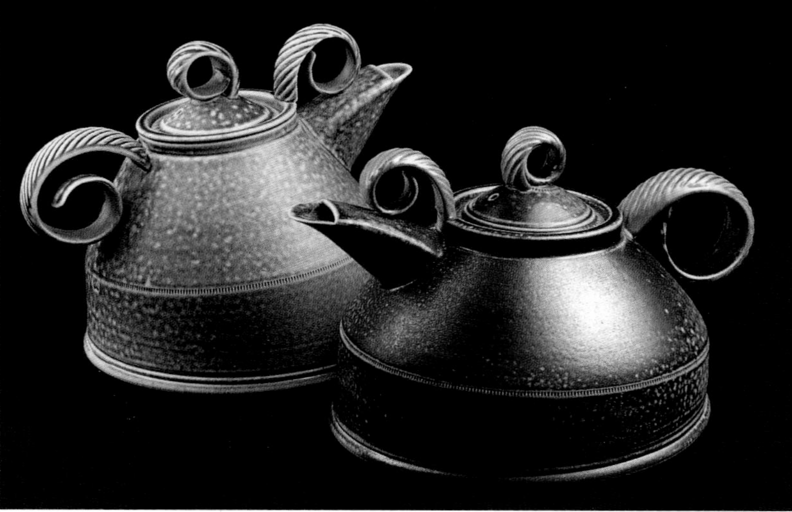

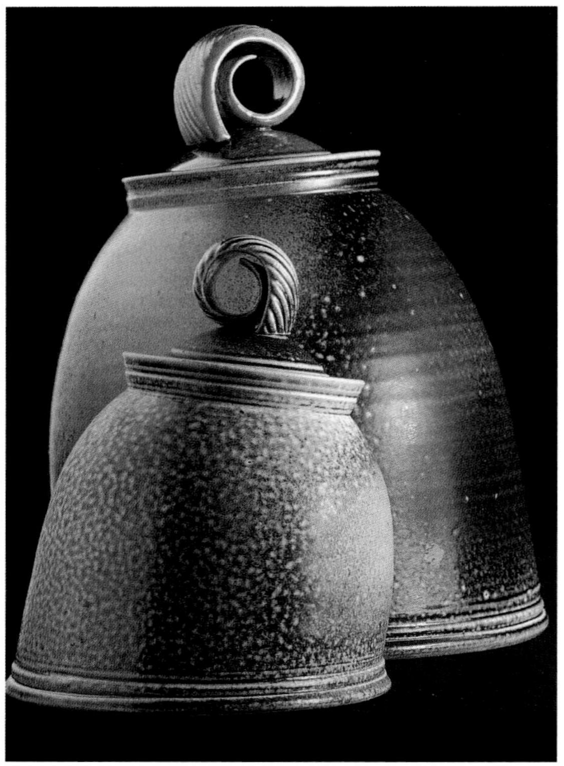

(TOP) Oval dish by Jane Hamlyn, 1988. Embossed slab base, thrown ring.

(BOTTOM) Teapots by Jane Hamlyn, 1996.

(RIGHT) Leaning jars by Jane Hamlyn, 2000.

initial use of the slab roller was to produce highly textured surfaces and a new range of forms. These incorporated thrown and altered walls with slabbed bases and modelled handles and feet.

Hamlyn's work has always had a strong individual identity in terms of surface decoration and colour, and a wide variety of forms. Throughout her exploration of salt glaze it has been the combination of making, firing, reassessing, and then remaking work that has extended her salt-glazing vocabulary and moved forward her interest in the relationship between form and process. She says:

> Salt glazing is my chosen method because, quite apart from the beauty of its effects, the technique allows an empirical way of working and a special kind of dialogue between kiln and materials; unexpected qualities, that can stimulate new ideas, are more likely to appear. My work moves between two particular areas which interest me. One is the close and intimate relationship between pot and person, maker and user, which can be found in smaller-scale objects and in which my careful and rather precise making requires a certain restraint of surface treatment and not too much interference from heavy salting. But I also love the seductive, elemental, luscious, dripping, melting qualities of salt, and the rich colours of its fluxing interaction with slips and oxides. These extravagant qualities are best exploited in the simpler forms and larger scale pieces. However, it is not easy or even always possible, to achieve both these effects successfully and simultaneously in the same firing in the same kiln! I try to have it both ways, but perhaps these conflicting interests represent certain aspects of my personality which also find expression in my pots!

Hamlyn says that she recognizes in herself both the need for sensibility and control, and the opportunity for exuberance and daring, and she sees that salt glazing can offer expression to both these desires. She has not wished to choose one effect to the exclusion of the other, but always wants the possibility of both. By skilful positioning of pots in the kiln, and by using clays of varying character, she manages to succeed in reconciling these apparent opposites. Talking about these qualities of risk, and the control of the salt-firing process, Hamlyn quotes from a lecture that she gave at a symposium in the Netherlands:

> Controlling the unpredictability of salt glaze is like breaking in a wild horse: it has to be handled so you can ride it, but you do not want to destroy its spirit. It must be understood that the degree of control required is obviously of great significance, because in salt glazing, the process is part of the aesthetic. For example, many potters have a perception of the right amount of salt. This is both a practical and an aesthetic judgement, which relates to a spectrum of risk. At one end the rich extravagance of melted silica (risking surfeit), and at the other end, the nuances of quiet restraint (risking monotony). The position the potter chooses on that spectrum is one of the factors that defines their work as aesthetic. It is not simply a question of high, medium or low salt, but how the decision is put to the service of the potter's intention.
>
> For the future, I cannot imagine making pots that are not salted, although I can imagine working with paler clays and more subtle surfaces, where the salt glaze would simply be used as a fine sheen and not as a thickly reticulated covering. And I think my forms will become simpler.

Maybe this will be the direction of work from her new gas kiln. The original oil-fired kiln, built in 1975, is reaching the end of its life, and this new one, completed in 2001, offers an opportunity for more new directions.

Micki Schloessingk

As a student, Micki Schloessingk took a year out of university to travel in India. There she discovered the traditional earthenware potteries, and on her return home she was determined to become a potter. Before starting the course in 1970 she went to work with Grattan Freyer in County Mayo in Ireland, and whilst there she found a small pot whose tactile quality, texture and colour captivated her. It was lightly salted and wood-fired, and had the name Tiffoche scratched on the base.

During her first year at Harrow, she sought out Gustave Tiffoche at his workshop in Brittany, France. She worked there during the summer holidays, and was inspired by the rich effects of the salt-glaze wood firing, and by the excitement and challenge of the process. She returned to Harrow to build a wood-fired salt kiln with two other students, Elenor Epnor from America, and Zelda Mowat, and the very first firing produced the most wonderful satiny surface qualities. However, there was no possibility of any further supplies of wood, and so they had to continue the salt firings with oil. As a student, Micki succeeded in developing a range of slips that produced rich oranges and reds – colours that she has continued to explore.

When the course finished in 1972, she returned to work with Tiffoche, and then gained further workshop experience in Spain; but it was yet another two years before she was able to realize her plans to build a wood-fired kiln for salt glaze. In 1974 she moved to Bentham in Yorkshire and set up her own salt-glaze pottery. She worked under her married name, Doherty, until 1979 when she reverted to her maiden name.

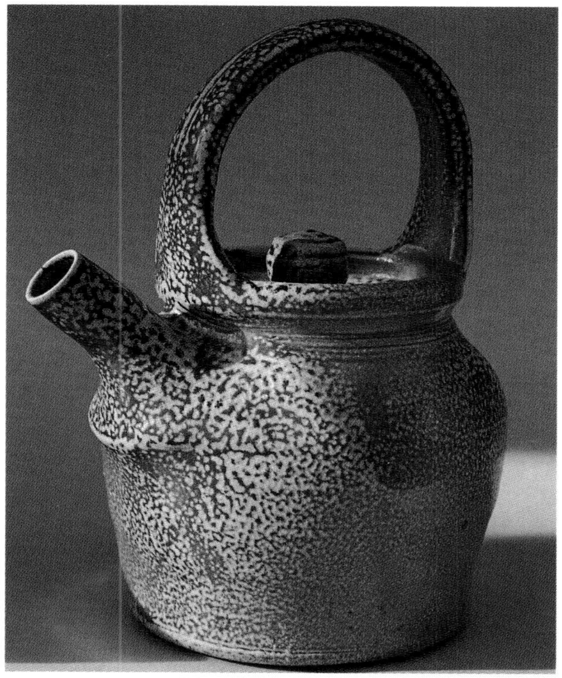

Teapot by Micki Schloessingk, 1986.

(RIGHT) Vase by Micki Schloessingk, c.1992.

(FAR RIGHT) Jug by Micki Schloessingk, 1995.

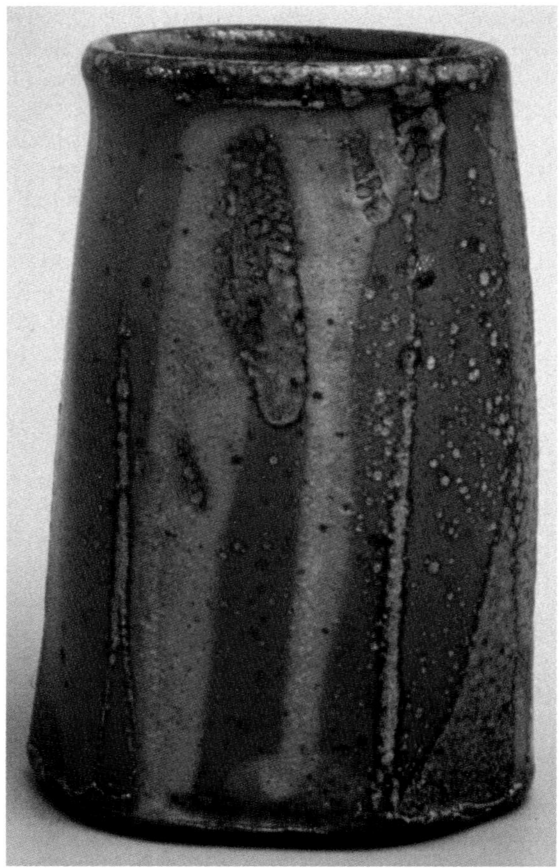

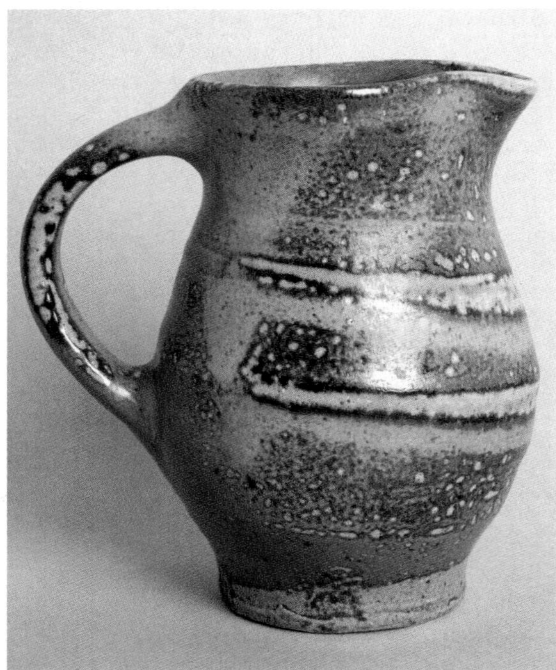

When she was at Mewith Pottery, Micki built a large, 2.1cu m (75cu ft) wood-firing kiln. It took up to thirty hours to reach temperature, and required a team of helpers to fire it. With great determination she continued making, juggling the needs of a young family with a complex and demanding potting process. Her early work was sold through the Craft Potter's Shop in London, and from her pottery in Bentham.

In 1987 she moved to the Gower Peninsular in South Wales. There she designed and built a smaller (1cu m/35cu ft) wood-fired kiln, with which she has worked for fourteen years.

Most of her work is functional, vigorously thrown tableware covered with slips, either dipped or poured or brushed. Lines, accentuated during the throwing, create soft curves reflecting shades of light on the salt-glaze surfaces of the bowls, jugs and vases. Certain pieces are softly distorted to deflect the passage of the flame and alter the effect of the vapour's path around their surfaces. Micki makes in series, whilst approaching each pot as an individual piece. Her forms remain simple, and echo the soft and sensitive way she handles the clay. She has worked constantly to explore the qualities of slips, and the combined effects of the wood ash and salt glaze. Taking risks with an unpredictable process, she has been rewarded with the most beautiful surfaces on her pots.

Micki Schloessingk never fails to express her enthusiasm and love of the process. The tactile quality of the pots is very important to her; she uses an impressive number of slips, and has an intimate understanding of each one. She says:

> Knowing the effects of the clay, the slip, the salt and the wood ash, and the process of the firing, determines exactly where I choose to place each pot. The packing of the kiln is a central and creative part of the process.

There is a great element of chance with wood and salt firing, so unpacking the kiln, too, is always accompanied by a mixture of excitement and anticipation.

Micki is in the process of redesigning and building a new wood-firing kiln, and she continues to consolidate her experience of salt glaze. She says:

> My biggest passion is for the warm colours that suggest fire, summer and deserts. I have a great love for the very light-fired salt glaze, for example old La Borne pots. Yet the pots which I often like the best from a firing, are those that

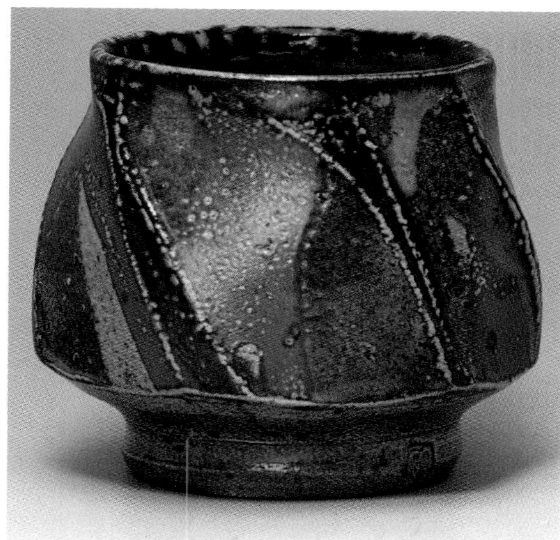

Teabowl by Micki Schloessingk, 1999.

are most heavily salted. My ideal, and the hardest challenge, is to apply minimal conscious decoration, and to allow the colours to come to life in the firing.

Micki's intimate knowledge of wood-fired salt glaze continues to deepen.

Sarah Walton

Sarah Walton first trained as a painter at Chelsea School of Art. Her second art training was as a potter, when she followed the Harrow Studio Pottery course between 1971 and 1973. There she found herself involved in the salt firings, and enduringly attracted to the warm colours so typical of the process. Between one year and the next, and on leaving Harrow, she worked briefly for David Leach and Zelda Mowat, before moving to Sussex in 1975; here she set up her own workshop to produce salt-fired work. She also built an oil-fired kiln with an 11cu m (40cu ft) setting space, and this is still in use today.

For the first ten years, Sarah Walton managed to earn her living from the sale of her pots and from occasional teaching. With an unremitting commitment to producing large numbers of pots single-handed, by the end of 1983 she had fired her sizeable kiln sixty-eight times. She says: 'Firing a salt kiln excited me enormously, with the sense of drama and connection with control and power. It was essential, at that time, to be party to such excitement.'

She produced functional wares – storage jars, jugs, bowls and teapots – all distinguished by profiles of clear, fluent lines. They were coated in simple slips that fired to produce seductive surfaces, a soft sheen and warm lustrous colours ranging from the palest peach and golden tans, to rich orange and red. She felt that the scale of any orange-peel effects broke up the forms of the tableware, and she found ways to avoid those effects of the salt vapour by using shields in the kiln pack, and by the choice of materials that made up the slips.

Sarah Walton remained loyal to the idea of function, but over time, her understanding of the meaning of 'functional' changed. From the beginning she had a heightened awareness and particular interest in form, and she used simple sgraffito lines, combing the surface, to reinforce the underlying forms of her pots. She had always seen that pots could be thought of as sculpture while still fulfilling their domestic functions, so she made pots without the wheel, experimenting with hand-building methods. She produced flower bricks that were oblong and square, and she also made large dishes, both oval and oblong: 'By 1983 I was working

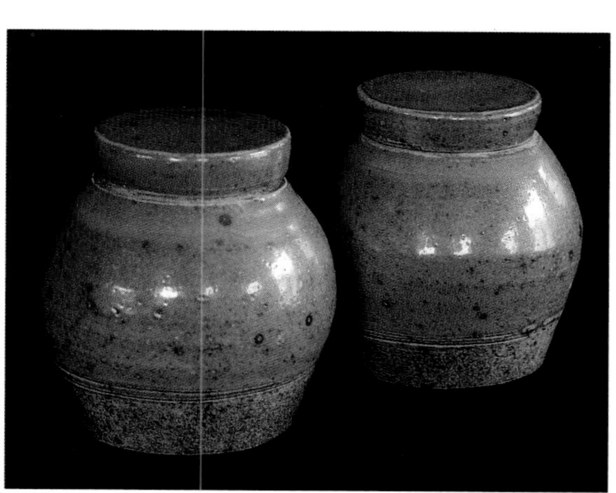

(LEFT) Lidded round jars by Sarah Walton, 1984. Part-dipped in orange slip.

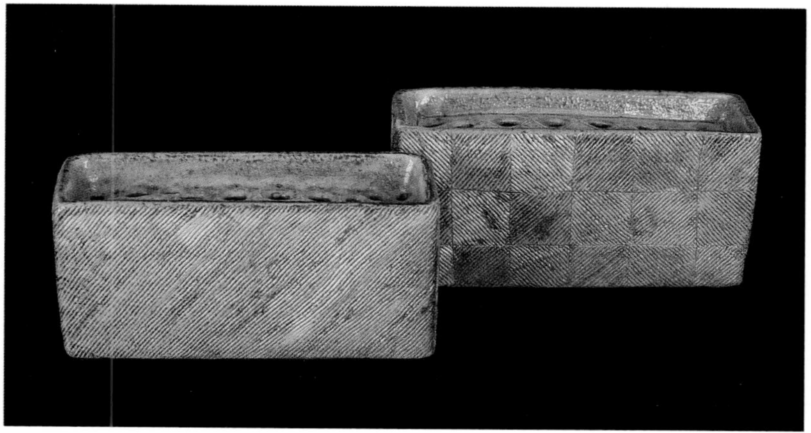

(RIGHT) Flower Bricks by Sarah Walton, 1985, 8 × 4 × 3in.

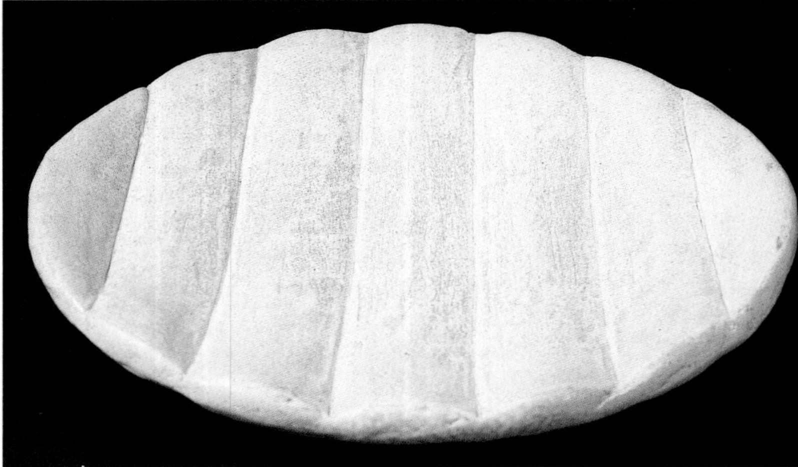

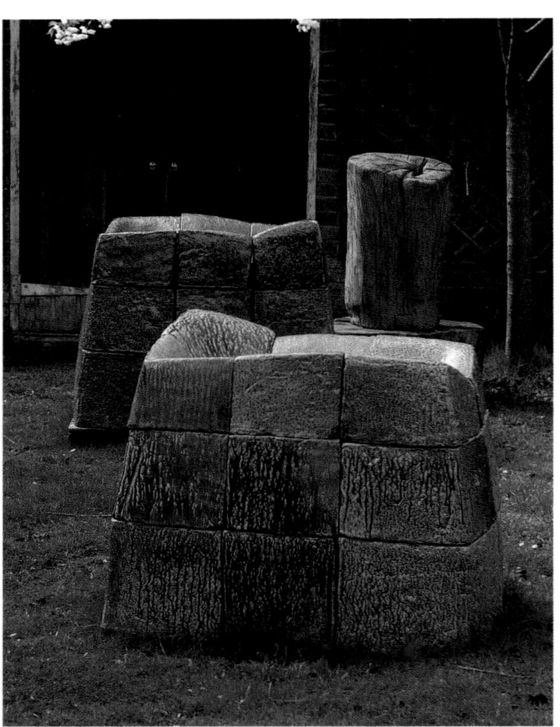

(TOP LEFT) Large dish by Sarah Walton, 1986. Porcelain

(TOP RIGHT) Two versions of 'Landscape' by Sarah Walton, 1991–99. 90cm long by 90cm high by 65cm wide. Constructed from eighteen sections. The details of each section can be seen as landscapes in themselves. The shadows are cast along the joints of the blocks, and the salt glaze drips and runs across the surfaces to suggest the shapes and textures of landforms and rocks.

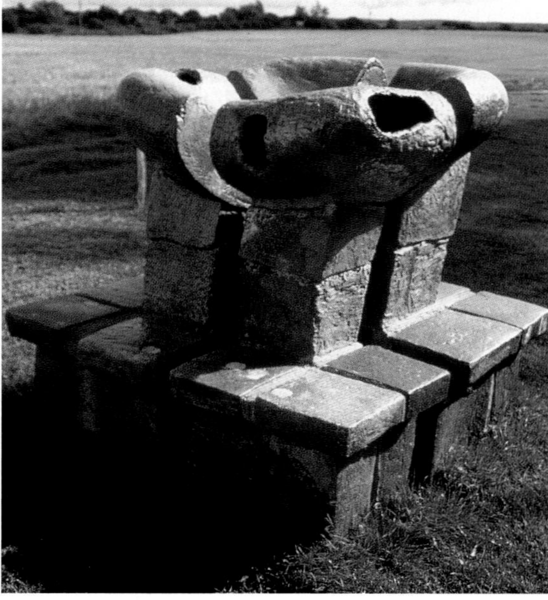

(BOTTOM LEFT) Metaphorical 'Self-portrait' by Sarah Walton, 1991–93; 135 × 135 × 135cm. Assembled from twenty-eight sections.

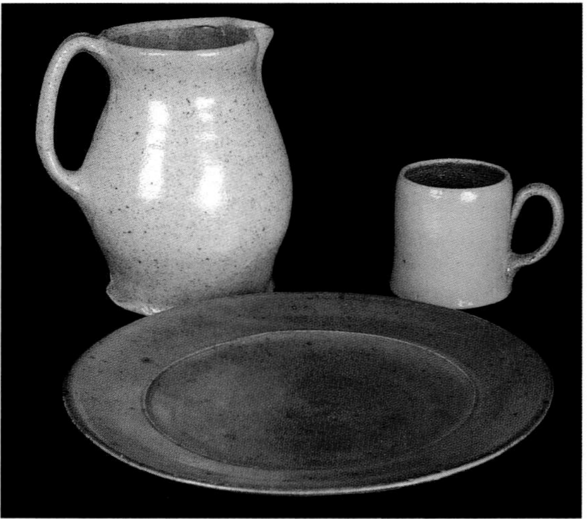

(BOTTOM RIGHT) Jug, mug and plate by Sarah Walton, 2000. Jug 9in high, plate 10in diameter, mug 3½in high.

on the surfaces of some of the forms after they had come from the kiln, using wet and dry carborundum paper, and aiming for the tactile qualities of greater sensuousness than before.'

The development of her ideas for larger sculptural pieces followed. In 1984 she started to make hand-built birdbaths on wooden bases for standing outdoors. Other, smaller pieces made at that time in white porcelain showed her interest in using light and shadow alone to reveal the form.

Sarah Walton has found inspiration from the forms of medieval and Korean pots, and from the Neolithic and Bronze Age cultures, in particular those of Greece, Cyprus and China. The Greek archaic sculptures and the architectural features of a Saxon church, a Norman font and cloisters are equally important influences on the sculptural character of all her work. So, too, is her early interest in chiaroscuro in painting and film, and the landscapes that she had drawn in Sussex and the Lake District.

Between 1991 and 1996 she stopped making any pots and concentrated on developing her large-scale pieces for outside. One piece, entitled 'Landscape', was made in eighteen sections and is 90cm long, by 65cm wide, by 90cm high (35 by 25 by 35in). She also worked on a massive piece entitled 'Self Portrait', measuring 135 × 135 × 135cm (53 × 53 × 53in); this stands in a big space, and is seen against the open landscape. The salt-glaze surface has been worked on to produce the qualities of stone aged by weathering.

In recent years, Sarah Walton continues to produce square birdbaths, and has also returned to making pots. She says they again have expressive potential for her. She has written:

> There are influences and there are also aims. I try for something tender, poignant and grave, something balanced, economic and resolved. Recently I've decided to use less slip than in years previous, in order to let the interplay of salt and reduction on the bare body be my sole means.

Michael Casson

With his passion for the history of pottery, Mick Casson's involvement in salt glaze stems from an interest in the early German salt-glaze pieces, and from his own strong sense of being European and his appreciation of European and Mediterranean pottery forms. His first peripheral participation in salt firings began at Harrow Art College where he taught the students on the Studio Pottery course, set up in 1963 by Victor Margrie and himself. He would watch the kiln-building and firing efforts of the students, who were encouraged by the infectious enthusiasm of Walter Keeler. Now and again, attracted by the pitted and varied surface qualities of salt glaze, one of Casson's pots would find its way into someone else's kiln.

In 1977 Mick Casson and his wife Sheila, also a potter, moved from their home and workshop in Buckinghamshire. Andrew McGarva, who had recently completed the pottery course at Farnham College, joined them in 1978, and their new pottery was established at Wobage Farm near Ross-on-Wye, Herefordshire. One of the reasons for the change had been the need to find a more suitable place to wood-fire, and the first wood-fired salt kiln was built in 1978/79.

Andrew had some experience of both salt and wood firings at Farnham and at La Borne in Central France, so a shared enthusiasm and commitment led them to build and fire several kilns at Wobage, including a double-chambered 51cu m (180cu ft) down-draught kiln that they worked with for nearly ten years. Through Andrew, Casson rekindled his love of peasant ware, the traditional once-fired country wares.

The immediacy of the making process with the firing was, for Casson, one of the most compelling attractions to vapour glaze. Over the first ten years at Wobage, he was involved with the building and firing of a series of kilns, and at any one time several might be in use for wood-firing, wood-fired salt, and oil-fired reduction stoneware. In 1983, he showed work in an

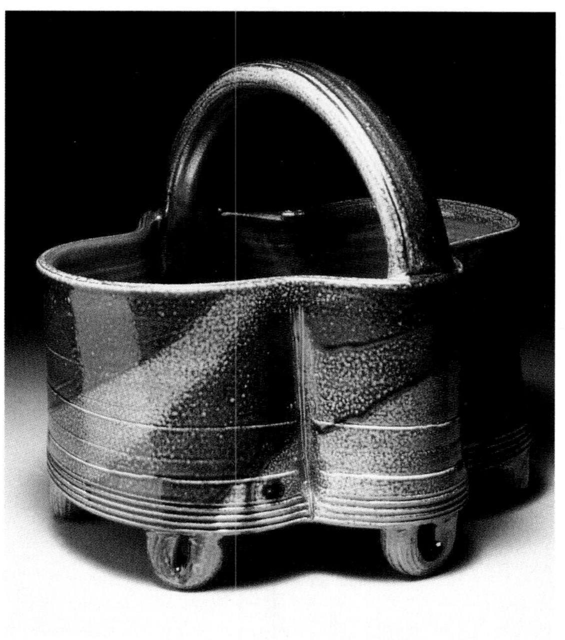

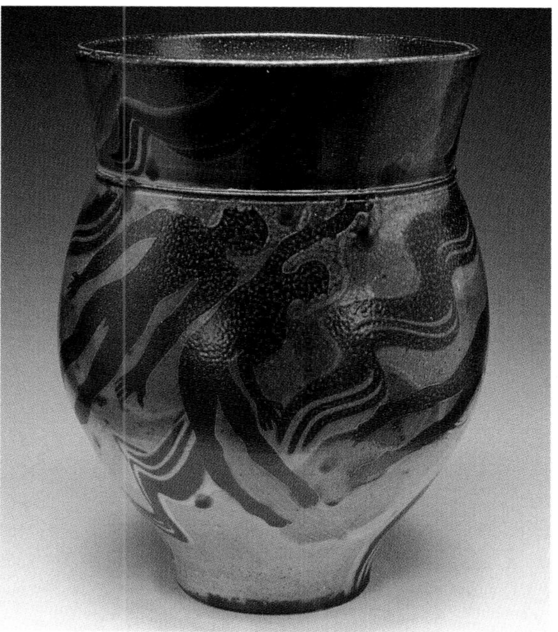

(FAR LEFT) Large trough by Michael Casson, 1986. 20in wide. Wood-fired salt glaze.

(LEFT) 'Swimmers' bowl by Michael Casson, 1989. Wood-fired salt glaze. Paper resist figurative decoration.

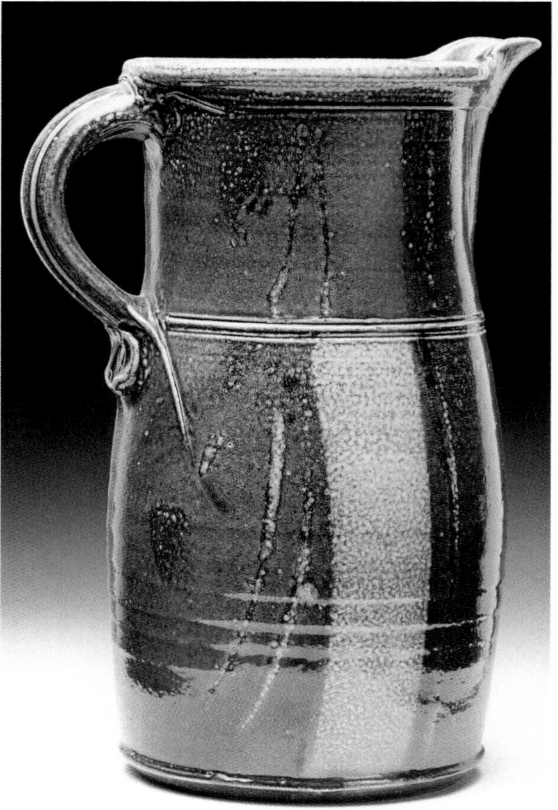

(RIGHT) 'Puisaye' jug by Michael Casson, 1995.

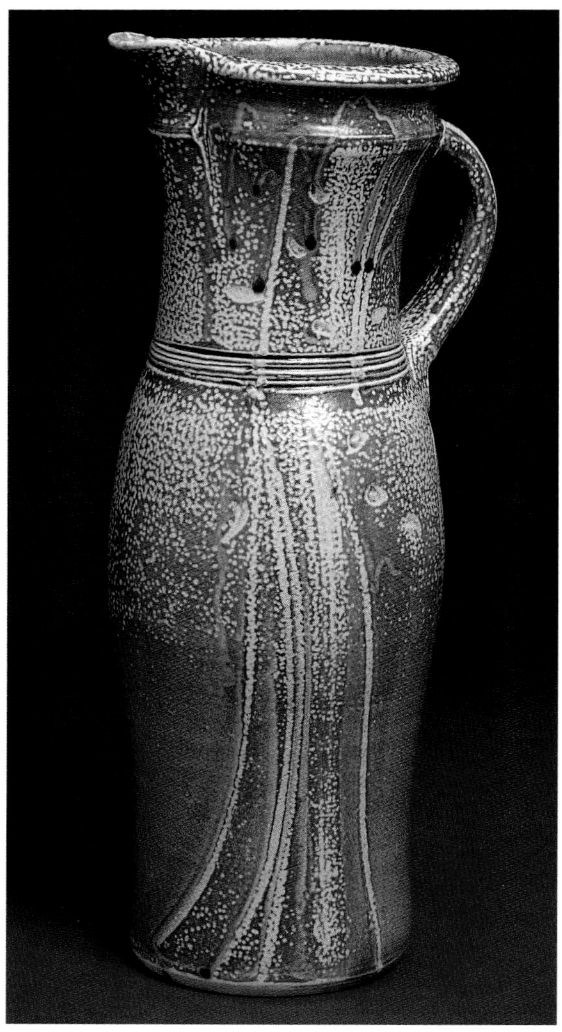

(FAR RIGHT) Jug by Michael Casson, 1995.

exhibition entitled 'Pots from Three Kilns'. In an article published at the time in *Ceramic Review*, the great collector W.A. Ismay wrote about Casson: '. . . he insists that what moves him into action is the exploration of materials and processes, the excitement of using different materials and different kilns, and grappling with their problems.'

There is no doubt that the combination of wood and salt suited his work admirably. His forms – in mainly jugs, bowls, dishes and lidded pots – are bold and strong, and his decoration – slips that are dipped, combed, brushed, trailed and incised – is generous and spontaneous. The path of the flame and vapour glaze invigorates the scale and character of his pieces. The random effects of the long flame of a wood firing have always had the greatest appeal for Casson. But regrettably the large wood kiln was too much for a single-handed effort, and after Andrew left to set up a workshop in France in 1990, Casson turned to firing the majority of his salt-glazed work in a gas kiln. Occasionally he has used a small, 6cu m (21cu ft) wood-salt 'fast-fire' kiln – but those firings still take up to fourteen hours.

At one stage Casson used the paper-resist method for figurative decoration, depicting swimmers moving around the outside of generously proportioned bowls. But he is happiest when he can apply the colours in a looser, freer way. His forms remain robust, and are decorated with slips in ways that echo his delight in the immediacy of the process.

At present, Casson continues to produce his vapour-glazed work in the gas-fired kiln. During the firing, as well as throwing the salt into the fireboxes, a small amount of soda is sprayed through various ports into the kiln. He still loves the effects of salt, but is equally enthusiastic about the effects of soda, as the soda vapour distribution through the kiln is more random and adds more of that chance of drama to the surface qualities of his work.

Recently, Jeremy Steward, with some assistance from other Wobage potters, has built a

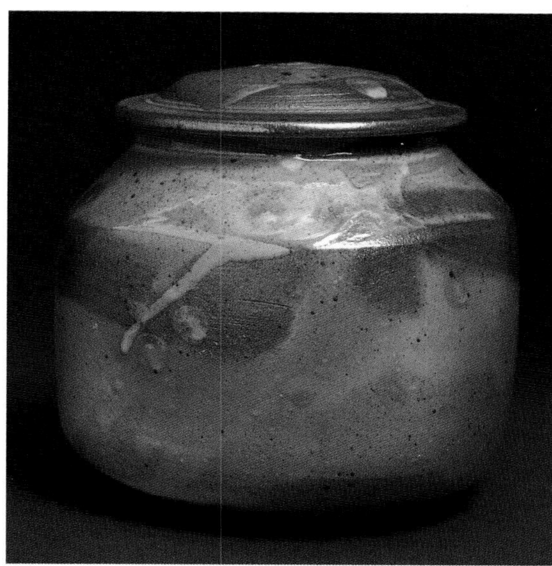

Lidded jar by Michael Casson, 1998.

large wood kiln at Wobage, the intention being to use it for soda firing. With this, Casson seeks to achieve far more of the random effect on his pots in the future. He anticipates using more glazes, or slips and slip glazes on the surface of the pots, and letting the fire and the wood and soda do the rest to help the vigour of the pieces he makes.

Peter Starkey

Peter Starkey started his training as a potter at Harrow School of Art in 1971. He remembers when Micki Schloessingk, in the year ahead, brought a pot from the salt-glaze kiln outside, into the students' room: 'It was a chestnut colour. It had a surface on it like a polished pair of boots. It was very beautiful.' Starkey is an enthusiast, and from that moment he decided that salt firing was what he wanted to do.

He had already encountered salt glaze some years earlier, when studying at Cardiff College of Education. He and another student had had an agreement with a local pipeworks, still salt glazing, to obtain unfired, extruded, round- or square-sectioned tubes for taking back to the college studios. One of the employees at the works used to bring a few pieces from his pottery evening class to sneak into the enormous domed kilns, in between the sewer pipes, and the two students had seen the fired results. Starkey was also familiar with the collection of German salt-glaze pieces in Cardiff Museum, and he knew about the Wrens' salt glaze at Oxshott, and of Guy Sydenham salt firing in Poole.

His real motivation at Harrow was to obtain the seductive surfaces that salt-glaze firings could produce. He recalls the fast learning curve for the students, who worked together to share their discoveries after each firing. Harrow established the salt revival firmly in the area of functional pots, and although it maintained the connection with utilitarian wares and salt, it was very different to the previous English tradition of thin-walled pots of refinement. The Harrow 'style' of pot came to be identified with a certain kind of domestic ware that had an essentially rustic quality – basically the character of the salt-glaze pots made by the students there. It was also true that those pots had a very strong sense of being made particularly for that process. Starkey considers that it is this quality of

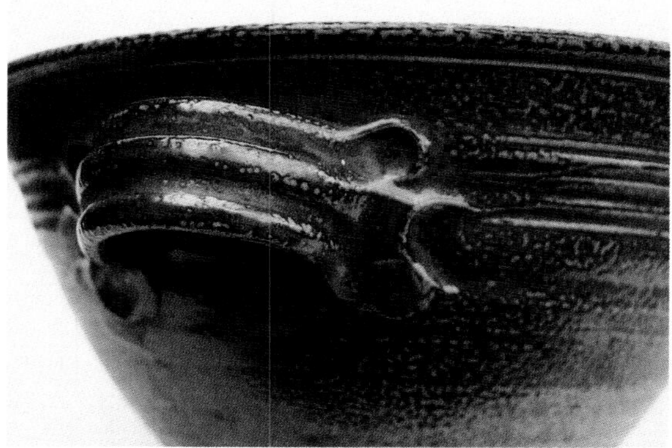

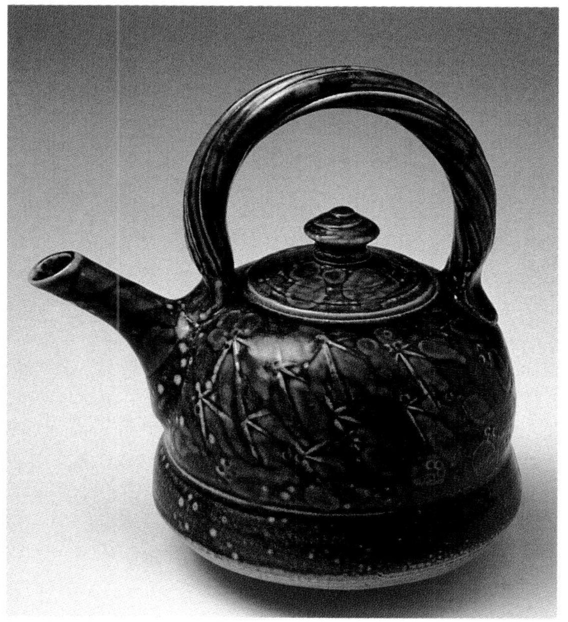

(FAR LEFT) *Detail of mixing bowl by Peter Starkey, 1972.*

(LEFT) *Teapot by Peter Starkey, 1989.*

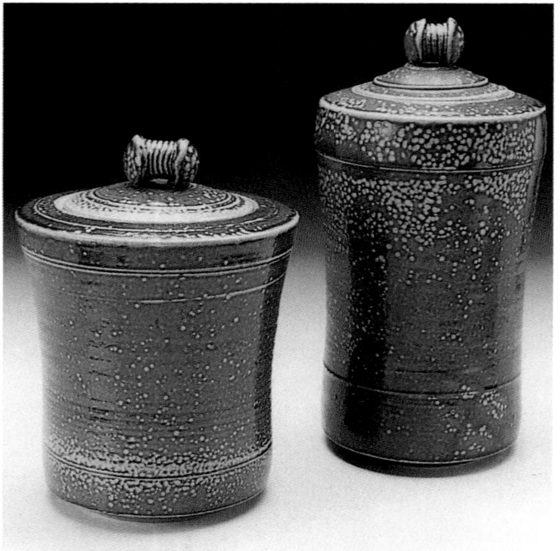

(RIGHT) *Jars by Peter Starkey 1996, 11in and 13in.*

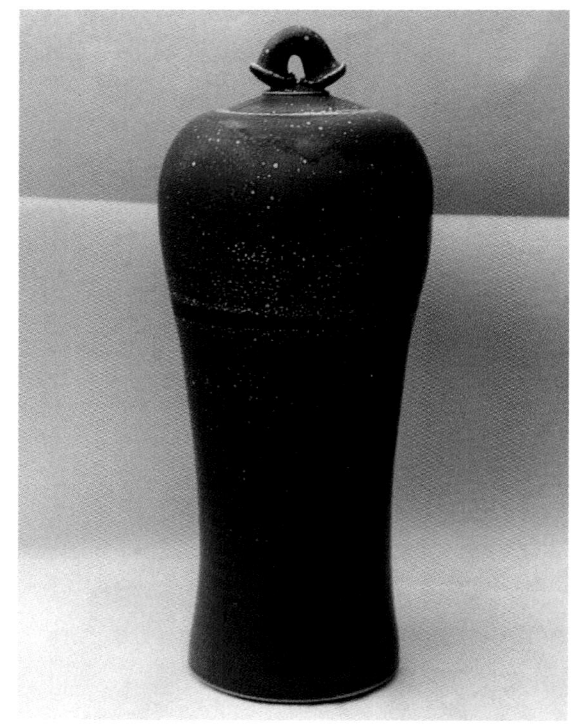

(FAR RIGHT) *Tall jar by Peter Starkey, 1998.*

'rightness' that will be found in all the most successful salted pots.

When he left Harrow in 1973, he set up his pottery and built his salt kiln at Hunworth in Norfolk. He then taught for a short time at Farnham College of Art before becoming the first manager of the Dartington Pottery Training Workshop in Devon, in 1975. It was while he was there that his book *Saltglaze* was first published, in 1977. Until then, information about the salt-glaze process for the studio potter was hard to find, and it was certainly an important landmark in the revival of salt glaze in Britain. It became the constant companion of a great number of students and potters who built their kilns for salt-glaze firings.

Starkey wrote the book as an enthusiast, and in doing so encouraged many other potters to enjoy the process for themselves. He wrote: 'For me, it [salt glazing] is the most exciting way of making pots, often very exasperating, but never dull or predictable.' He left Dartington in 1979 to teach full-time at Cardiff College of Art and Design, where he later became head of the Ceramics degree course.

In the years after Harrow, Starkey was producing a distinctive range of wonderfully robust table- and kitchenware. Made with a direct and practical approach, the work had a splendid simplicity of form. The functional country-style wares included bread-crocks, lidded jars, casseroles, bowls, colanders and jugs; some pieces were covered with a heavy orange-peel texture, others were dipped in slips to produced various orange and tan colours, coming from the kiln with smooth satin surfaces. He used simple scored lines and parallel ridges to define the edges of the forms and to break the surface of the salt glaze.

He continued to build kilns and salt fire his work, and he developed a number of slips, introducing various blues as well as oranges on the pots he now makes. Over time the qualities of his pieces have become more refined, but they still hold the authority that signifies the passion of a potter engrossed in the entire process.

In the salt-glaze revival of the 1970s, Starkey and the other salt-glaze potters were, to a great extent, aiming to recapture a look of something they had already seen or found. In his book he wrote: '. . . there is an unlimited opportunity for extending the scope and range of the [salt-glaze] technique in a very personal way.'

At the beginning of the twenty-first century he still believes this. He is a teacher as well as a maker, and he believes that the full potential of vapour-fired surfaces remains wide open for exploration. For that to happen the journey must start from a different standpoint, distanced from the conventional concept of salt glaze. It must lead away from its predictable use on traditional forms, and of course that will mean taking risks and playing with the unknown.

A Personal Perspective: Rosemary Cochrane

In 1979 I started the degree course in 3D Design in Wood, Metal and Ceramics at Manchester Polytechnic, now Manchester Metropolitan University. Pottery was my real passion, and in my second year I joined a third-year student to share her firings of a salt kiln. I saw it as an opportunity to be involved in something that I was unlikely to continue after leaving college. In my final year I was the only student in the department interested in salt firings, and with the help and encouragement of my tutors, David Murphy, Chris Jenkins and Alex McErlain, I continued working with salt glaze.

When I completed the course I moved to live in South Wales, set up my workshop, and in 1984 built my salt kiln. I continued salt-glaze firings, exploring the orange-peel surface textures, and learning how to repeat the qualities I liked best. Since college days, Alex McErlain has remained a firm friend. He has helped with the design and building of two kilns, and is a regular summer visitor, sharing firings and exchanging thoughts about salt glaze.

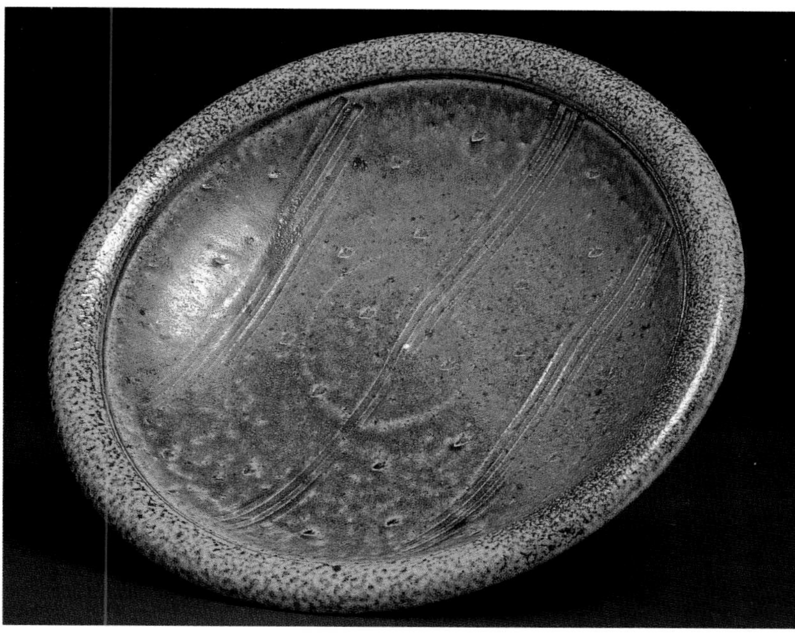

(ABOVE) *Dish by Alex McErlain, 1990s. Salt glaze over ash glaze.*

I was always clear that I wanted to make functional pieces and, even before I returned to college as a mature student, I was aware of the salt-glaze potters whose work was shown in exhibitions and in the Craftsmen Potters' shop. In my own workshop I began to produce a range of domestic ware, using slips that

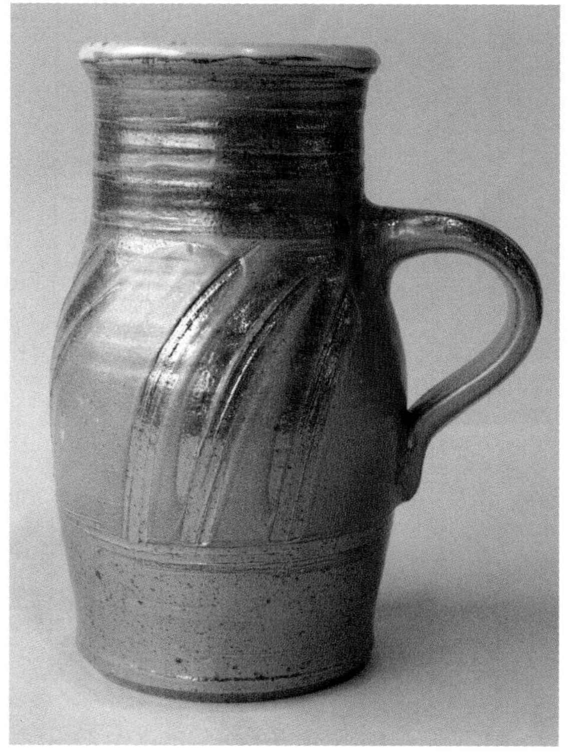

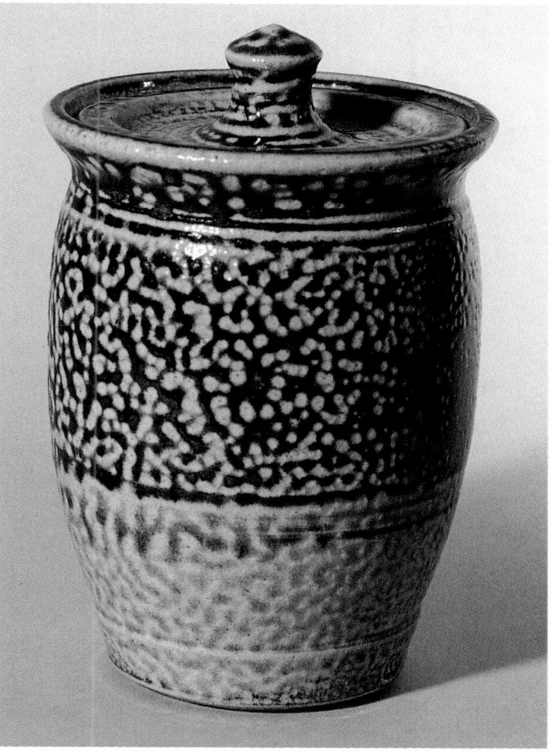

(FAR LEFT) *Jug by Rosemary Cochrane, 1981.*

(LEFT) *Lidded jar by Rosemary Cochrane, 1988.*

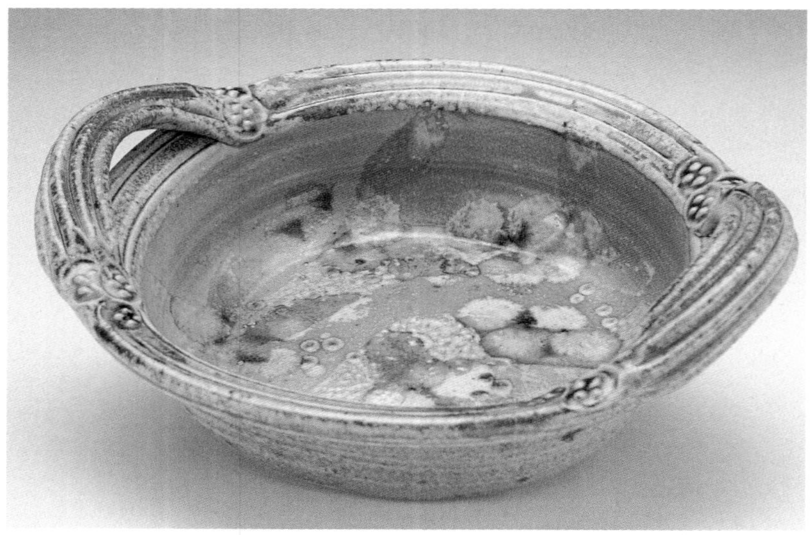

Dish with handles by Rosemary Cochrane, 1989.

I have had over 100 salt firings, exploring ways in which salt will combine with my ideas for colour and decoration for tableware. More recently I have become interested in some of the more unexpected vapour surfaces, which can push the boundaries of function. Entwined in my fascination for salt glaze are the colours, textures and patterns of the landscape, the changing moods of the seasons, and the effect of the elements on natural forms. Salt firing mirrors life, in that unpredictability is coupled with a need for control, disappointments can be opportunities to learn, and the unexpected can bring delight. For the present I enjoy developing my relationship with salt glaze, capricious companion that it is.

encouraged a dramatic, heavy orange-peel in contrast to the quieter surfaces of the clay body. I developed ideas from looking at old salt-glaze pots, reinterpreting the techniques and forms in my own way.

Then a visit to Suzy Atkins' salt-glaze pottery in France brought a real change in my work. I saw her coloured salt-glaze pieces, and knew that I wanted to find more colour for my own work. Instead of uninterrupted areas of slips, I began to create surfaces of loosely applied brushed and trailed pattern, which the effects of the salt firing could enliven.

Inspiring Salt Glaze

There are many other makers whose salt-glaze work is an inspiration. Some chose salt glaze from the start of their ceramic careers, others adopted the process after successfully working with another glaze process. Their work will be illustrated throughout the following chapters, which deal with making for salt glaze, kilns and salt firings.

(BELOW) Bowl by Rosemary Cochrane, 1993. Brushed and trailed slips with sponged cobalt and rutile oxides.

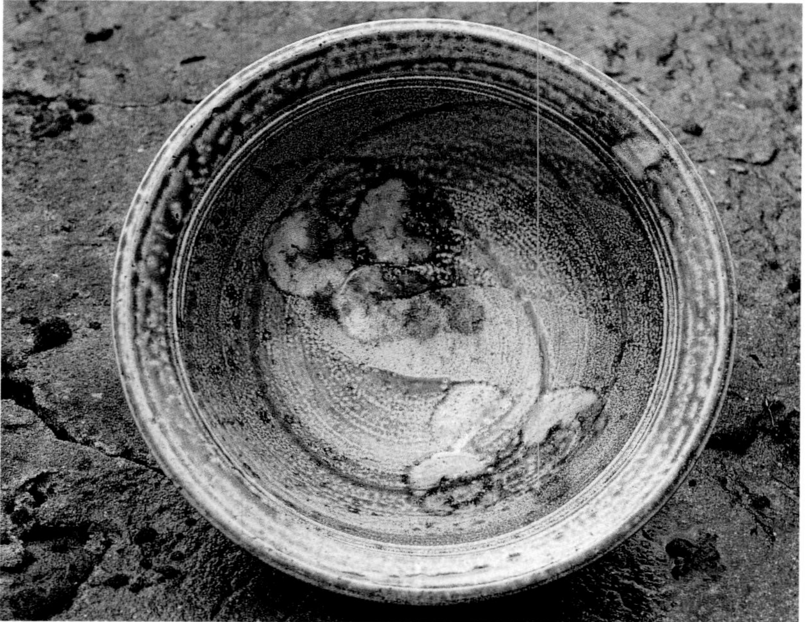

Detail of 'Landscape' jugs by Rosemary Cochrane, 2000. Various slips brushed, poured and trailed.

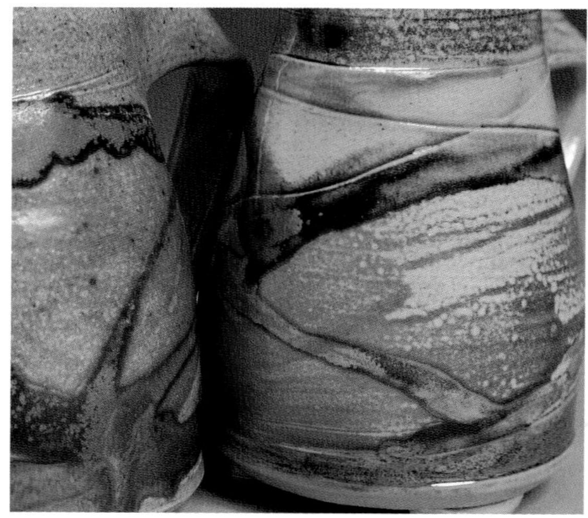

II

Salt Glaze in Practice

6 The Science of Salt and Soda

In this chapter, the science of the vapour glaze process using either salt or soda is explained. Any concerns about the process are investigated, and unwarranted and exaggerated fears dispelled. Traditionally it has been only salt that was introduced into the kiln to produce the glaze, but in the second half of the twentieth century, soda compounds came into use as alternative agents. Together they are given the term 'vapour glaze'. During a firing, the initial chemical reaction of salt and soda is somewhat different, but the appearance of the glaze produced by either vapour agent is only subtly different.

In either case, the process of salt or soda glazing is unpredictable. When there is such a myriad of surface qualities and colours to be found by using one of a countless number of conventional glazes, why choose vapour glaze? Whether you are seduced by the surface qualities of salt glaze, captivated by the colours, or excited by the process, the decision to make high-fired salt or soda glaze implies a response to all of these things. It is then that the science can become alchemy.

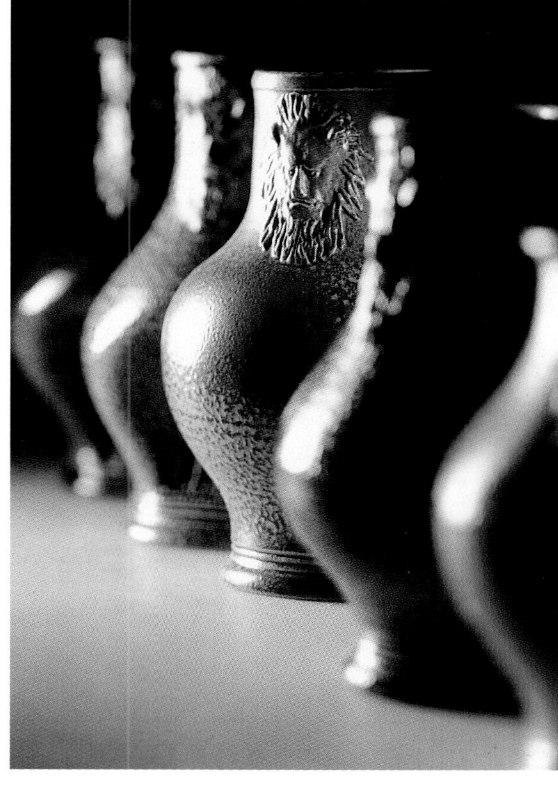

'Leomines' by Steve Harrison, 2000. Part of 'Salt 2000', a limited edition collection of salt-glaze stoneware made for the Lion Salt Works Trust to celebrate the millennium. The last open-pan salt works in Cheshire has been restored as a working industrial museum. (Lion Salt Works Trust)

The Salt-Glaze Process

When damp common salt – sodium chloride – is thrown into the kiln at high stoneware temperatures, it breaks down into sodium oxide and hydrogen chloride, an active gas that immediately volatilizes and distributes the sodium oxide throughout the kiln. The sodium makes contact with the clay and joins with the silica and alumina at the surface of the pots to form a glaze: sodium alumino-silicate. The hydrogen chloride is involved in a chain of reactions, which result in the production of hydrochloric acid and the return of the majority of the components to salt.

In fact salt melts at 800 °C, and the chemical decomposition takes place above 1,100 °C. Water is added to the salt in order to create steam, which encourages a quick breakdown of the salt. As the salt moves from the solid to the gaseous state, it increases its volume up to twenty times, and it is this forceful pressure that distributes the vapour around the pots in the kiln. All combustible fuels have some water content, and propane gas in particular. For this reason it is possible to introduce dry salt into the kiln and still create the same effective chemical reaction.

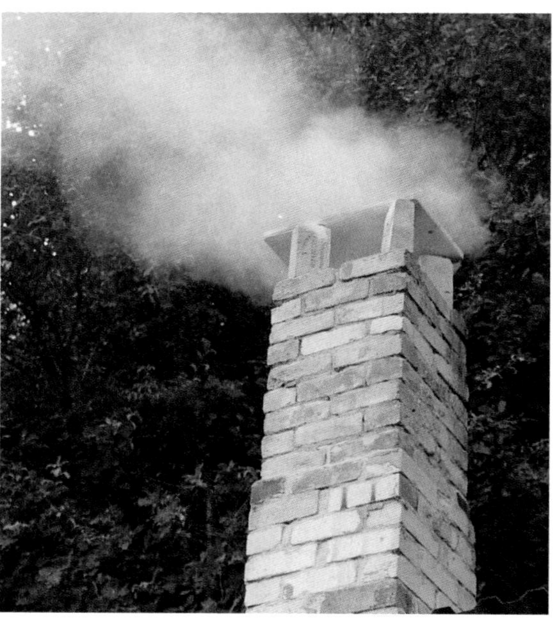

Flue emissions from a studio potter's kiln during salting. There are various ways in which the firing can be carried out to minimize the fog and also neutralize the emissions.

SALT

Sodium chloride is the chemical compound NaCl.

The decomposition of sodium chloride in a hot kiln
Over 1,100 °C

$$\underset{\text{salt}}{2NaCl} + \underset{\text{water}}{H_2O} \rightarrow \underset{\text{sodium oxide}}{Na_2O\ (gas)} + \underset{\text{hydrogen chloride}}{2HCl\ (gas)}$$

Salt firing:

- Salt is introduced into the kiln.
- In the presence of water it dissociates into sodium oxide and hydrogen chloride.
- Some of the sodium oxide reacts with alumina and the silica of the clay to form sodium alumino-silicate, the glaze.
- The remaining sodium oxide recombines with the hydrogen chloride and escapes from the kiln as salt.
- The surplus hydrogen chloride combines with the water vapour to produce hydrochloric acid.

Only a very small proportion of the salt that is introduced into the kiln is used to form the glaze. Much of it re-crystallizes around the top of the chimney as it escapes from the kiln. The remainder of the salt particles are held in solution in the water droplets of the steam. Together with an extremely small amount of very dilute hydrochloric acid, the salt leaves the kiln as a white mist that condenses on contacting the cooler atmosphere outside. Being hygroscopic, the salt content attracts further humidity and causes the mist to become heavier than the surrounding air. It falls gradually to the ground, where it hangs still or drifts as a white fog.

Environmental Concerns

The scale at which salt glaze is carried out by studio potters nowadays is infinitesimal compared with the level of industrial production of salt glaze in the past. These days, the contribution that salt glazing makes to air pollution, although temporarily visible, is hardly more than that made by any other kiln firing. During the revival of the salt-glaze process in studio pottery, various misconceptions regarding the nature of the emissions brought about a period of scare-mongering. In spite of this, it is only right that anyone involved in vapour firing should be given the facts, and should make their own informed opinion. The view generally taken is that many of our human activities add to environmental pollution, and the contribution made by potters' firings, whether vapour glaze or not, is, on the scale of things, exceedingly small. By comparison, for instance, we could do far more to help the global situation by taking steps to reduce our daily use of the petrol-driven motor car.

Early Pollution Problems

In the past, the process of salt firing was carried out in the centre of towns where there would be a concentration of salt kilns within a small area. In such circumstances salt firing caused a problem.

The Trail of Smoke and Fumes

From the earliest days of salt firings, there are contemporary descriptions of smoke and fumes belching out of the kilns as they were baited with salt. Objections to the nuisance and unpleasantness led to the early sixteenth-century German salt potters of Cologne being driven out of their city. In Britain in the mid-eighteenth century, the largest concentration of salt-glaze kilns was in Burslem in North Staffordshire, and they were just as noxious: the large quantities of smoke that resulted from the coal used to fuel the kilns combined with the fog from the salting to produce a thick dark smog. Here is a contemporary description from the *History of the Staffordshire Potters*, written by Simeon Shaw in 1829:

> The vast volumes of smoke and vapours from the ovens, entering the atmosphere, produced that dense white cloud, which from about eight o'clock till twelve on the Saturday morning (the time of the 'firing-up' as it is called) so completely enveloped the whole of the interior of the town, as to cause persons often to run against each other; travellers to mistake the road; and strangers have mentioned it as extremely disagreeable, and not unlike the smoke of Vesuvius . . .
>
> This temporary inconvenience entailed on the district the character of being unhealthy, but the contrary is the fact; as may be seen every day in the very old persons living; and proved by the Bills of Mortality. [It seems that the residents were prepared to accept the inconvenience, as he also reports:] The benefits accruing from the great demand for the salt-glazed white stone ware, caused the inhabitants to tolerate the method of glazing, altho' for about five hours each Saturday, fifty or sixty manufactories sent forth dense clouds of vapour that filled the valleys and covered the hills to an extent of several square miles.

A Combination of Problems

By the mid-nineteenth century the Lambeth area of London had taken over prominence in the production of salt glaze. At one time over eighty kilns were being fired regularly. The bulk of production was in the heavy clay industry, and in the manufacture of pipes, bricks, chemical vessels as well as bottles for ink and blacking. Lambeth must have been a particularly unpleasant area to live in, as bone boilers, breweries, manure yards and candle-makers were amongst the other culprits causing the foul air. The burning of coal in both the home and industry was a major source of the yellow fogs of London and other cities. In Lambeth, the potteries were using coal to fire the kilns and create smoke, but were adding to the problem with their production of salt-glaze stoneware.

Early Legislation

The causes of industrial pollution began to be tackled when the first Smoke Nuisance Abatement (Metropolis) Act was passed in 1853. In 1855, the Nuisance Removal Act included fumes, although initially glass and pottery works were exempted; however, this was only until the Smoke Abatement Act of 1856. Further controls of noxious vapours came into effect under the act of 1864, and this led to the establishment of the Alkali Inspectorate. But before the emissions from stoneware potteries came under closer scrutiny, the Inspectorate dealt with the much more significant and most damaging emissions of hydrochloric acid. These came from the alkali industry that was employed in decomposing salt for the production of soda compounds. (The cleaner Solvay process has since replaced the original method.)

For several years the fog from salt kilns continued to wrap itself round the streets of towns wherever there were concentrations of stoneware potteries. In Lambeth, numerous letters and reports were written concerning the nuisance, but they only partly succeeded in effecting changes, and only half-hearted attempts were made to reduce the problem – largely because the manufacture of salt-glaze wares was far too lucrative a business ever to bow to public pressure alone. It is ironic that the production of the millions of sewer and drainage pipes should be a major contributory factor in improving the sanitation of the cities, but at the same time added to the problem of air pollution.

Complaints and arguments against the polluting effect of the emissions from the salt kilns no doubt contributed to the setting up of the Royal Commission on Noxious Vapours in 1876. This was to deal with a much wider national concern for industrial pollution. In Lambeth the residents gave evidence, mainly directed against Doulton's salt-glaze kilns. Henry Doulton was quick to offer his defence of the firing practices, and what he considered as only brief and occasional inconvenience. In spite of the commissioners' recommendations, it was not until nearly twenty years later, in 1895 – only two years before Henry Doulton's death – that stoneware potteries eventually came under the responsibility of the Alkali Inspectorate. Even then the actual emission levels were not controlled, although later chimneys were required to be higher.

'Clean Air'

Legislative controls over the industrial emission of hydrochloric acid gas were tightened in the Works Regulation Act of 1906. Finally, the various Clean Air Acts of the 1950s and 1960s brought to an end salt-glazing on an industrial scale.

The production of salt-glaze drainpipes and bottles had already declined, as plastic pipes replaced stoneware ones and cheaper pressed-glass bottles were now supplying the market's need.

Environmental Issues

Burning Fuel

Any firing derives its heat at some cost to the environment. Burning a combustible fuel such as wood, oil, coal or gas uses up resources and produces a variety of polluting emissions. Burning a fuel efficiently by firing in an oxidized atmosphere will create carbon dioxide, the main greenhouse gas that contributes to global warming. A reduction firing decreases the fuel-to-air ratio, giving insufficient air for efficient burning, and will produce carbon monoxide, hydrocarbons and free carbon, the particles of which can be seen as a sooty smoke.

There is also a significant presence of sulphur in coal and fuel oil, and when they are burned, the toxic gases of sulphur dioxide and trioxide are given off as a visible blue haze. Small amounts of the nitrogen oxide group of gases are always the product of any high temperature burning, and will contribute to acid rain. Other relatively insignificant organic compounds are produced from the fuel, and the clay itself is sure to contain impurities, albeit barely traceable in the kiln emissions. All of this is without the salt or soda.

Speculation and Misconceptions

The earliest studio potters, who experimented with salt firings at St Ives, held the very misguided idea that salt firings caused the emission of chlorine gas. Bernard Leach in his *The Potter's Book*, published in 1940, describes the salting there:

> This caused a dense white smoke to pour out of the kiln and down the Land's End road, to the alarm of the stokers, who rushed out of the pottery fearing to see passers-by fall in their tracks overcome by the chlorine fumes.

Their fears were unfounded, and certainly unnecessarily dramatic. But unfortunately others also held this misconception, and further erroneous statements continued to be made over the years. The situation became increasingly confused, and soon the problem of emissions from studio potters' salt kilns was inflated out of all proportion.

For a long time, environmentalists' concerns have been focused on the effect of greenhouse gases and acid rain. Studio potters would be correct in identifying the polluting greenhouse gases and low acid emissions produced by any kiln fired with a combustible fuel, along with the still very small but additional levels of acid emissions from salt kilns. But with the renewed interest in salt firing in the 1970s, it was all too easy to unjustly target salt kilns, and to condemn the plumes of dense white mists as excessive pollution. Unfortunately, the erroneous idea concerning chlorine gas from salt firings persisted, and when soda was proposed as the alternative to salt, the emphasis was on the elimination of the chlorine gas that was never present.

Introducing Soda

The outcome was that potters began to experiment with the alternatives to salt as a way of introducing the sodium into the kiln. Soda, in the form of sodium bicarbonate or sodium carbonate, had already been suggested as an alternative to salt, in the book *Ceramic Glazes* by Cullen Parmelee in 1948. In America the use of sodium carbonate was producing good results, and in other countries, including Britain, others were soon following suit. Since then, many contemporary salt-glaze potters have chosen to use soda rather than salt, enjoying the opportunity to vapour-fire in an urban situation, without any visible cloud of mist.

Soda Firing

When soda compounds are introduced into the hot atmosphere of the kiln they release sodium oxide, which combines with the silica and alumina of the clay to form the glaze, as with salt. The further by-products of sodium carbonate are carbon dioxide, and sodium hydroxide. Hydrogen chloride, the acid fumes of salt that

SODA

Soda is the general term describing the sodium compounds. These are the ones that can be used in a vapour firing:

- Sodium bicarbonate, also known as baking soda: $NaHCO_3$
- Sodium carbonate, also known as soda ash: Na_2CO_3
- Sodium carbonate in the form of washing soda: $Na_2CO_310H_2O$

The decomposition of soda in a hot kiln

Over 860°C

Na_2CO_3	$\rightarrow$	Na_2O (gas)	+	CO_2 (gas)
sodium carbonate		sodium oxide		carbon dioxide

Over 270°C

$2NaHCO_3$	$\rightarrow$	Na_2O (gas)	+	H_2O (gas)	+	$2CO_2$ (gas)
sodium bicarbonate		sodium oxide		water as steam		carbon dioxide

Soda Firing

- Sodium carbonate is introduced into the kiln.
- In the heat it splits into sodium oxide and carbon dioxide.
- Some of the sodium oxide reacts with the alumina and silica in the clay to form the sodium alumino-silicate: the glaze.
- The remainder of the sodium oxide combines with any water vapour present to form sodium hydroxide: caustic soda.
- Sodium carbonate does not recombine to its original form, as salt does.

produce the fog, are avoided. Sodium carbonate melts at 850 °C but has a very low vapour pressure, while sodium bicarbonate melts at 270 °C and has a higher vapour pressure. For this reason the soda products are usually introduced into the kiln in ways that will facilitate its distribution among the pots. A saturated solution of one, or a combination of the soda compounds, is made up in boiling water and sprayed into the kiln, although this must be done with great care to avoid a potentially dangerous expansion of the water into steam.

Current Legislation

In the UK, the Environmental Protection Act of 1990 once again tackled the problems of those processes that use potentially harmful and dangerous substances. The new, stricter regulations were aimed at industry, and in the field of ceramics it was aimed at large-scale producers of heavy-clay goods. Today, the only remaining commercial operation involving a salt kiln, and paying for a licence to salt, is the Errington Reay Pottery at Bardon Mill in Northumberland.

Stacking pots for a salt firing in the coal-fired beehive kiln built in 1932. Errington Reay Pottery at Bardon Mill, Northumberland. Established in 1878, in Victorian days the salt-glaze business earned its reputation for high quality sanitary ware, drainage pipes and ornamental domestic ware. Now production is of garden pots and domestic storage jars. (Hexham Courant)

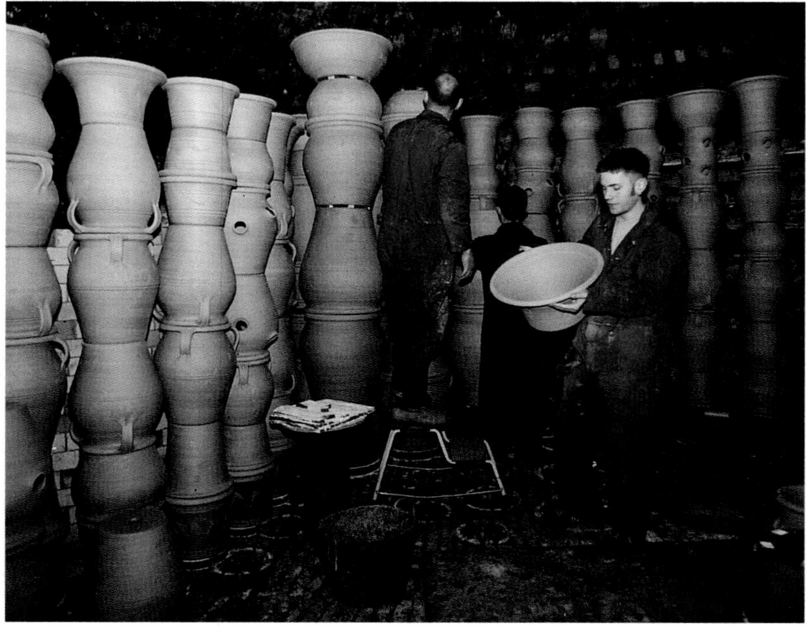

The Implications for the Studio Potter

Small craft businesses involved in the small-scale production of salt-glaze ceramics were advised to apply for either exemption, or authorization, to be allowed to continue using the process. It is the one time that the words 'trivial' and 'insignificant' are welcomed as a description of the activity of a salt-glaze pottery. Each potter's situation must be assessed individually, and it continues to be advisable for anyone salt glazing to contact the HM Inspectorate of Pollution and to seek exemption from the legislation. Wood-firing kilns that annually consume over an estimated ten articulated-lorryloads of timber also require registration and authorization. However, this can be considered well beyond anything likely to be undertaken by the studio potter.

Regaining a Proper Perspective

Over the past few years, several potters have collaborated with chemists to set up experiments in an attempt to measure and evaluate the emissions from salt and soda kilns. An article recording the tests made in Britain by the potter Peter Meanley and chemist William Byers was published in *Ceramic Review*, issue 157, in 1996, and it was considered that the conclusions went a long way to lessen the anxieties over the environmental concerns over the gases emitted from salt firings.

The most recent research has been undertaken by Wil Shynkaruk, a member of staff in the ceramics department at Utah State University, in America. He considered that: 'claims that soda firing is safer than salt firing mean little without a direct comparison between the by-products of soda firing and those of salt firing.' He conducted his original research at the university, and presented his paper at the 1997 annual conference of the National Council on Education in the Ceramic Arts, in Las Vegas, Nevada. He outlined his studies in an article printed in *Ceramics Technical*, No.5, 1997.

Only a brief summary of the research is given here. In simple terms, the average quantities of salt and soda needed to produce a heavy orange-peel are compared, according to the average emissions from each. The fuel-emission pollutants from either firing are assumed the same, and are therefore excluded from the equation. The final list compares the averages of the input, the amount of sodium reacting with the clay to form the glaze, and the output. The results are evaluated in terms of the quantity of pollution. Thus, from the salt kiln the by-products are found to be salt and hydrochloric acid, which contribute to acid rain. From the soda kiln the by-products are gauged to be relatively greater, and are identified as carbon dioxide, which will contribute to greenhouse gases; sodium peroxide, which is unstable and converts into a number of substances; and sodium hydroxide, a highly corrosive base.

What is 'Significant'?

Shynkaruk concludes that the calculations '. . . clearly show that a soda kiln produces more pollution than a salt kiln.' However, in his final conclusion he says '. . . the amount of pollution produced by salt or soda firing is insignificant when compared with the hundreds of kilograms produced by combustion alone.' On the basis of his measurements, and with comparative examples of pollution created by the motor car and aircraft, he ends: 'Clearly the only significant grounds that exist to determine whether to fire straight gas, salt or soda, are the aesthetic ones.' In some countries legislation may still be the deciding factor.

Gil Stengel moderated the panel discussing sodium vapour glazing at the Nevada Conference, and brought together the evidence in her article 'Salt and the Atmosphere', *Ceramics Technical* No. 7, in 1998. She concludes that '. . . both salt and soda firing have broad possibilities for aesthetic research, and with some simple precautions in place can be widely enjoyed and safely practised.'

Minimizing the Effects

Fume Washing

Under the Alkali Inspectorate, the effort to clean up industrial pollution focused on the removal of the acidic content of residual gases before they escaped into the atmosphere. In this way, the most assiduous studio potter can certainly remove the worst of the acid air pollution emitted from the salt kiln.

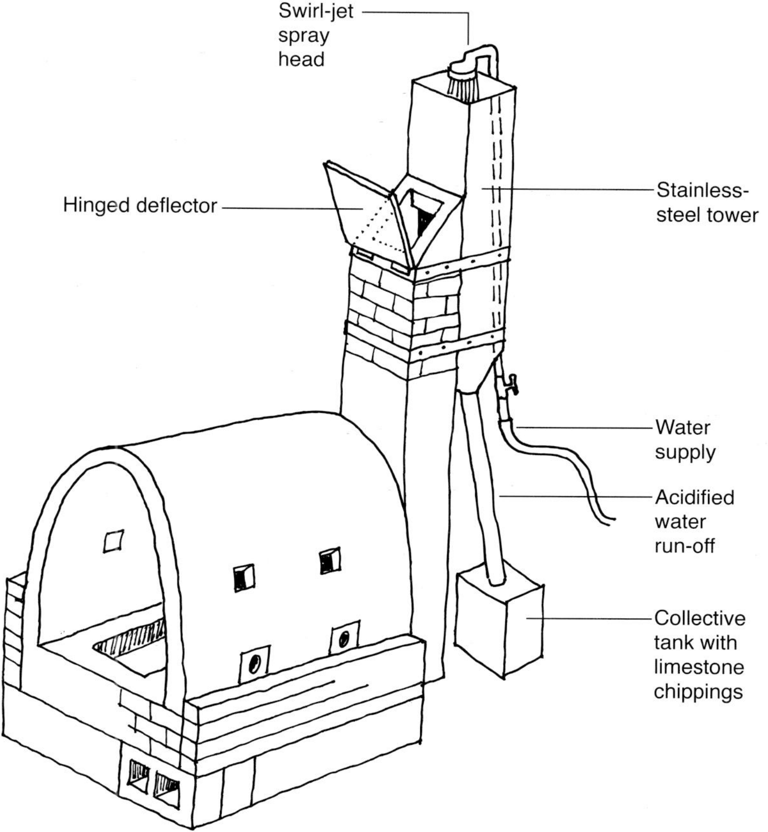

(ABOVE) Diagram of a 'scrubber' system for fume washing.

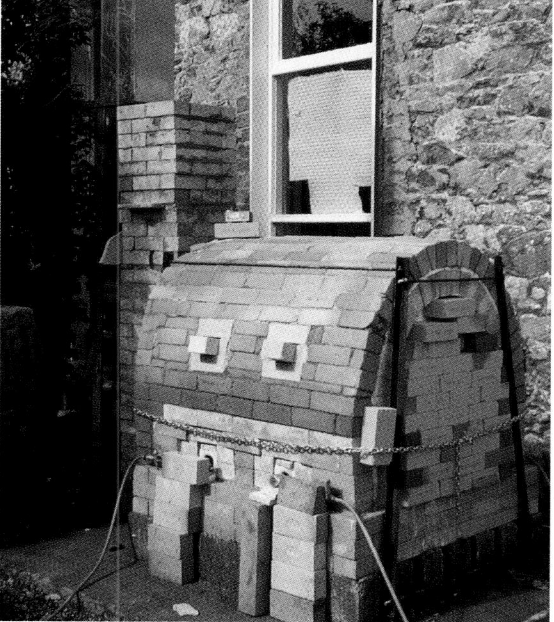

Kiln with a stainless-steel flue for a 'scrubber' system. (Gus Mableson)

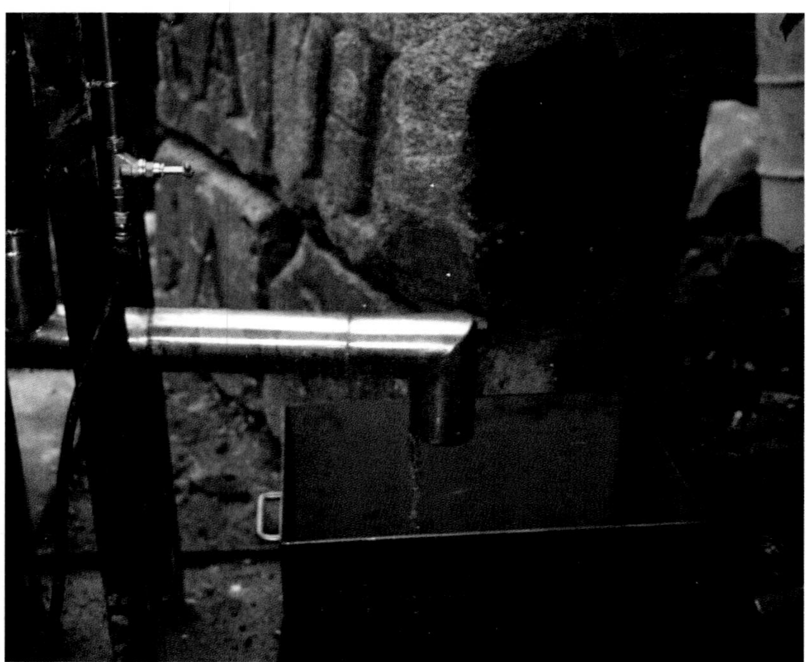

Tank for collecting 'washed' fume gases. (Gus Mableson)

A 'water scrubber' or 'purge chimney' will help to neutralize the acid emissions. In the 1950s, Denise and Rosemary Wren sought advice from the Gas Board on building their first coke-fired salt kiln, and part of the installation included a 'scrubber'. Since then, the use of the device has been demonstrated in a number of countries; for instance, Gus Mableson has fitted the apparatus to several of the kilns that he has built in Ireland. It works like this: as the acid fumes from the salt kiln emerge from the chamber, they are deflected into a washing tower. There they are sprayed with a fine mist of water which, together with the acid, condenses into dilute hydrochloric acid; this is then neutralized over a bed of limestone chips. The level of corrosive vapours released into the atmosphere is thereby considerably reduced.

Health and Safety

The immediate hazard during salting is exposure to the vapour emissions. To reduce the risks of its potential for harm, those people who need to work around the immediate vicinity of the kiln should take sensible precautions. Closing all the openings of the kiln at the time of salting will do much to prevent the fumes escaping into this area. Obviously great care should be taken to avoid breathing the fumes, and the best way to do this is to wear a proper respirator.

More Efficient Salting

There are several ways of salting that can make better use of the salt and at the same time reduce the less desirable effects of the process. A large proportion of the salt – as much as 98 per cent – that is thrown into the kiln is in fact not taken up to produce the glaze. If salt is introduced later, rather than earlier in the firing, the residual salt in the kiln will be used to form some glaze, and it follows that less additional salt need be introduced. Also, rather than introducing the salt in just a few bulk baitings, a more efficient way would be to put in small amounts over an extended period of time. The pots will be exposed to the salt vapour for longer, good results are achieved, and a less dense fog is created.

Finally, introducing the salt as a saturated brine solution has the benefit of not only using less salt, but also virtually eliminating the fog. (The alternative ways of salting are covered in Chapter 9, and the ways to introduce soda are explained in Chapter 10.)

So . . . Salt or Soda?

Current legislation and consideration for any neighbours may well determine the location of the kiln, and whether to use salt or soda. In Britain it is unlikely that the planning authorities would grant permission for any salt firing in an urban area. It is also improbable that in such a location the Pollution Inspectorate would ever allow an exemption from the legislation. Apart from that, any vapour firing that produces a fog in an urban area is going to be a nuisance, and likely to cause offence to neighbours.

The Last Word

Perhaps most importantly, and to make the process worthwhile, the potter who is resolved to become involved in the salt- or soda-glaze process needs to make pieces that genuinely call for the virtues of a vapour firing. When they do, the wonderful unique surface qualities will demonstrate the value of the process. The best pots taken from the salt or soda kiln can be breathtaking and uniquely beautiful.

7 Making for High-Fired Salt Glaze

The results that come from a salt kiln are ultimately determined by decisions made during the firing and cooling of the kiln, but making a pot or sculpture that is intended for vapour firing involves a continual awareness of the entire process. It begins with the choice of clay.

CLAYS

The early European salt-glaze potters had little option but to work with locally available materials. This gave their pots a distinctive appearance that would be identified with each particular area. Today we are spoilt for choice, and any number of ready-prepared clays is available from the suppliers, or clays with particularly desirable qualities can be imported from other countries. Some potters choose to mix their own individual clay recipes using raw materials selected from an infinite list. What constitutes 'good' clay for salt firing depends very much on how the final colours and surfaces are envisaged.

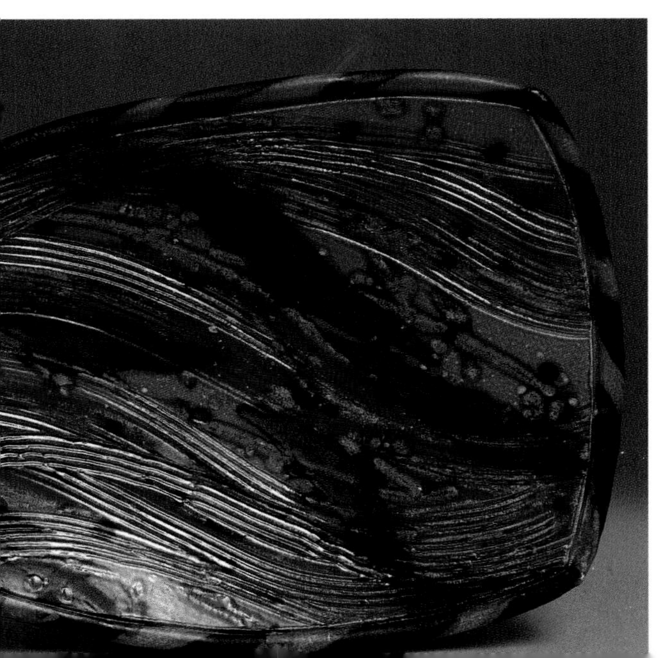

Studies of the suitability of various clays to take a salt-vapour glaze were carried out by scientists in the early 1900s, and in the 1940s further research was undertaken in the United States on behalf of Borax Consolidated Ltd. The work was commissioned in an attempt to standardize the products of an industry primarily concerned with the cheap manufacture of heavy clay pipes. Much of the information has formed the basis of our understanding of the properties of clays for salt firing. A summary of the data is published in the Borax Consolidation booklet entitled *Ceramic Glazes*, and the general principles are included in the following section.

Today's studio potters have the freedom to use the qualities that were then dismissed as undesirable. In one sense any clay can be considered for salt firing, because within contemporary ceramics any one of the entire range of surfaces – from white and shiny to black and matt – can be regarded as an acceptable finish when appropriately employed.

Temperature Response

The way a clay will react to the salt can be predicted by first looking at the firing range and vitrification point, and secondly, by an elementary analysis of its chemical content. Most of the clay manufacturers publish all this information. The higher the vitrification temperature of the clay, the better the reaction with the vapour. Although salt melts at 800 °C, for a salt glaze to form the clay body must mature above 1,100 °C, as that is the temperature at which the salt begins to volatilize. Earthenware and low-temperature salt firings are discussed in Chapter 10, but stoneware clays and porcelain are the

Dish by Rosemary Cochrane. Slab formed with rolled rim and scored lines. 'T' material clay, body stains and slips.

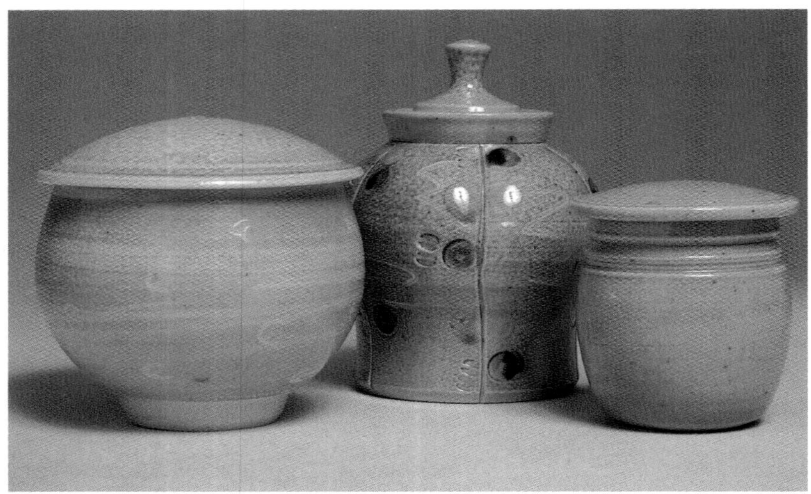

Porcelain lidded pots; pale slips. Left to right: Alex McErlain, Jane Hamlyn, Rosemary Cochrane.

choice for high-fired salt glaze. Porcelain bodies do vary in their response to salting, but the best results show a wonderful brightness, although the glaze is less likely to orange-peel and will craze where thicker. The white body offers a perfect base on which colour can be applied.

Apart from the temperature response, amongst the many hundreds of stoneware bodies available, there are two other critically significant properties of clay that will influence the nature of its reaction to the salt. These are the ratio of the two principal elements of all clays, alumina and silica, and then the iron content.

The Key Components of Clay

The Alumina and Silica Ratio

One part alumina to four parts of silica is considered to be the best ratio for the formation of a classic salt glaze, although anything between one part alumina to three to five parts silica can produce good results, depending on the other compounds in the clay body. However, an excess of silica in the clay body, while adding to the quality of the salt glaze, may have an adverse effect.

The various forms and phases of the silica in any firing is a complex subject, but in a salt firing a high silica content, combined with a longer firing cycle held at the top temperatures, can make a piece more brittle, liable to dunting cracks, and unsuitable for functional ware. Conversely, in vitrified bodies where much of the silica is involved in the melt, the remaining alumina and silica regroup as mullite, greatly strengthening the body.

SUMMARY OF THE EFFECT OF ALUMINA AND SILICA

- The chemical formula for alumina is Al_2O_3.
- Alumina acts to stabilize the glaze and is a highly refractory element of the clay.
- The higher the alumina content, the more the salt will be resisted, and the more matt the finished surface.
- Alumina has the effect of encouraging rich orange colours.
- The chemical formula for silica is SiO_2.
- Silica is found as quartz and flint, and is also a fundamental ingredient of clay.
- The silica in the clay is the glassmaker. It reacts with the salt and, together with the alumina, it produces the glaze.
- In simple terms, the higher the silica content, the thicker that the salt glaze will form, and the shinier the pot will be.

Iron Content

After the alumina to silica ratio, the second important component of the clay is the iron content. The different compounds of iron oxide, and the variable way these respond to other materials and to the firing schedules, have a dramatic effect on the colours and surface: this is fundamental to understanding the results from a salt firing. The lower percentages of iron in paler firing clays give a fired colour from white, through gold, to tan. Between 2 and 5 per cent of an iron compound will produce a range of browns, and up to 8 per cent will give mahogany to metallic black. The higher the firing temperature, the more noticeable the effects of the iron; for instance at 1,280°C, less than 4 per cent of iron will produce a very dark brown.

To appreciate the powerful effect of the iron content of the clay, it is helpful to be aware of the two simple forms in which it is found. The most likely iron-bearing clay colours will be red or brown, seen in various natural clays that also contain other trace elements and impurities.

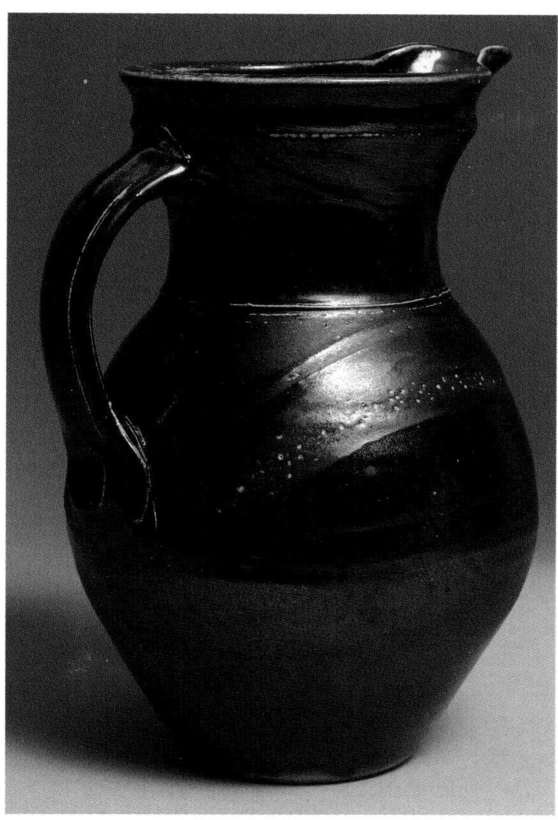

Jug by Michael Casson, 1986/7. The body has a very high iron content for salt glaze. Leeds fireclay and Keuper red marl with sand. The thin slip is 50/50 SMD ball clay and china clay.

The more usual normal state of iron oxide is red iron oxide, also called ferric oxide: this is the red of terracotta clays. The iron in an unfired clay that contains decomposed organic matter is likely to be in the form of black iron oxide, also called ferrous oxide. The obvious black colour of any clay is mostly carbon, and this colour will override the colour of both forms of iron oxides.

In the early stages of a firing the clay will be oxidized. Much, but not all of the iron content, regardless of its original form, will be converted to red iron oxide, and a high percentage of iron in this ferric state will tend to resist the salt. The brightest fired-colour range of red, orange and yellow comes from the varying proportions of iron in oxidation, but in reduction all these iron colours change to grey. Above 900 °C, reduction of the kiln atmosphere will continue to affect the iron, as more of the red ferric oxide is easily converted to the ferrous oxide. In turn, this black iron oxide becomes a flux, reacting with the silica to fuse the clay body, and integrating with the silica and sodium vapour as they combine to form salt glaze. Any black iron oxide integrated in the body melt is likely to remain in this reduced state.

The temperature at which reduction takes place is all-important. To be effective, reduction of the clay body needs to take place before, or at least by, the earliest stages that the glaze begins to form. This may be a problem in the salt kiln. The fireboxes are the hottest part of the kiln, and any residual salt there will begin to volatilize early. This prevents some of the clay body, in the cooler parts of the kiln, from being well reduced. After the salt glaze has formed, oxidation and reduction will only be effective in changing the oxides on the surface of the pieces. Cooling in oxidation will brighten the colours of the glaze, as the black iron oxide on the surface re-oxidizes and converts back into the red iron oxide form. Cooling under reduction will retain the grey colour, but can cause unattractive dull colours on the white and paler clays.

There is one further disadvantage of a high iron content in the clay. During salting, the temperature around which vitrification occurs is held for a considerable time. Too much iron oxide in the clay body can encourage the formation of a very dense vitrified body, and the pots will develop a poor resistance to thermal shock. Decreasing the iron oxide content will improve the resistance to thermal shock. It also has the effect of freeing more silica to react with the salt vapour, producing a brighter glaze.

SUMMARY OF THE EFFECTS OF IRON OXIDES

- The chemical formulae for the different forms of iron oxide:
  Black iron oxide, also called ferrous oxide, is FeO.
  Red iron oxide, also called ferric oxide, is Fe_2O_3.
- High percentages of red iron oxide in the clay will tend to resist the salt.
- The brightest colour range comes from the iron in oxidation, red iron oxide.
- Reduction converts the red iron oxide to black iron oxide and therefore the colours to grey.
- A mottled brown will occur in a neutral atmosphere or if the timing of reduction or oxidation has failed to convert the iron fully to either its ferric or ferrous form.

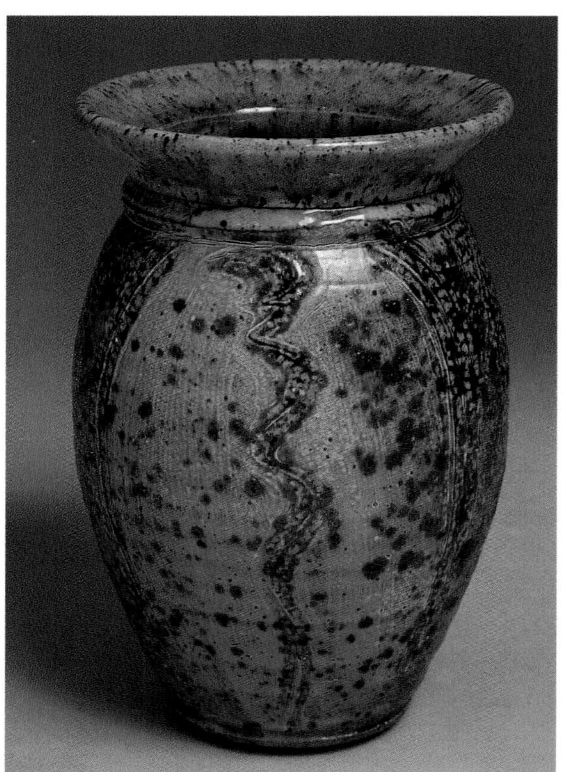

Vase by Alex McErlain. Orange slip over a coarse, high iron-bearing clay. For a distinctively bold effect, finely ground fireclay will add texture and colour to a clay body. It contains particles of iron in the form of iron pyrites, which create a heavy, dark speckling that can be wonderfully dramatic when it is combined with the orange-peel of the salt glaze.

Additional Components of Clay

All but the purest clay will contain traces of a number of other materials, and the manufacturers' tables of clay analyses will indicate their presence. They can affect the fired colour and the surface response to the vapour. Calcium oxide together with iron oxide colours the glaze yellowish-green. A small amount of titanium oxide in the clay brightens the salt glaze. Over 3 per cent of magnesium oxide can cause the surface of the glaze to be dull or crystalline, while a smaller proportion will combine with alumina to produce orange flashing.

Modifying a Clay Body

Additions to the clay body can help to balance the properties and achieve the required qualities. Silica, in the form of fine sand or finely ground flint, improves the glaze thickness and shine. The size of the silica particles affects the degree of orange-peel, but if they are too coarse they will cause a rough finish to the salt-glaze surface. Too much silica will cause the fired pot to shatter on cooling.

Nepheline syenite is sometimes added to clay for salt firing. It contributes alumina and silica in the ratio of approximately one to three, but it also contains a small amount of sodium oxide, which acts to produce a smoother glaze surface. The quality of the glaze surface can also be improved by blending one of the soda compounds into the clay. Soda ash or sodium chloride can be added in quantities of up to 0.5 per cent of the other dry ingredients.

Coming to a Conclusion

After all the analyses and principles, the best way to find out how a clay body will react to the salt glaze is to fire it. Your own trials and actual examples, combined with written references, will give you the best grasp of the subject and will open up opportunities for new surface qualities from salt vapour. Whether pieces are to be thrown or hand-built, are functional or sculptural, the desired aesthetic qualities will need to be balanced against the working properties of the clay.

Manufacturers' Prepared Clay Bodies

Ready-prepared clay bodies are the starting point for many potters. The following is a selection, and by no means a definitive list, of those found suitable for salting. It should be borne in mind that potters have individual requirements. Blends of these clay bodies are made, sometimes with a mix of clays from different manufacturers, and in some cases up to 15 per cent silica sand is added. Further clay bodies mixed from raw materials are listed, with additional slip and glaze recipes at the end of the chapter.

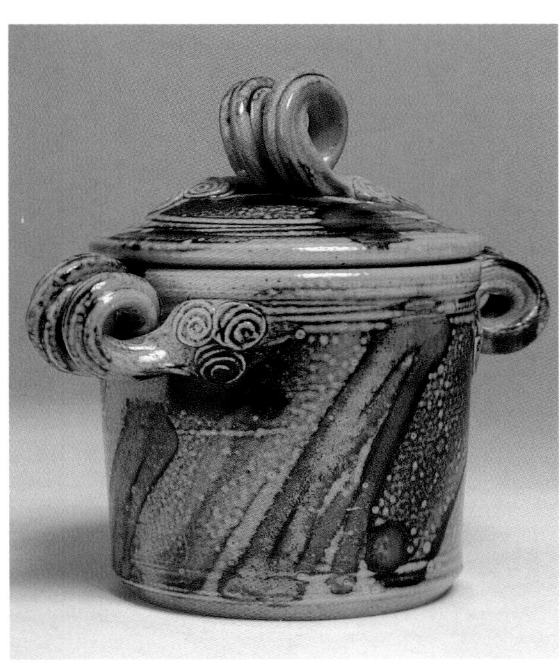

Lidded pot by Rosemary Cochrane. Various slips brushed over white stoneware clay.

Potclays Ltd

1104 Red St Thomas
1106 White St Thomas
1145 White Stoneware
1123 Special HT
1120 Buff body
1149 HF porcelain

Used individually or mixed in various proportions.
Also 1106 White St Thomas 50/50 with 1141 Super Earthenware
Surprising and interesting results from 1148 Bone China.

WBB Vingerling

Various, available through UK agents Pottery Crafts Ltd.

Commercial Clay Ltd

Super White Stoneware
TS Stoneware
Mixed in equal quantities.

Sandstone
Mixed with the above in equal quantities.

Valentine Clays

Audrey Blackman porcelain
'Scarva' Earthstone
TS Stoneware mixed with 'Scarva' Earthstone
Smooth White Stoneware B17C mixed with 20 per cent Special Fleck.

W. J. Doble Pottery Clays

DWSP White stoneware
DSS Reduction stoneware
Mixed in various proportions.

SLIPS

A slip is liquid clay, a mixture of clay and water, and the use of slips for colouring and decorating the surface of clay objects is as old as pottery itself. The wonderfully fluid traditional use of slips in Britain is seen on the slip-decorated earthenware pieces from many old country potteries. But there is little historical precedence of slips being used in that particular way on early salt glaze in Britain, and the traditional earthenware slip techniques remained with the small country potters. When salt firing was adopted for mass-produced stoneware, and developed on an industrial scale later on, the use of slip was confined to being a simple dipped coating that would give a satisfactory final colour to the salt-glaze products.

Unfired slipped ware by Michael Casson.

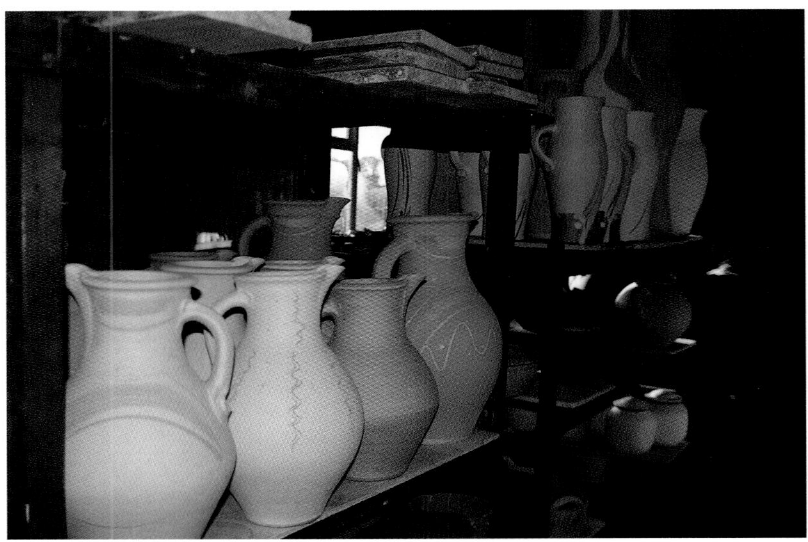

Since the time of the art pottery studios, and the later growth of studio potteries and individual expression, the use of slips has been explored in diverse ways by both earthenware and stoneware potters. It now plays a big part in the effects produced by contemporary salt-glaze potters, being a very immediate way of working with clay, and well suited to the salt-firing process.

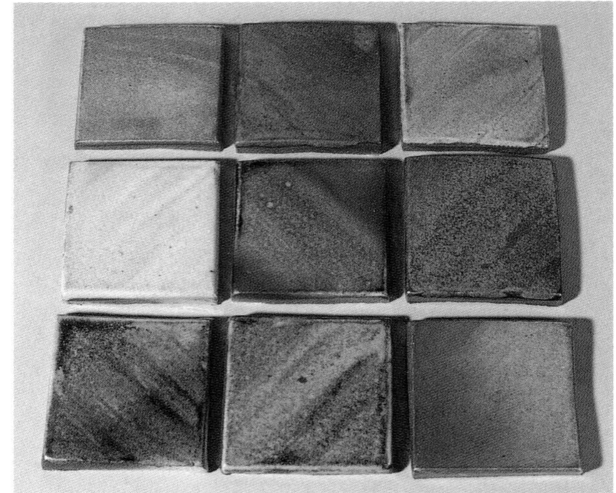

Tiles. Altering the proportions of china clay and ball clay, and adding various percentages of colouring oxides, will open up the tests.

Extending the Range and Response

There is a great deal to understand about the nature of salt glaze and its interaction with the wide choice of ceramic materials that can be used to make up slips. Slips greatly extend the opportunities for colour and texture and, by starting with a simple set of variables, it is possible to develop slips that give a wide range of surfaces, from traditional orange-peel through to dry matt.

Testing Slips

Assuming an elementary understanding of the essential ingredients, a useful and practical way to test slips is empirically – that is, based on observation and experiment – as the very nature of salt firing will produce many unpredictable variations: it can never be an exact science. The exploration of colours and textures from slips can begin with various ball clays. Just as in the clay body, the variable proportions of alumina, silica, iron oxide and traces of other materials in the different ball clays will produce many subtleties of colour and texture.

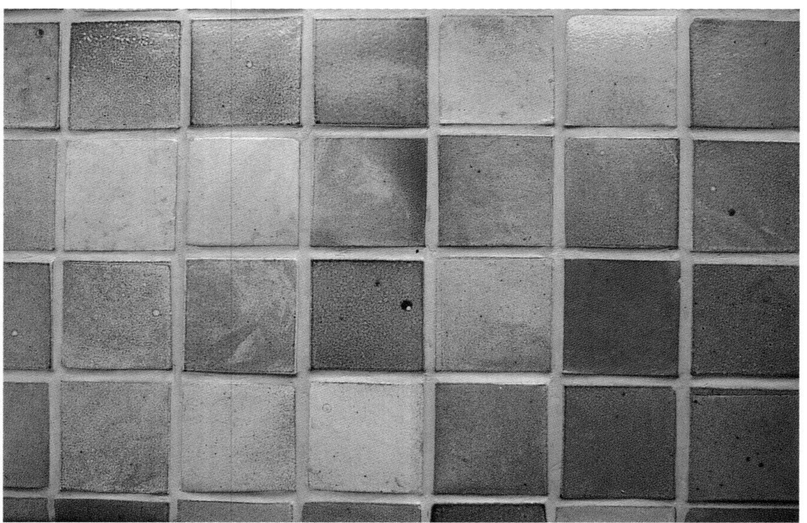

Tiles by Rosemary Cochrane. 50/50 ball clay and china clay slips, using a variety of ball clays, fired in various parts of the kiln, give a wide spectrum of warm colours. 'T' material clay body.

Tests can start with a choice of three or four different clay bodies. Any number of slips can be made up using different ball clays in a simple mix of half china clay and half ball clay. China clay contains a high percentage of alumina and is used to produce a range of yellows, oranges and reds. These slips can be applied as a thin dip, and can then be double-dipped for comparison, although the thickness of the slip is less critical than the amount of salt. Several samples of each combination of clay and slip, placed in various parts of the kiln, help to give a more complete evaluation of their nature.

Adding a Flux

The less flux the slip or engobe recipe contains, the more refractory it will be, resulting in an opaque-satin or matt surface. As the proportion of the flux content is increased, the more transparent the finish. Feldspar and china clay can form the basis of a slip, and increasing the percentage of feldspar discourages the formation of the orange-peel texture. When a flux forms a high proportion of the mix, the classification of the recipe moves from an engobe to a glaze. All other fluxes will produce a diverse variety of responses to the salt vapour. Up to 10 per cent of calcium carbonate, lithium carbonate, zinc oxide, or barium carbonate can also be used as a flux to modify the slips.

As the tests proceed it will be necessary to monitor the clay content of the slips, as this affects the shrinkage rate and the stage at which

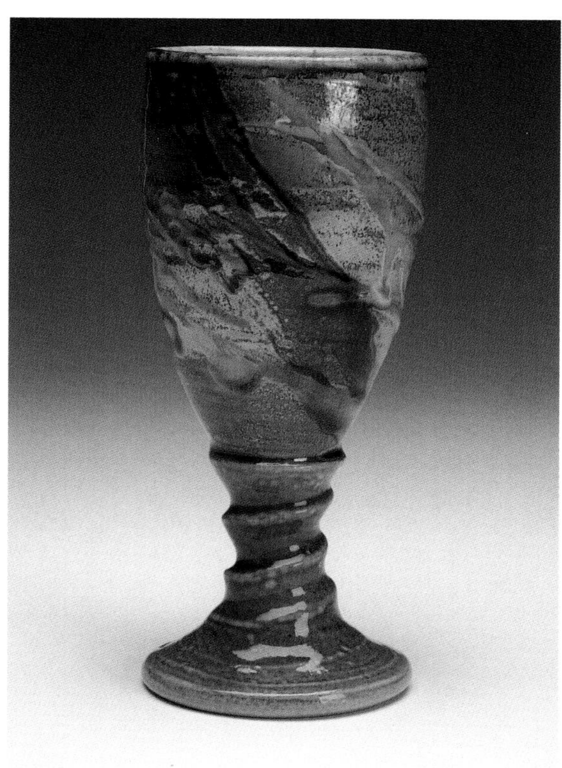

Champagne goblet by Stuart Whatley. High alumina and shino slips with trailed slip glazes and some rutile.

ENGOBES

An engobe is a slip that contains comparatively more flux than a normal slip. It must contain sufficient clay to give adhesion before the firing. It contains a different balance of the three ingredients that go to make up a glaze: silica the glass-maker, flux the melting agent, and alumina, which binds the glass and flux together in the firing.

An engobe lies between a slip and a glaze, both literally and in composition.

it should be applied. Clay-based slips are generally applied to soft or leather-hard clay and will contain at least 50 per cent clay. Those that are high in alumina, or with only 30–40 per cent clay, will be better applied to dry ware. With only 20 per cent of clay, the mix becomes half way between a slip and a glaze. This will need to be applied to dry clay or bisque-fired ware. The shrinkage rates of the slip and clay body must be compatible, and recipes may need to be adjusted.

These can only be guidelines, and trial and error is the only way to establish the best ways to make the recipes compatible with the clays. Different combinations of materials and clays are infinite, just as the problems that may be encountered when applying and firing slips. This topic is not specifically one of salt glaze, and there are several books listed in the bibliography that cover the subject.

Something Different

While the wonderful classic salt-glazed surface of shiny orange-peel remains one of the main attractions to the process for many potters, there are other vapour surfaces to be exploited. The general rules are made to be broken, and there may be potential in any of the qualities that materialize. Forget the ball clay and china clay base, and start with something completely different. Experiment with line blends of several different combinations of materials, tested over a range of clay bodies, to find out more about the interaction of slips and salt. The effect of the salt on materials such as calcium and magnesium compounds, and on the range of minerals with crystal-forming properties, is open to further exploration.

Keeping a Record

The permutations are endless. Without a good system to record recipes, and results from different firings, the tests will become frustrating and meaningless. This early research is the foundation for developing a personal palette and range of surface qualities that you enjoy, and a range of reliable and versatile materials with which to work. There is an opportunity to put trials into every firing, and the challenge to explore beyond the safe and familiar can be rewarded with the excitement and success of discovering the unexpected and truly beautiful.

After initial tests, use the mixes on large pieces, set them much more widely around the kiln, and investigate the effect of overlapping slips. Eventually it will not be simply a matter of chance by which the process happens and the effects are created. However, remember that a different kiln will almost certainly not produce the same results, and unpredictability will always play its part. Just when you think you begin to understand what is happening, the kiln will throw out surprises that only providence can explain.

All recipes have been quoted as given by individual potters. Some are batch recipes in weights or by parts. Others are given as percentages or convenient numbers.

Personal Experiences

Mirka Golden-Hann and Joseph Lynch

Golden-Hann and Lynch are graduates from the University of Westminster (Harrow Campus). When they left college in 1999, they set up their first pottery workshop and built a salt kiln:

> The vast research of clay bodies and slip recipes that we undertook during our studies at Harrow is one of the most valuable aspects that we brought with us to our new workshops after leaving university. The colours we are getting out of our new salt kiln are much different to the ones out of the well-salted kiln at university. But the unpredictability that transcends any research is one of the main attractions of this wonderful process of salt firing.

Interested in vivid colour, Mirka says:

> I tested various shades of blues, greens, reds, pinks and yellows, using not only coloured oxides but also commercial stains, ground and broken glass, and pieces of various metals. Joseph used colouring oxides in base slips, but was largely interested in earthy colours, testing mixtures of natural clays and ash. We became interested in pinks and yellows and oranges, achieved by close packing pots, and piling pots one on top of another – a less rigid approach to kiln packing. The work was very labour intensive, but altogether we were able to test several clay bodies and glazes and hundreds of slip recipes.
>
> The warmer colours tend to occur where high alumina slips with a low percentage of iron resist the salt. Tests were based around china clay, the main source of alumina, which was blended with a variety of other clays – ball clays, fire clay, fusible red clay and bentonite, and so on. Line blends with 10 per cent increments were used, and the results were both a graphic description of alumina, silica and iron oxide in combination with salt, and a lively palette of warm, earthy and often vivid flame colours.

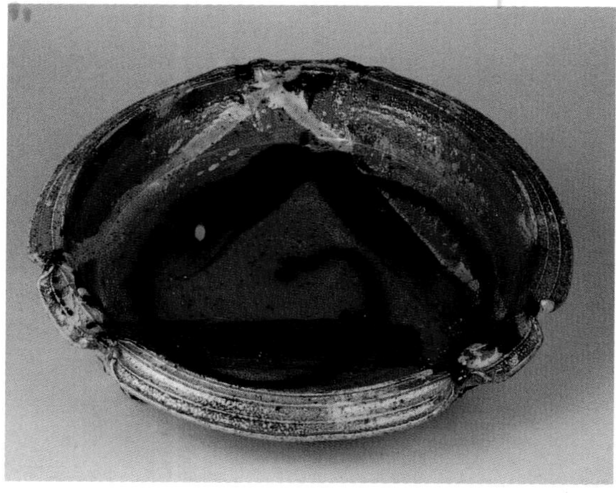

Large dish with feet by Mirka Golden-Hann, 1999.

RECIPES

Off-white base slip to which colorants can be added:

China clay	30
HV ball clay	40
Flint	15
Nepheline syenite	15

New Harrow body as brown slip, gives good pronounced 'tiger-skin':

HVAR ball clay	40
Fireclay	20
Red clay	4
Potash feldspar	4

Industrial white earthenware as a slip:

Hyplas 71 ball clay	25
China clay	25
Flint	35
Cornish stone	15

Micki Schloessingk

Micki salt glazes in a wood-fired kiln, and has developed an exceptional understanding of a wide range of slips for use on her work. The

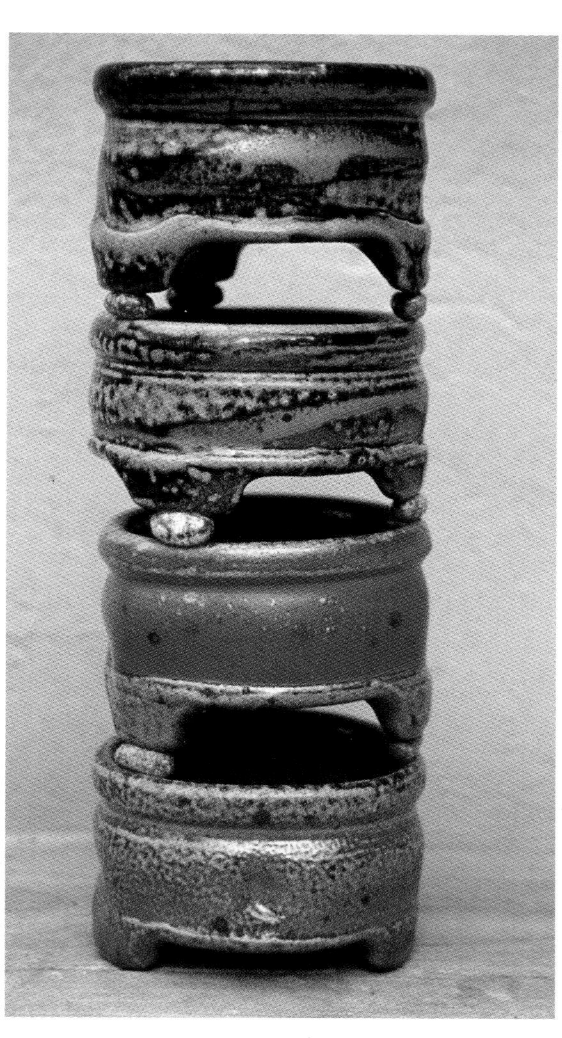

Stack of pots by Micki Schloessingk, 2000. Each part influences the other parts: 'Let me explain . . . I know that this slip, if it is on the top, will go brown; this one is almost pure alumina and is very dry, and happy here, in another place it would not work. The next slip has a nice melt, it has some tin in it and goes a nice orange-peel, and I can put it on the bottom of the pile where it gets less salt.'

way the kiln is packed is an essential part in making the slips work well; she describes the procedure thus:

> High china clay slips give a range of colours from light salmon through to dark brown. They may come out light orange on a porcelain body, salmon on a mix of porcelain and St Amand clay, and a rich dark red-brown on the clay high in iron pyrites. The colour and texture of the slip depends on the relationship between the iron content in the body, the amount of reduction, the exposure to salt and fly ash, and the temperature reached. When there is a heavy fly ash deposit as well as strong exposure to the salt, the red is leached from the slip, which then takes on an ash green orange-peel.
>
> I use a number of slips in which I mix small proportions of porcelain or nepheline syenite or iron-bearing clays – such as AT – with grolleg china clay. I may then use a slip with up to 50 per cent nepheline syenite on the inside of a stacked bowl, while I use a slip with only 10 per cent nepheline syenite on the exterior surface, and end up with a similar glaze and texture inside and out. I experiment with adding anywhere up to 10 per cent titanium oxide to produce a range of slips that explore the yellow to ochre-brown colour range. Titanium also has the effect of breaking up the surface of the slip well, helping create a good orange-peel texture. I have come to a number of my slips by the triaxial test method.
>
> Note that a slip that works well in one salt kiln may fire quite differently in another, so I would encourage exploration and experiment and risk-taking.

COLOURING

In addition to the oranges and reds from alumina, and the range of colours – light tan through browns to black – produced from the iron oxide in the clay body or slips, any of the usual colouring agents will give colour from vapour firings. The early traditional use of cobalt oxide is seen on German pots, together with manganese, which produces shades of purple to brown. Oxides can be applied as a wash, sprayed or added to the slip or clay. The strongest colours are obtained where the glaze coating is thin. A heavy salting will leach out the colours.

Colouring Oxides

The typical percentages of oxide, appropriate for adding to slips or engobes, follow the usual suggested guidelines. A few, however, are worthy of particular mention. Copper oxide, for instance, becomes very volatile in the salt kiln, and even if it is contained within a glaze mix it will easily contaminate other pots; used in quantity it remains in the kiln fabric and affects following firings. For a reduced copper-red, the timing and holding of the period of reduction is critical, and in a salt firing it is not easy to achieve as an overall colour.

Cobalt oxide combined with rutile gives a vivid green; cobalt and titanium oxides com-

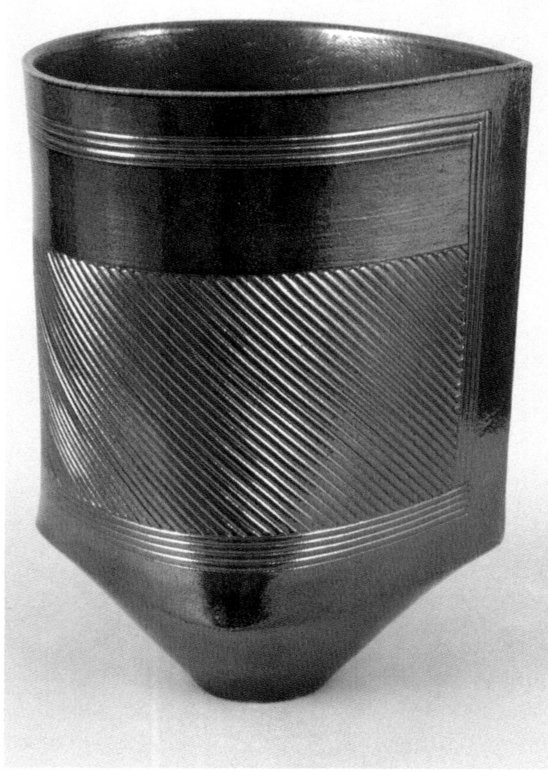

Deep pot by Ruth King, 1999. Made in one piece, 29cm. Incised decoration and turquoise slip band, over-sprayed with 50 Feldspar and 50 AT (high iron) ball clay ± ¼ per cent cobalt oxide slip.

bined produce a soft light green. Yellow is obtained by mixing barium, titanium and nickel oxides. Both titanium oxide and rutile, the naturally occurring form of titanium oxide, promote a crystal formation that makes a dense sheen of yellowish-brown. Lithium and titanium oxides combine to give colours from mahogany red to bright yellow.

Results are always dependent on the set of circumstances: the thickness of application, the amount of salt deposit, and the firing atmosphere. In salt firing the unpredictable element is the final touch that gives success or disappointment, so it can be worth repeating a recipe, or re-firing a piece, to give the flames and vapour a second chance.

Curl handle detail of oval dish by Jane Hamlyn. Lustrous effect from titanium dioxide painted over blue slip.

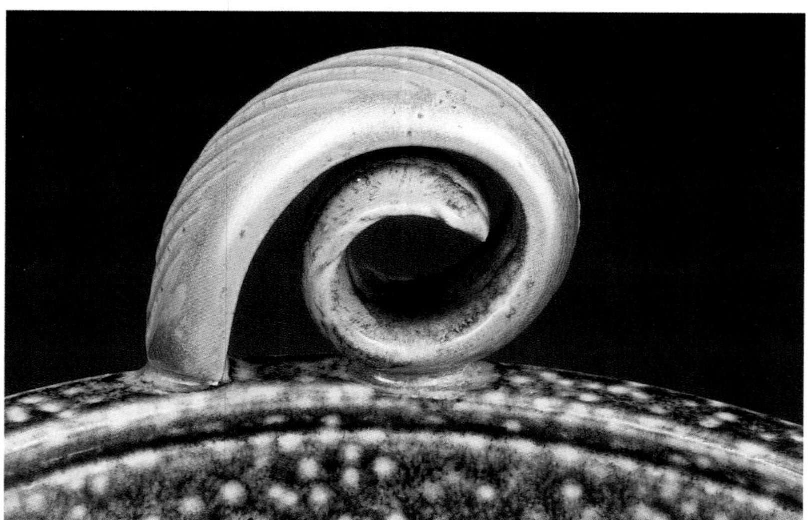

COLOURING STRENGTHS FOR OXIDES

1–3% cobalt oxide (CoO): pale blue to deep bright blue

2–8% manganese dioxide (MnO_2): purple to brown

3–8% copper oxide (CuO): green in oxidation, red in reduction

1–3% chromium oxide (Cr_2O_3): green

5–10% vanadium pentaoxide (V_2O_5): mottled yellow

3–15% titanium dioxide (TiO_2): a crystal-forming opacifier

Note that both rutile and ilmenite are different crystal forms of titanium oxide:

5–20% rutile (TiO_2 plus small amount of iron)

3–8% ilmenite ($FeOTiO_2$)

Jane Hamlyn's Blue Slip

Depth of colour depends on the thickness of application and the exposure to salt.

Nepheline syenite	6
AT ball clay	13
SMD ball clay	25
Rutile	1%
Cobalt oxide	1.5%

Titanium dioxide painted on top of this blue slip sometimes gives a greeny-gold crystalline lustre, but it is unpredictable.

Daniel Boyle's Slips

> I use slips of different vitrifying temperatures and, with the use of a spray gun, layer them on top of each other, putting the most vitreous on the top, and firing to make the one on top fluid, leaving the undercoat stable to create a base colour. The vanadium under-slip encourages

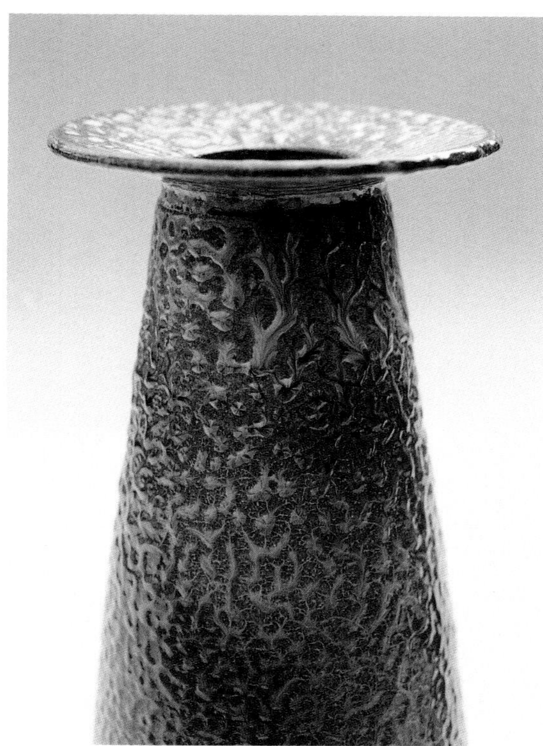

Detail of tall candle holder by Daniel Boyle. Textured and rivered surface.

the top slip to break and move, exaggerating the salt-glaze effect. For example, the titanium slip fires smooth on its own leaving a pearl finish, but with the vanadium slip underneath becomes a textured and rivered surface. The titanium and 'blue' together create a lustrous green.

VANADIUM PORCELAIN SLIP

(based on a David Leach porcelain recipe)

China clay	55
Potash feldspar	25
Quartz	15
Bentonite	5
Vanadium pentoxide	10

'SALT' SLIP

China clay	17
Ball clay	19
Flint	24
Nepheline syenite	31
Standard borax frit	9

Add oxides:

(Blue) cobalt carbonate	3
(Moonshine white) titanium dioxide	9

Other Colouring Pigments

Both under-glaze colours and body stains have the potential to give exciting results in vapour firings. Although not all colours will work in the volatile atmosphere of a high temperature salt firing, the manufacturers of these products are usually happy to advise. An oxidizing rather than a reducing atmosphere will favour some of the more subtle colours. Stains can be mixed in the slip, or brushed or painted on the surface of a white slip or clay body. To make their application easier, they can be mixed with a flux or a low temperature frit.

Peter Meanley's Research

As a part of his research into the nature of salt glaze, Peter Meanley undertook a series of 300 tests in 92 firings. The kiln was 0.4cu m (14cu ft), fired with propane gas. He chose Potclays 1145 White Stoneware as the clay body, and mixed the colours in a variety of slips, using colouring oxides and stains. In the main the slips were sprayed onto the pots, which had

(BELOW) Fish dishes by Frank Hamer. The pieces were similarly decorated with a slip of HVAR ball clay coloured with various stains and oxides over a blended body of Potclays Reduction and White St Thomas stoneware. The effect of the salt-glaze firing, in which the colours have burnt out and been overwhelmed by the iron content, compared with a similar piece fired as it is normally, under reduction in a gas kiln.

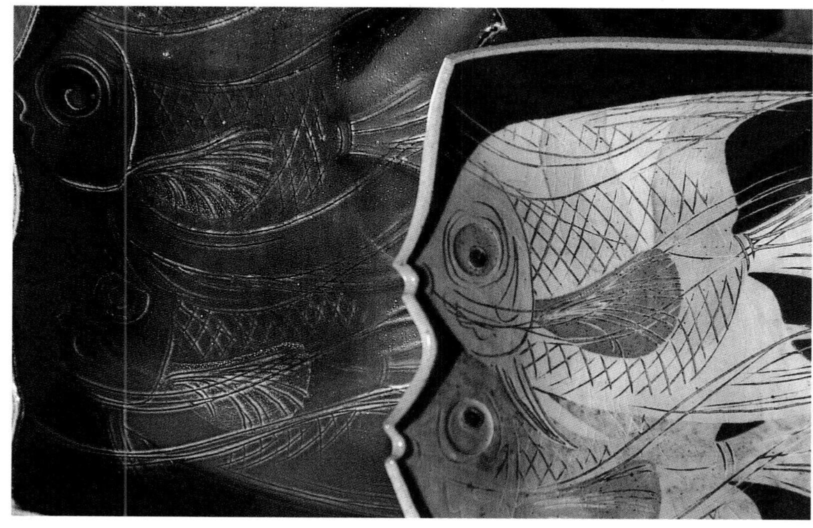

been biscuit fired to 1,000°C. He also sponged, poured, brushed or squirted the slips for the more complex decoration. An analysis of his work is outlined in his article published in *Ceramics Technical* 9, 1999. Only a very small selection of his recipes are shown as examples.

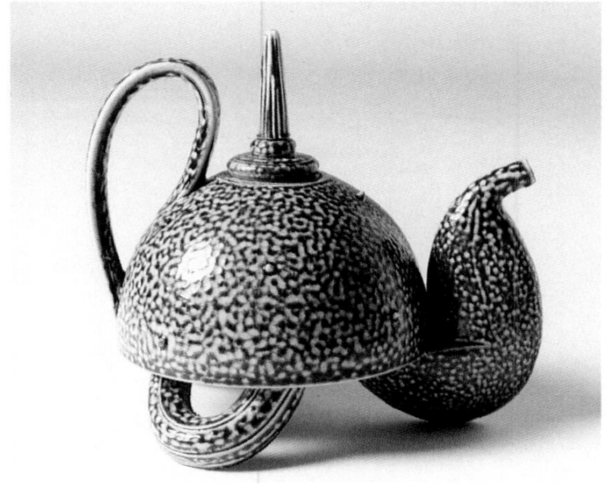

Teapot by Peter Meanley, 1997. 21 × 14 × 16cm. Thrown, press-moulded spout, extruded handle, thrown foot. Three parts cobalt-stain slip and one part turquoise-stain slip, sprayed (see recipes).

BASE SLIPS MIXED WITH VARIOUS STAINS OR OXIDES

Used with 10 parts Scarva stains: B106 for blue cobalt, B115 for turquoise.

SMD	80
Grolleg	20

or

SMD	50
Grolleg	50

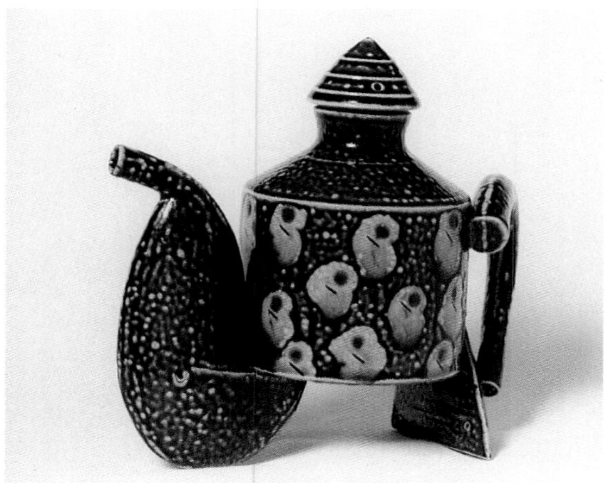

Teapot by Peter Meanley, 1999. 24 × 12 × 19cm. Yellow and purple and green slips with sprayed base slip coloured with manganese, chromium and cobalt (see recipes).

Base colour

SMD ball clay	80
Grolleg	20
Cobalt carbonate	0.75
Manganese dioxide	12
Chromium oxide	1

Hymod S.M (74% silica) ball clay mixed with various combinations of oxides to give:

Yellow

Red iron oxide	15
Quartz	10

Purple

Cobalt carbonate	0.5
Manganese dioxide	6.0

Green

Cobalt carbonate	0.5
Chromium oxide	2
Quartz	10

Colouring Clay

Another way of introducing colour is to colour the clay, and interesting and unexpected colours will come from salt-firing clays mixed with body stains. It will always be necessary to make tests, to find out what works for each individual choice of materials and kiln.

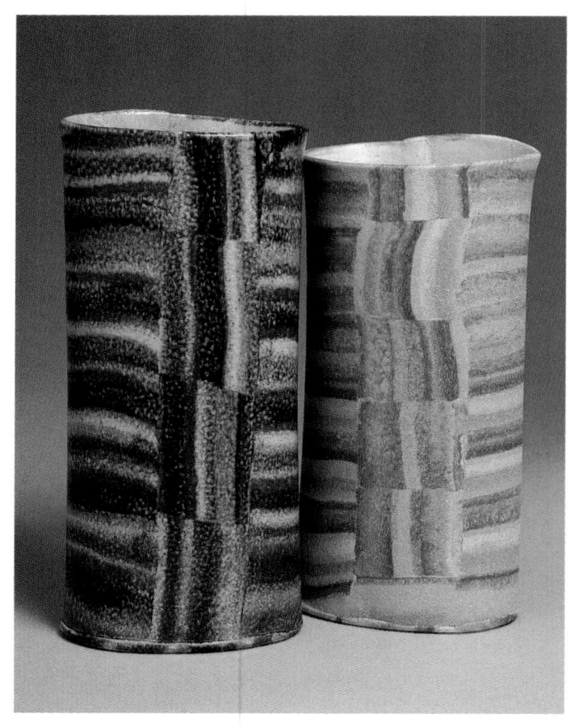

Vases by Jo Connell. Jo blends various proportions of body stains and oxides with 'Scarva' Earthstone. Her hand-built pots are normally fired to 1,260°C in an electric kiln with the colours as shown on the piece on the right. On the left are the effects of an almost identical piece from salt firing to 1,280°C, which produced a surprising and distinctly different colour response.

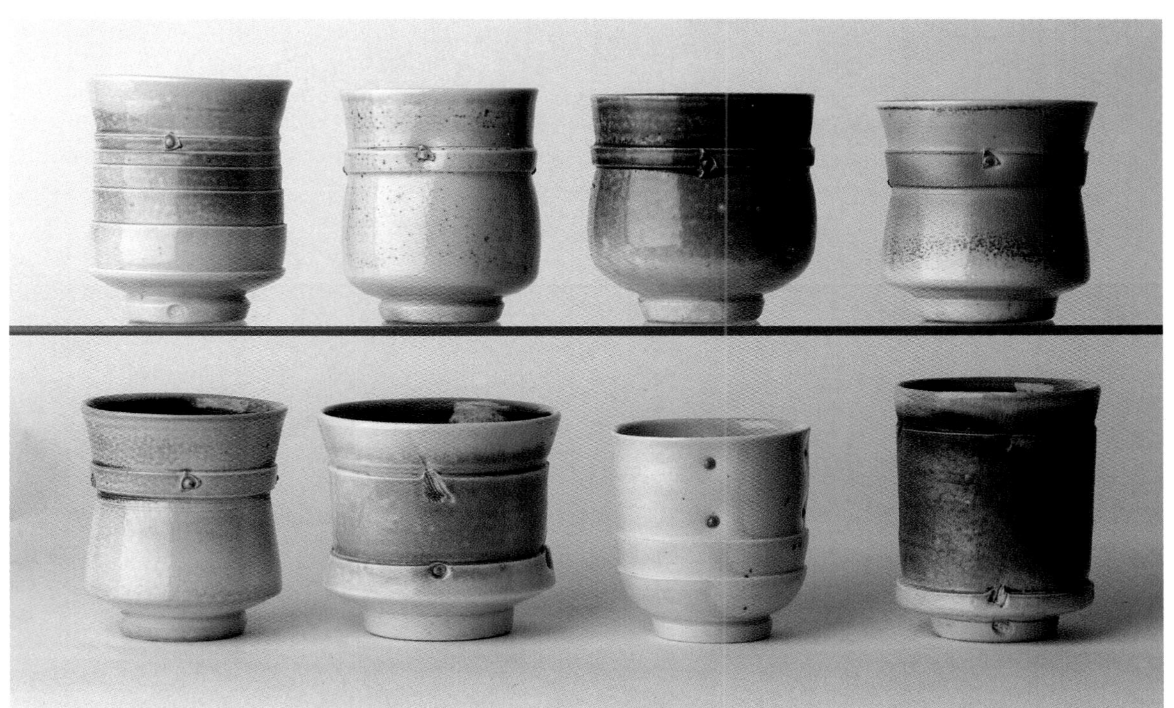

Eight tea bowls by Jack Doherty. Porcelain clay with copper-stained clay, soda-fired.

Jack Doherty's Work

Jack Doherty works with a choice of three prepared porcelain clay bodies:

Valentines Audrey Blackman porcelain

Limoges 1400 porcelain

Potclays 1149 Harry Fraser porcelain

> The clay bodies all have very different properties and are used for different forms. The colours are achieved by adding coloured clays or slips. I use a clay or slip stained with 2 per cent copper carbonate, which is added to the inside of the form. The copper will migrate through the clay body, reacting with the soda and marking the outside of the form.

All the work is once-fired in a propane gas kiln. Doherty's soda firing is described in Chapter 10.

GLAZES

The salt vapours will not reach into steep-sided or lidded items in a salt firing, and so it is usual for a 'liner' glaze to be used for the interior of such pieces. The salt glaze will cover the rims and reach into the upper part of a deep bowl or cylindrical piece, and where there is no lid, can interact with the liner glaze to produce interesting effects. A glaze can be used decoratively on the outside of a piece, adding to the different surface qualities. It may be useful to make use of a glaze in those parts of the kiln where the pieces are least affected by the salt. Any stoneware glaze can be tried in order to find one that suits the colours and surfaces of the work.

Raw Glazing

The use of raw glazes is part of the directness of approach that makes the salt-glaze process so attractive. Raw glazing is done at either the leather-hard or dry stage, and the glaze will usually contain between 30 and 100 per cent of clay. As with any problems regarding the application of slips and engobes, those that may be encountered with raw glazing are not specifically ones of salt glaze. Raw glaze is a subject of its own, and covered in other books listed in the bibliography.

Sarah Walton Recipes

Cardew Green gives an opaque pea green to a dark transparent green. Firing temperature is 1,240° to 1,300°C; a raw glaze:

Potash feldspar	33.3
Whiting	14.3
Talc	6.9
Red clay	29.2
Quartz	20.0

Jane Hamlyn Recipes

All recipes are designed for raw pots.

Blue exterior glaze:

Potash feldspar	1
Cornish stone	1
Ball clay	1
Cobalt carbonate	0.5–1% to taste

'Shino' liner glaze:

Nepheline syenite	33
AT ball clay	33
Potash feldspar	33

Shino Glazes

A 'Shino' glaze has a high nepheline syenite content, and is often used for the inside of salt-glaze functional ware. In enclosed forms, a deep orange colour is drawn from the iron in the clay body, complementing the orange colours of ball-clay slips. The glaze can be easily adapted for application to either raw- or biscuit-fired pots, and gives a range of blues with added cobalt oxide or carbonate. On the outside of salt-glaze pots it gives a smooth surface.

Nepheline syenite	60	70	50	75	40
AT ball clay	40	30	30	10	20
China clay	–	–	20	15	–
Petalite	–	–	–	–	40

There are numerous permutations of the recipe, but nepheline syenite is the essential ingredient. The first one is definitely suitable for raw glaze. Depending on the clay body, the others may suit either dry raw or biscuit application.

'Tenmoku' Glazes

These are high in iron oxide and normally fire dark brown to black. They are transformed by the salt firing into various strengths of paling green, as the salt leaches out the colour.

From Michael Casson

Tenmoku glaze gives from yellow to black, for raw or biscuit application.

Paul Barron recipe:

Potash feldspar	55
'Local' clay	35
Whiting	10
Red iron oxide	2.5

For the 'local' clay, try using local red clays. Mick uses Humber clay, a brick/tile works clay.

Other Glaze Recipes

Magnesium glaze for inside, raw (when the pot is bone hard), or biscuit.

Magnesium carbonate (light)	2
Cornish stone	33
Whiting	7
Hyplas 71	4
China clay	6

From Walter Keeler

Interior glaze for biscuit-fired ware.

Phil Wood recipe:

Cornish stone	70
Woolastonite	30
Red iron oxide	8

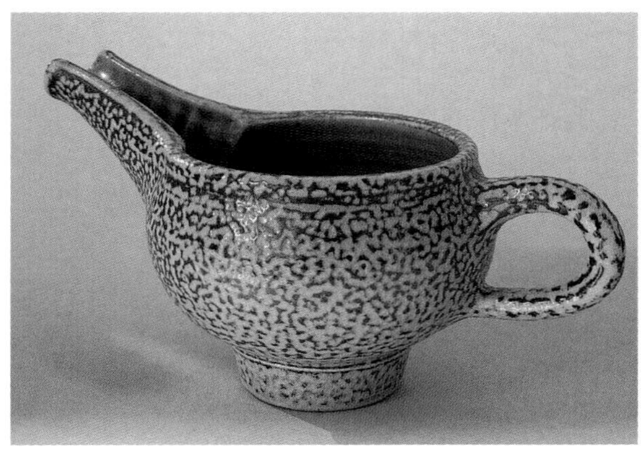

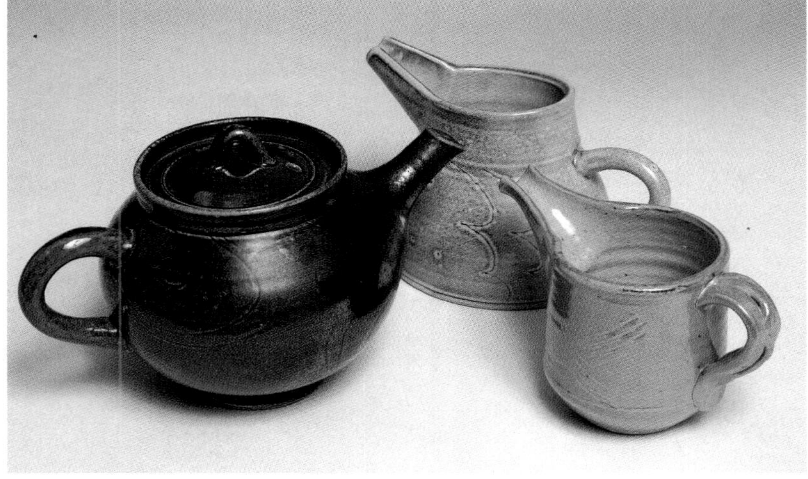

(ABOVE) Teapot and two jugs by Sheila Casson, 1989. Sgraffito decoration. Outside 50/50 nepheline syenite and Hyplas 71 ball clay, with 1 per cent red iron oxide and 0.5 per cent cobalt for dark blue, 3 per cent rutile for light tan. Inside magnesium glaze.

(ABOVE LEFT) Jug by Shiela Casson, 1998.

From Rosemary Cochrane

Base glaze recipe for inside or outside, on dry raw- or biscuit-fired wares, suitable for the addition of colouring oxides.

Ball clay	6
Potash feldspar	10
Dolomite	4

'Autumn orange' glaze, for application on dry or biscuit, inside or outside pots, giving a wide variety of results from matt speckled orange to glossy olive-green.

Hyplas 71	5
Nepheline syenite	3
Whiting	1.5
Flint	0.5
Red iron oxide	0.5
Titanium dioxide	0.25
Bentonite (optional)	0.25

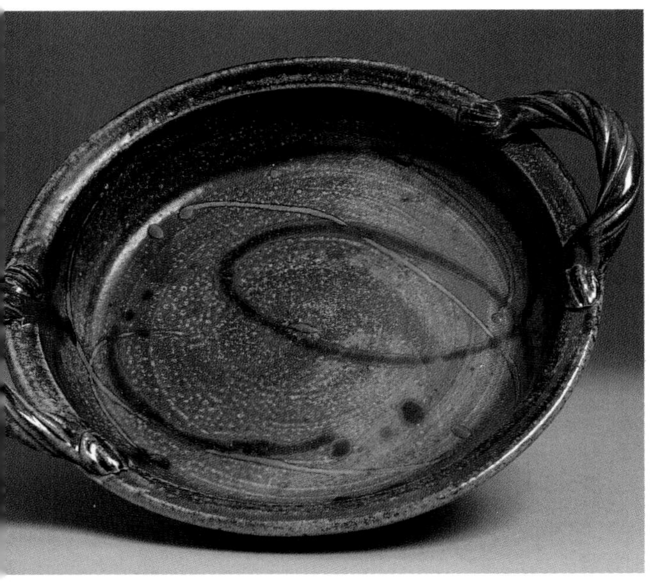

(LEFT) Dish with handles by Rosemary Cochrane, 1999. 'Autumn orange' glaze and trailed blue shino.

FORM AND DECORATION

The vapour deposits glaze amongst the wares in such a way that chance will always play its part in the creation of a salt-glaze piece. But a maker who is mindful of the whole salt-glaze process is more likely to produce a piece that will be truly successful in capturing the combination of lucky happenings during a firing.

Consideration of Form

The salt glaze lands readily on the rims, shoulders and upper parts of taller pieces. Also the bold nature of the orange-peel surface, which is encouraged by the heavier deposit of salt, sits well on a strong simple form. Any form that has been faceted, manipulated or distorted in other ways, will deflect the passage of the flames and vapour and affect the way the salt is deposited.

Phil Rogers

Phil Rogers set up his first pottery in 1978, and was drawn to making salt glaze many years later. He regards simplicity of form and decoration as an essential part of the success of a salt-glaze piece. His pots, while retaining a feeling of the plasticity of clay, have a strength and presence. He uses the wheel to make the forms; some are then squared off, or given marks that reinforce those made in the spinning

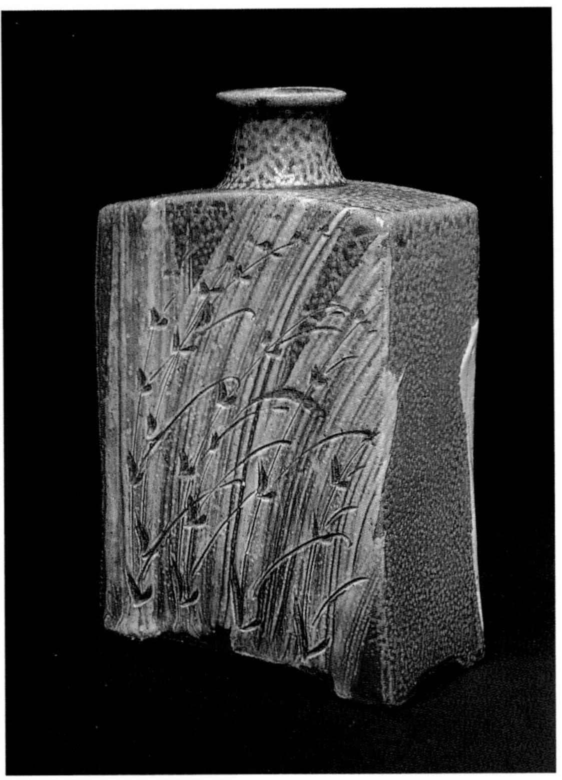

(RIGHT) Press-moulded bottle by Phil Rogers, 2000. 10in tall. Made with a clay body high in iron (4 per cent). The bottle is dipped into a thin slip of local earthenware clay and allowed to dry a little. A thick white slip (25 per cent Molochite, 75 per cent SMD ball clay) is brushed on with a coarse Hakame brush that allows the brush marks to stay visible. The pattern is drawn through the thin, white, local-clay slip to reveal the dark body underneath.

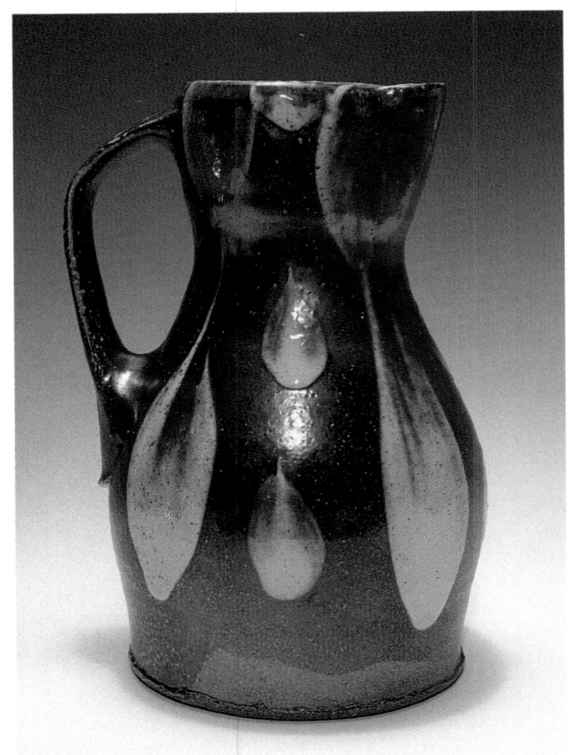

(FAR RIGHT) Jug by Phil Rogers, 2000. 10in tall. With the same combination of slips, the slip has been brushed onto the jug with a large soft brush in one movement from top to bottom.

and turning. Brushed slips, and sometimes incised or impressed decoration, are added to the surfaces. The salt glaze picks up the movement of the pieces and plays with the slipped surfaces to enhance the whole. His pots display a complete integration between the form, glaze and surface pattern.

Ray Finch at Winchcombe Pottery

Salt glaze has always been a sideline from the main wood-fired stoneware at Winchcombe Pottery. The first salt kiln there was the combined effort of two young enthusiasts, Toff Milway who had recently completed the Harrow course, and Alex McErlain who was working at Winchcombe in the early 1970s. Ray Finch has continued to remain interested in salt glaze, and fires his small 0.56cu m (20cu ft) gas-fired salt kiln four or five times a year. He says: 'I enjoy salt glaze as a contrast to our usual glazed stoneware. On the whole I favour a definite orange-peel quality, and I like the warm yellow and brown colours which remind me of the slipware I once used to make.'

Over the years, Ray has produced some beautiful salt-glaze pieces, including several

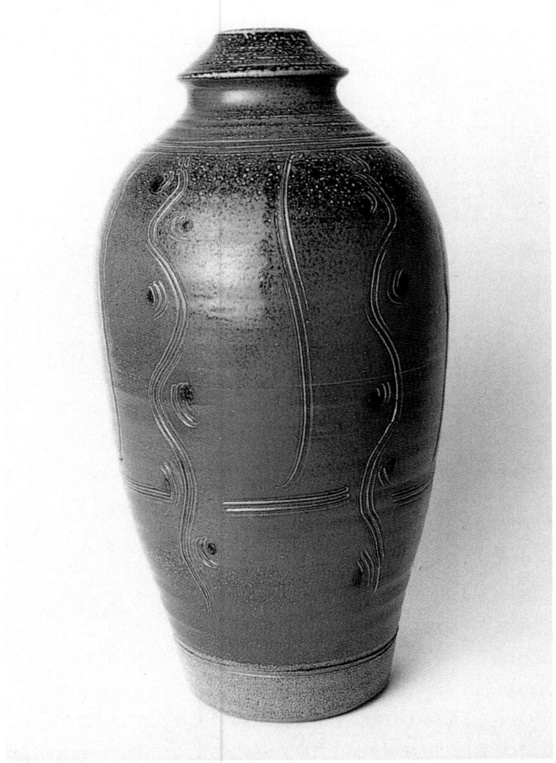

Jar by Ray Finch. Orange slip with sgraffito decoration.

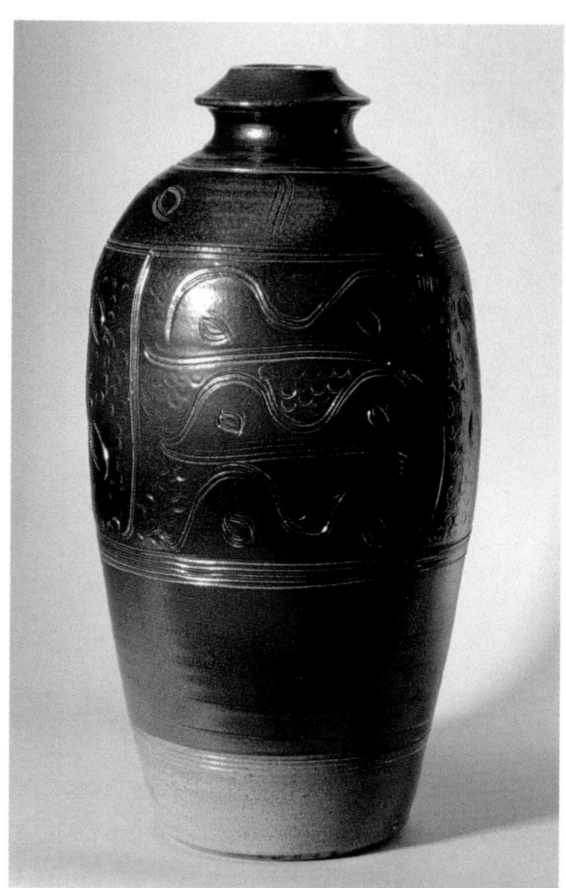

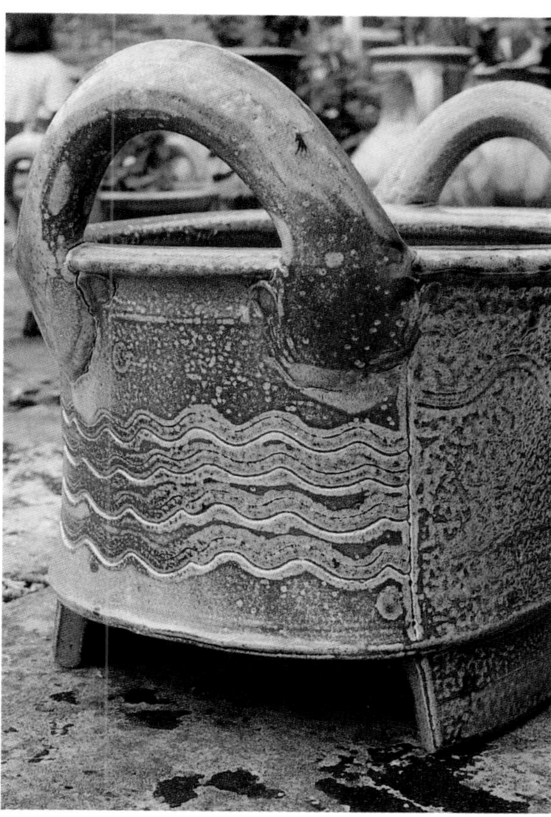

(FAR LEFT) Jar by Ray Finch. Brown slip with green flashing, sgraffito decoration.

(LEFT) Detail of garden trough by Michael Casson, c.1987.

magnificent cider jars, using simple slip coatings, sometimes with sgraffito or incised decoration. His craftsmanship is masterful and, combined with his love of slipware, makes his pieces perfect for the salt-glaze process: strong direct forms, with a simple, fluid use of slips. The salt glaze completes their beauty.

Decoration

Whether the work is functional or sculptural, some techniques respond especially well to the effect of vapour glaze. Many of these have already been mentioned in the early section of the book, which looks at old salt-glaze pots. The contemporary maker has the freedom to interpret any of the traditional styles in a personal and innovative way. Sprigged decoration was used to great effect on traditional wares, and the same technique has been used on contemporary pieces. Any details are brought into focus by the thin coating of the clear salt glaze. Stamping or pressing a texture across the form can also make an effective surface that the salt will pick out.

The simple application of an all-over covering of slip, or the plainest of all surfaces, the clay body itself, can be transformed by salt glaze. Equally effective are the random effects of pouring a slip across a form, or a very controlled application. Sgraffito, and combing through the surface of the slip to reveal the clay body beneath, are techniques well suited for decorative salt glaze. Alternatively, the surface of the clay can be treated like the canvas of a painting. Layer upon layer of surface decoration, slips, engobes and glazes can be applied, scraped off, scratched through and brushed over, creating textures and colour which the attack of salt vapour will enrich.

In the contemporary scene there are certainly many very different and appealing salt-vapour surfaces. Such variety implies that any attempt to define what might be regarded as 'the finest salt-glaze work' is going to be a subjective judgement. But in whatever ways colour and decoration are used, the best salt-fired pieces will be the result of carefully considered form and use of materials, with the added ingredient of the chance magic in the firing.

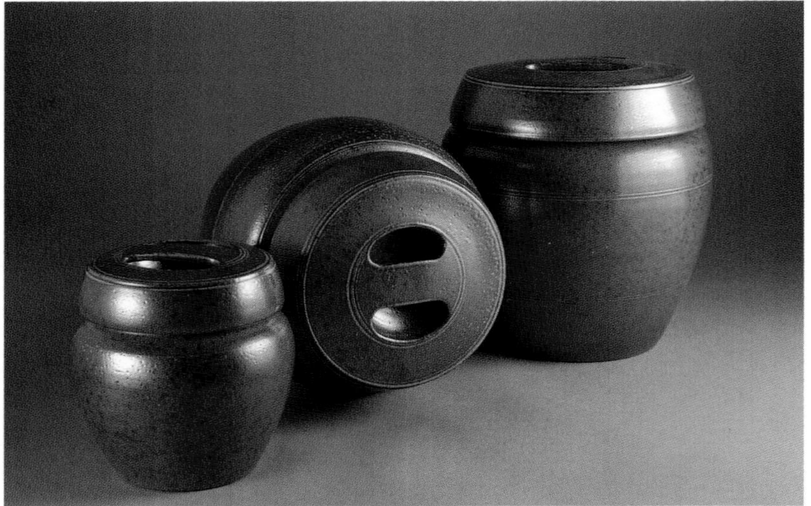

(Above) Group of lidded bins by Toff Milway, 2000.

(Right) Group of functional ware by Toff Milway, 2000.

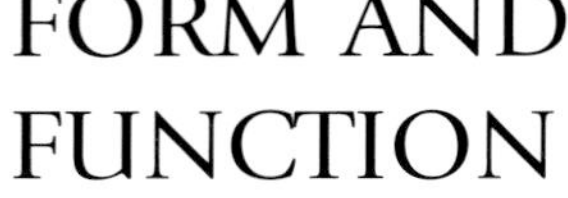

FORM AND FUNCTION

Making functional ware for salt glaze goes beyond the usual concerns that ensure the items are useful and fulfil their purpose – a hygienic surface, a teapot that pours and so on. The finest salt-glaze functional ware combines form, function and the additional attention that the process requires. With only a few exceptions, functional ware has been at the foundation of twentieth-century British salt glaze; in particular two potters who originally engaged fully in production ware, as opposed to series of pots, found inspiration in the old Nottingham and Brampton wares.

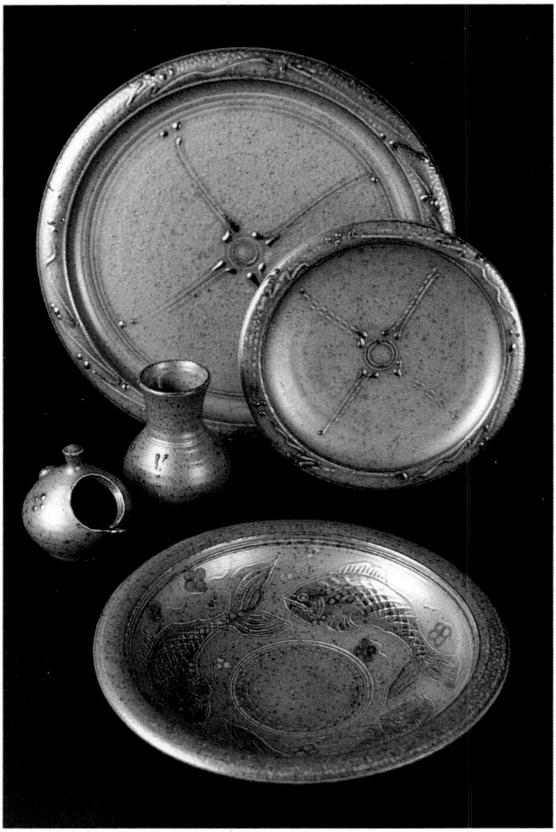

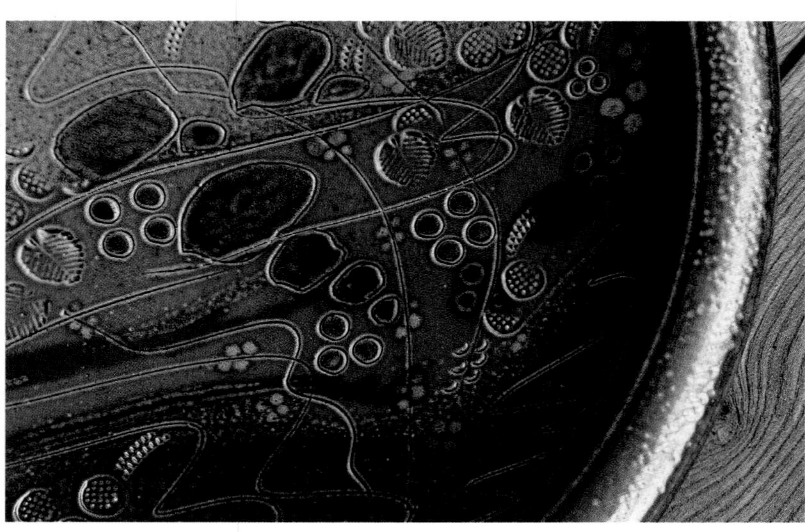

Detail of 'Field Flower' plate by Toff Milway, 2000.

Toff Milway

Toff Milway joined the Harrow course in 1970. There he was introduced to kiln building by Walter Keeler, and was inspired to make high-fired salt glaze by Gwyn Hanssen. Salt glaze became his passion, and although he spent some time abroad, he continued to produce salt-glaze pots – even while working in Lesotho in Southern Africa. In 1985 he established his own salt-glaze studio workshop in the Cotswolds. He has developed his own distinctive style of functional pots, which reflects his enjoyment of good food and his enthusiasm for life.

The pots range from those with strong, smooth and quiet surfaces to others that belie a very simple range of raw materials with their riot of decorative surface textures and colour. Toff uses a variety of decorative techniques, including dipping, pouring and trailing the liquid clay slips on a very fine ball clay-based clay body. The qualities of the old Nottingham wares are called to mind with his use of rouletted lines and sgraffito, and the light coating of glaze. The elegant lines of his jugs and containers combine the traditions of English slipware and practical country pots. He remains dedicated to the practical use of his pots, and his work shows an instinctive response to the qualities that salt glaze can offer for functional surfaces.

Toff's work displays a beautiful range of subtly salted surfaces, and is a wonderful example of the wide variation that can be achieved with only a few carefully selected materials. These are offered to the salt vapours in a closely attended firing. He says:

> I use one clay body based on a blend of two fine ball clays, with additions of fire clay for speckle, molochite to extend the firing range and adjust shrinkage, and some nepheline syenite added to control the free silica. Texture in the clay is achieved by the addition of various grades of fine sand, according to the effects required. I work with two main slips, with a further blue slip for trailing and one for banding. I use only one glaze, and that is for the interiors that are required to be smooth and hygienic.

Clay Body

BKSL	30
HVAR	30
Fireclay	20
Molochite	15
Nepheline syenite	2.5
Red sand	2.5

Glaze

Inside (liner) glaze SHZ 67

Nepheline syenite	30
Cornish stone	8
Potash feldspar	17
67 Hyplas clay	25
Dolomite	9
Zirconium silicate	3
Silica	5
Yellow ochre	1

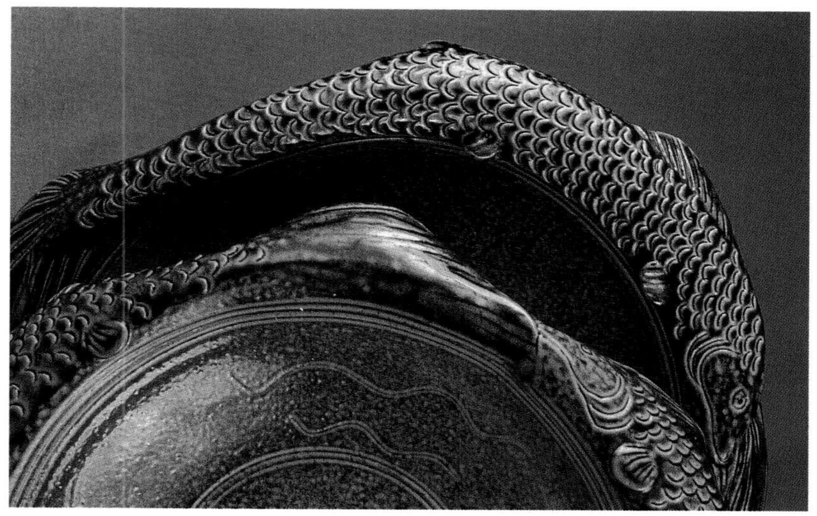

Detail of two fish-handled dish by Toff Milway, 2000.

Slips

Fireclay slip

Fireclay	45
China clay	45
Potash feldspar	10

Porcelain slip TK2

Potash feldspar	36.5
AT ball clay	36.5
(Hyplas 67 for white)	
China clay	18
Silica	9

Blue slip B61

Sodaspar	14
Potash feldspar	6.5
China clay	33.5
Quartz	24.5
Fireclay	19
Hyplas 67	1.5
Cobalt	0.7
Black iron	0.5
Manganese	0.5

Blue banding slip BB25

Sodaspar	25
Potash feldspar	25
China clay	25
Silica	25
Cobalt	1
Red iron	2
Manganese	0.5

Detail of teapot and plate by Gus Mableson, c.1989.

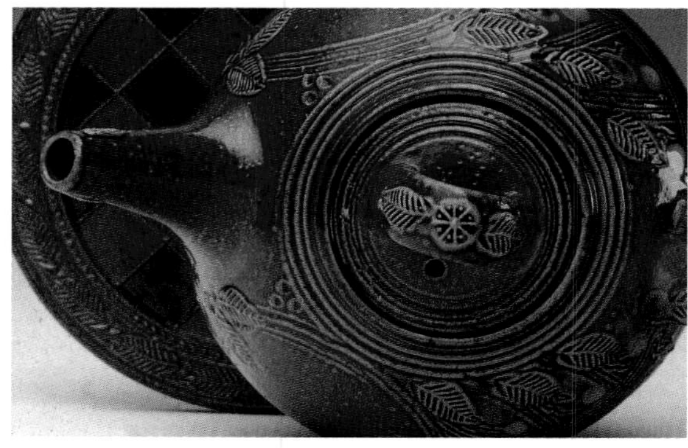

Gus Mableson

Gus Mableson established his first workshop in Northamptonshire in 1978, producing salt-glaze functional pieces, including architectural commissions. Traditional Nottingham wares were a huge influence on his early work. He decorated his pots using a number of tools: metal roulettes, plaster stamps giving low-relief designs, and wooden tools for drawing and scratching marks in the clay, which were then picked out by the salt glaze. Since he moved to Ireland in 1990, Gus Mableson has been involved in building four salt kilns; but he has only recently started to make his own salt-glaze pots again, using a 2.26cu m (80cu ft) wood-fired salt kiln built at Thomstown, County Kilkenny, shared with a group of seven others.

Clay Body

Potclays 1120 (buff body)

Slips and Glazes

Blue slips

1120 clay
¾% cobalt oxide

Tan slip

AT ball clay	2
Nepheline syenite	1

Blue shino (used on the outside of pots)

Nepheline syenite	5
AT ball clay	2
Cobalt oxide	½%

(RIGHT) 'Sconce' by Maureen Minchin, 1987. 40cm high, 'T'material, with variety of slips and glazes.

(BELOW) Blue teapot and plate by Gus Mableson, c.1989.

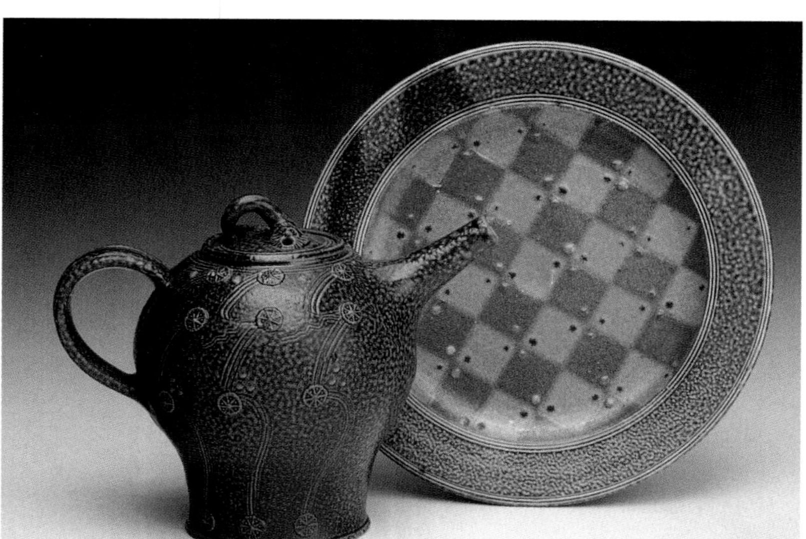

Dartington 1980s

An interesting number of recipes come from the days that Andrew Osborne, Jennie Hale and Maureen Minchin were on the Dartington Pottery Training Workshop course. Several potters took time to experiment with their own

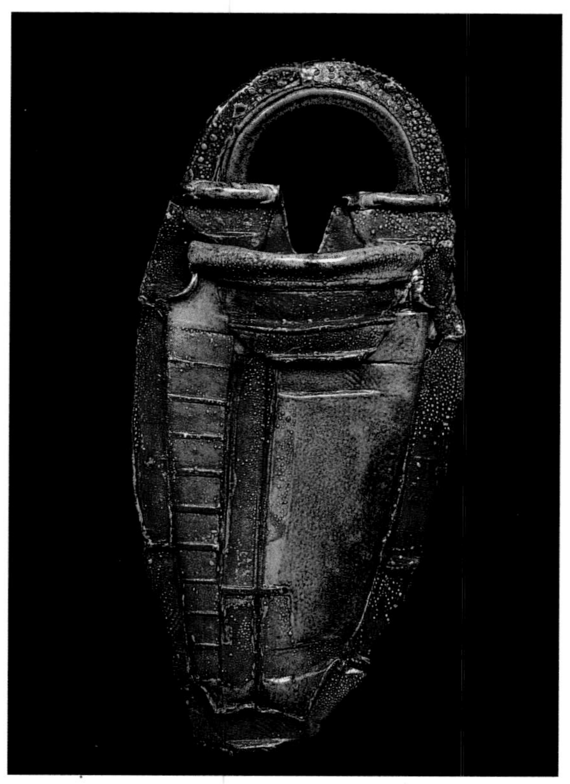

work, and became involved with firing the salt kiln there. Several went on to make salt glaze at their own potteries.

Clays

Franco's porcelain salt body

Grolleg	50
AT ball clay	25
Feldspar	15
Silica	10
Fine grog	5
Bentonite	5

Petro's clay

TWDV	3
HVAR	9.5
Leeds fireclay	1.5
Fine grog	0.5
China clay	0.5
Potash feldspar	0.5

Maureen's clay

Hyplas 71	70
Grolleg	20
Nepheline syenite	8
Molochite	6

Andrew's clay

Hyplas 71	50
AT ball clay	50
with 5% added sand	

Slips and Glazes

Paul's earthenware

HVAR	83.6
Nepheline syenite	16.5
Cobalt oxide	2

Annie's Blue, also used thick for trailing

SMD	50
China clay	50
Quartz	10
Cobalt carbonate	0.75

Dark blue-black

SMD ball clay	80
Potash feldspar	10
Quartz	10
Cobalt carbonate	1

Further Recipes

From Michael Casson

CLAY BODIES

Harry Davis type, at times added 5–8% sand and/or molochite.

Hyplas 71 ball clay	75
ECC Porcelain powder china clay	24
Cornish stone	1

A lighter iron-bearing body

Hyplas 71 ball clay	35
AT ball clay	35
China clay	8.5
Keuper Marl red	8.5
Fireclay (Leeds)	8
Sand	5

SLIPS

Blue slip on raw (thicker) or biscuit

Nepheline syenite	50
Hyplas 71 ball clay	50
Cobalt oxide	1
Iron oxide	2
Chrome oxide (gives a variation)	0.25

Orange slip (must be thin to avoid crazing)

China clay	30
Nepheline syenite	10
Calcined china clay	15
TWVE ball clay	25
EWVA ball clay	25
Quartz	5

Jeremy Steward

Wood fires with soda.

Clay Bodies

Two recipes mixed from dry ingredients:

Hyplas 71	50kg (112lb) (2 bags)	–
Hymod AT	25kg (56lb) (1 bag)	–
HVAR	–	76kg (168lb) (3 bags)
China clay	25kg (56lb) (1 bag)	25kg (56lb) (1 bag)
Fireclay	1.8kg (4lb)	3.6kg (8lb)
Sand	7.4kg (16lb)	5.4kg (12lb)
Nepheline syenite	3kg (7lb)	3.6kg (8lb)
Potclays keuper red	2.7kg (6lb)	–

Slips/Glazes

Shino types

Hymod AT ball clay	36
Nepheline syenite	27
Potash feldspar	27
China clay	10

or

Nepheline syenite	35
TWVE ball clay	45
China clay	20

Liner glaze (olive green)

Iron-bearing stone dust	25
Granite dust	17.5
Hyplas 71	30
Wood ash	24
China clay	3.5
Bentonite	3

Sarah Walton

For hand building:

Hyplas ball clay	50	(2 bags)
Fireclay	37.5	(1½ bags)
China clay	12.5	(½ bag)
Sands, grogs and molochite		15–35%

CONCLUSION

Clay, slip and glaze and recipes are endless. These are selected from ones that have proved reliable for the named makers, but taking risks and trying different combinations of materials is a way for makers to extend the possibilities of the vapour-glaze process.

8 Kilns

Any serious kiln-building project involves a considerable investment of time and money, and before embarking on building a new kiln it is advisable to consult specialist books on the subject, and gather first-hand information by visiting and talking to other potters. The following section offers some help and advice on ways to approach building the kiln for vapour firings. The vapour agent, salt or soda, and the way in which it is introduced into the kiln, have a bearing on the choice of building materials and other aspects of kiln design. There are a number of specific questions to be addressed during the planning stage, and the answers to these are interdependent and will be specific to each situation.

Making Plans

The Location of the Kiln

Assuming that any necessary permissions and approvals have been granted, both the safety and practical aspects of the site must be considered together. If the kiln is built outside there will certainly be plenty of air circulating around it, but adequate shelter will need to be constructed to protect it, and those working around it, from the elements. Packing and firing a kiln while being battered by inclement weather is not an essential ingredient of salt glaze. Outside there will be plenty of space in which to work, but all the kiln furniture will need to be stored dry and reasonably close to the kiln.

Outbuildings serve well as kiln sheds, but there must be ample ventilation through open windows and doors to ensure that any fumes from the kiln cannot accumulate. Avoid siting the kiln too close to the inner walls, or in a corner with inadequate space to move easily around it. As the firing progresses, the outer walls of the kiln give off considerable heat, and it can become very difficult to manoeuvre in a hot tight space, especially around the flue, to check the spy-holes, adjust the damper or attend to the burners. Awkward situations can be avoided in the initial planning stages.

Additional space is needed around the kiln not only to store the kiln furniture and 'wicket' bricks, but also to bring the pots and to prepare for the firing. The bigger the kiln, the more space is required. How the fuel will be delivered, stored and how it will reach the kiln, needs to be worked out at the same time as determining the site.

Fuels

Any high temperature vapour firing needs a live flame from a combustible fuel, the options today being wood, oil or gas. Each has its

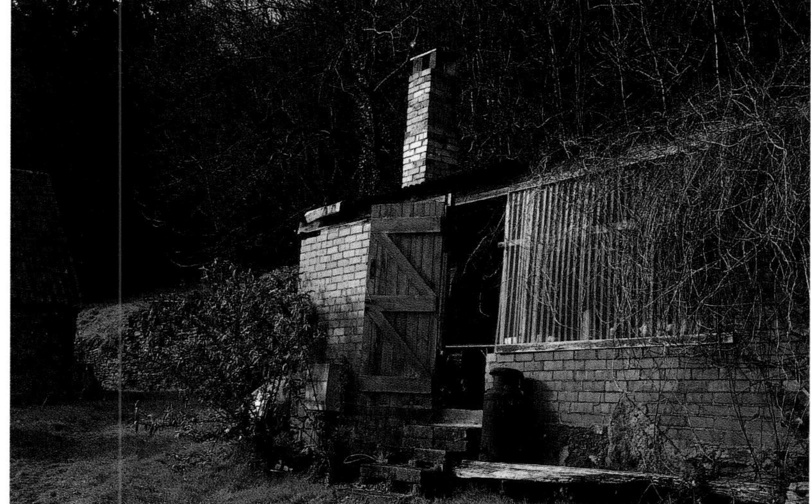

The salt kiln at Rosemary Cochrane's pottery was built in a redundant chicken shed.

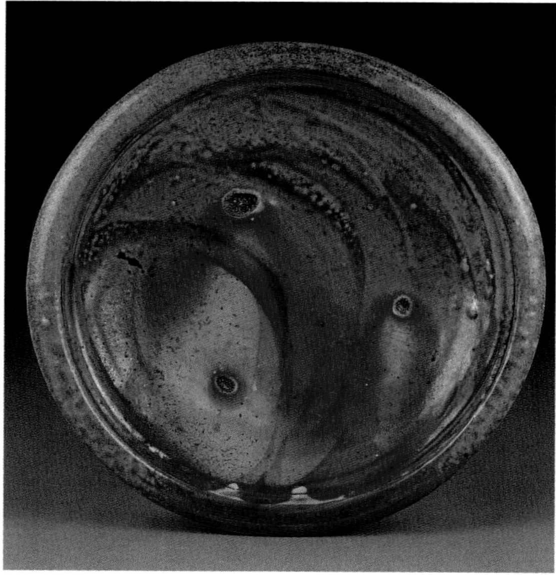

Deep plate by Jeremy Steward. 10½in. Wood-fired soda glaze.

advantages, disadvantages, and different aesthetic merits. In Britain, approximately half the potters engaged in vapour firings are using gas, and the remainder use oil and wood, in roughly equal numbers.

The glaze qualities from a successful wood-fired salt or soda kiln can be the richest and most exciting of all. The combination of the flames and ash deposits produce both subtle and dramatic surfaces that no other firing can. Undoubtedly any wood-fired kiln is best suited to a rural location, as smoke is an unavoidable part of the process. Readily available timber supplies, adequate space for delivery, and covered storage for seasoning and drying the timber all have to be organized. Furthermore a wood firing can be a long and exhausting event and is best undertaken with a small team of willing helpers.

Oil burns with a long, hot flame that favours the distribution of the salt vapour and an even control of the kiln atmosphere. Colours in salt glaze can be enriched by traces of impurities in oil. But it is also possible that oil will contain small amounts of sulphur, and this can be the cause of unpleasant deposits on the surface of the pots. The cheapest source of oil is to recycle waste sump or drain oil, but it is certainly the dirtiest to handle and burn. Heavy fuel oil, such as for a domestic central heating system, is generally the choice for firing a kiln. Oil needs to be stored in a large capacity tank and gravity-fed to the burners.

All burners work on the same principle, using a supply of forced air to produce a fine spray of oil. They range from home-made fittings, to those that are sophisticated and expensive. Electricity is needed to power the source of pressurized air that atomizes the oil, and in a rural area where the power supply may not always be

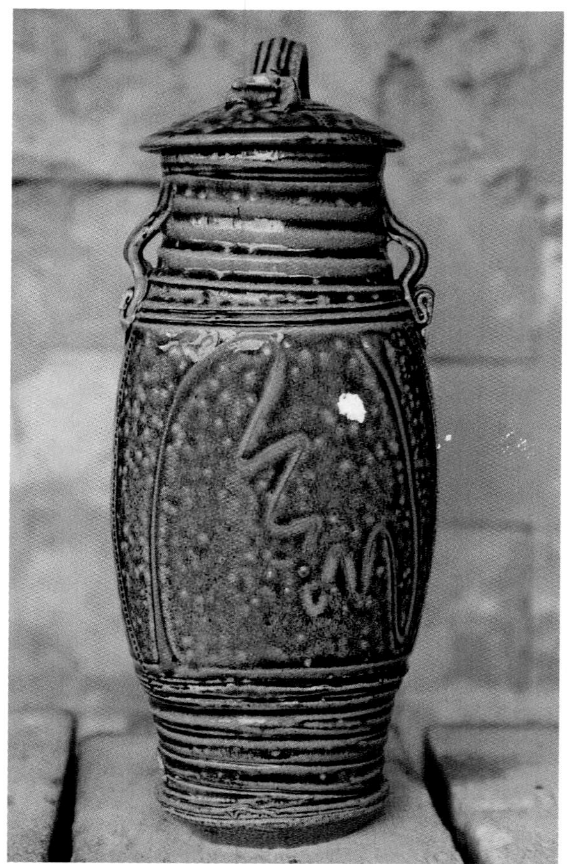

(RIGHT) Tall, lidded jar by Barry Huggett. Gas-fired salt glaze.

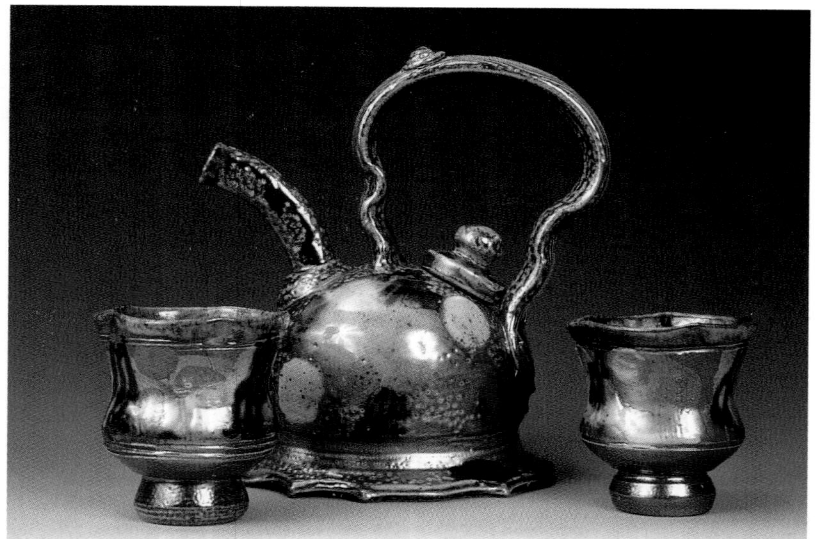

(BELOW) Teapot and two tea bowls by Richard Dewar. Oil-fired salt glaze.

reliable, it is advisable to have a generator standing by. There is only one way to fire with oil without using a source of forced air and that is with a system of plates onto which the fuel drips, vaporizes and burns.

Gas may be either propane, or natural/mains: as the majority of vapour kilns will preferably be sited in rural areas, the most likely gas supply will be propane, either bottled or from a large storage tank. Gas bottles are heavy and need safe storage. Once the choice of building materials and the size of the kiln have been decided, the manufacturers will be able to advise on the number and size of suitable burners. The fittings, pipes, regulators and burners must be assembled in consultation with a qualified person. Gas is relatively easy to control for oxidation and reduction, although depending on the kiln design and number of burners, some potters find that the generally shorter flame length can inhibit vapour distribution. Introducing suitable-sized lengths of wood into the firebox at stages during salting can help to enliven the flame-path. Oil can also be used to the same effect, by setting up a pipe above the gas burner to drip-feed oil onto the gas flame.

Costs

In terms of the comparative fuel costs, it is not possible to be precise. Those of oil and gas fluctuate from year to year and according to the world market. The source and price of wood supplies, including delivery, will be specific to any one area. The size of the kiln, and the type of brick used to construct it, will obviously affect fuel consumption, and good insulation will undoubtedly conserve heat.

The Size of the Kiln

For those who wish to try vapour firing on an experimental scale, the solution is a small, simply constructed kiln. Ideas for a test kiln are given later in the chapter. Such a kiln can also be useful for firing small batches of work, and a portable version useful for demonstration firings. But if the fascination with salt glaze leads to a serious commitment to the whole process, then deciding how big or how small a kiln to build will involve thinking about the way you like to work.

Unless the plan is to fire large sculptural forms, a kiln with a large capacity means that a considerable volume of work must be produced to fill it. Predictably firings will be less frequent. This may suit some potters and can be a spur to making, but to others it can seem a daunting task, and a struggle to maintain the momentum of a comfortable cycle of making and firing. A large kiln also means that each firing will represent a big investment of work. The chance to experiment with the kiln atmosphere, and other variables during the firing, will risk everything. On the other hand, too small a kiln could become a frustration and may not be an economical use of fuel.

Inevitably, any maker's level of production is going to vary throughout the year, and a good compromise would be to build the first vapour kiln to a size that will allow an average of a firing every six to eight weeks. It is invaluable to be able to fire again with the experience of the previous firing still fresh. For this reason, it can also be useful to have the firings back to back. Furthermore, if the kiln is outside, firings in quick succession are a good way to take advantage of better weather, and to avoid wet and cold winter firings.

Building Materials

In the years of the salt-glaze revival, many salt kilns were built from scavenged refractory materials not best suited to salt firings. Understandably, students who build kilns at colleges do not have much interest in their long-term survival, and it can be assumed that the life of the salt kiln is short. Moreover, there is rarely any money to spend on new bricks. Many salt kilns lie abandoned after perhaps only twenty firings, poorly maintained and flawed in their design and structure.

Nevertheless, although the vapour does attack the interior of the kiln, it is certainly possible to maintain the fabric of the kiln so that it will last for a very long time. There are salt kilns built of the better kind of heavy brick which are still in use after over 200 firings. Such a kiln will have been regularly repaired, and some sections rebuilt. Opting for the least destructive method of introducing the vapour agent will also help to preserve the kiln. The alternative ways are discussed in Chapter 9.

Interior of salt kiln. Build-up of salt glaze on 'scavenged' high-silica bricks. Deterioration of unsuitable mortar running down brickwork around the salt port. Bag wall collapsed into firebox.

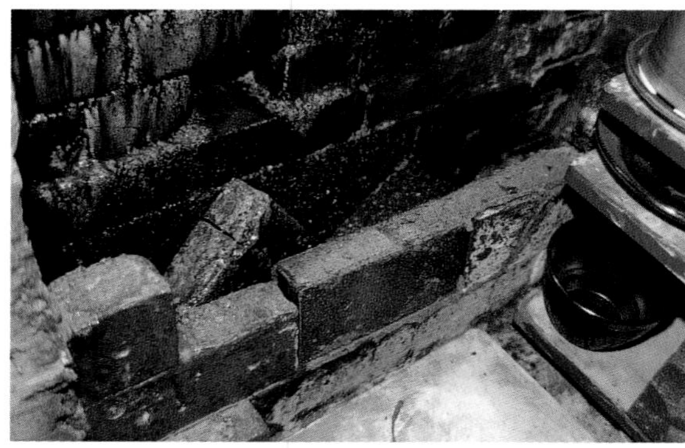

Choice

For a long time it was generally agreed unwise and a waste of time and money to use any type of lightweight insulating bricks for the interior of a salt kiln. It was thought they would be less able to withstand the vapour attack, and would deteriorate very quickly. In some cases this proved to be correct, but in others the opposite was also found to be true. Vapour kilns built of lightweight bricks are still standing after years of constant use, and there are also examples of trolley kilns, built for vapour glaze firings with high temperature insulation bricks, which are still in reasonable repair.

Today it is considered practical to have the choice of either heavy firebricks or lightweight insulating bricks for either a salt or a soda kiln. The over-riding difference is in the initial cost of building materials – but even if funds are limited, it is still worth considering both the options, as considerable fuel savings can be made with the right choice of insulating brick. Whatever the final choice of brick for the main structure of the kiln, it is always recommended that the best grade high-alumina heavies be used for the fireboxes and the most vulnerable parts of the kiln around the salt and soda ports.

Heavy Firebrick

Many free bricks from second-hand sources, such as the dismantled kilns of brick works and the lining bricks of furnaces, may still look to be in excellent condition. However, one serious drawback is that they will almost certainly have a high silica content. They are designed for industrial kilns and furnaces, and are less able to withstand the relatively rapid heating and cooling and repeated firings of the studio pottery. They will also attract the salt vapour, become heavily coated in glaze, and deteriorate rapidly. The brickwork will slag, and the lower structure of the kiln will weaken quickly.

Heavy firebricks, or 'heavies', come in different categories and grades. Manufacturers normally classify them as super, high, intermediate and low duty, and within these classes there are different basic types, each made of a different composition. Either of the middle-duty ones should prove suitable for high stoneware or porcelain temperatures. If you are able to purchase new 'heavies', the ones recommended for the interior of a salt kiln should have a high alumina content of at least 40 per cent, or better still, 60–63 per cent; but any higher, and the percentage of alumina makes the brick more porous and prone to deterioration. Within that choice, there will be several grades at different prices.

The two usual methods of manufacture are dry press, or stiff mud, and they produce bricks of differing qualities. Dry-press bricks are the most uniform, and will expand and contract with the least spalling. The stiff mud process produces a brick that is described as dense, and able to withstand slagging. Note that all heavies are extremely hard, and difficult to cut and shape without machinery. They take up a lot of heat, have a high rate of heat conductivity, and will need a backup layer of insulating bricks on the outer face of the kiln. Many potters still choose to use hard bricks for the inner construction of their salt kilns, and dense firebricks are unquestionably the only choice for the fireboxes.

Lisa Hammond's 90cu ft trolly kiln used for soda firings. The walls and arch are built of insulating bricks; heavy bricks for the base and fireboxes.

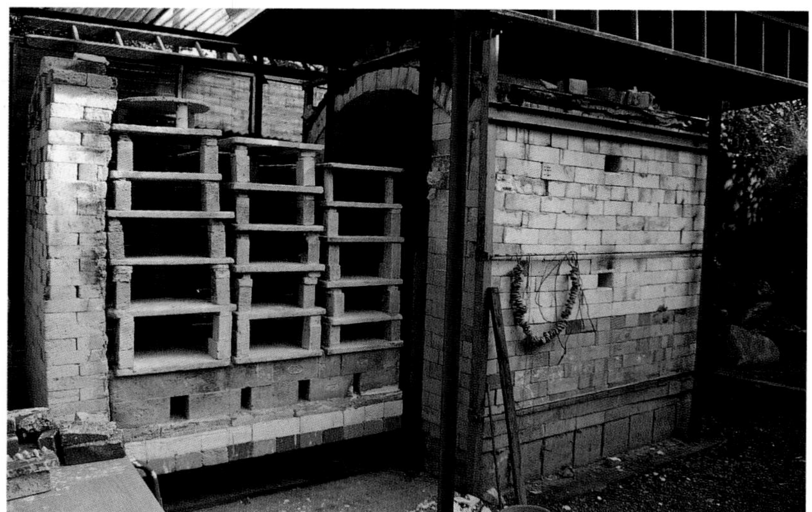

Insulating Firebrick

There are several different types of lightweight insulating brick. Hot-face insulating bricks withstand high temperatures and are used for the interior of a kiln. High temperature insulation bricks, or HTIs, can also be used, but are slightly different in that they are not necessarily load-bearing. IFB is another abbreviation for 'insulating firebricks'. All insulating bricks are manufactured with a mix of refractory clay, and a filler which burns out, or a specially structured aggregate. Either method produces a brick that is easily cut and is up to 85 per cent lighter than a dense, heavy firebrick. They neither store nor absorb much heat, and having a low conductivity, the heat loss is considerably reduced.

Insulating firebrick is categorized by temperature, so the number relates to the maximum service temperature: the higher the service temperature, the denser the brick and the lower the insulation properties. A 26 grade has a maximum service temperature of 2,600 °F – that is, 1,427 °C. This would be suitable for the hot face of the vapour kiln, and is a valid option for salting methods using dry salt or sprayed solutions. However, it is strongly advisable that samples be tested over several firings in another salt kiln, before the final purchase is made. This should confirm that they are not prone to spalling or melting, and are likely to be a satisfactory choice. Investigations continue into the suitability of different insulating bricks for salt and soda kilns.

Peter Meanley's three-year, post-doctoral research is underway, funded under the Arts and Humanities Research Board of UK Universities. His aim is to try to identify the conditions, materials and appropriate application of resists to give salt and soda firers the confidence to build their next kilns with insulation materials. So far the research indicates that there is unlikely to be a definitive formula for success. However, the nature of the bricks and the methods of applying the resist are both critical, and maintaining a watchful repair and renewal system will always remain important.

Mortars

Even if the kiln is to be a permanent structure the bricks can be laid dry, but any mortar mix that is required in building the salt kiln should be made with a high alumina fireclay, as opposed to one that is high in silica. The wicket is dismantled and rebuilt for each firing, and although this, too, can be dry-laid, it needs to be sealed. Two parts sand to one part fireclay makes a suitable mix, and remains friable and easy to clean off. This is also used to seal gaps that appear during the firing, and for clamming up at the end. May Ling Beadsmoore's experience of air-setting cements in the construction of her kiln is described in later pages.

The Wicket and Outer Insulation

The lightweight lower grades, 16 or 20, are useful as a back-up brick. Diatomaceous bricks can also be used as an outer insulating brick. The 'wicket' is the entry into the kiln chamber through which the pots are introduced, and is bricked up during firing. There is some benefit in using hot-face insulation bricks for the wicket, as they are lighter and easier to handle.

The refractory industry is continually updating and revising its list of products. The cost varies according to quality, and the suppliers can provide manufactures' technical data sheets, and advise on your requirements. Superior quality insulation bricks from both Europe and America can be a good investment for the ultimate high-tech kiln.

Arch Insulation

The vapour-glaze process prolongs the firing, and a good layer of insulating material is essential to reduce heat loss and conserve fuel. The

Laying the base of a salt kiln using the minimum of mortar. Catenary arch former in background.

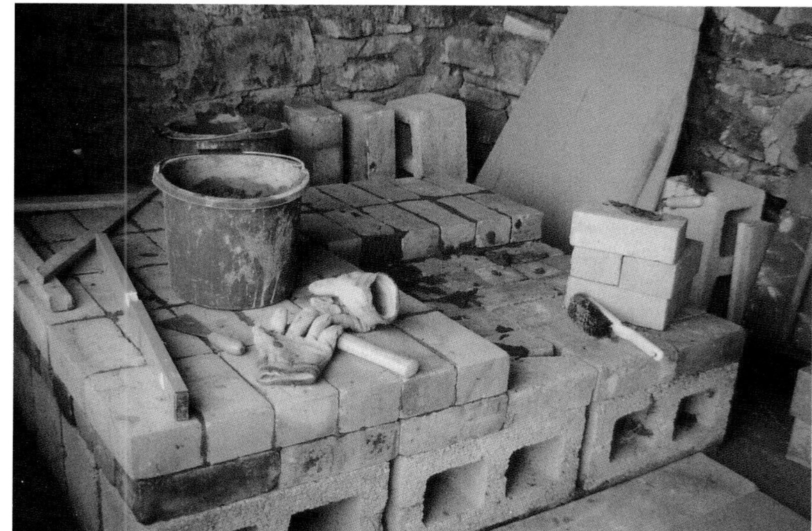

arch can be covered with sheets of fibre blanket or extra coatings of an insulating mix made up with sand, vermiculite, sawdust and fire clay. The proportions for such a mix vary widely, but in principle the sand and fireclay, with a small amount of water, comprise the binding agent and make up the smaller part of the mix.

It is important to protect any timbers in the ceiling or roof from the heat, and additional insulation board should be used to shield and safeguard the vulnerable area above the kiln. Heat loss from the kiln continues long after a firing is complete, and could ignite dry timbers when the kiln is left unattended.

Ceramic Fibre

A European directive now classifies most refractory ceramic fibres as category 2 carcinogens, and also as an irritation to the skin. With these potential risks and hazards to health, every precaution must be taken when it is handled and used. There is no ban on its use, but the British Health and Safety Executive have published their recommendations in an information document. There are alternative products available that can be used, but as a sensible precaution, protective gloves and a facemask should be used when handling any fibrous material.

Castables

Castables are made up of alumina and aluminium-silica coarse aggregates which, when mixed with water in the correct proportion, will harden in thirty minutes and set to a very hard and resilient cement. These refractory products are invaluable when building the salt kiln, and for repairing various sections. As the fireboxes are the hottest part, and also sustain the most attack from the salt, a lining of high-alumina castable will protect this area.

In time, and particularly if heavy, damp salt is introduced over the firebox, even the castable will break down under the salt attack. An accumulation of glaze liquefies and runs into any porous or jointed surface in each firing. However, before the bricks themselves have been subjected to the salt-glaze penetration, the castable can be chipped out and replaced with a new lining.

Castables can also be used to construct the arch of the kiln, but the experience of using castables ranges from highly successful to disastrous. An arch cast as one piece will have great strength and good insulating properties and, in principle, no joints through which the vapour can penetrate and erode the structure. But problems start if stress cracks develop, or if there are large interlocking sections and construction joints open up during the firings. In these circumstances not only do the vapours enter the casting through the cracks, but bits of castable fall onto the pots.

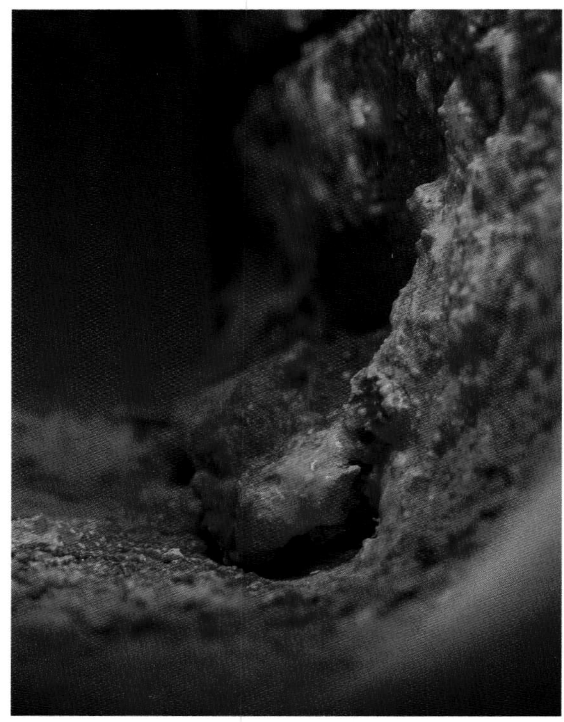

Firebox castable lining in need of repair.

A further drawback is the porosity of high-alumina castable. This makes it susceptible to the salt-vapour attack, more so as the calcium in the cementing agent acts as a strong flux, causing the surface to melt and peel off. A denser, high alumina refractory is called for, but also one that will not crack with the relatively quick heating and cooling of the studio potter's firings.

The choice of castable is therefore critical. As there are many products available it is advisable to consult with the manufacturers or suppliers. All castables have specific instructions on how they should be mixed and applied, and the product's performance depends on this.

Refractory Suppliers

Refractory materials are those that are resistant to high temperatures and suitable for kiln building, for kiln shelves and for other kiln furniture. At the start of the twentieth century the manufacture of refractory bricks had virtually ceased in Britain, and they are now imported from various other countries. The main regional suppliers of refractory products can be found in local directories. Some overseas manufacturers have regular agents in Britain.

Kiln Design

Down-draught kilns are generally easy to control, and give the best circulation of heat and vapour for a salt firing. They are often designed with burners that are diametrically opposed, in order to achieve a good overall flame path and even distribution of heat. A catenary arch kiln, or a box-shaped kiln roofed with either a sprung or catenary arch, are both suitable designs for the salt kiln. The chimney must be high enough to take the salt vapour emissions away from the area immediately around the kiln. Air and damper controls must be able to produce extremes of oxidation and reduction.

SIGNIFICANT POINTS FOR KILN DESIGN AND BUILDING

Specific considerations for building a vapour kiln:

- Refractory materials available
- Budgets for building
- Fuel and fuel costs
- Intended life-span of the kiln
- Salt and or soda

Considerations to incorporate into the structure:

- Salt ports
- Soda ports
- Salt drip system
- Reinforcement around the vapour ports
- Repairable combustion area from where the salt can be distributed
- Protection of the firebox
- Ways to repair or reconstruct the fireboxes
- Repair and support of the bag walls

Factors to favour the long life of the kiln

- Choice of appropriate materials
- Good brickwork
- Hard firebrick fireboxes lined with castable
- Sufficient substantial steel bracing
- Routine repair
- Least damaging method of introducing the salt
- Efficient and economical use of salt

Salt Ports

Salt ports are incorporated at the building stage as loose bricks in the kiln walls. Traditionally they are sited over the fireboxes, either above the burner ports or through the side of the kiln, but the final decision will depend on how the vapour agent is to be introduced. It is a good idea to leave the options open, and to make provision for salting or soda glazing in more than one way. A greater number of loose bricks will be needed for spraying soda, but whether the spray is a salt or soda solution, the best location for the ports may be a matter of trial and error, and will depend on the kiln itself. Insulation bricks are lighter and easier to handle during the process.

Bracing

The base of a kiln will tend to move as it expands and contracts on firing and cooling. In the case of the vapour kiln, the sodium will penetrate any crevices and cracks and cause further deterioration of the fabric. It is especially important to brace the base of the kiln with a substantial metal frame, as well as restricting any likely movement of the arch, front to back. The sodium vapour will attack any metalwork, which should be treated with aluminium paint to keep it from corroding.

Protecting the Kiln Interior

Although many potters would advocate that it is best not to coat the inside of the kiln with anything, there are various remedies that can be adopted to reduce the attack of the salt or soda vapour on the kiln. The first is to apply a proprietary zirconium-based resist that is marketed in Britain under the name of 'Furnascote'. It is

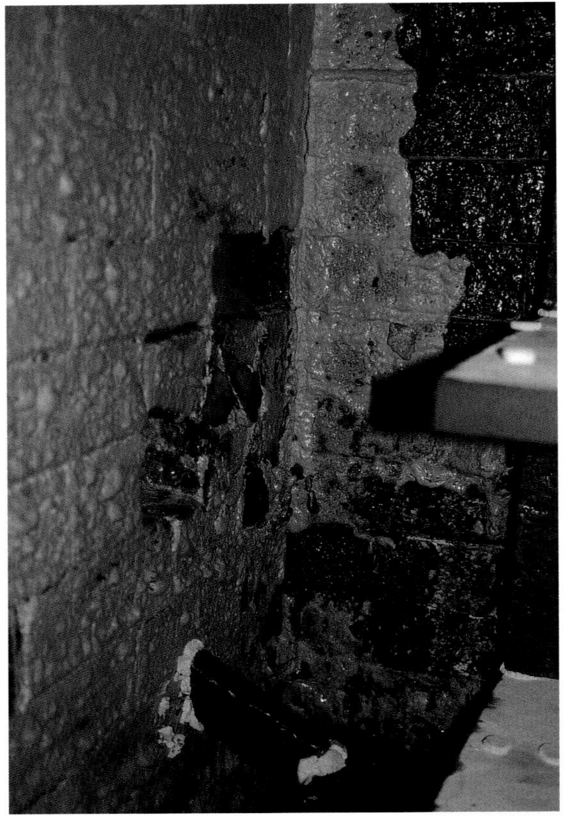

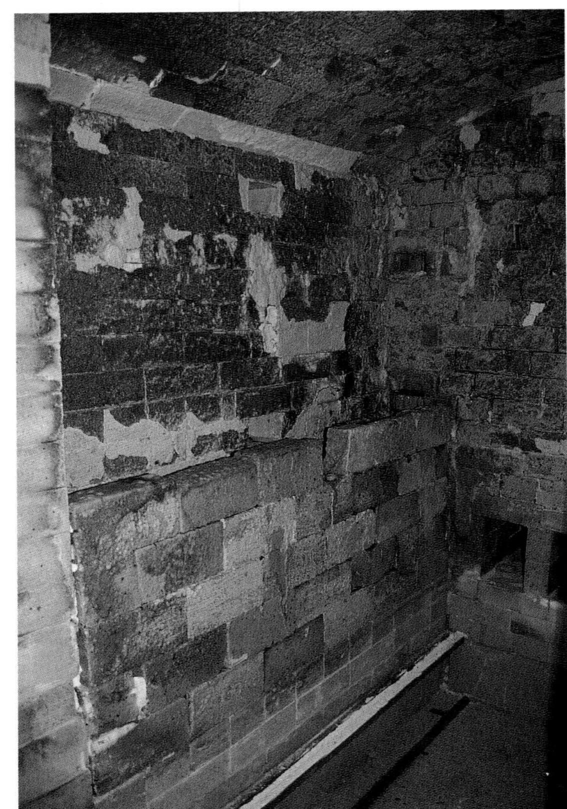

(RIGHT) Deterioration of protective coating in gas-fired salt kiln.

(FAR RIGHT) Deterioration of protective coating on insulation bricks in gas-fired soda kiln.

impossible to either recommend or condemn this, as the experience of potters varies hugely whether they use salt or soda: some have found there is a high risk of the resist flaking off and falling onto the pots during subsequent firings; others have had few problems and are convinced of the advantages the protection has given to the interior of their own kiln. It is certainly important to use it in exact accordance with the manufacturer's directions.

Any resist that is high in alumina will repel the salt vapour. Peter Meanley has used a fine-grained mix of 5 parts calcined alumina, 2.5 parts molochite 130s grade, 2.5 parts china clay and 1 part silicon carbide 220s grade; this is mixed with water and applied in a thin wash before any firing. By dipping the brick in the wash, the coating will cover all the hot face edges of the brick. A series of successive coatings should be applied in following firings, and as the layers accumulate, the areas where it begins to loosen can be tapped off and the coating reapplied.

In Peter's small kiln, 0.4cu m (14cu ft), two coats were worked into the hot face of HTI bricks. Although after successive firings there is some shelling from the walls, it has been considered successful in protecting the bricks from the penetration of vapour attack for over seventy firings. The kiln interior had become very irregular, and kiln cement mixed with alumina hydrate has since been applied to the entire surface. The 'bubble alumina 34' bricks in the firebox are the only ones apparently untouched by the salt.

Another remedy is to spray or paint the inside of the kiln with a coating of a simple stoneware glaze mix before the first salt firing. This will seal the surface of the bricks and help to prevent the direct attack from the salt. The build-up of salt glaze on top of the applied glaze can cause drips to run off the top of the arch onto the pots, although in fact this can be a problem with heavy bricks that are not high in alumina, whether they have been painted or not.

Care and Repair

Emphasis has been placed on the need to look after the structure of the salt kiln, and it pays to heed the early signs of deterioration and to

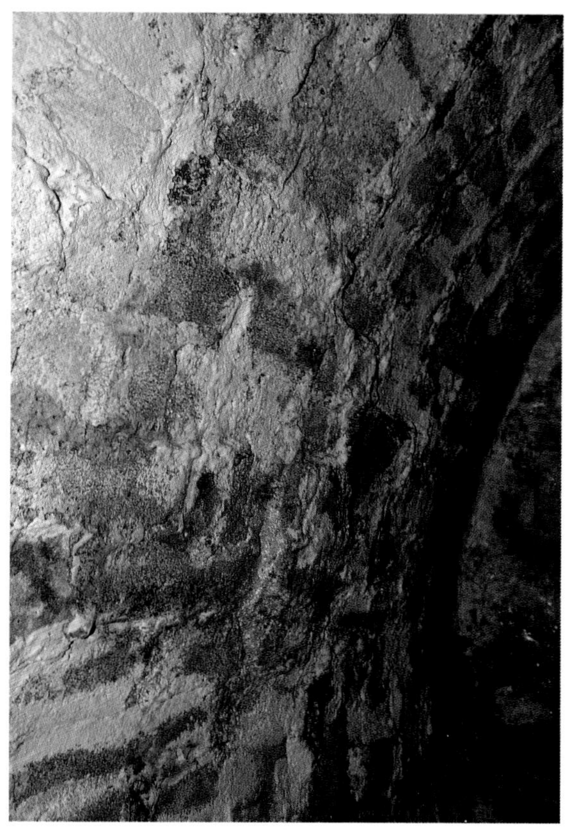

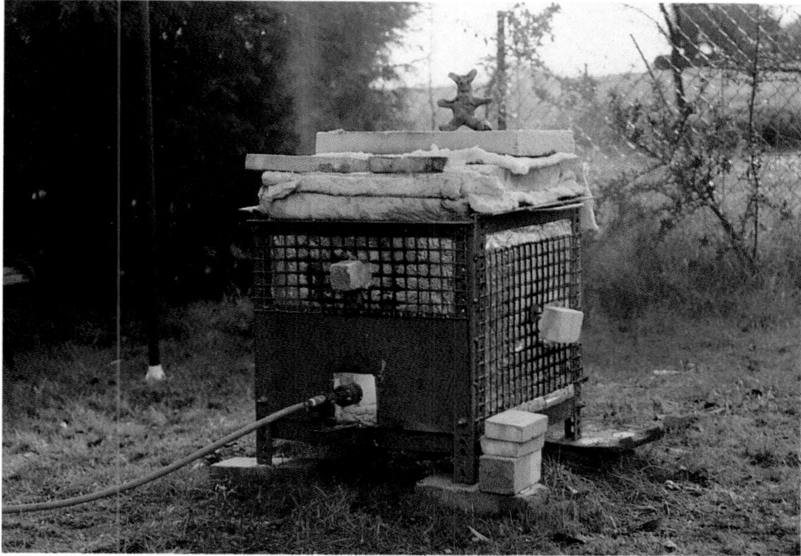

versions have been constructed and fired, and have survived the salt. This type of kiln is suggested for experimental and occasional use – although every care should be taken when handling ceramic fibre, particularly in the construction stages. Steve Harrison has built a test fibre kiln that he uses for demonstrations and workshop days, and for the occasional urgent order.

(FAR LEFT) A well repaired arch of a salt kiln built of heavy bricks.

(ABOVE) Steve Harrison's fibre salt kiln in action.

patch, repair or rebuild as soon as possible. The bag walls may start to lean and need to be supported in some way. If they are dry-laid, with bricks dipped in an alumina resist, they will be relatively easy to separate, and can be turned around to reduce the effects of excessive heat on the firebox side. Less frequent repairs will include replacing the refractory castable lining of the fireboxes.

There is a variety of patching materials based on alumina and kiln cement to repair a salt kiln. Ted Hamlyn has developed one that has been used to maintain the Hamlyn's kiln for over 200 firings. It is made up of a mix of high alumina cement available from any builders' merchant, with the addition of unmeasured amounts of molochite, crushed-up hard brick, and 'T' material, a clay with a high molochite content.

First Salt Kilns

Small Fibre Kiln

Salt glaze is not often associated with small, lightweight, portable fibre kilns, but several

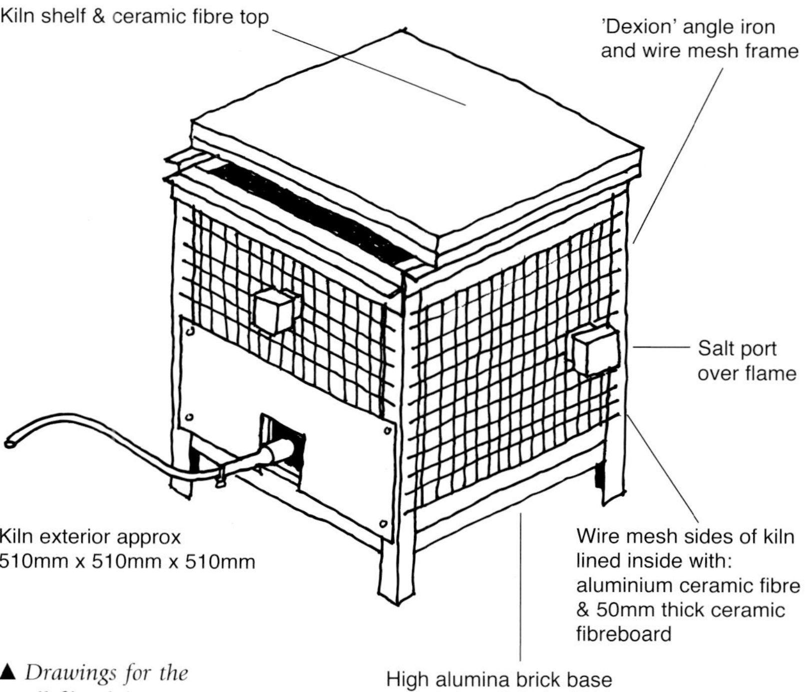

▲ *Drawings for the small fibre kiln.*

(RIGHT) Catenary arch kiln under construction. High-alumina heavy bricks.

A cube is built with angle-iron and an iron-mesh frame, and is then lined with ceramic fibreboard, ceramic fibre blanket and aluminium foil on the outside. The base of the kiln is made of high alumina bricks. 'Furnascote' should be applied thinly to the inside of the kiln before it is first used. Good maintenance is essential to preserve the lining. 'Furnascote' and 'Higlaze' should be applied as necessary and in response to each firing. Steve has not yet had to re-line his kiln after forty firings. The appropriate BTU rating of the burner will depend on whether it is for natural or propane gas.

For a more permanent site, a similar-sized kiln can be constructed using insulating bricks contained within a simple cube of angle iron, but without the need for the wire mesh.

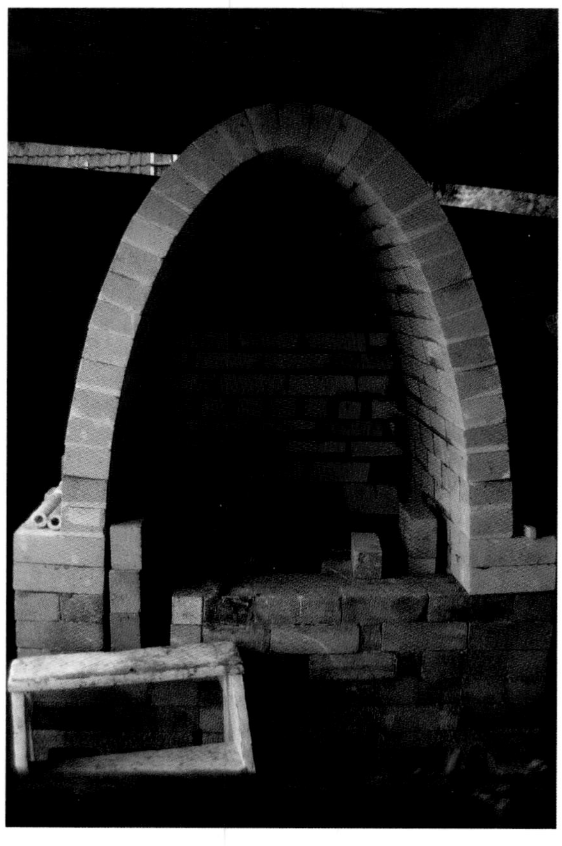

'Fast-Fire' Salt Kiln

Plans for this kiln from New Zealand have been circulating for some years. Jane Hamlyn was impressed when she saw it in action at George Halliday's salt-glaze workshop near Christchurch. It can be fired with gas or oil, requires a total of 250 bricks, and claims to have been fired in four hours using 20ltr of oil.

▼ Drawings of the brick-built 'fast-fire' kiln.

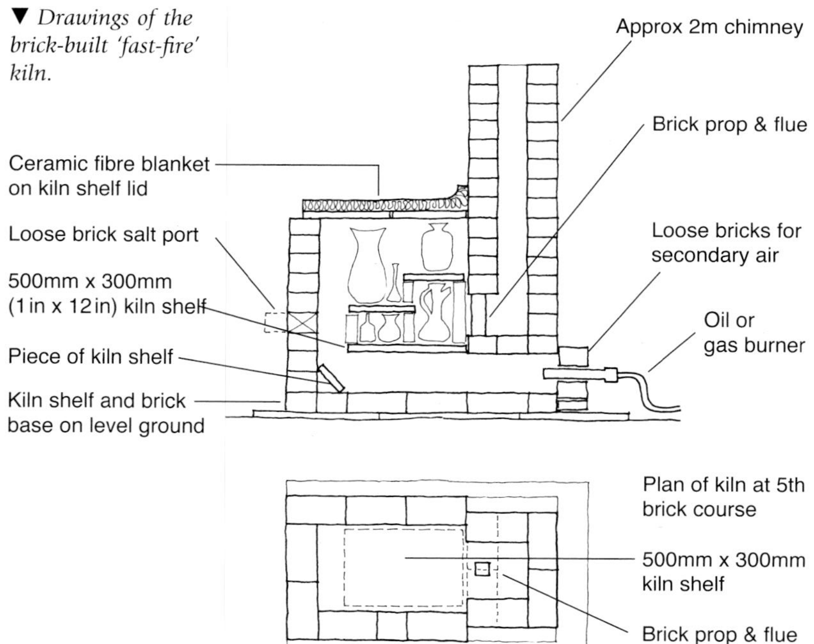

Catenary Arch Salt Kiln

A catenary arch is derived from the curve made by suspending a chain between two fixed points, the inverted curve becoming the arch. It is a particularly strong structure, although for a salt kiln the arch must be braced from front to back; also, because the front and back walls are not tied into the arch brickwork, there is a tendency for a gap between to open out. It has the further disadvantage of being awkward to pack, since the curve reduces the height available at the sides of the shelves, and the diminishing width makes it difficult to place pots on the top shelves.

Small Wood-Fired Salt Kiln

The 'Stubbs-Schloessingk' prototype kiln was built and fired at the 1977 International Potters Festival at Aberystwyth. Micki Schloessingk wanted to develop a kiln that was easy to fire single-handed and would be efficient in its use of fuel and energy. Paul Stubbs helped with the design of a kiln that was fairly simple to build

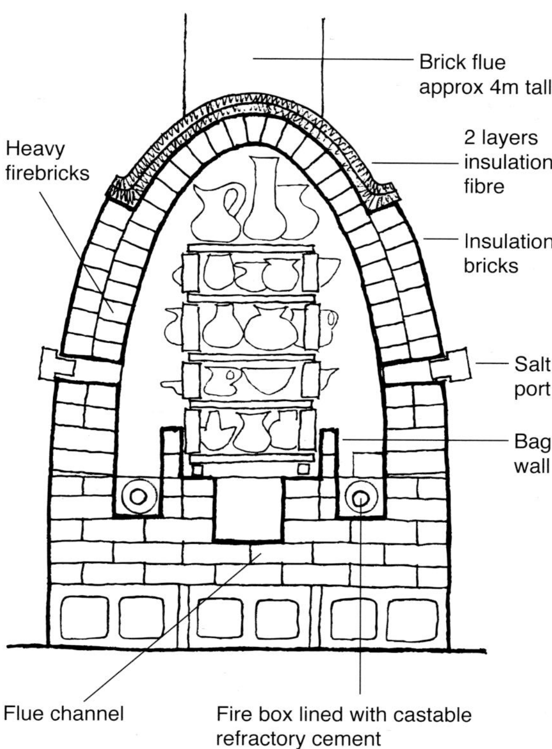

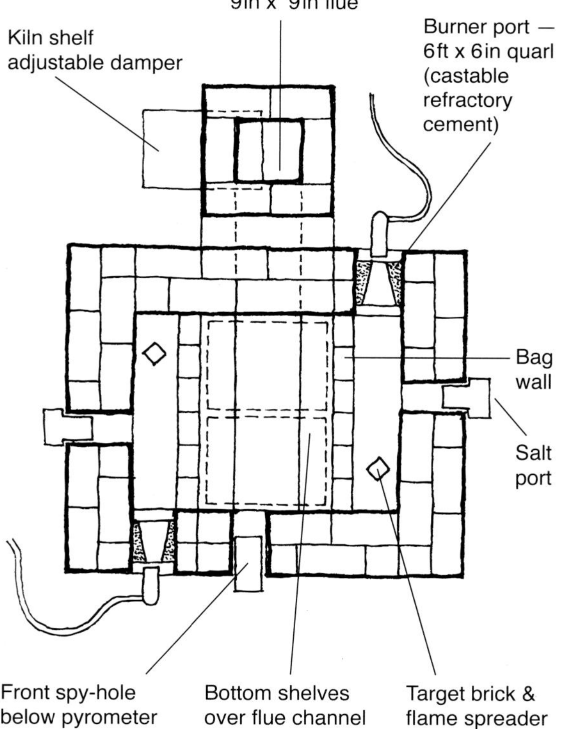

and would be easy on the stoker. A full account and plans of the kiln appeared in *Ceramic Review* No. 170, 1998.

(FAR LEFT) Drawings of the catenary arch kiln used by Rosemary Cochrane.

Production Pottery Salt Kilns

Toff Milway

Toff has been a production salt-glaze potter for nearly two decades, and his experience is of particular interest to those who hope to build a salt kiln that will have a long life. Generally he is seeking a smooth salted surface, but he is also mindful of the damage that the salt has on the kiln fabric. He uses relatively low levels of salt in the firing process, and because of this he finds that the maturity of the kiln and the residual salt it holds is all-important. He says: 'Re-bricking the bag wall or replacing old shelves with new is enough to throw out the balance and can give rather dry effects. Unfortunately, the destructive effects of the salt necessitate regular replacement of shelves.'

The kiln is of a sprung-arch, down-draught design with salt pits beneath the burners. It is fired on liquid petroleum gas with three burners rated at 69,000BTU each, and operated at a maximum of two bar. The first kiln, built in 1986, was rebuilt in 1998 after 150 firings. The chamber is 1.53cu m (54cu ft), and the packing space about 0.85cu m (30cu ft). Originally a 26-grade, soft hot face insulation brick was used for the main body of the kiln, with 28-grade for the firebacks in the bag wall area, super-duty heavy bricks in the firebox area and hearths, and a back-up of 25-grade overall on the outside. Although the interior bricks were affected with a glaze from the salt, it was the 28 higher-grade bricks in the firebacks that had creviced, cracked and spalled the worst. The effect of the salt had also penetrated between the walls in the area around the burner ports, and they were near to collapse.

All the bricks had originally been coated with a glaze wash that survived about ten firings before the outer layer of the bricks began to peel off. This protective treatment was not repeated in the rebuild, and instead the proprietary kiln wash 'Furnascote Non-Vit' and 'Higlaze' was

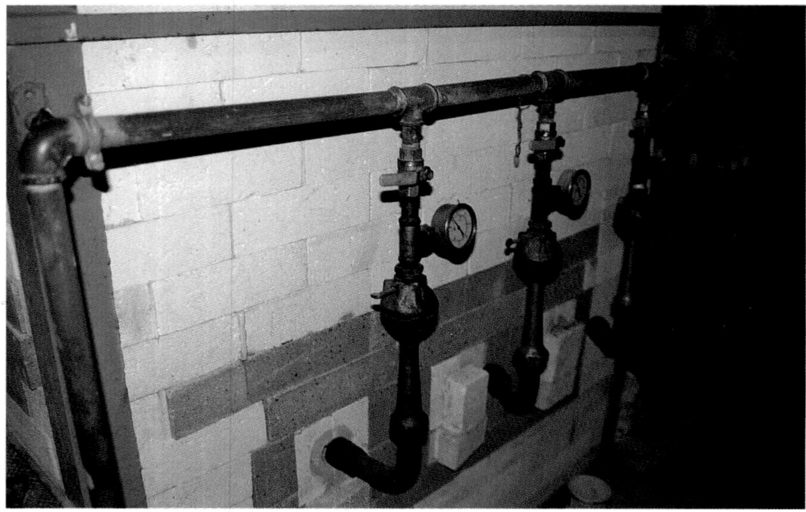

(ABOVE) Toff Milway's gas-fired salt kiln showing heavy brick reinforcement around the salt and burner ports. Salt pits are beneath the burners.

(RIGHT) May Ling Beadsmoore's down-draught, gas-fired soda kiln. Approximately 1cu m, fired with eight Aeromatic Barter burners.

tried. It fell off in sticky sheets after fifteen firings. The 26-grade insulation bricks have been replaced throughout the chamber, and high alumina heavy bricks used to strengthen the areas around the salt and burner ports. Although a kiln shelf is used to protect the top of the stack during the firing, up to 10 per cent of the kiln contents are spoilt by pieces that flick off the walls and roof and land on the pots.

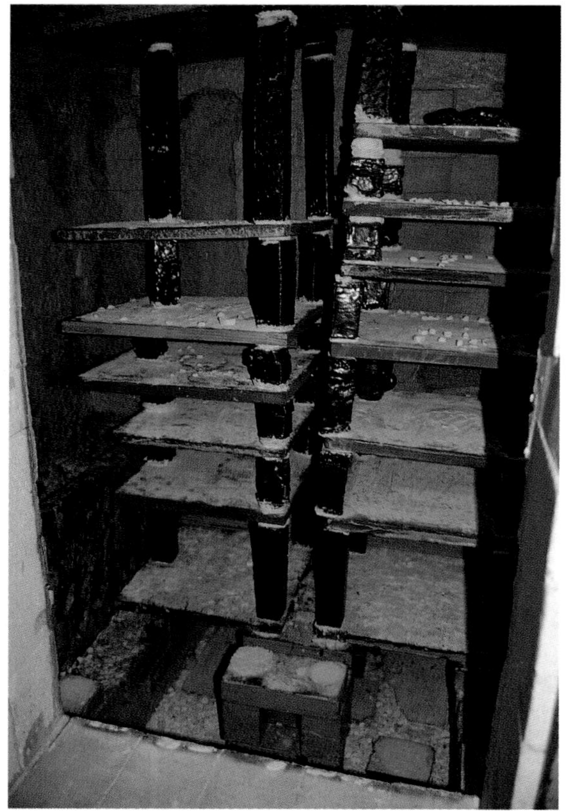

Interior of Toff Milway's salt kiln.

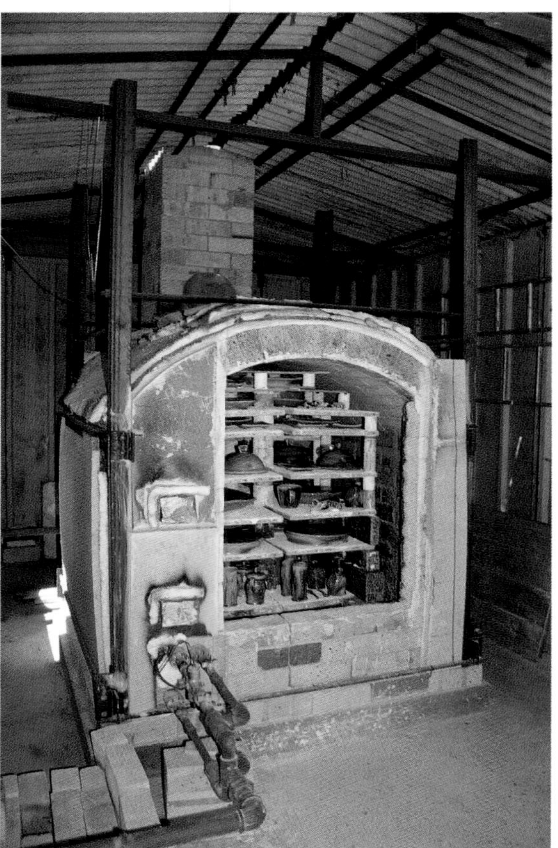

May Ling Beadsmoore

May Ling's 0.76cu m (27cu ft) soda kiln was built from single-skin firebricks with air-setting mortar, and insulated with 25mm (1in) ceramic fibre blanket and 25mm (1in) 1,260°C ceramic fibreboard; 2mm (1/10 in) ceramic fibre paper was pushed into the expansion joints, but has since dissolved. Firebricks were chosen for their longevity and low maintenance, even thought they soak up a lot of heat and firings are relatively expensive.

Two different types of firebrick and mortar were used: for the walls, 42 per cent alumina firebricks with 'wet air-set cement' were used, and after thirty firings this adhesive has melted and run, and there is a crusty build-up on the bricks. For the arch, 60 per cent alumina firebricks with 'BR5 Sairset Ready Mixed' were used, and after thirty firings the bricks and adhesive are almost as new, with no soda build-up. The bricks have spalled slightly, but the adhesive has shrunk very little and has resisted the soda. The air-setting mortar develops a strong bond throughout the entire brick joint.

'Low Tech' to 'High Tech': Suzy and Nigel Atkins

A number of salt-glaze potters in America and Europe have built their recent kilns using the very latest refractory materials, incorporating sophisticated features and firing with high-tech equipment. At present no one in Britain has such experience.

Suzy and Nigel Atkins give a straightforward comparison between producing salt glaze using a traditional kiln, and their more recent experience using a high-tech kiln. Suzy originally trained at Harrow during the 1970s. She set up a pottery in France, with her husband Nigel, making functional salt-glaze ware.

The old kiln was a 3cu m (106cu ft) down-draught kiln with two Swirlamizer induced-air gas burners. The kiln was built with nine spy-holes, plus one usually set in the wicket. The inner walls were built of 43 per cent alumina heavy bricks, with an outer coating of insulation bricks and Rockwool insulation held in place with chicken wire. The useful volume of the kiln was 2cu m (70.6cu ft). Salting took 18kg (40lb) of coarse wet sea salt, manually loaded onto angle irons and thrown into the fireboxes. Suzy and Nigel appreciate that this was a very cheap, medium-sized kiln that served them well once they got to know it; in the end it became increasingly erratic, capable of superb firings, or neatly destroying all the decorated ware in the kiln.

The advantages of the old kiln were its initial cheapness, and its occasional capacity to produce quite astonishing results. The disadvantages were that it was impossible to control in the face of changing meteorological conditions. Salt distribution was uneven, with two areas being so over-salted that they were finally abandoned, losing a tenth of the kiln volume. It was also labour intensive: building and dismantling the wicket alone took seven days each year. Bad firings resulted in seconds and worse; and lastly, the gas consumption was uneconomic.

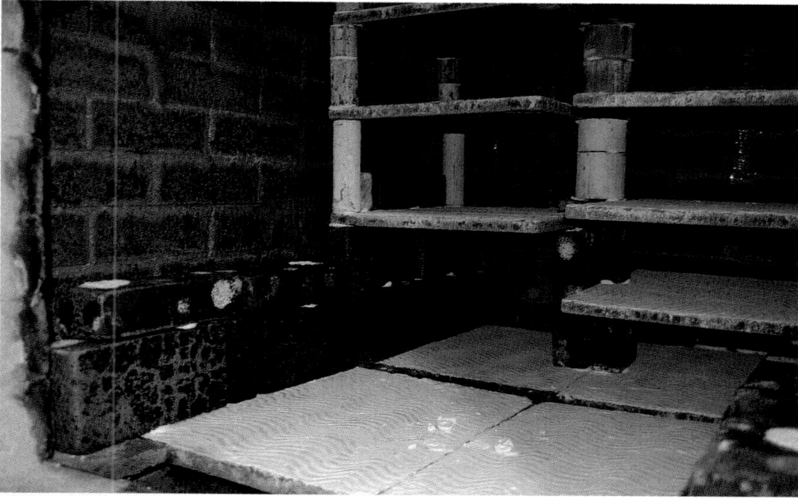

Interior of May Ling Beadsmoore's soda kiln showing bag wall built into the shelf stacks each firing.

The new high-tech kiln has 1cu m (35cu ft) of useful volume heated by four North American forced-air burners. There is no chimney, but down-draught gas evacuation occurs as the kiln fires under positive pressure, expelling exhaust gases into a hood and an exhaust duct above the rear vent. The kiln is built of 60 per cent alumina bricks coated with Polybond zircon-based wash, backed by two layers of insulation bricks and insulation felt. There is a full-width door on the front of the kiln, and one spy. The damper in the rear duct is left permanently open.

The new kiln uses 8.5kg (18.7lb) of fine sea salt, blown into the kiln through refractory steel tubes set just above the flames of the burners. In principle this kiln is a very expensive, reliable, controllable production tool, with normally a long life and thus eventually a low cost per cubic metre fired. It is nevertheless a complicated piece of delicate technology, which requires constant attention and very precise adjustments in order to produce constantly fine results.

Its advantages are listed as easy to load and unload, very reliable automatic control, tiny production of seconds, remarkable glaze results

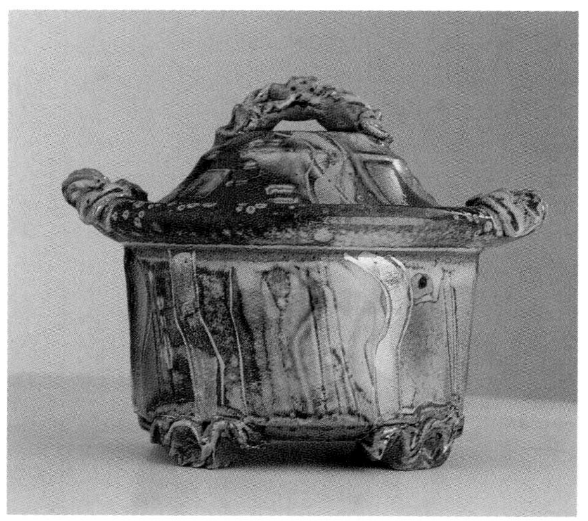

Serving dish on feet by Suzy Atkins, 1990. Fired in the old kiln.

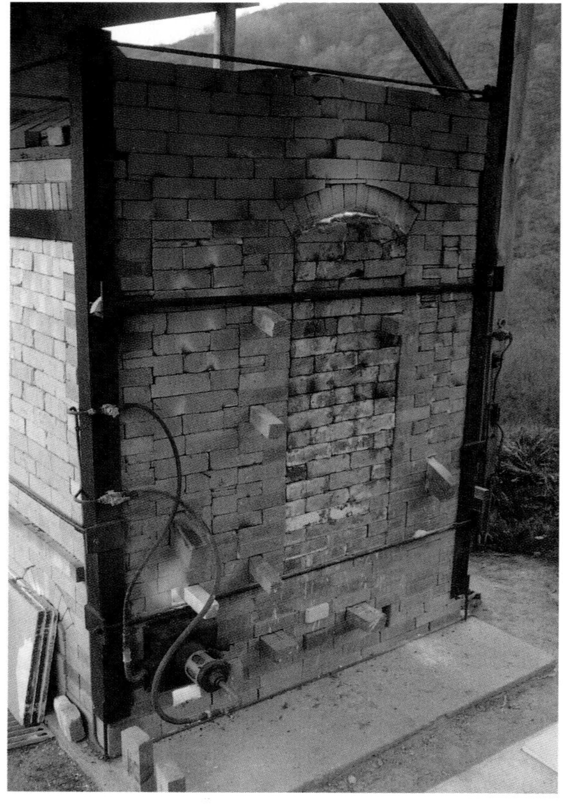

Atkins' old oil-fired kiln.

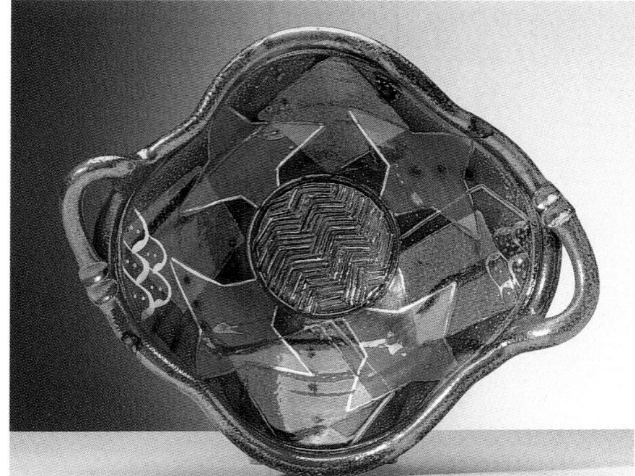

(RIGHT) Dish with handles by Suzy Atkins, 2000. Fired in the new kiln.

on all slips and excellent salt distribution. The disadvantages are its vast initial expense, it is very sensitive to regulate, and there is complicated technology to master.

It is unlikely that anyone would invest in a high-tech salt kiln before building a more conventional, cheaper kiln. However, some of the materials and a simplified technology could be useful for a smaller-scale operation.

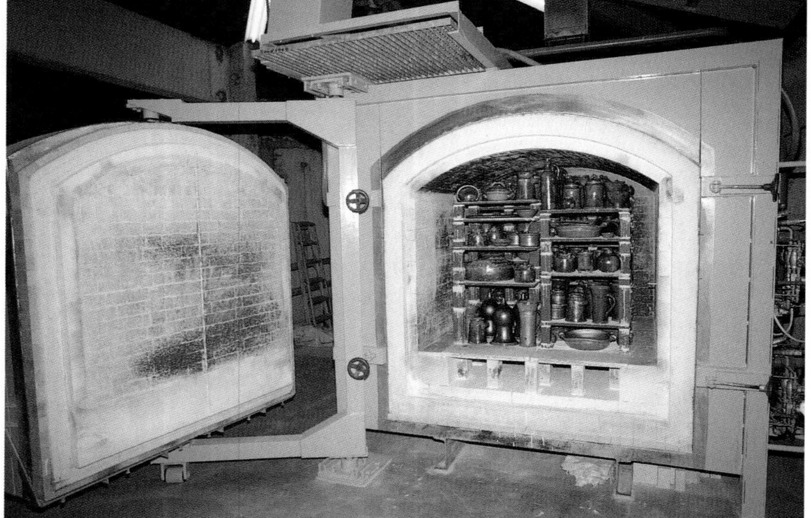

Atkins' new high-tech, gas-fired kiln.

In Conclusion

The problems that are intrinsic to any high-fired vapour kiln revolve around the detrimental effect of the sodium and its inevitable attack on the kiln structure. The perceived difference to the wear and tear of salt and soda kilns is well founded. Soda firings may seem to be less destructive on the soda kiln's fabric because the fireboxes are spared a concentrated attack of an accumulation of sodium. Soda is nearly always introduced as a sprayed solution. When salt is introduced as a brine solution, instead of as damp salt dumped into the fireboxes, the deterioration of the salt kiln is considerably reduced.

Apart from agreement on the use of heavy firebricks for the fireboxes, it is difficult to be categorical about building a salt or soda kiln, and this is borne out by the wide variety of successful vapour kilns. The experiences and views of vapour-glaze potters can vary as widely as the materials they have used, and as the combination of factors at work. Trials continue on the effect that salting has on different insulation bricks and coatings. In one sense they can never be entirely conclusive because of the many variables that are always involved in the way that a salt firing is conducted.

9 Packing, Firing and Salting

Rosemary Cochrane's kiln, wicket down and ready to unpack.

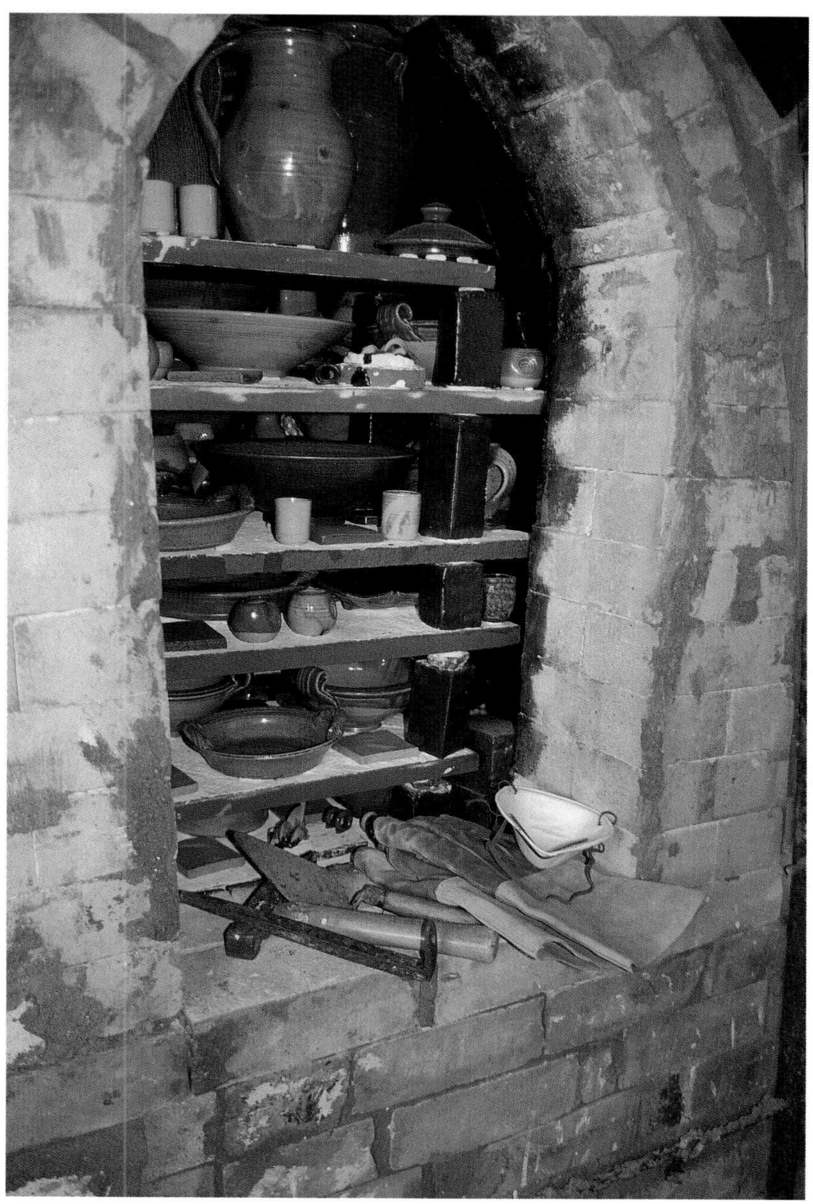

Before any type of coating is applied to the inside of the new salt kiln, it is recommended that the kiln is first fired with pots for an ordinary stoneware glaze firing, without the introduction of any vapour agent. This allows for an initial shrinkage and movement of the bricks, before the sodium starts to attack the fabric. The firing will also give a preliminary indication of the way the kiln behaves. Then preparations for the first salt firing can begin, and the resist or seal applied if that is the choice. Right from the start, it is well worth the time and trouble to attend to any deterioration of the fabric of the structure between each firing.

Preparations for Salt Firing

During a salt firing the vapour will seek to create a glaze on any accessible, receptive surface in its path, unless it is washed with an agent to resist the salt, or held separate with wadding. 'Batt wash' is used to coat the shelves and props, and 'wadding', a dough-like mix of similar non-fusing materials, is used to hold the pots off the kiln shelves, to prevent a lid from sealing to a pot, and between pots that are being fired rim to rim. It is also used between the kiln props and shelves.

Shelves

Shelves made from silicon carbide will last longest in a salt kiln, but they are very heavy, cost a great deal more, and the nitrate-bonded ones that are suitable for a salt firing are not

BATT WASH AND WADDING

Batt Wash Recipe

From Jane Hamlyn:
First, mix a packet of cellulose wallpaper paste to a stiff jelly; then mix . . .

alumina hydrate	4 parts
ball clay (low iron)	1 part

. . . to a thick cream.
Mix together the jelly and cream.

Wadding Recipes

Jane Hamlyn:

0.9kg (2lb)	alumina hydrate
227g (8oz)	china clay
113g (4oz)	ball clay (low iron)
28g (1oz)	grog 80s-dust

Add 113g (4oz) plain flour, and mix with water to a paste.

Gus Mableson:
2 parts flour
2 molochite
2 alumina
1 china clay

The small quantities of flour are added to make the wadding dough more pliable. Wadding should roll out easily to whatever shape is required or can be extruded, from a hand extruder or cook's icing bag, directly onto the base of the pots. If it contains flour, once the water is added it will go mouldy within a few days unless it is stored in the freezer.

Other Mixes:
50 alumina
50 china clay/kaolin

(For kiln furniture, dust the shelves in alumina for improved resist.)
6 alumina
1 china clay
+ Bentonite

(For batt wash or wadding.)
60 alumina
30 china clay
10 flour

(Wadding.)

available in Britain, and have to be ordered from Europe. Most salt-glaze potters are still opting to use 25mm (1in) thick, standard kiln shelves – although those made from sillimanite, with over 60 per cent alumina, are likely to be a better investment.

Generally, shelves should be coated with a resist known as batt wash: this can be applied, according to preference, as either a thin or a thick coating. Apply a thick mix using a wallpaper-paste roller or by dabbing it onto the shelf with a wide bristled brush. A thick application applied smoothly can be scored with a tile-cement plastic comb while it is still wet. This will dry to a hard, textured surface, and if the pot is placed without wadding, it will be resting on many tiny raised pimples of alumina, which will keep it from fusing to the shelf in the firing. The undersides can be left untreated.

Between firings, the shelves may need recoating with batt wash. Layers can be painted on accumulatively, or the shelves can be scraped clean before the new wash is applied – either way the shelves only last for about ten firings. Most begin to spall and flake on both sides, which considerably reduces their original thickness: obviously there must be a calculated risk in continuing to use them. The alternative to batt washing is to carefully sprinkle each shelf with alumina, 80s grade, after the shelves are positioned in the kiln.

The bottom shelves are set on pads of wadding, or rested on pieces of batt-washed, broken kiln shelf, separated by pads of wadding. The height of the bag walls and the first layer of pots can make a big difference to the way the heat and vapour is distributed. Trial and error will determine the best configuration for each kiln.

Props

It is essential that the props on which the shelves are supported are reliable. High-alumina heavy firebricks, cut to various sizes, make the best props: these can be dipped or coated in batt wash so they are more easily knocked apart after a firing. A flattened wad on either end of each prop keeps the shelves from sticking and makes unloading easier. Any small pieces of broken kiln shelf, used to raise the main props higher, should also be coated and wadded.

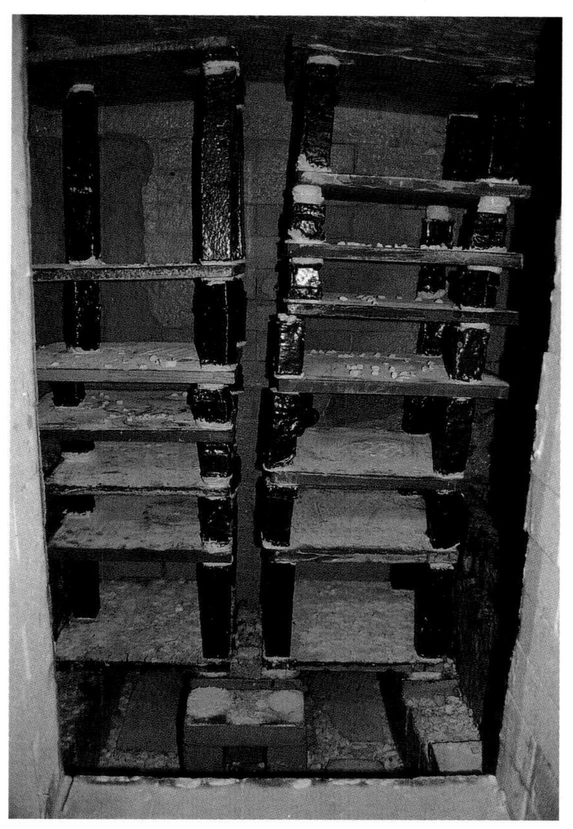

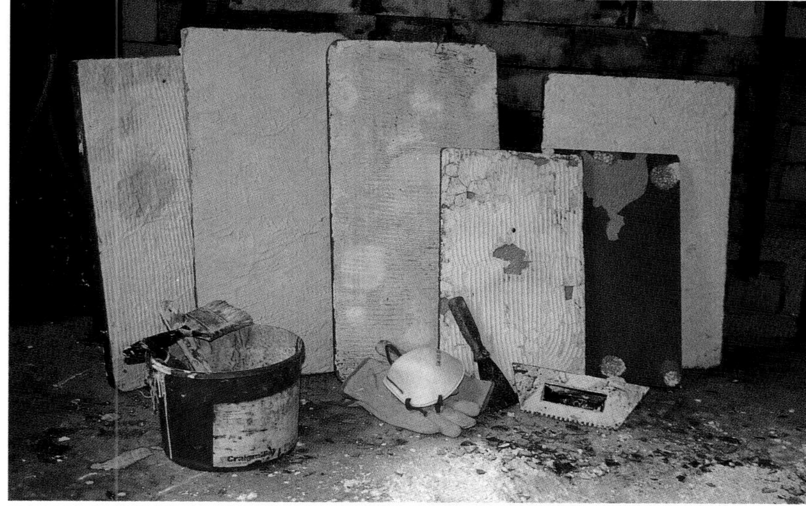

(ABOVE) *Sorting and preparing kiln shelves for a firing.*

(ABOVE LEFT) *Toff Milway's kiln. The shelves can be left* in situ *for several firings if a regular arrangement for the kiln pack suits a standard production of pots. Note the shelves that protect wares from the flaking roof, and shelves dusted in alumina.*

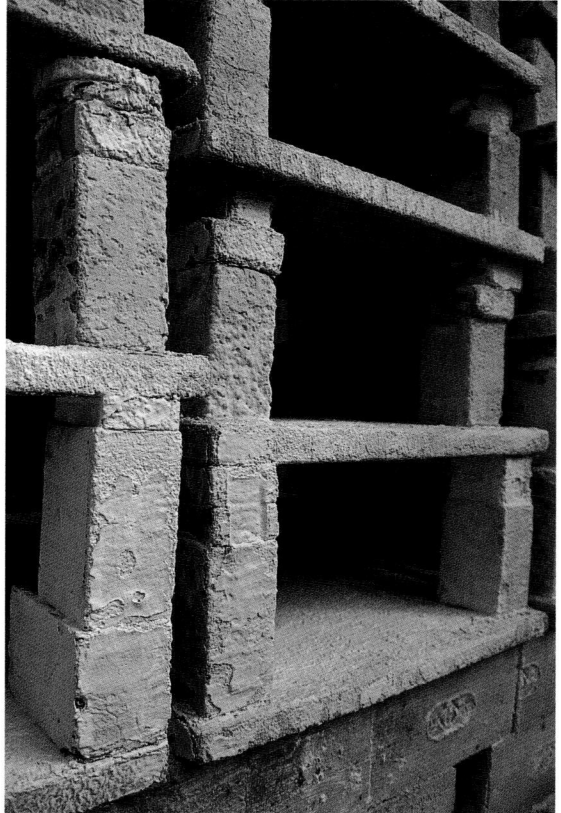

Kiln furniture well coated in batt wash.

CHECKLIST BEFORE PACKING THE KILN

- Clean out and repair the kiln as necessary.
- Check the shelves, clean and apply batt wash.
- Prepare the draw rings and cones.
- Mix the wadding.
- Identify pots for special places in the pack.
- Refer to notes from previous firings.

Packing the Kiln

Packing the salt kiln takes longer than other kiln packs and, as a fundamentally important part of the salt-glaze process, it is worth a lot of thought and care. Stretching, twisting, bending and lifting can put a strain on the back, so it is sensible to minimize the difficulties, and also have the kiln props and shelves conveniently close by.

Placing the Pots

Although a heavily textured, batt-washed surface can eliminate the need for wadding, it is more usual for pots to be placed on wads for a salt firing. Turn any salt-glaze pot over, and find pleasure in the marks that tell of the moment the pot was placed on the kiln shelf and offered to the fire and salt. Bowls can be stacked inside one another with wads or shells holding them apart, and the scars that are left become an acceptable feature of the firing. Interesting

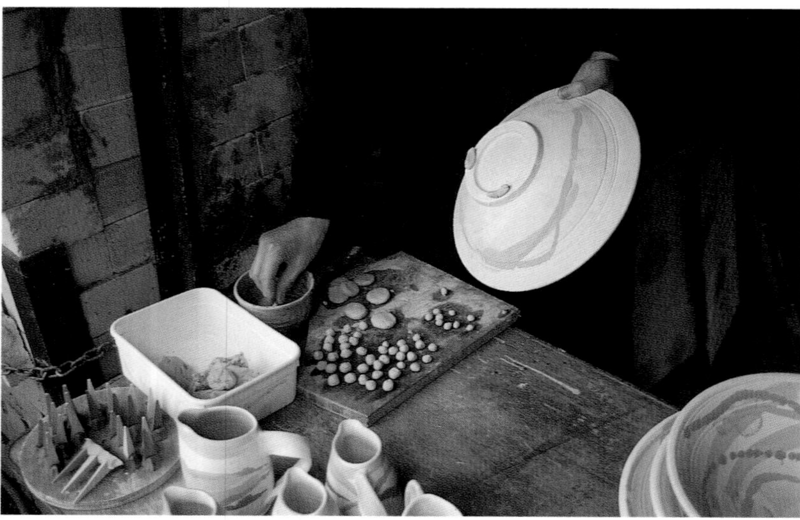

Wadding the pots. Lightly pressing the ball of wadding onto a damp sponge will make it stick more readily to the base of the pot.

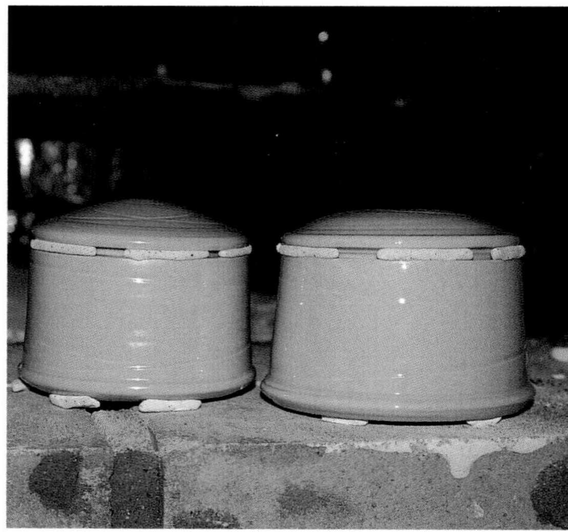

If the pot is finely thrown, closely set wads will prevent the lid warping. Well spaced pieces of wadding can be used on thicker, more robust rims.

effects can result from placing pots of salt or combustible materials in small dishes amongst the pieces. Wood, ash, charcoal or any organic material will cause flashing and local reduction. Wrapping grass, or fabric soaked in salt water, or wire around individual pots will leave distinctive marks, too.

Each pot will need at least three small balls of wadding attached to the base. If the resist on the shelves is inadequate and the pots are placed without wadding, they will risk being damaged by 'plucking'. This can happen when the pot is lifted out of the kiln after the firing, when part of the base is left attached to the shelf. Lids and pots must be held separate by wads. Alternatively, a simple wash of alumina and china clay, brushed onto the rim, will prevent the lid from fusing to the pot.

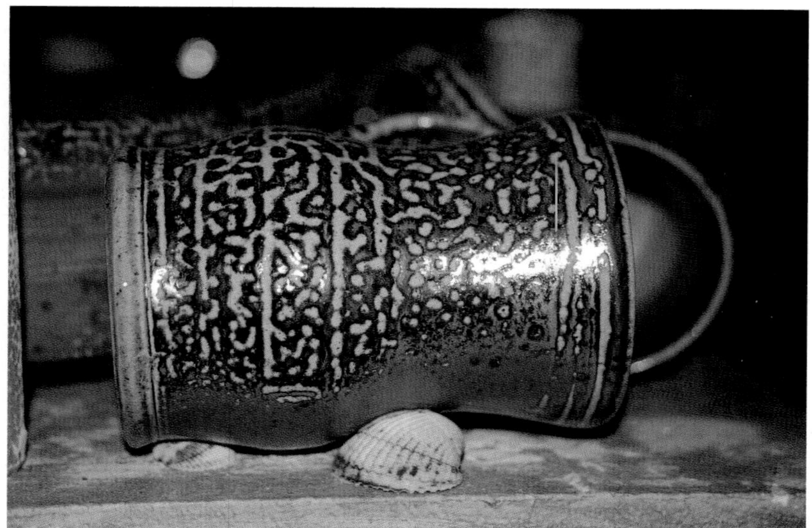

Micki Schloessingk uses cockle shells to support some of her pieces. Shells are rich in calcium and will resist the salt, and the scars make a dramatic reference to the way the pots were fired.

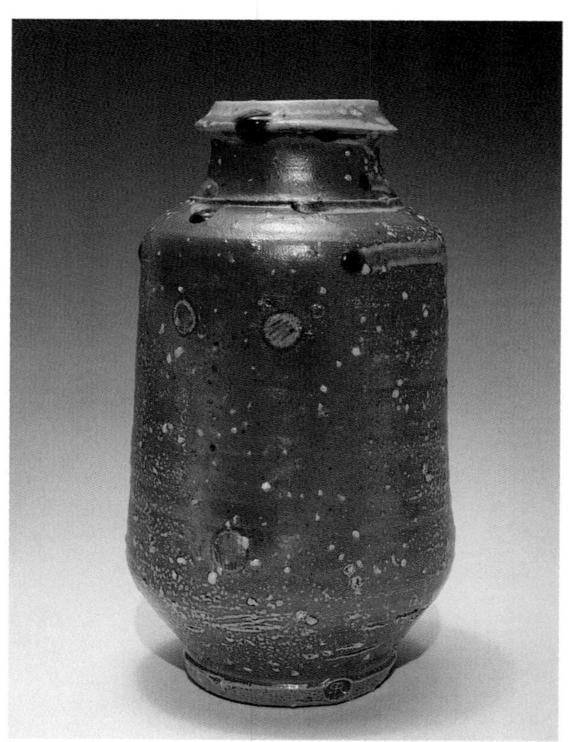

Vase form by Phil Rogers, 2000. 11in tall. This piece has feldspar chips wedged into the body, and has then been fired on its side resting on cockle shells. The intense colour comes from salt starvation and a high alumina slip. There is an ash glaze inside and over the rim.

Every stage in the salt-glaze process has its effect on the pieces, but the position of each pot in the kiln is the final and deciding factor. Imagine the passage of the flames and vapour as each pot is placed into the kiln and the shelves are supported on the props. At first it will be, at best, a guess as to how the salt glaze will develop, and variety is inevitable and wonderful. With experience, however, the kiln can be packed to take advantage of the particular effects that are likely to occur, and slips and glazes can be developed for the different conditions.

The pack will be more open than for any other type of firing, to allow the salt vapours to reach around the surfaces. A few guidelines will help: first, shelves should not sit too close to the pots below. Low kiln fillers are useful to place around the base of larger bowls. Flat ware can be fired on plate stackers that are well batt-washed, and with adequate space allowed between the stacks. Deliberate crowding of pots can produce matt surfaces that are just as seductive as a rich orange-peel.

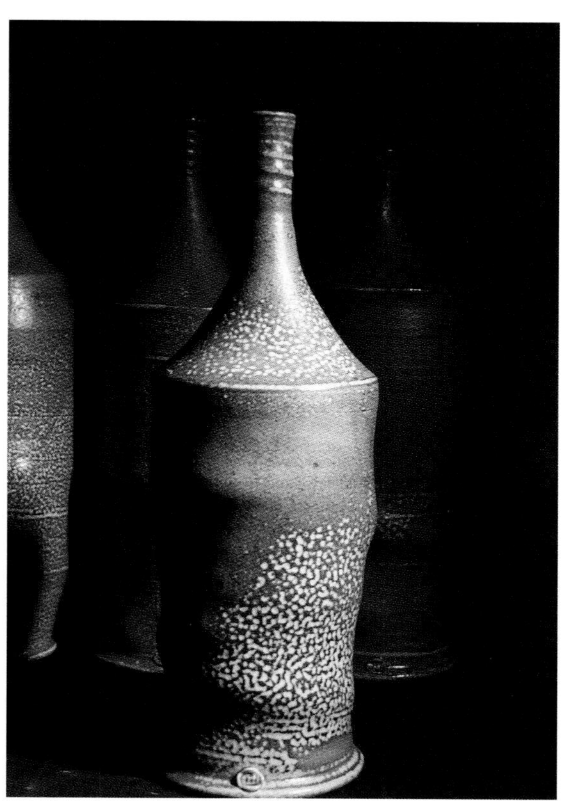

Bottle forms by Steve Taylor, 1999. 'Scarva' smooth Earthstone clay body with a china clay slip applied on the dry piece. Their position at the top of the kiln caught a wonderful variation of salt vapour effects, from dry to heavy orange-peel.

The Spies

As the shelves are placed in the kiln they need to reach the correct levels for the thermocouple and the spy holes: these will be at the back or side of the kiln, and in the wicket at the front. A permanent mark on the outside of the front of the kiln serves as a reminder. The thermocouple may be in a fixed position, but if not it should be inserted in more or less the same place at each firing, in order to make meaningful comparisons between the firing schedules. It is most useful to indicate the temperature trend, whether up or down.

Cones

These must be clearly visible through the spies. Although the pyrometer will indicate the temperature, cones are vital for measuring the heatwork inside the kiln. Placed in different parts of the kiln they will also indicate any variation of temperature. The salt vapour will cause the cones to melt at a rate different to that specified, but salt-glaze potters learn to use them as significant indicators for the various stages in the salt firing. The cones should include, as a minimum, one for reduction, and three around the top temperature. The specific choice will depend on how the kiln is to be fired, but as a general rule, more cones are better than too few.

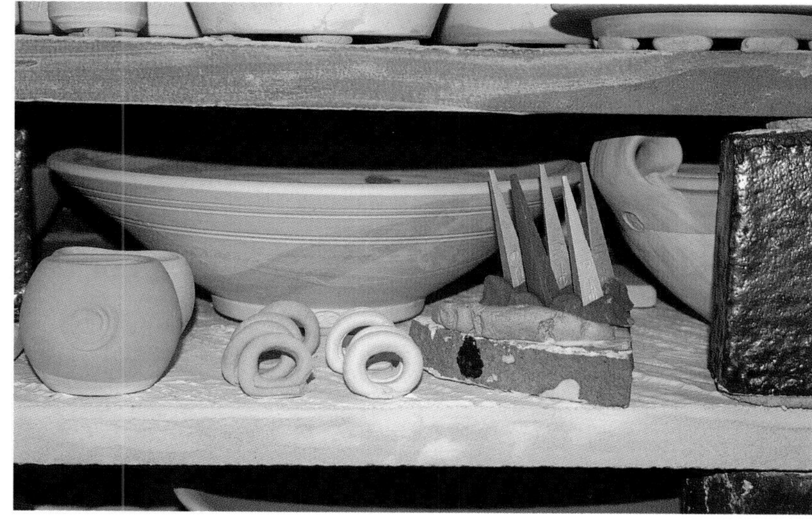

The cones should be set so they can be watched clearly through the spies. A shaped pad of wadding will help prevent the melted cones from spilling onto the kiln shelf. Make the draw rings large enough to be drawn from the kiln, allowing for shrinkage during the firing. They must be carefully placed so they can be taken from the kiln during the firing. A dab of batt wash on the bottom of the rings will ensure they lift out of the kiln easily.

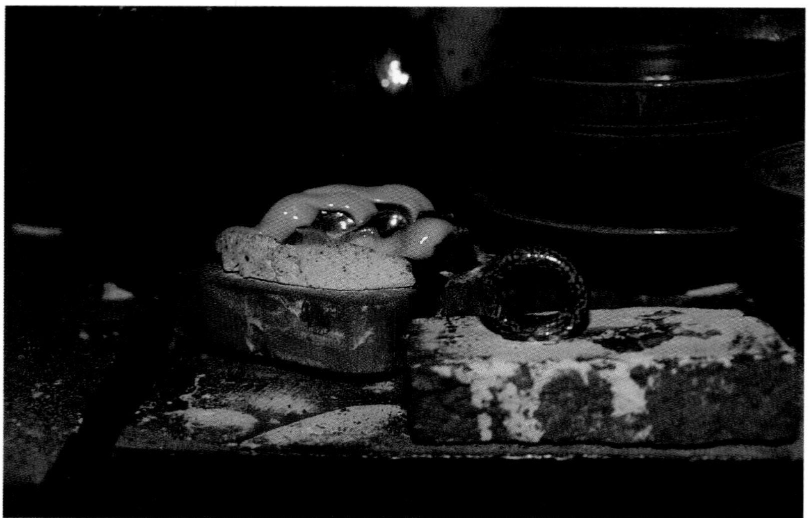

Cones after the firing.

'Draw Rings'

Drawing out trial rings of clay from the kiln is the long-established way of judging how the salting is proceeding. The 'draw rings' should be made from the same clays that have been used to make the pots, and the comparative feel of the rings will be the guide to the progress of the salting. If both smooth and coarse clays are being fired, it will take longer for the glaze to smooth out on the coarser one, and this will give a better indication of the length of time required for the final soak, before the firing is finished.

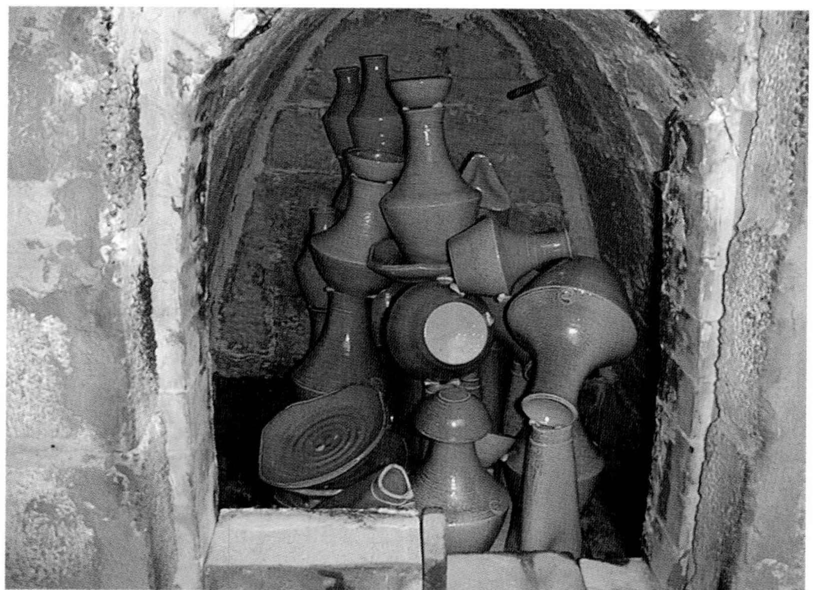

A successful salt firing of a tumble-stacked kiln by Lolly Torbensen at the Glass and Ceramics School, Bornholm, Denmark.

A 'Tumble Stack'

The bold and brave might like to try a 'tumble stack'. The least number of shelves are used, and pieces are piled up high, one on top of another, separated with wads; these also help to keep the pile steady. Larger pieces and sculptural objects may well lend themselves to being stacked without shelves. The early, cheaply produced bottles were always fired in this way, and marks left on the pots would be considered part of the process, neither making a piece a second nor giving it any special merit. Today the studio potter sees the scars from such a firing as a feature.

Using Saggars

Saggars are made from highly refractive clay and have holes cut into their sides, thus allowing the salt to reach the pots within. Experimenting with a variety of combustible materials, and perhaps with the addition of small quantities of oxides placed within the saggars around the pots, will give different effects. Saggar firing can be well controlled, as the partially enclosed space has its own mini atmosphere. A description of low-fired salting in saggars can be found in Chapter 10.

Bricking Up

Once the kiln is packed, the front wicket must be built up. Coating the hot face-edges of the bricks with alumina, should prevent them from sticking together during the firing, and makes dismantling the wicket easier. Heavies can be backed up with insulating blocks. The wicket is quicker to build and easier to dismantle if these are dry-laid without mortar; furthermore, because the kiln structure moves, the wicket space does not remain the same. Pieces of insulating brick are easy to cut and ideal for filling gaps; they are also useful as loose bricks for the spy holes and salt ports, cut to fit tightly against the surrounding wall of the kiln. When bricking up is complete, the outer joints should be sealed with a wet mix of 'compo' – one part fireclay to two parts sand.

CHECKLIST BEFORE FIRING

- Check fuel levels.
- Check salt/soda supply.
- Salt 'shovel' and containers.
- Gloves, mask and goggles.
- Draw-ring rod.
- Thermocouple and indicator.
- Mix sand and fireclay for wicket and gaps.
- Kiln log.

The Effects of Firing

No two kilns fire the same, and even the results from one salt kiln can vary considerably from one firing to the next. It takes time to get to know the idiosyncrasies of a kiln and to gain a degree of control through experience and intuition. However, to a great extent the paths of flame and vapour can never be controlled, and it is this predictable unpredictability that makes salt firing so exciting.

The interaction of the clay and salt is a complex process, but the atmosphere during the firing, and the cooling cycle at the end, are the two major factors that determine the likely results. This explains the colours of the early German salt glaze, and is initially described in Chapter 1.

The Kiln Atmosphere during Firing

The design of the kiln and the way it is packed will determine the movement of the flames, the heat distribution, and the passage of the salt vapours during the firing. The way the gases are pulled through the kiln affects the atmosphere within it. During the firing the atmosphere within the kiln can be oxidized, neutral or reduced, and it is regulated by controlling the amount of air reaching the flame. Alternating periods of reduction and oxidation occur naturally in a wood firing as the fire is stoked. With other fuels this is achieved by either manipulating the damper or adjusting the burners. The colour of the fired pot is dependent on the way the elements of the clay, and the iron oxide content in particular, combine with oxygen – a subject already covered in Chapter 7.

OXIDATION AND REDUCTION

Oxidized firings: an oxidizing atmosphere is achieved by allowing an excess of air into the kiln, by opening vents and allowing a free passage of air.

Reduction firings: a reducing atmosphere is achieved by slowing down the passage of air through the kiln by restricting the flue and closing the vents. Smoke can be an indication of insufficient oxygen and a reduced atmosphere in the kiln. Under reduction, the air supply is cut down and, in an attempt to burn more efficiently, oxygen will be taken from the oxides in the clay body and slips.

The Kiln Atmosphere on Cooling

Heat is retained for a long time by a kiln built of heavy bricks, or by one that is densely packed, and the natural cooling cycle will be slow. The faster cooling cycle of a different kiln can produce different effects: as explained in Chapter 7, the atmosphere in which the kiln is cooled determines the final colours; also the rate of cooling has the potential to affect the crystal structure and the final strength of the pots. The kiln can be crash-cooled, once the burners have been turned off, by allowing cold air to be sucked into the kiln. In this case the rapid initial cooling period will create an oxidized atmosphere in the kiln. If the intention is to maintain a slower and reduced atmosphere at the end of the firing and during cooling, the kiln must be tightly sealed on the outside to prevent any air entering the chamber.

Firing Schedules

This is my own (the author's) firing schedules: I fire my functional pots in a 0.85cu m (30cu ft) catenary arch kiln built of heavy firebricks, using propane gas. Usually the pots have been biscuit-fired. The evening before the firing the damper is pulled out, and the burners are lit and left on a low flame to dry out and warm the kiln. Until the flue warms up there is no through draught; the spies are therefore left partly open so that the damp air can escape. Last thing, I shut the burners off, seal all openings and close the damper to keep the heat in.

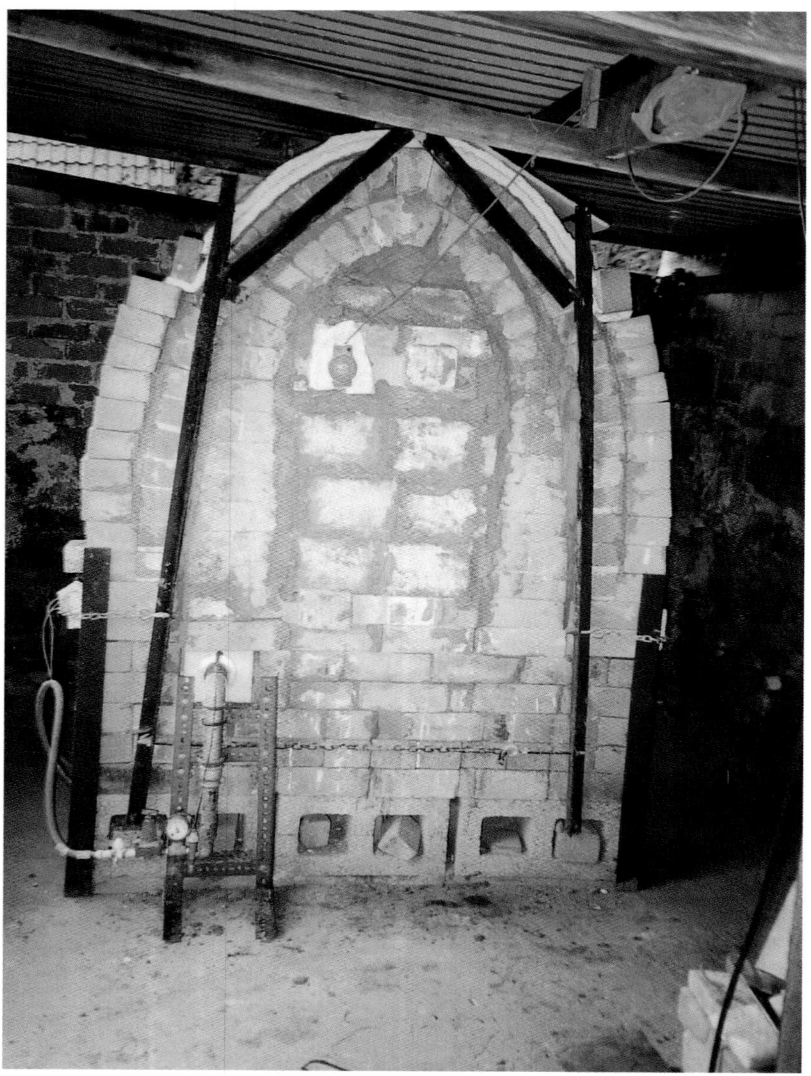

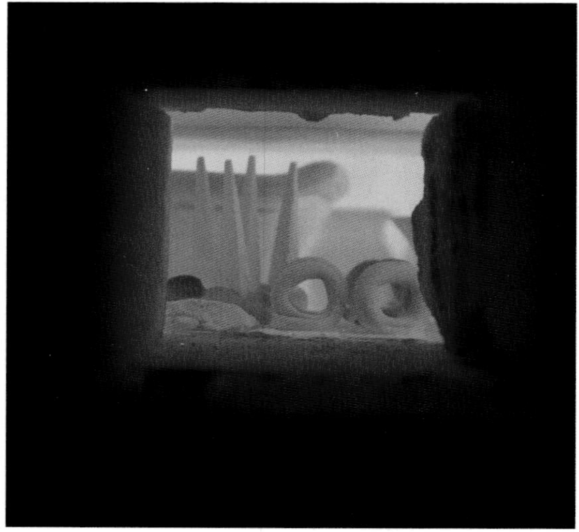

(ABOVE) Watching the cones through the spy.

(LEFT) The author's catenary arch salt kiln in the early stages of firing.

(BELOW LEFT) The performance of the cones during firing, as recorded in the kiln log.

Red^{n}. Ox. Salt

ORTON CONES	06	1	8	9	10	11	
°C	995	1145	1235	1260	1280	1300	
TOP BACK	1040	1112	1228	1245	1260		
	1055	✓	1240	1260	✓	1285	
TOP FRONT	1020	1112	1228	1235	1260		
	1055	✓	1235	1250	✓	1285	
BOTTOM FRONT	1069	1112	1240	1260	1285		
	1120	1140	1250	1280			

If it is a cold night, or it is a raw firing, I will leave the burners on low all night. To do this safely it is important to have a flame failure device so that, should the flame blow out, the kiln will not be filled with gas.

Assuming that all the pots have been biscuit-fired, at 7 o'clock the next morning I pull the damper out and relight the burners, gradually increasing the gas pressure over the next few hours, to maintain a reasonably fast temperature rise. By about 10.30am, 900°C will have been reached, and the burners will be full on at 5 or 6psi. An hour later the pyrometer is showing around 1,000°C, and the first cones will be bending. Cones in different parts of the kiln indicate if the kiln is firing unevenly. I use three sets of Orton cones, 06, 1, 8, 9, 10 and 11, top back, front top and bottom. I wait until all the first cones are down, and it is usually noon when I am able to start reduction.

Reduction

I reduce the atmosphere of the kiln by pushing the damper halfway in, and I also use loose bricks in the flue to slow the draw through the kiln. After many firings and trying different ways, I find that this is the simplest and most successful combination of adjustments by which to control the atmosphere of my kiln. I aim for a medium reduction, indicated by a short flame out of the top spies, and I maintain this for half an hour as the temperature continues to rise at a very much slower pace. The damper is then adjusted for a lighter reduction.

When the pyrometer is reading 1,160°C, I can see salt crystals whitening the baffle on top of the chimney, and also the faintest haze of the salt fumes. At this point the residual salt in the kiln has begun to volatilize and interact with the clay. I aim for a neutral or oxidizing atmosphere in the kiln, to prevent this early salting from sealing in the grey reduced body.

By 2.30pm the temperature will have reached 1,200°C, and will continue to climb until the 1,235°C cones are melted. The pyrometer does not always read the expected temperature, but it is the heat-work that is the better guide to what is happening inside the kiln. I rely on the behaviour of the cones to judge the time for salting. Even though the residual salt may already be affecting the cones, I know that they will behave in a constant way from one firing to the next.

Preparing to Salt

While waiting for the cones to bend, I weigh out 4lb [1.8kg] of salt into each of two buckets, one for each salt port. I add about half a pint of water to dampen each batch of salt. Damp salt holds together and is easier to load into the kiln. I use a 'shovel' made from angle-iron fixed to a length of wood. There is a T-piece on the handle, which stops the shovel from being pushed too far into the kiln, and the salt is tipped into the firebox.

Salting

The moment to salt comes when at least two of the 1,235°C cones are down. As far as possible throughout the salting I keep the spies clammed up to prevent the fumes from getting into the kiln shed. Anyone around the kiln is advised to wear the recommended masks as protection from breathing in any fumes. If the salt is too damp as it is being thrown in, it can spit and blow out at the salt port, so it is essential to be prepared and well protected. Sleeveless tops, bare legs and sandals are not a good idea.

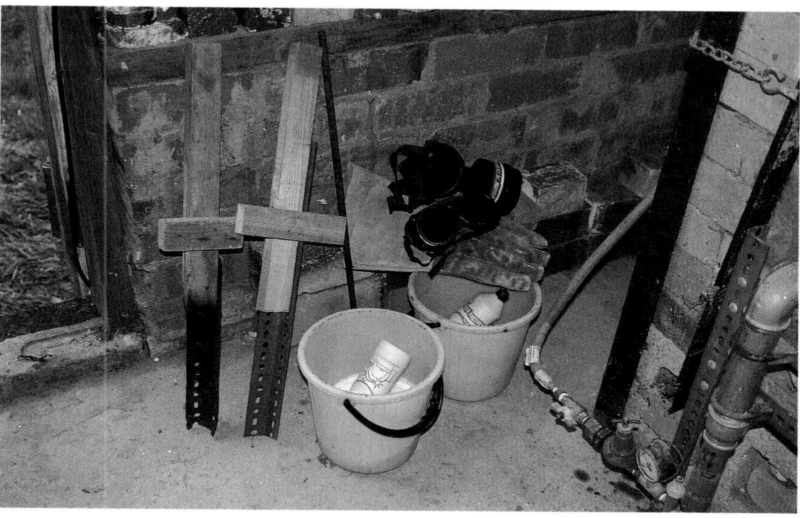

Salt and 'angle-iron shovels'.

Armed with long gauntlets and goggles, the salting begins. The burners are not adjusted during the salting period. I may adjust the damper, to hold a light reduction, but this will depend on the temperature. Each load of salt causes the temperature to drop before it starts to slowly climb again. I look for a pattern of

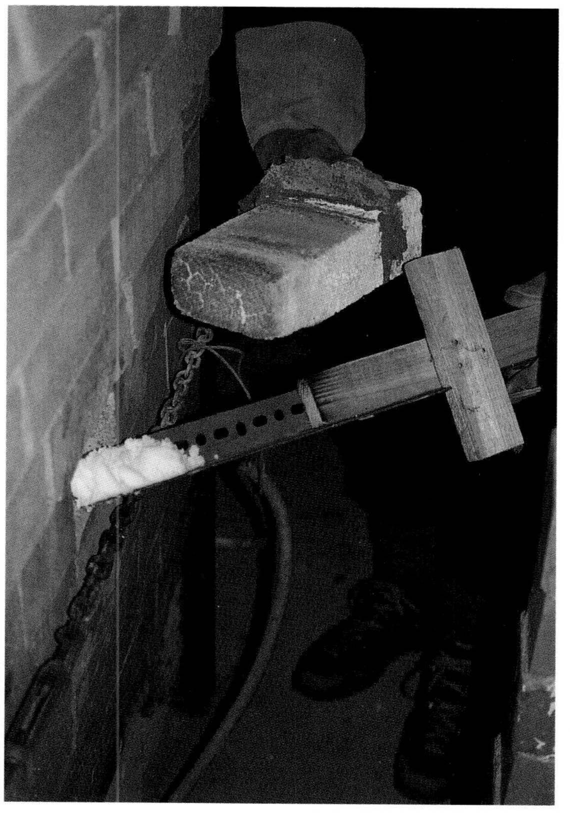

Salting. A small amount of salt is loaded onto the angle iron and tipped into the kiln, one scoop each side.

salting to maintain the temperature, or better still achieve a slight overall rise.

Salting starts between 3.30pm and 4pm, and takes at least two hours. I prefer to salt little and often. This not only helps to prevent temperature loss, but the results depend on the length of time to which the pots are subjected to the salt, rather than the quantity of salt that is used. If it is daylight I watch the emissions coming from the chimney. When they have reduced to a light mist I repeat the salting. This usually means ten minutes between salting. I keep a watch on the remaining cones as they bend and fall. After an hour and a half of salting the pyrometer may read anything between 1,250°C and 1,280°C.

Assessing the Progress

The first trial rings are drawn from the kiln when two-thirds of the salt has been used. I like to be able to compare rings from different parts of the kiln. As they come from the kiln they are placed out of the way to cool, then after a few minutes they can be handled. With experience this is the only trusted way to judge how much salt is needed to form a good glaze. I may decide to use more, or sometimes less than the quantity I originally weighed out. Draw rings do not show their final colour; this is produced during the final cooling. The last salt goes in around 6pm, with the pyrometer reading between 1,270°C and 1,290°C. I leave some rings in the kiln to draw later, after the soak.

Soaking

The final soak will be for at least one hour, with the damper reset for a neutral or an oxidizing atmosphere. The salt ports can be sealed up, but the firing needs to continue until the glaze has settled smoothly, and any gritty feeling is gone. The temperature is encouraged to rise, and is then held at 1,290°C or even 1,300°C until the last ring is taken out and the salt glaze declared perfect. If the firing has gone to plan it will have taken twelve hours, and the burners will be turned off at 7pm.

Crash Cooling

I choose to let the kiln crash cool in an oxidized atmosphere, with burner ports open and damper full out. It takes about one hour to drop to 1,000°C. This brightens the colours and

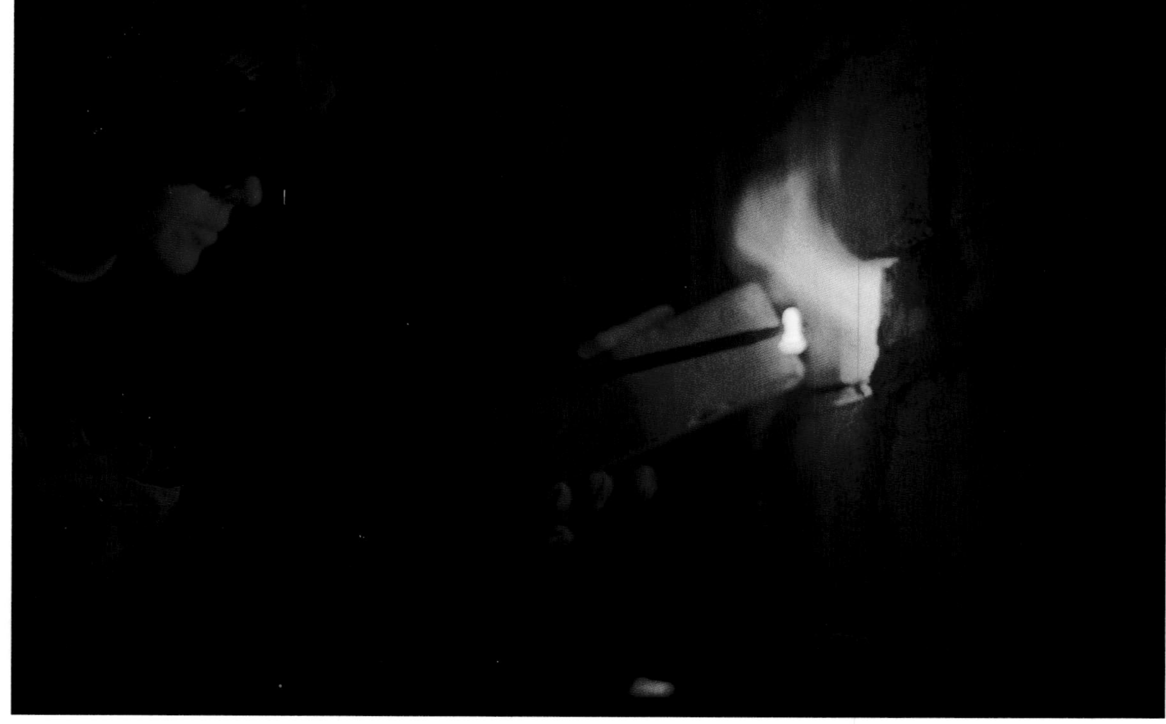

Drawing a ring by inserting an iron bar through the ring, then carefully lifting it out of the kiln through the spy hole. It feels like a fairground game, and you lose the prize if the ring escapes and falls off – inevitably dropping into the open bowl on the shelf below.

returns the rich brown colours. Finally, all loose bricks and ports are clammed up, by trowelling the mortar mix around the joints and sealing over the burner ports. The damper is pushed full in, and the kiln left to cool for thirty-six hours. Two days later it will be unpacked in the afternoon. There are always surprises: the results can be wonderful, while another firing will bring only disappointment. Either way, any one firing always encourages me on to the next.

More on Salting

Type of Salt

Common salt is available in various forms. The one most used for salt firings comes in dry vacuum-packed sacks, obtainable from agricultural suppliers or wholesale outlets. Rock salt may have impurities that may affect the results of a firing. Salt crystals or flakes will have more volume by weight than fine-grained salt, but whether this makes any difference is debatable, and will depend on how the salt is used.

How Much Salt?

Whatever the type of brick and possible coating, the first firing will certainly take a great deal more salt than following firings. It is difficult to give an average weight of salt required for a firing, as it will very much depend on the clays, and the effects that are looked for, and the way the salt is introduced. Using between 225 and 450g (8oz and 1lb) of damp salt for each 0.2cu m (cubic foot) of the kiln is a very general guide for producing the traditional orange-peel surface. It is quite possible to reduce this amount of salt by extending the period of salting, by using small amounts for each baiting, and by adopting one or a combination of the other ways of salting.

Alternative Ways of Salting

Damp Salt

Some potters throw handfuls or cupfuls of dry salt into the hottest part of the kiln, but damp and straight into the firebox, either loose or in packets, seems to be the way most commonly used in Britain. The idea of using damp salt has developed with the idea that the additional water helps the sodium chloride dissociate more quickly. (The chemical reactions are explained fully in Chapter 6.) The drawback is that damp salt is heavy, and most of it lands in the firebox where it accumulates in considerable quantities. As it seeks out the silica content of the bricks to form a glaze, this build-up of salt attacks the structure of kiln in the area of the firebox. So it is necessary to maintain constant repairs to prevent fast and devastating deterioration that will quickly shorten the life of the kiln.

So how can the salt be introduced into the kiln to prevent this particular problem?

Dry Salt

Blowing dry salt into the kiln is a relatively recent means of introducing it. A system employed successfully by Gus Mableson in Ireland is to use forced air from a compressor to blow fine-grained salt through a sandblasting spray gun, directly into the kiln, over the top of the flame. The results on the pots appear to be as good as those from the more usual method of throwing damp salt into the firebox, but as the salt does not accumulate in the firebox, it does not suffer the same damage. There is also the advantage that less salt is required – 6kg (13lb) of salt are used to achieve a good glaze cover on the contents of a 1.7cu m (60cu ft) kiln. More sophisticated systems incorporated into the burner are being used by salt-glaze potters in Europe.

A Brine Solution

Chris Jenkins devised this method in the early 1980s, at Manchester Polytechnic, where the students' salt kiln was in a city location. The kiln had a packing space of 0.34cu m (12cu ft) and was already well salted. The saturated salt solution was drip-fed from 1,200°C, an operation that would extend over four to five hours. Depending on the pack, around 3.5 to 4.5 litres (6 to 8 pints) of saturated brine solution was used each side, using a maximum total of 3.6kg (8lb) of salt.

A T-piece was fitted onto the oil line, and brine was drip-fed by gravity, together with the oil, to the home-made forced-air burners. It was regulated with a mini-clip, in the same way as the oil. The two liquids flowed together, but unmixed, along the transparent plastic tubing. Quantities were judged right when there was 25mm (1in) of oil followed by 13mm ($^{1}/_{2}$in) or less of brine. A dramatic chugging noise was created as the brine interrupted the oil flow to the burners. Intermittently salt would clog up the ends of the burners, blocking the flame passage, and had to be knocked off in a tricky manoeuvre with a long iron rod.

Jugs and bowl on the top shelf by Alex McErlain. Kitchen pots on the lower shelf and the table top by Rosemary Cochrane. These were salt-glazed by 'drip-feeding' brine into the kiln, all from firings in the 1980s.

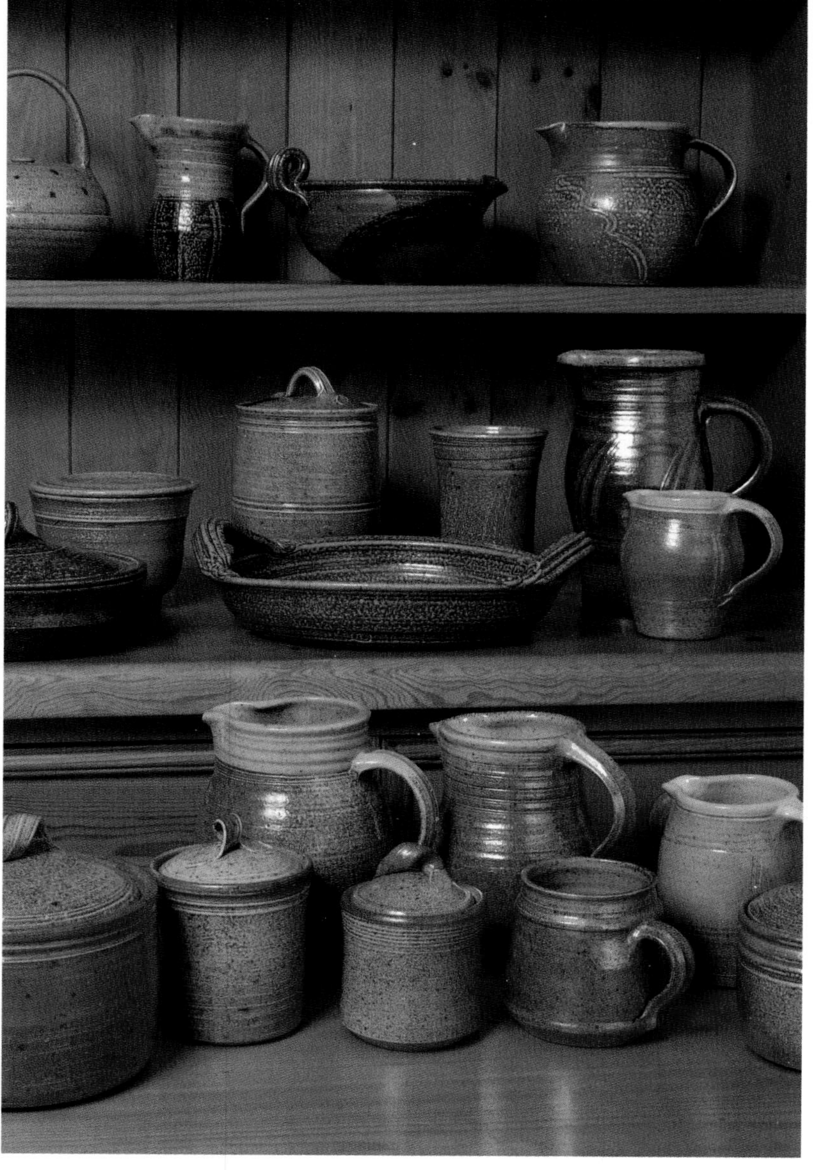

In my own first kiln, 1.4cu m (50cu ft) oil-fired, I would drip-feed brine continually from 1,250°C, until 3½ litres (6 pints) had been consumed through each burner. Before the drip-feed had finished, small quantities of loose salt were also introduced through salt ports over the fireboxes; a total of 3.6kg (8lb) each side, at ten-minute intervals, over an hour and a half. It would have taken a very long time to achieve a good glaze cover on the pots in such a large kiln using only the brine solution, but by combining two methods of salting I considerably reduced the salt attack on the fireboxes. Aesthetically the results were completely satisfactory, and I never had to forfeit orange-peel textures. In my second, smaller, gas-fired kiln, I returned to salting by introducing damp salt, but I am reconsidering other ways of spraying in the salt solution.

The drip method has been developed independently by various potters since the early 1970s. Margaret Gardiner, salt glazing on the Harrow Studio Pottery course in the 1970s, looked for an option to throwing in the salt. She has now refined the system to resolve the problem of salt crystallizing on the end of the tube. Her set-up consists of a plastic container of saline solution suspended up high: from this, 8mm plastic tubing carrying the brine and regulated with mini-clamps, leads to 4mm metal pipes. These are balanced just above the burner jets. The pipes are encased in 6mm tubes that can be slid backwards and forwards, to knock off the salt lumps.

Practical Benefits

Maybe salt-glaze potters like the excitement of throwing in salt. But if we are prepared to sacrifice that part of the drama of the process, there are considerable benefits to be gained.

Drip-fed salting has the distinct advantage of being kinder to the kiln fabric, and although the length of the firing will be extended, the fumes are dissipated over a longer period of time and therefore there is no emission of a dense white fog. Even so, it is probably unwise to proceed with heavy reduction whist the brine is being fed into the kiln, even though the water is being introduced into the kiln very gradually, and there is little chance of an excessive explosive force of steam building up inside the kiln.

The other alternative is to spray the salt solution into the kiln, using a garden spray. But this will need to be a very frequent activity over a long period of time if a classic salt glaze is to form. In combination with other salting techniques, the spraying or drip-feeding methods are practical options with considerable benefits.

In a wood firing, the salt or soda can be introduced on slats of wood, or as brine-soaked bundles of twigs. There is also no reason why a small amount of wood could not be used to introduce the vapour agent into a gas- or oil-fired kiln. This could produce interesting effects from the additional brief periods of reduction as the wood ignites, and from local deposits of ash.

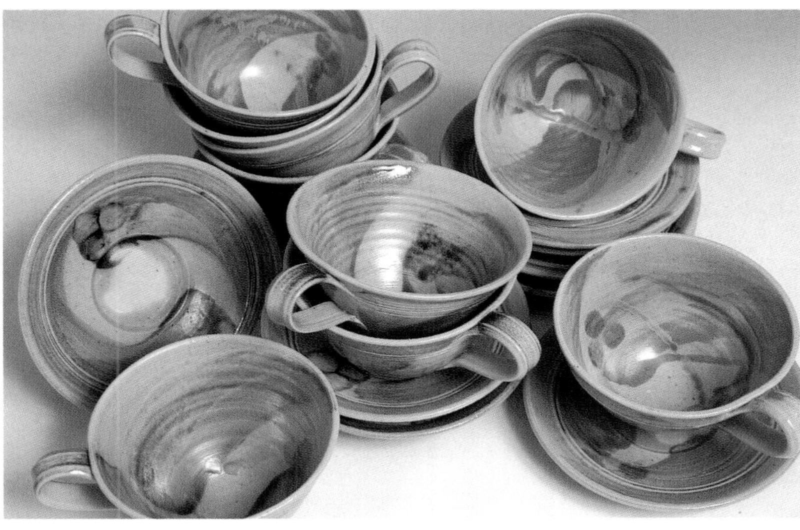

Cups and saucers by Rosemary Cochrane.

Unpacking the Kiln

It is a tremendously exciting moment when the wicket is taken down and finally the pots are unloaded from the kiln. The kiln has replied to your part in the salt-glaze process, and each unpacking will be the time to gather information on which you will build for future firings. Make notes, as you cannot afford to miss any

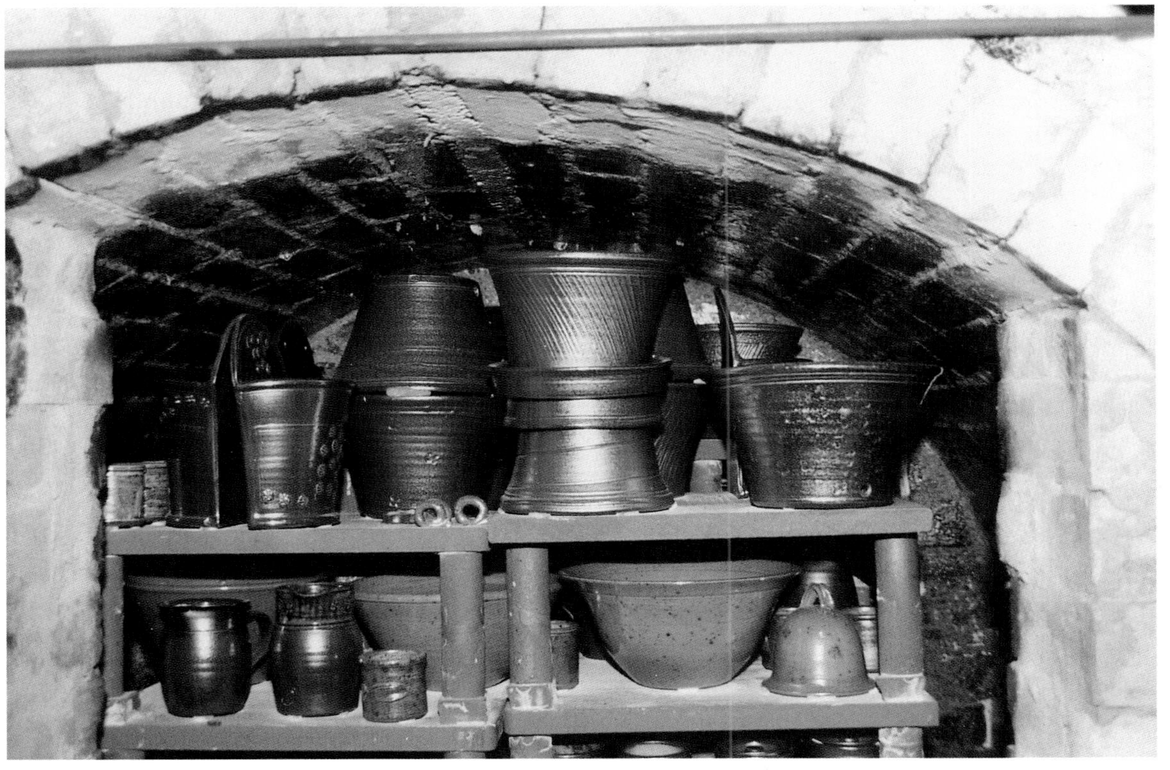

The dark results from the first firing can be a total surprise. All the pieces are discoloured by the release of ferric oxide from the kiln wall. The lighter clays with a low iron content become gold or orange-red, and the darker clays mahogany brown or even darker. It was a phenomenon dreaded by those German potters who prized the grey-blue surface of their salt glaze.

chance to understand the process. Linger over each pot as it comes from the kiln, and try to make sense of the forces that work within the kiln. It is the opportunity to learn about the kiln's performance, to notice any hot or cold spots, local areas of oxidation or over-reduction, what passage the salt vapours take.

The kiln's first high-temperature salt firing is guaranteed to be one of trial and error, and in retrospect it often proves to be the longest and most drawn out of the kiln's entire firing history. But it is only the start of an evolving process. Firings can be exciting and exasperating, but when they come right, the rewards are in the rich, unique surfaces of salt glaze.

Dramatically Dark

There is one particular exchange that occurs between bricks and pots during the first firing, and to a much lesser extent, for a further couple of firings. A considerable amount of iron oxide is released from the bricks, and transferred by the vapour onto the pots in the kiln. Unless it is understood that the volatile release of such a significant amount of iron only happens once, the results of the first firing can distort your understanding of how to control the effects from the kiln in the future. The dark colours in this first firing have little to teach about the real nature of the clays and slips, or the success or failure of first attempts to control the atmosphere of the kiln. Judging the true effects of the different stages of oxidation and reduction will be part of the learning experience of each firing after the first one.

Problems

There are some qualities that may appear on salt-glaze pots that are both puzzling and undesirable. 'Christmas glitter' is used to describe an unfortunate phenomenon that can appear randomly and unexpectedly and for no apparent reason, and which can ruin either a few or a considerable percentage of pots from a firing. What happens is that minuscule flakes of glass lift off the surface when the afflicted pieces are handled, suggesting that the glaze has not fused to the clay. No one has the definitive answer as to why it does this: even though all the variables of clays, slips and glaze recipes, position in the kiln, type of fuel, atmosphere and cooling cycle have been assimilated, there is still no single theory that can be put forward to explain it. It is undoubtedly a combination of several circumstances. If it does occur it is reasonable to look carefully at all the possible contributing factors in an attempt to avoid it in future firings. As a last resort solution, it can be removed by putting the piece through the dishwasher.

'Carbon trap' is another problem that escapes a full explanation. Glazes and slips containing nepheline syenite seem more prone to be affected by it. It appears as a grey smudge or shadow within the slip or glaze: the carbon may be sealed in the clay as the residual salt begins to vaporize, or it is a result of partial reduction during early stages of cooling. It is not always easy to determine whether the greyness is in the glaze or in the clay; and although it is difficult to explain, there are examples where re-firing has radically changed the affected pieces.

A Selection of Firing Schedules

Results from a salt-glaze firing are very kiln-specific, and in spite of using the same clays and slip combinations, the colours and surfaces will nearly always turn out differently. However, it is always helpful to know how another similar kiln is fired and salted.

Jane Hamlyn

The following notes describe a salt firing of raw pots in an oil-fired kiln:

> A thirty-six-hour firing because pots are raw. Pre-heating with one small gas burner overnight, second gas burner on in morning. From mid-afternoon a wheelbarrow of wood is fed through the salt ports to form a bed of ash in the firebox. This procedure ensures a very slow warm-up, and no bloats from re-absorbed moisture; it warms up the chimney gradually and gets a draught going. The bed of hot ash near the front of the firebox also prevents the burners – on low – from blowing out.
>
> The two Dine oil burners are turned on low at about 5pm, with the gas pilot still on. Ted

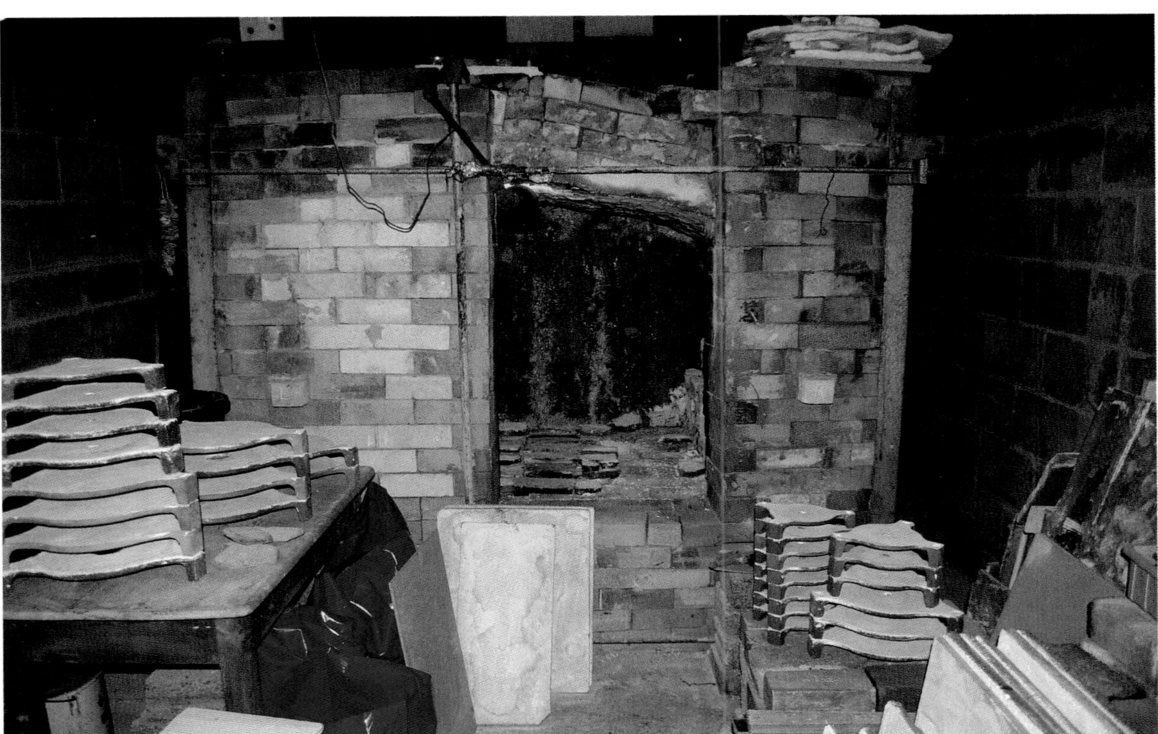

Jane Hamlyn's kiln. Shelves and plate stackers batt-washed and prepared for packing.

goes to bed around 8pm and I stay up for the first shift, checking things are safe and gradually turning up the oil burners. Ted takes over in the morning and does all the serious business. Usually the firing is over by midnight.

There are Orton cones in the door, plus two sets at the back: 991, 1200, 1235, 1260, 1280, 1300 degrees Centigrade. Cones may not be exact in a salt kiln, but they are consistent and we fire to the cones. We also have two pyrometers in the door: top digital and bottom analogue. Pyrometers can register a drop in temperature, which is useful, and also a gradual rise, which is reassuring.

A standard reduction firing proceeds until the 1200 cone begins to go. Re-oxidize for an hour, then start salting at 1260. 10kg (22lb) damp salt at 500g (8oz) each side takes about an hour. Soak until 1280 over at front and 1300 flat at back. Shut down and clam up.

Ours is a rather long-winded firing, and people (often students!) have suggested ways to speed things up; but the kiln is lined with heavy brick, which heats up slowly, and we have learned to love it – and it has stood the test of time. We do it our way!

Toff Milway

Toff's kiln is described in Chapter 8. Here he describes a salt firing of raw pots with propane gas:

> The kiln is fired clean to 1,000°C, and will be held at this to ensure that there is an even temperature throughout and, since it is raw fired, to burn off any carbon. A heavy reduction is held for about 15 minutes, and a lighter reduction is then maintained until after the first salting: this starts at about 1,120°C, when the body starts to vitrify. The salting continues in a neutral to oxidizing atmosphere for up to two and a half hours, by which time cones 9/10 are down. The last stage of the firing is a clean burn in oxidation for a further two hours, letting cone 11 fall. A final twenty minutes is in strong reduction, helping to give the lustrous effects on the pots. The kiln is then crash cooled in oxidation down to 1,000°C before being clammed up. Great attention is paid to the reduction, as the least tendency to oxidation causes dramatically unfavourable results, perhaps due to the very fine clay body, whose character is only drawn out under ideal reducing conditions.

Mick Casson

A salt firing with some soda, in a propane-gas kiln. All the work is biscuit fired. There is a total of four burners.

27 May 2000. One burner lit overnight from 10.30pm to 8.30am, very gentle flame. 28 May, 8.30am. Temperature reads 239°C. Firing proceeds, with a one-and-a-half hour soak at 800°C. Reduction begins at 3.50pm. with cone 05 down, and pyrometer reading 1,035°C. Reduction continues for three hours to 1,225°C. Salting begins at 6.50pm, when cones 7 are going over. Salt is introduced over each burner in a long-handled metal 'spoon'. 2lb [900g] charges at five-minute intervals, alternate ports. 24lb [11kg] of salt is in after one hour. A ring is taken, and an additional 4lb [1.8kg] introduced at 5-minute intervals. After a total of 28lb [12.7kg], salting stops at 8.00pm. Then soda spray carried out for 15 minutes; 400g [14oz] of sodium carbonate into 2 litres [3 pints] of water. 8.25pm, 1,251°C soda stops. Clean burn, 50 minutes soak at end of soda/salt. At 9.15pm, 1,270°C, all cones slumped over including cone 12 at top. Burners OFF. Temperature crashed with all bungs, ports and damper open. 10.30pm, 971°C. All basted up. Damper closed.

May Ling Beadsmoore

These notes describe a soda-glaze firing with raw pots. The kiln is approximately 0.76cu m (27cu ft), fired with natural gas on eight 'Aero-matic Barter' burners. The kiln is illustrated in Chapter 8.

15 October 2000
kiln packed, 6.45pm pilot lights lit.

16 October 2000
3am 60°C
Two burners lit. Steady 100°C rise every hour as burners are turned on and gas pressure increased gradually.
1.00pm 1,040°C
Top 06 cone flat, bottom 06 cone starting to fall, reduce with damper part-in.
Two and a half hours of reduction and slow temperature rise.
One and a half hours of alternate oxidation/ reduction to achieve a temperature rise.
5pm 1,204°C
Bottom cone 8 straight, top cone 8 only just starting. Start spraying solution of 4kg [8.8lb] soda crystals in at the burner ports.
6.00 1,204°C
Check draw rings are similar to previous firing. Soda input complete.
Bottom cone 9 straight, top cone 9 started.
6.30 1,204°C
Short reduction; have theory this will make colours even better.
6.45 1,204°C
Oxidized soak.
7.50
Top cone 10 bending, bottom cone 10 started, burners down.
8.05 1,175°C
Crash cool. Damper out, bungs left in.
8.10 1,155°C
Bungs removed.
8.50 970°C
Ports close to pots closed, as some pots beginning to look red/black.
9.20pm 914°C
Kiln sealed up.

19 October 2000,
10am, 87°C.
Kiln opened and unpacked.
Results: really good i.e. good colours and textures and no technical faults.
(Think reduction after soda worked well.)

Wood-Fired Salt Glaze

In-depth descriptions of salt-glaze firings in wood kilns can be found in books recommended in the bibliography. Wood-firing schedules are particularly kiln-specific, but the way the salt is introduced will be of interest. In several cases the salt-glaze potters introduce the salt quite late in the firing, when 1,280°C is reached and Orton cone 8 is down. The way of salting varies from damp salt in parcels, thrown into the fireboxes, to a combination of loose salt in the fireboxes with some salt solution sprayed through the spies.

In their soda-glaze wood-fired kiln, Jeremy Steward and Petra Reynolds start applying the soda once cone 5 is over and the pyrometer is

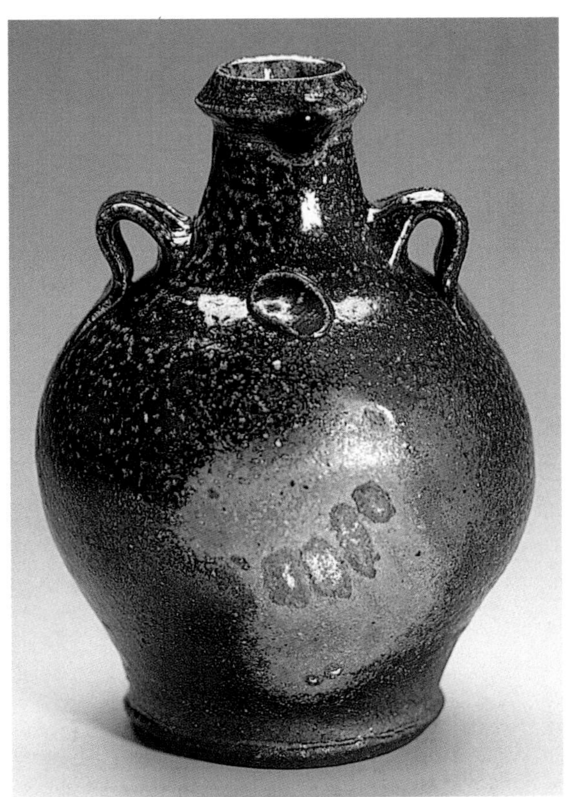

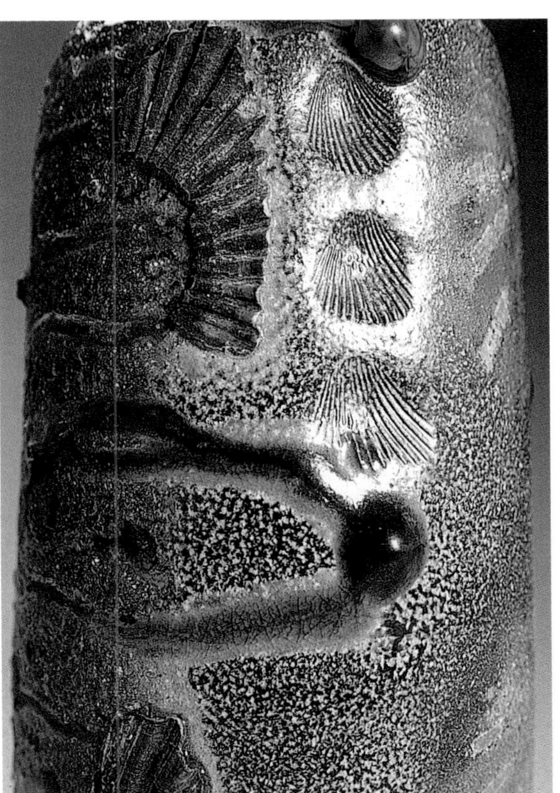

(FAR LEFT) Scarred bottle by Tim Hurn, 1999. Tim wood fires a 150cu ft anagama kiln, and although he does use salt, the heavy salting effects are quite localized. He stirs up the firebox in order to combine the ash with the salt, so as to produce rivers of glaze. The pots are stacked on one another, with wads of fireclay and sawdust and scallop shells.

(LEFT) Firebox bottle by Tim Hurn, 1999. Detail.

reading 1,180–90°C., 4.5 to 5kg (10 to 11lb) of sodium carbonate – washing soda – is applied to thin slats of wood, and introduced to alternate fireboxes over about one and a half hours. 1.5kg (3.3lb) of soda is then sprayed in solution using a garden spray, providing a more even distribution of glaze to areas outside the flame paths.

It is sometimes difficult to identify where the effects of the wood firing dominate those of the salt glaze. Several potters who wood fire, introduce comparatively small amounts of salt into their kilns for localized glaze effects.

10 Alternatives

Residual Salt

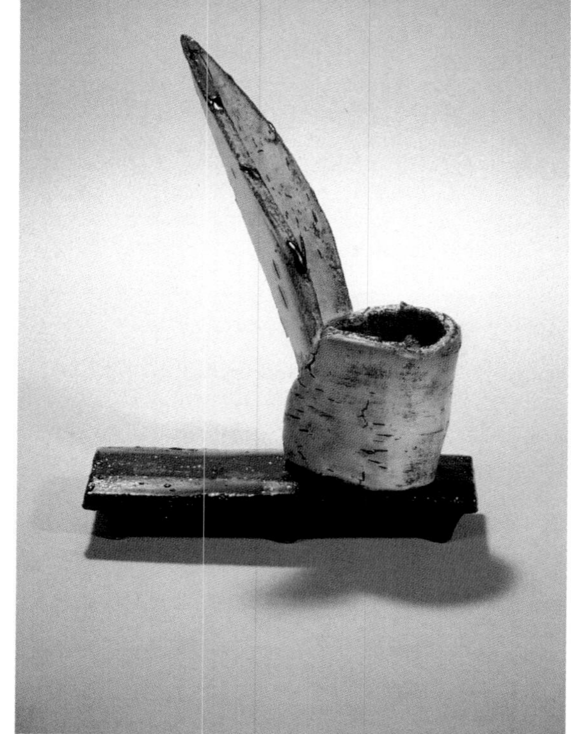

'Road Runner I' by Richard Launder, 1994. Sculpture 20 × 22cm. Residual high salt 1,300 °C. High-iron clay body, high alumina and silica slips. Multi-fired.

Any salt that has remained in the kiln after a full salt firing will volatilize and produce a glaze in the next firing. In a residual salt firing the kiln is fired to the normal schedule, but the temptation to introduce more salt is resisted. The pots will be lightly salted, without any dramatic orange-peel qualities, but by using appropriate slips and engobes a subtle range of salt-glaze qualities can be discovered.

The amount of residual salt in a kiln will depend on the way in which the salt was introduced in previous firings. The greatest amount remains after salting by throwing in quantities of damp salt, when much of it will have been deposited in the fireboxes. On the other hand, only a small amount of residual salt will remain after drip-feeding or spraying in a salt solution, or from blowing in dry salt. Two, or even three residual firings might be possible before the vapour effects become too weak to be noticeable; it depends what is wanted from the firing.

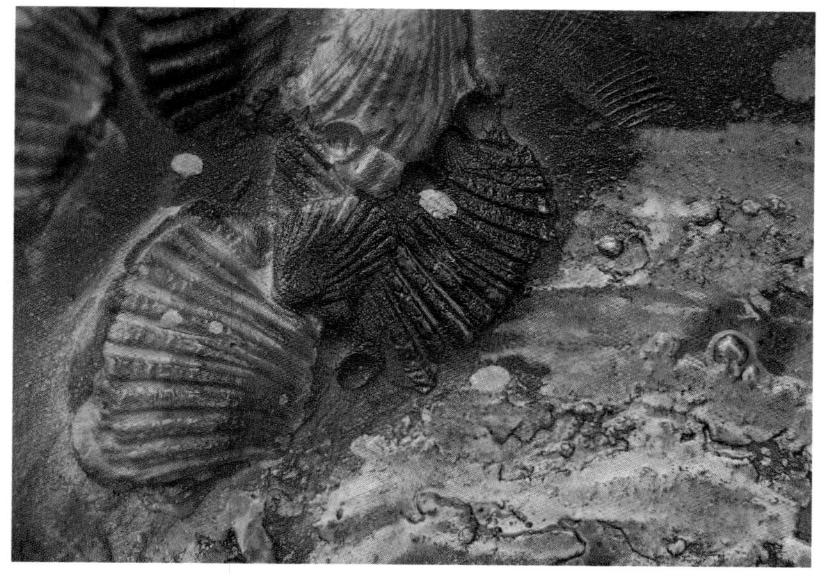

Detail of dish by Rosemary Cochrane, 2000. From the 'Water-worn' series. Residual salt firing to 1,280 °C.

It is not true to say that the salt kiln cannot be used for stoneware glaze firing. It can, but the residual salt will, to a varying degree, affect the glazes. Residual firing provides an opportunity to combine the use of stoneware glazes with more lightly salted and flashed surface qualities. Ash glazes are a good place to start, but exciting results will be found through taking risks and applying other glazes, engobes containing fluxes, and slips for drier colour surfaces.

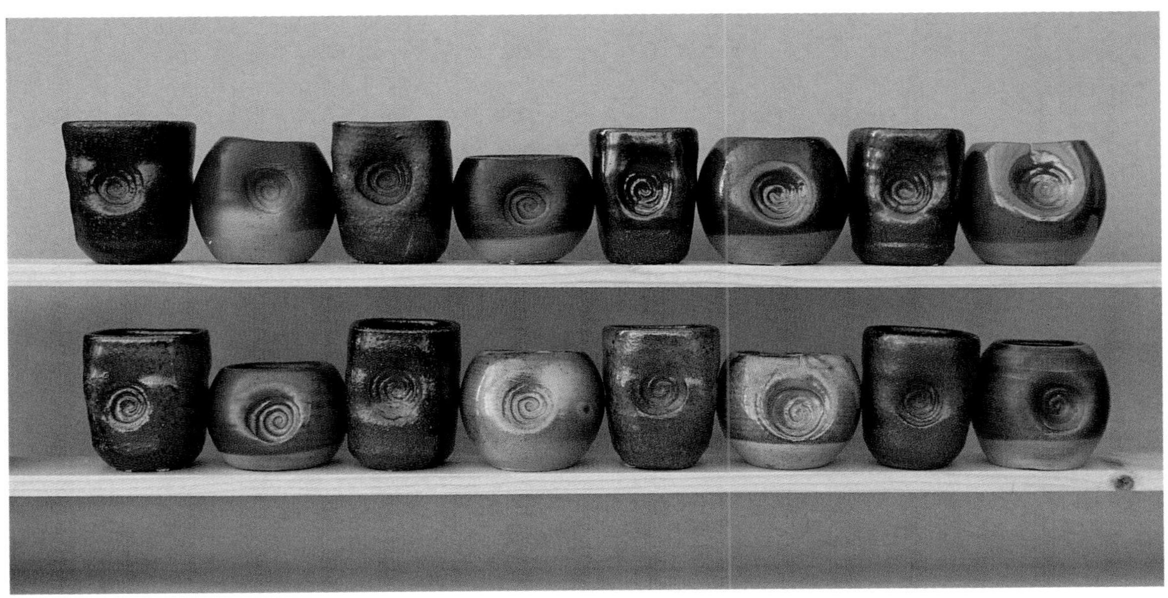

Trials from a residual salt firing. The square pots are high-iron clay (2.25 per cent), the round pots low-iron (0.7 per cent). Top row: slips 1 to 4; bottom row: slips 5 to 8. The light salt glaze from this firing inhibited the development of colour in most of the slips, with the exception of slip 1, the AT/CC slip, on the pale firing clay. Slips that contained a flux were more inclined to show colour, and were clearly less inclined to be dry.

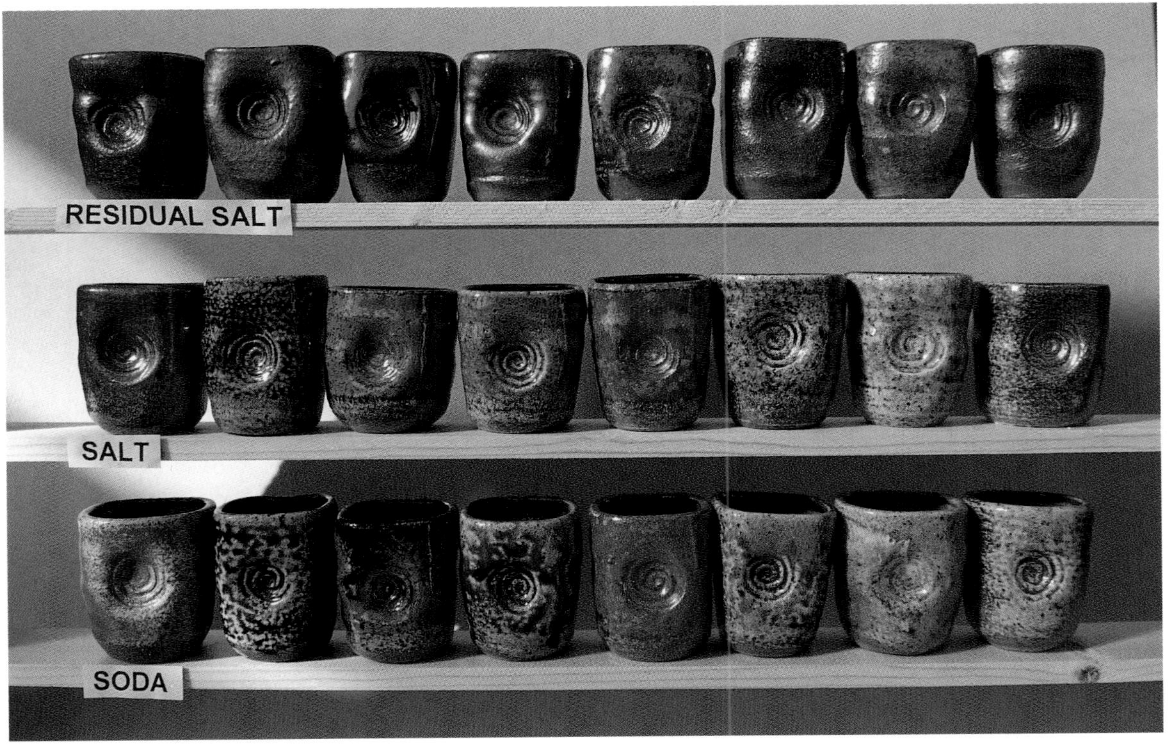

Comparison of trials from residual salt, full salt and soda firings on the iron-bearing clay A. Left to right: slips 1 to 8.

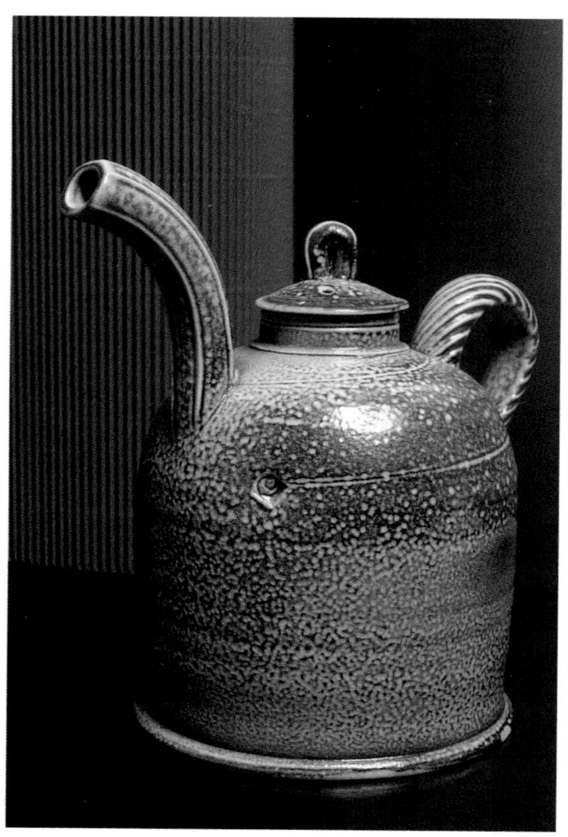

Teapot by Rebecca Harvey, 1999. Soda glaze. Thrown with extruded handle and spout.

Alternative Vapour Agents

Soda compounds are the alternative vapour agents. Soda can emulate the classic orange-peel surface of salt glaze, but as an alternative to salt glaze, soda glaze also has its own specific characteristics.

Salt and Soda Compared

Salt volatilizes quickly and easily, and it can be introduced into the kiln in a dampened state, directly into the fireboxes. As we have seen, dumping quantities of salt into the kiln during salting results in a destructive attack in the firebox area, in particular; also a thick white fog during the salting period is inevitable with this method. The salt can be blown in by force in its dry state, or mixed with water into a saturated solution and dripped or sprayed into the kiln; these methods cause the least attack on the kiln fabric and avoid the plume of thick white mist. Salt can also be placed in small pots around the kiln for localized vapour-glaze effects, without causing any visible mist.

There is a choice of soda compounds, though none of them decomposes or volatilizes as easily as salt. Soda can be introduced into the kiln by any of the methods used for salting, but is generally better dispersed in a saturated solution in boiling water, sprayed through a number of ports around the kiln. The most severe attack on the kiln is seen around the spray ports. Other methods of introducing the soda include mixing sodium bicarbonate with damp sawdust and using a burner/blower unit to blow it in; or mixing up a paste of sodium bicarbonate and sodium carbonate, which solidifies and can then be crumbled and scooped into the fireboxes. Most significantly, there is no cloud of fog produced from a soda firing, and in certain circumstances this can be the over-riding factor in the choice between salt and soda. The pollution issues and the chemical reactions are described in previous chapters.

The aesthetic differences between salt and soda glaze come as a result of the way in which the vapour is dispersed within the chamber of

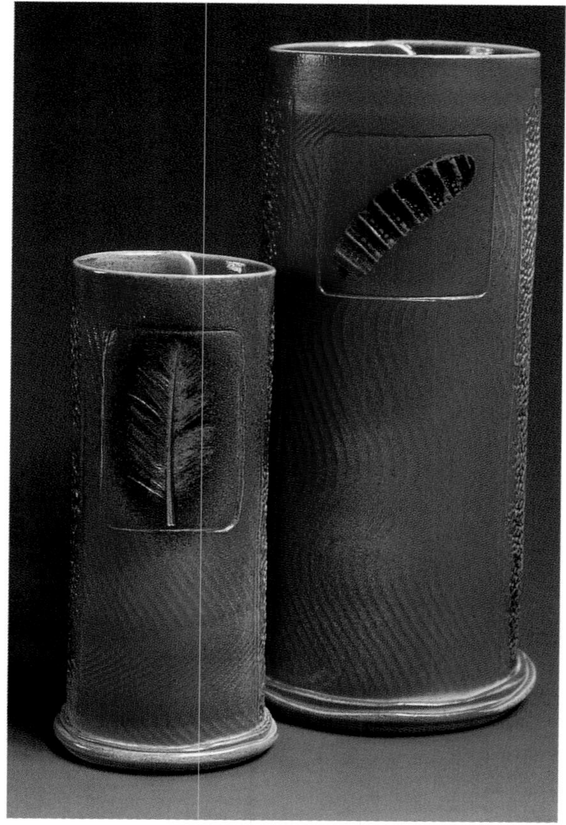

Vases by May Ling Beadsmoore, 2000. Height 16cm and 21cm. Soda glaze.

the kiln. The soda vapours are less readily distributed, and this encourages the flashings of a heavy deposit of orange-peel glaze, as well as leaving dry, unglazed areas on the pots.

Salt does usually give a more even coverage, and the finish of salt glaze generally shows crisper, sharper detail; the effects of soda, on the other hand, have a softer and more blurred quality. Any of the vapour agents offer rich and varied surface qualities and have the same alluring attraction. Some potters add variety to the firing by settling for a combination of both salt and soda, and a mixture of methods for introducing each of the elements.

Trials Comparing Salt and Soda

A series of tests were made in order to confirm the differences between salt and soda firings, and to identify the nature of any other variations. May Ling Beadsmoore supplied a quantity of her usual clay mix and slip recipes, and undertook to fire the tests in her soda kiln. (Her kiln and a typical firing schedule are described in Chapter 9, and her work is profiled in Chapter 11.) All potlets (below) were prepared at the author's (Rosemary Cochrane's) workshop, and the tests for salt glaze were fired in her salt kiln.

The Clays used in Tests

'Salt' clays A and B are those used by the author (Rosemary Cochrane).

A. Square-shaped potlets; 2.25 per cent iron content of clay.
   Potclays Reduction St Thomas (1104) and White St Thomas (1106) 50/50 mix.

B. Round potlets. 0.7 per cent iron content of clay.
   Potclays White stoneware (1145).

'Soda' clay C used by May Ling Beadsmoore.

C. Bottle-shaped potlets, low-iron content clay. Commercial clays TS Stoneware and Super White 50/50 mix.

(Clays B and C gave very similar results)

Slip Recipes used for Tests

'Salt' slips 1 to 4 are those used by myself, the author.

1. Salt Orange
   50 AT ball clay (high iron content)
   50 china clay
2. Salt Blue
   70 Hyplas 71 (ball clay)
   30 china clay
   2.5 cobalt carbonate
   1.5 red iron oxide
3. Salt Green (from Suzy Atkins)
   25 Hyplas 71
   25 potash feldspar
   3 rutile
   1 cobalt carbonate
4. Salt Pale Blue (from Suzy Atkins)
   70 nepheline syenite
   5 AT ball clay
   25 Hyplas 71
   1 cobalt carbonate

'Soda' slips 5 to 8 are those used by May Ling Beadsmoore:

5. Soda Rich Orange
   60 AT ball clay
   20 FFF feldspar
   10 whiting
   10 flint
   10 rutile
   5 red iron oxide
6. Soda Blue
   60 AT ball clay
   20 FFF
   10 whiting
   10 flint
   2 cobalt carbonate
   2 copper carbonate
7. Soda Iridescent
   60 AT ball clay
   20 FFF
   10 whiting
   10 flint
   10 rutile
8. Soda Grey
   70 AT ball clay
   20 FFF feldspar
   10 flint
   2.5 copper carbonate
   2.5 manganese dioxide

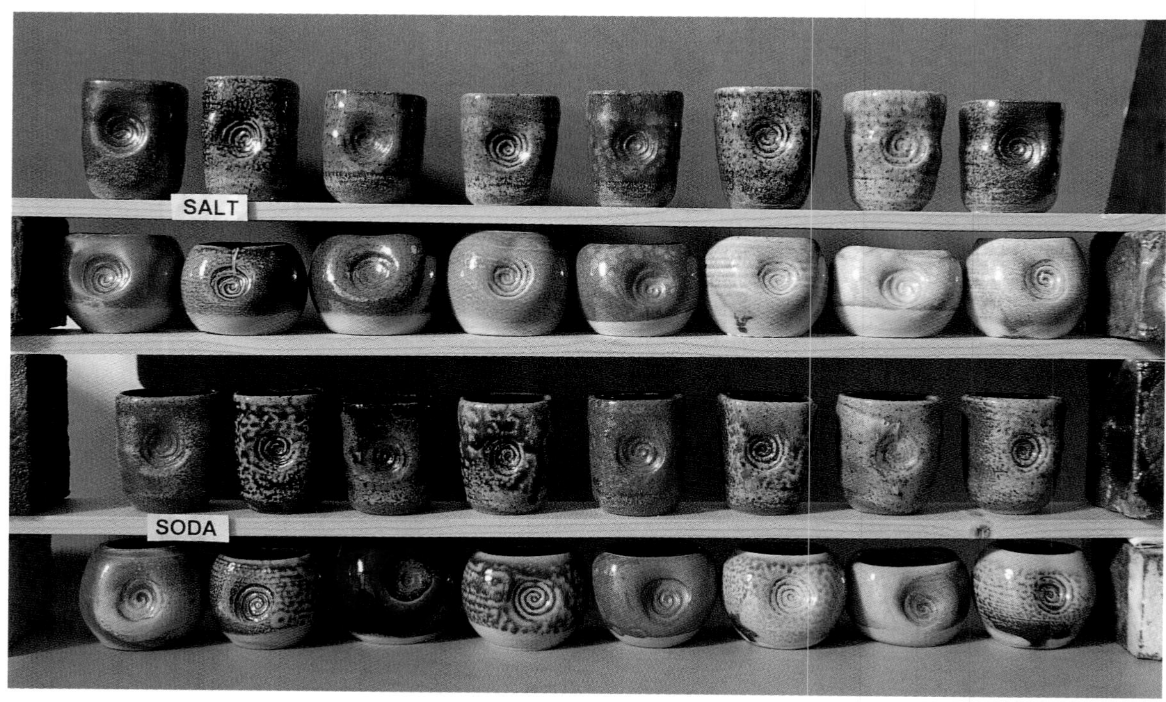

Comparison of salt and soda trials on 'salt' clays A and B. Left to right: slips 1 to 8. Top row: 'salt' clay A, salt fired. Second row: 'salt' clay B, salt fired. Third row: 'salt' clay A, soda fired. Fourth row: 'salt' clay B, soda fired.

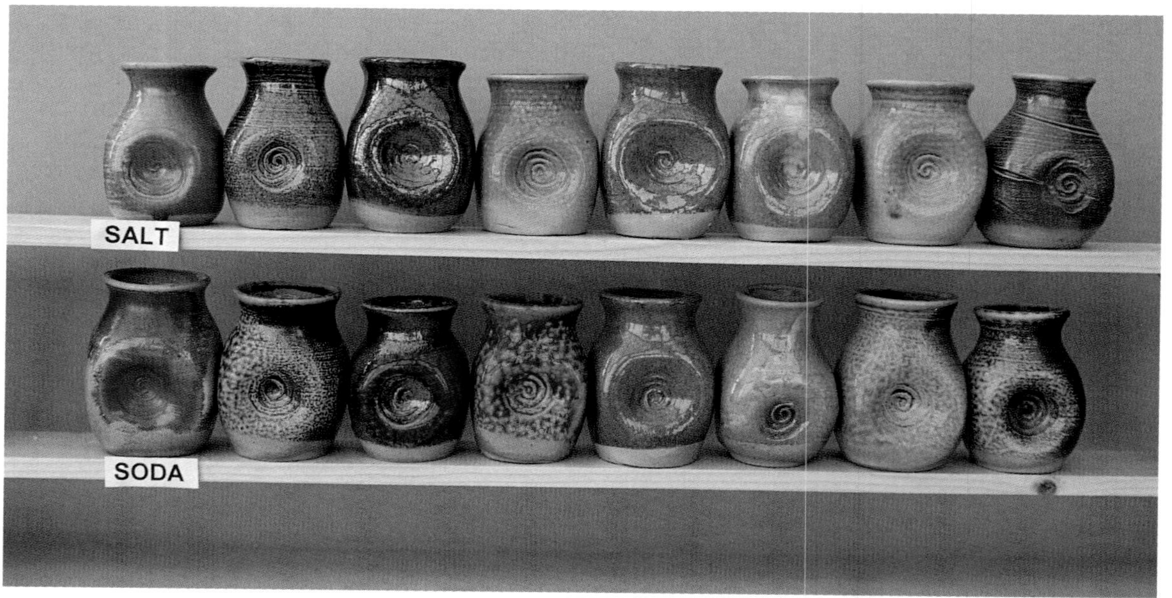

Comparison of salt and soda trials on 'soda' clay C. Left to right: slips 1 to 8. Top row: salt fired. Bottom row: soda fired.

SALT AND SODA COMPARED

The trials involved three clays, and ten slips. Four of these slips were recipes used in salt firings, and four were recipes used in soda firings. Up to three samples of each slip, on each clay body, were placed arbitrarily throughout the salt and soda kilns. Both kilns were gas-fired, to a similar firing schedule, under light reduction, and up to 1,300°C, cone 11.

- The salt glaze was more evenly distributed than the soda glaze.
- The soda glaze was more random, and the shielded areas of the pots remained unglazed and without a colour response.
- Some colours were brighter on the soda-glaze pots than on the salt-glaze pots.
- One slip in particular had a distinctly different colour response in the soda firing, and cobalt oxide content dominated the rutile content.

SODA COMPOUNDS

Soda is sodium oxide, and is a general term that covers the sodium compounds included in the list below. These may be considered suitable for soda glaze.

- **Soda ash** (sodium carbonate) Na_2CO_3
- **Washing soda** (sodium carbonate) $Na_2CO_3.10H_2O$
- **Baking soda** (sodium bicarbonate) $NaHCO_3$

Borax is a source of boron oxide with sodium oxide, and can be used in combination with any of the sodium compounds. Used with salt it can lower the temperature at which vaporization will occur. It is not only a flux but also a glass former. It brightens the colours and helps promote a more fluid, smoother glaze finish.

- **Borax** $Na_2B_4O_7.10H_2O$

The Nature of Soda Glaze

With even more variable results than salt glaze, the random nature of the glaze is one of the attractions to soda firing. The dramatic effect of the heaviest flashing contrasts with the driest areas that occur on the side that escapes the vapour. The forms need to be visually strong in order to be able to receive the impact of the random soda vapour without being overwhelmed. The variable effects from soda can be less desirable on functional ware. Adding a flux to the slips will help to ensure the surfaces will have a more even surface quality.

Early Soda Glaze

In Britain the first experiments with soda glaze took place alongside salt firings at Harrow in the early 1970s. They were carried out by a few students, who built a small soda kiln. An article by an ex-Harrow student, Ann Shattuk, in a 1975 issue of *Pottery Quarterly*, describes the tests that she was undertaking on vapour glazing with soda. In it she suggested that either one could accept soda-glaze pots for what they are, colourful and often just flashed with glaze, or alternatively one could try to turn soda into a viable alternative to the salt process and attempt to achieve the same results as with salt.

Behind much of the early research into soda glaze, undertaken in America and Britain and later in Australia, was the aim to find an alternative to salt glazing in urban areas. For some, this remains the only interest in using soda. But there is something missed if every attempt was made to minimize the special nature of soda vapour. The random qualities of soda firing have yet to be fully exploited, and the potential lies in the development of the surfaces for sculpture and non-functional ceramics.

Pioneers in Soda Glaze

LISA HAMMOND

Lisa Hammond was a student at Medway College between 1975–78, when she was introduced to salt glaze during a kiln-building course with Ian Gregory. She set up her first pottery, making salt glaze, in Greenwich, London, in 1980, remaining there for five years. She was

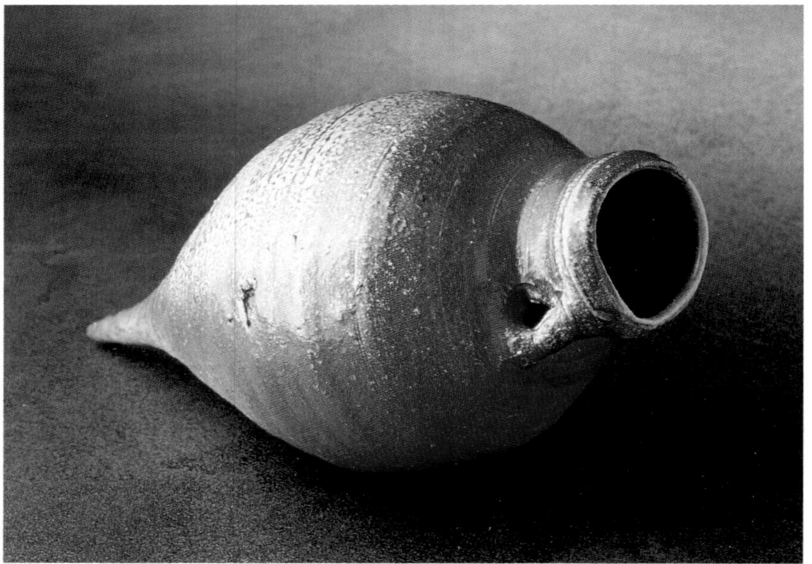

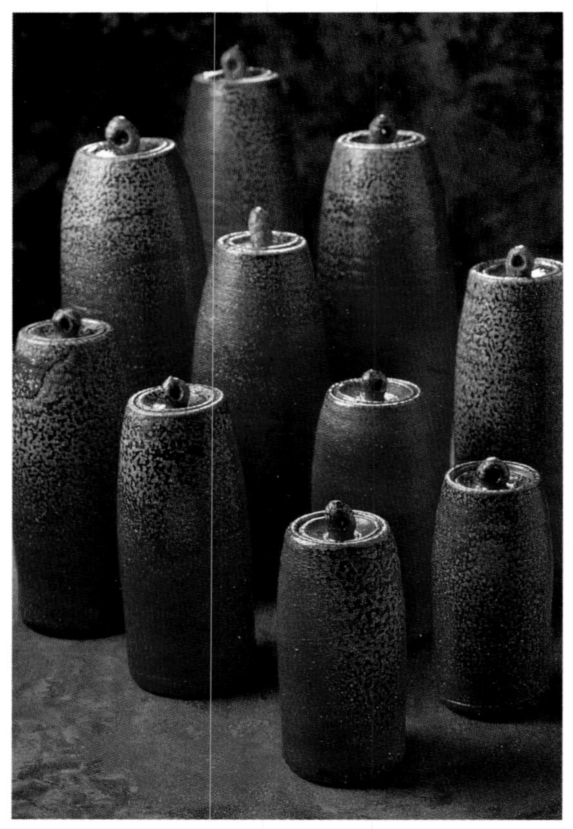

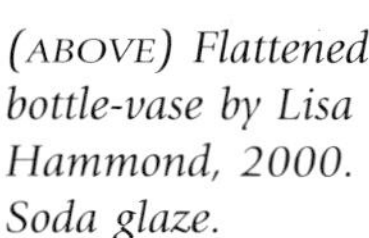

(ABOVE) Flattened bottle-vase by Lisa Hammond, 2000. Soda glaze.

(ABOVE RIGHT) Lidded jars by Lisa Hammond, 2000. Soda glaze. Heavily flashed on one side, with lighter coating or dry surface on the other. Uneven distribution of vapour is certainly a more pronounced trait of soda firing.

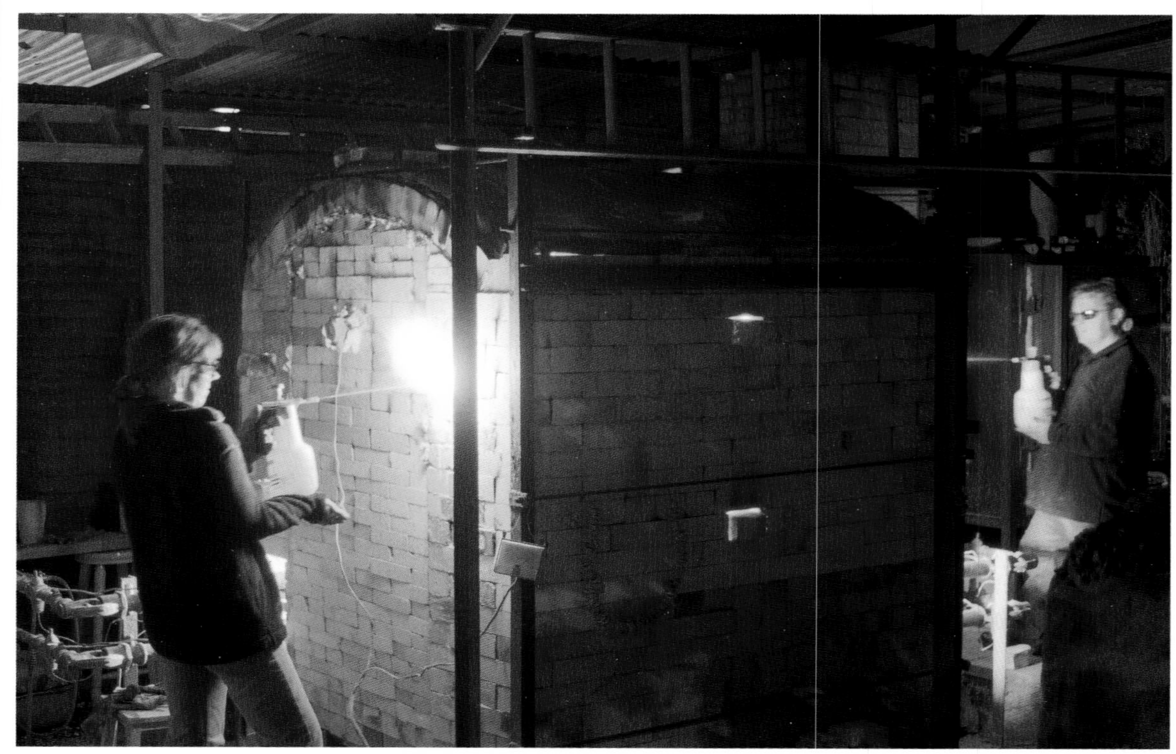

Firing Lisa Hammond's trolly kiln. The soda is sprayed into the kiln over a period of up to two and a half hours, during which the damper position is changed a number of times to vary the flame path and vapour distribution.

conscious of the un-neighbourly effects of the fog in an urban environment, caused by the salting. In an attempt to reduce the problem, she began testing different ways to introduce both salt and soda into her kiln. At the same time, students at the University of London Goldsmith's College, where she taught, were beginning a period of pioneering work with experimental soda kilns.

When she established her second pottery workshop in Greenwich in 1994, Lisa Hammond was committed to soda firing. She built a large, 2.5cu m (90cu ft) trolley kiln, using lightweight, high-alumina bricks, and fired with natural gas. Her experiments with soda taught her that it has a tendency to sit on the bottom of the chamber, and is less inclined to volatilize. So she sprays the soda in as a solution of sodium bicarbonate, and also throws in a handful of damp rock salt at the end of the firing. She stacks the wares so the vapour can circulate through the kiln. But she also places each one carefully to make the most of the 'flashed' effects, as these are what she wants for her strong, simple, functional forms.

RUTHANNE TUDBALL

Ruthanne Tudball works in a way that retains the soft fluidity and plasticity of clay in her forms. She wanted to choose a glazing technique that would enhance and emphasize the marks and rhythms of the making. Salt would have been an obvious choice, had it not been for her concern for the environment (the likely pollution caused by salt and soda firings are debated in Chapter 6). Feeling on this issue at that time led her to start experiments with spraying sodium compounds into the kiln at Goldsmith's College, where she studied ceramics between 1987 and 1989. She also discovered an article by American potters in a 1978 issue of *The Studio Potter*, that discussed soda glazing, and the use of sodium carbonate to get salt-glaze effects.

Her method is to mix 1.3kg (3lb) of sodium bicarbonate with hot water, and this is sprayed at cone 8 to 10 in her 1cu m (35cu ft) kiln, in small amounts every 15 minutes over about two hours. There is an oxidized soak for 1½ hours at the end of the firing, and she crash cools to 950°C.

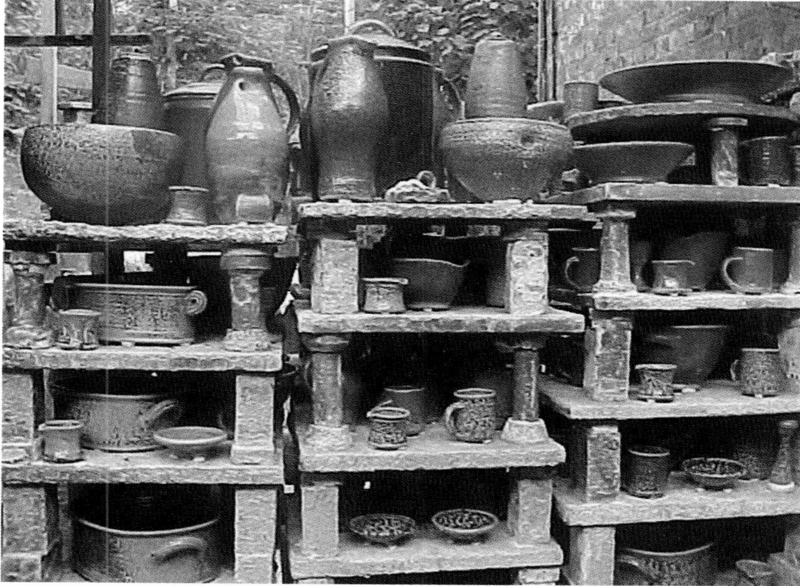

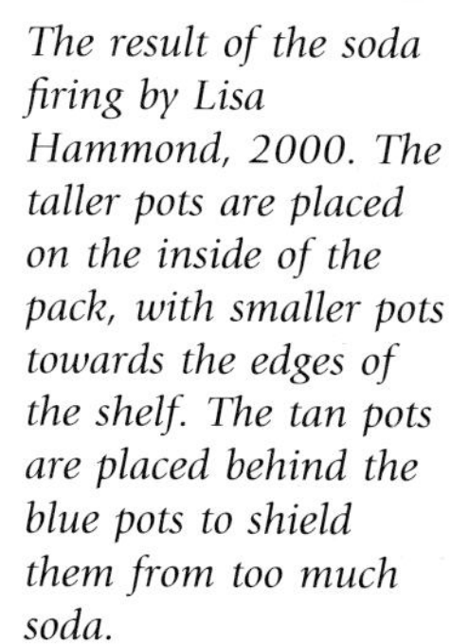
The result of the soda firing by Lisa Hammond, 2000. The taller pots are placed on the inside of the pack, with smaller pots towards the edges of the shelf. The tan pots are placed behind the blue pots to shield them from too much soda.

Ruthanne Tudball is one of the leading soda-glaze potters in Britain, and her energy and enthusiasm for the process has encouraged others to explore it for themselves. She says:

> Sodium vapour glazing has the wonderful attribute of bleaching edges and therefore emphasizing any mark made in the clay. I am particularly drawn to the surface qualities that

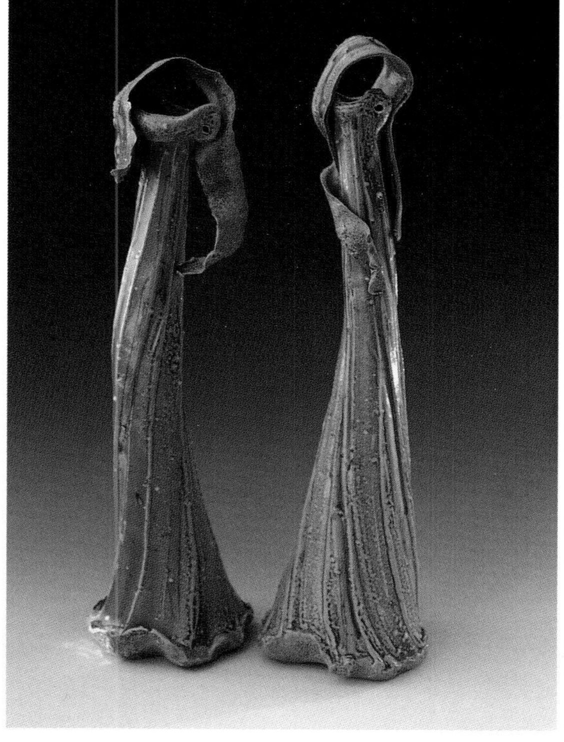

Dancing bottles by Ruthanne Tudball, 2000. 43cm and 45cm high. Soda vapour glaze. Faceted and slip-decorated, fired to 1,300°C.

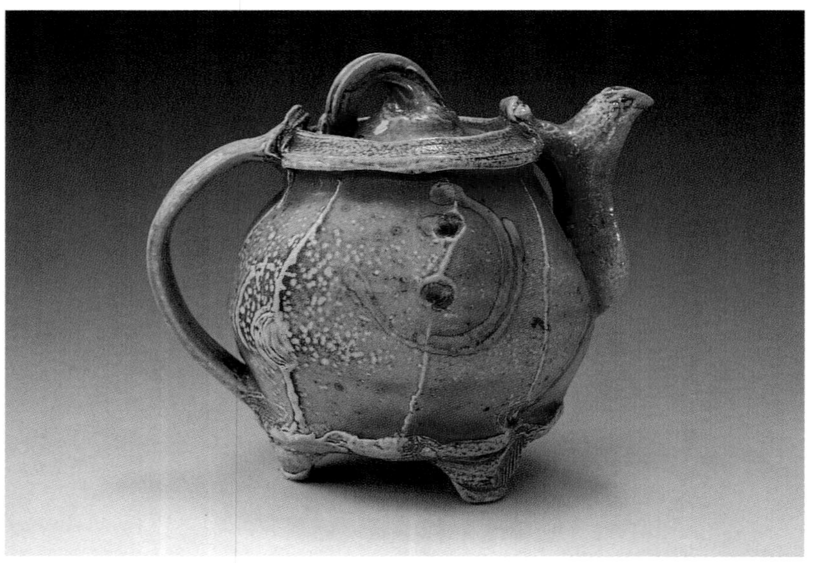

Teapot on three feet by Ruthanne Tudball, 2000. 18cm high. Soda vapour-glaze stoneware, 1,300°C. Faceted, with finger marks, slip decorated.

using sodium bicarbonate gives to the fired clay. There are shiny, matt and bleached areas, and darker shadowy areas tracing the path of the flame and the sodium vapour being carried by it through the kiln, giving each pot a unique surface.

Her book *Soda Glazing* was published in 1995, and gives practical advice for anyone specifically interested in soda firing.

JACK DOHERTY

Group of pots by Jack Doherty, 2000. Soda glaze.

Doherty fires with soda to use the qualities of a glaze that reveals and accentuates the marks created during the making. The use of soda rather than salt is deliberate:

> I enjoy the flashing effect as the vapour drifts through the kiln. I am not looking for heavy orange-peel surfaces, but am trying to enhance the clay with a fairly thin glaze. The kiln atmosphere is reduced from 1,000°C until the end of the firing. I mix 2kg [4.5lb] of sodium bicarbonate with hot water, and spray the mixture into the kiln at cone 8. This takes about one and a half hours. The firing then continues until cone 10 is down.

His use of colour is described in Chapter 7.

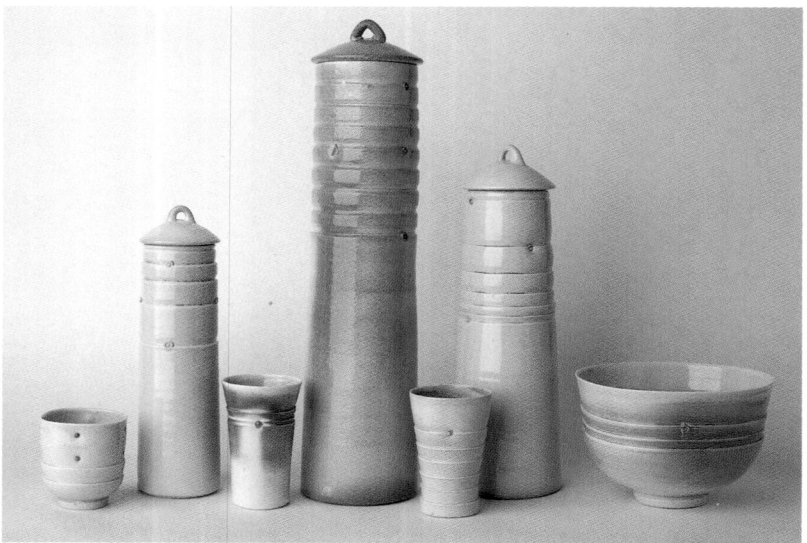

Alternative Temperatures

The use of vapour agents in the lower temperature ranges can produce salt-glaze earthenware, and it also extends the conventional qualities of the salting process to include vapour surfaces, as distinct from a vapour glaze.

Salt-Glaze Earthenware

The idea of salt-glaze earthenware might at first seem an anomaly. Salt glaze needs a mature, vitrified body, and earthenware usually remains open and porous. But a clay body can be made up of materials that will fuse and become dense around the temperature at which salt volatilizes,

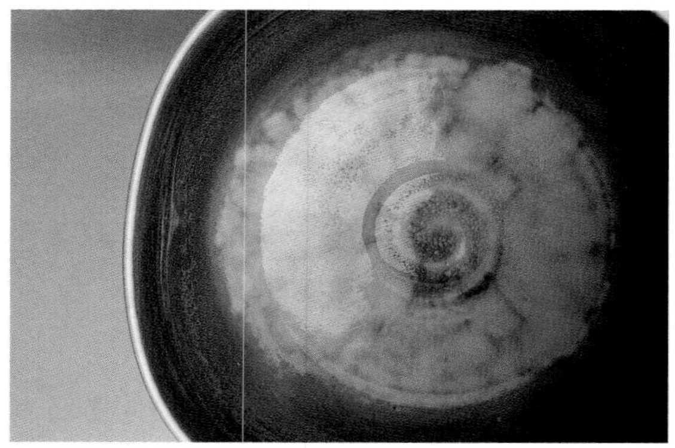

(ABOVE) Detail of inside of bowl by Jack Doherty, 2000. Soda glaze over various applications of copper oxide.

namely 1,100°C. In such a case, this can be termed salt-glaze earthenware – that is, salt glaze achieved in the medium temperature range, between 960°C and 1,180°C.

RICHARD LAUNDER

Richard has pushed the boundaries of the salting technique in many directions. His article on salt-glaze earthenware was published in *Ceramic Review*, issue 70, in 1981. He describes preparing trials for a suitable body for this medium temperature salt glazing, by mixing red and white earthenware and stoneware clays, with additions of white ball clay and silica sand. Varying proportions of clay will give a range of colour from dark brown to a pale cream. Too high an iron content – over 8 per cent – will repel the salt vapour and produce a dark metallic finish, and also cause bloating.

Slips can be prepared and tested in the same ways as for high-fired salt, but the addition of fluxes and frits will help to encourage a melt on the surface of the pots. The most successful glazes for the insides of the pots will need to be based on a low-temperature flux such as borax frit, and if the pots are to be once-fired, the raw glaze will need to contain a good proportion of clay.

As borax volatilizes at a much lower temperature than salt, it can be an advantage to use a mixture of salt and borax. Launder wrote:

> Mixtures of salt and borax should be used for temperatures below 1,100°C . . . Although salting can take place as low as 940°C, the minimum temperature for a good glaze appears to be 1,040°C (using a mixture of salt 85 per cent, borax 15 per cent).

For his own work he didn't use borax, finding that the temperature range 1,120° to 1, 140°C suited the clays and slips he had developed.

Low-Temperature Salt Firing

The function of the salt at low temperatures, below 1,000°C, is to draw out subtle nuances of colour inherent in both the clay body and the slip. The clay body will remain dry and matt.

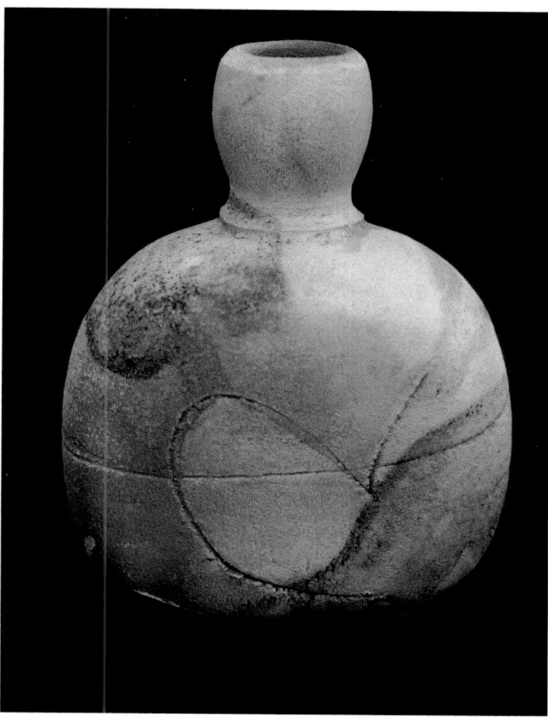

Bottle form by David Miller, mid-1980s. Low temperature salt. 28 × 20cm. Thrown, squashed, applied neck. White and copper slips.

DAVID MILLER

David Miller is one of the few British potters who, in the past, used low-temperature salt. He wrote about his progress in this experimental firing technique in an article in *Ceramic Review*, issue 85, in 1984. He biscuit-fired the pots to 980°C and then applied a thin layer of vitreous slip. A small percentage of copper carbonate was added to one mix of the slip, which was then applied to selected areas of the pots. His recipe for a base slip is:

Applied thinly (milk consistency) to biscuit pots fired to 980°C

Gerstley borate	7
Alkaline frit	3
Flint	20
China clay	40

Add copper oxide 1–2 per cent, or copper carbonate 2–3 per cent.

Further Guidance

The following guidelines are for firing low-temperature salt. A simply constructed small kiln will make it possible to explore some

'Standin' Cuneiform' by Richard Launder, 1992. Low-fired salt, sawdust and wood fired at 1,000°C. 25 × 19 × 19cm. Carved, modified brick clay, high silica slip and alkaline frit and copper.

extraordinarily rich effects, of a different nature to conventional salt glaze. A rudimentary updraught kiln will be suitable, such as the fibre one described in Chapter 8, or a similar one built of insulation bricks.

The stacking has a critical influence on the heat and vapour distribution. Salt and copper carbonate mixed with salt is best wrapped in packets and placed amongst the pots. The initial temperature rise to 700°C can be rapid, after which the firing needs to be slower to allow the salt vapour to work. A complete firing, to a maximum temperature of 1,000°C, will take around four hours. Only time and trials will bring a degree of understanding and control over the response of different clays and slips with coloured stains. This technique is one for taking chances, and for individual trials and expression. It is one in which to indulge with an open mind.

'Terra sigillata' is particularly receptive to low-temperature salt vapour. This is a slip made from very fine clay particles, that gives a very smooth surface to a clay body, and interesting responses can be produced using either red or white clay. The introduction of other carbonates and low-temperature fluxes into the kiln will produce more variation, and shielding the pieces from direct contact with the fuming materials will allow the vapour alone to interact with the pots. A salt solution can be sprayed through the burner port or directly onto the pots to enrich the effects of the salt vapour. Low-temperature glazes, such as those used for 'raku' firings, can be used in combination with the salt.

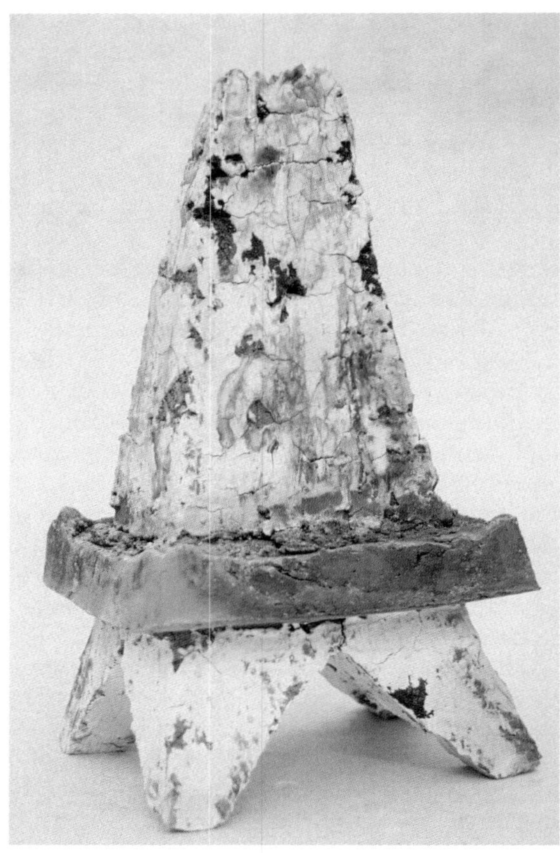

'Water-worn' dish by the author Rosemary Cochrane, 1999. Low temperature salt with copper.

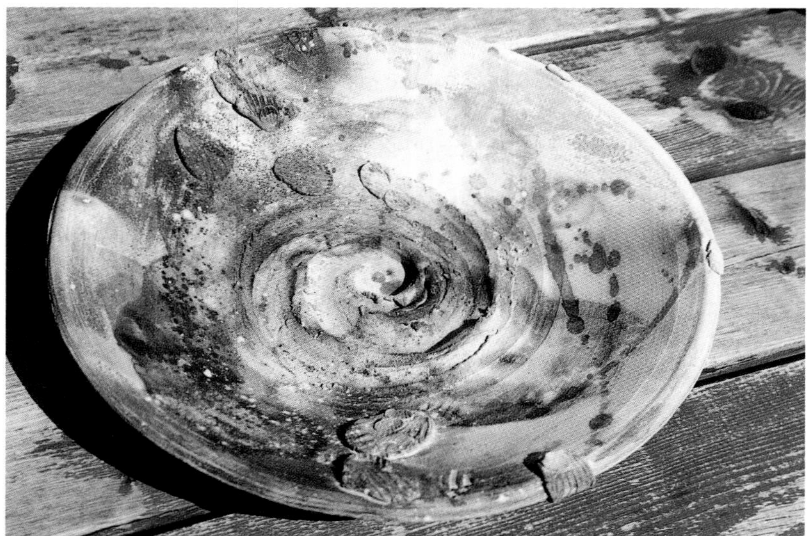

The permanency of unglazed, low-fired pieces can be uncertain if they still have an open porous body and are left in a damp place where they can absorb moisture: the surface of the piece will gradually flake away, in the same way as an old stone wall as the salts are drawn out into the atmosphere. The problem can be avoided, however, by burnishing the clay surfaces before firing, and afterwards keeping the pieces in a dry place. It also helps to fire to a slightly higher temperature, though not so high as to cause a glaze to form.

A word of warning: even when only small amounts of metal oxides and carbonates are used to create a volatile vapour in the kiln, some of the vapours will be released into the atmosphere around the kiln, and every precaution should be taken to avoid inhalation of any of these fumes. A respirator should be worn throughout the fuming procedure. The manufacturers will give advice on the appropriate filter to fit. Protective goggles also should be worn.

Firing Larger Pieces: with Ian Gregory

As a figurative ceramic sculptor, Ian Gregory has devised a way of making the larger pieces, which are intended for low-fired raku/salt, on HTI bricks and ceramic fibre blanket. This forms the base of a kiln, and he then builds the kiln around the work, first positioning three sides around the piece, then constructing the firebox for two gas burners, and finally adding the fourth side and the lid. Heavy-duty clips hold the sides together. Small pots of salt are placed around the piece, sometimes mixed with sawdust for various effects from firing to 1,020°C. A large version of the flat-pack fibre kiln can be erected using stacks of panels and with the addition of a small chimney, and can be used to fire to high temperatures.

Low-temperature Firing with Christine Gittins

Christine Gittins explores the effect of copper and salt on a burnished clay surface fired with sawdust in a saggar. She uses a white clay body that shows the final subtle pink and grey colours obtained in the saggar firing to their best advantage. Her pots are wheel thrown, turned and burnished when leather hard. After bisque firing to 1,000°C, the pots are re-fired in an earthenware plant container that serves as a saggar.

To create the colours, a mixture of copper carbonate and salt is introduced into the saggar. The salt is not allowed to come into direct contact with the pots: instead, small containers with the mix are packed carefully amongst the pots in the saggar. For more dramatic results, copper wire is wound around the pots to create spiralling black lines. The pots are placed randomly, but supporting each other, with smaller pots between the larger ones, and the gaps in between loosely filled with sawdust. The saggar is sealed tightly with ceramic fibre and a kiln shelf on top. The second firing is done to 800°C, after which the pots are cleaned and wax polished.

Another word of warning: although Christine uses an electric kiln, she always does a bisque firing between the saggar firings, and is fully aware that the life of the elements will be much shorter than would normally be expected. During the saggar firing any fumes should be avoided, and good ventilation around the kiln is essential.

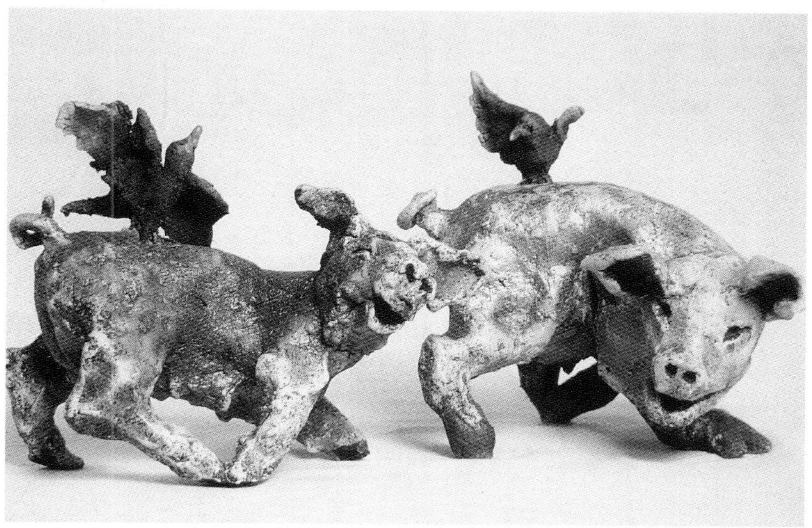

'Pigs and Crows' by Ian Gregory. 10in high, 15 × 6in wide. Low salt fired to 1,100°C. High silica earthenware clay. Bowls of salt and copper oxide to fume the pieces.

Sawdust Firing with Salt

In principle, any loosely built box of bricks, or an old metal drum pieced with holes, will serve as a sawdust kiln. Biscuit-fired pots are placed on a base layer of sawdust, and the spaces between are filled with sawdust, or sawdust wrapped in twisted sheets of newspaper, small

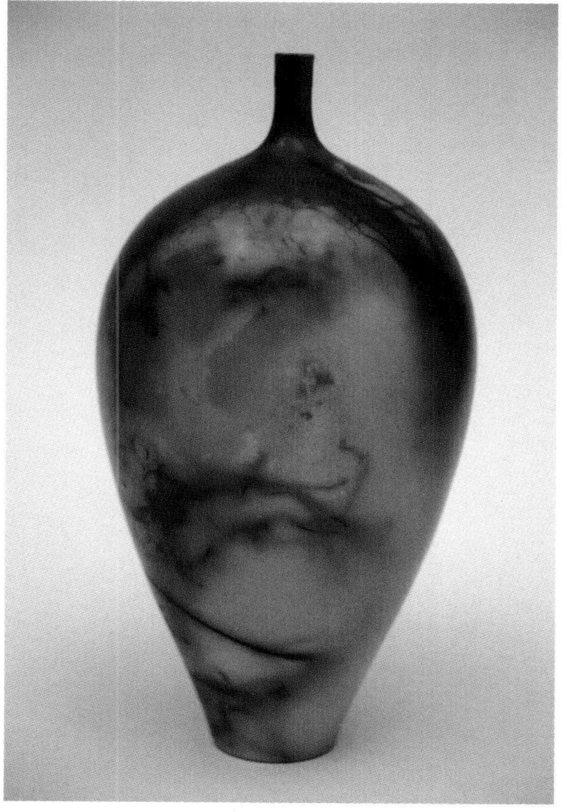

Bottle form by Christine Gittins, 2000. 32cm high. Low temperature, saggar-fired.

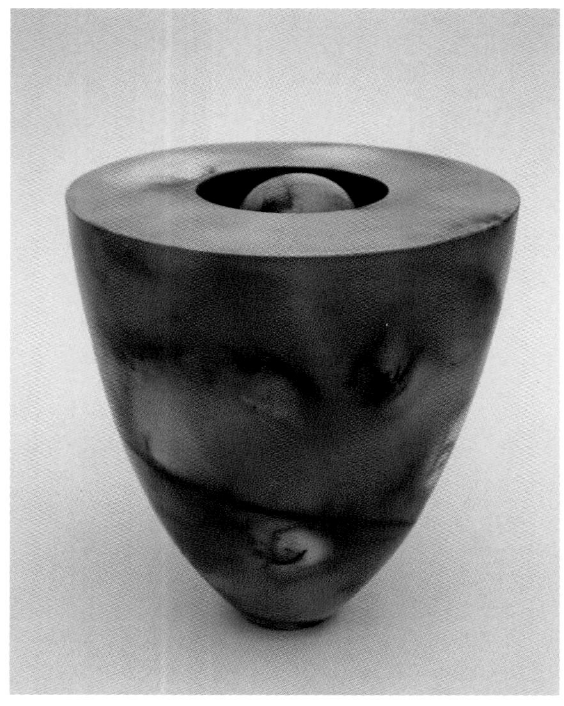

Double-sided vessel with sphere by Christine Gittins, 2000. 23cm high. Low temperature saggar-fired.

pieces of wood, and a final top layer of newspaper and sawdust. Small packets of salt and copper carbonate are placed between the pots and amongst the sawdust. In this type of stacking the fire can be lit at the bottom, through the holes in the kiln, and then left to smoulder overnight, with a metal lid covering the top.

If the sawdust is packed inside and around the pots without any extra paper and wood, the salt and copper mix can either be sprinkled in with the sawdust, or the packets of the mix placed amongst it. The top layer of sawdust should be deep so that when it is set alight it can build up a good heat. The kiln is covered with a loose lid and left to smoulder overnight.

Using these methods, unpredictable and exciting flashings of dry surface colours – reds, pinks and yellows – are formed on the pieces. A pale clay will show any colour response best, and burnished pots give an additionally smooth, tactile surface. Much more about sawdust firings can be found in books and articles specific to the technique.

Serendipity

Salt, soda, high temperature, low temperature, heavy orange-peel texture, dry matt surfaces: these are just the start of the alternatives within vapour firing. Added to which is the magic ingredient, serendipity. The unpredictability of vapour firing means that once a potter becomes involved with vapour firings, the element of surprise and the opportunity for delight will always be part of the process.

III
Inspirations for the Future

11 Vapour Glaze in the Twenty-First Century

A survey carried out by the author during the research for this book shows that in Britain today, at the start of the twenty-first century, there are around fifty potters committed to vapour-glaze firings. Of those, fewer than ten are using sodium compounds, the rest use salt. With a few exceptions, the majority of those potters are producing functional ware with the classic vapour-glaze surfaces.

In Britain, the number of colleges at which the ceramics courses can offer kiln-building experience and the opportunity for experimental firings out of the studio is diminishing. Since the 1970s tighter budgets and more rigorous Health and Safety regulations have brought about changes. Among the recent generation of studio potters, only a small number have taken up salt or soda glazing in a serious way, and are able to earn a living with their chosen craft. Functional ware is still at the heart of the work of these makers, who carry the tradition of vapour-glaze firings in Britain into the twenty-first century – yet each is using the process to achieve an individual and contemporary style of work.

May Ling Beadsmoore

May Ling trained to become a studio potter at Derby University, where she first built and fired soda kilns. Since 1996, when she built her own gas-fired kiln, she has produced her own contemporary range of soda-glaze tableware. She deliberately tries to exploit the characteristics of soda-glaze firings in the way the pieces are made. Her wheel-thrown forms are often dimpled with the impressions of shells, and slightly distorted in ways that will catch the variable nature of the vapour glaze. She uses a white clay body as the background for bright colours, which she achieves by spraying slips onto the dry, unfired pieces. The random flashes of the soda glaze pick out the direction from which the slips have been applied, creating watery-looking surfaces on the pots. Her hand-built forms have a textured finish, and retain soft curves and softened edges, further enhanced by the soft, blurred qualities of the soda glaze.

May Ling is attracted to soda glaze for several reasons. Vapour firing itself is exciting

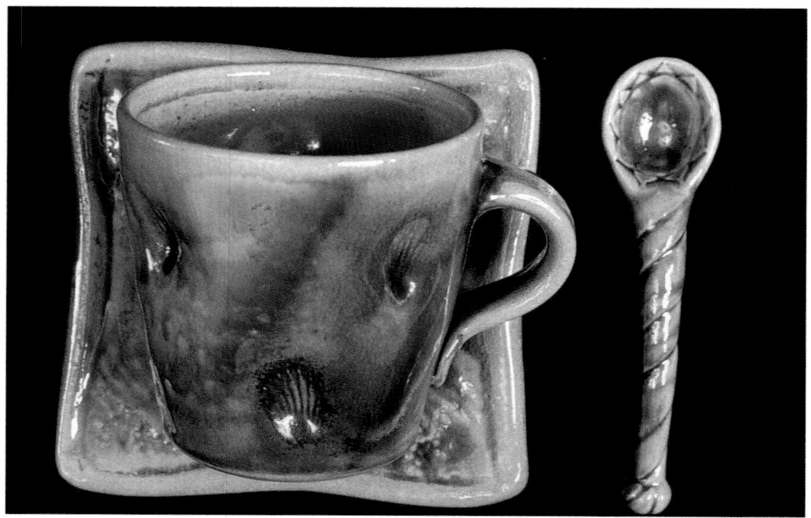

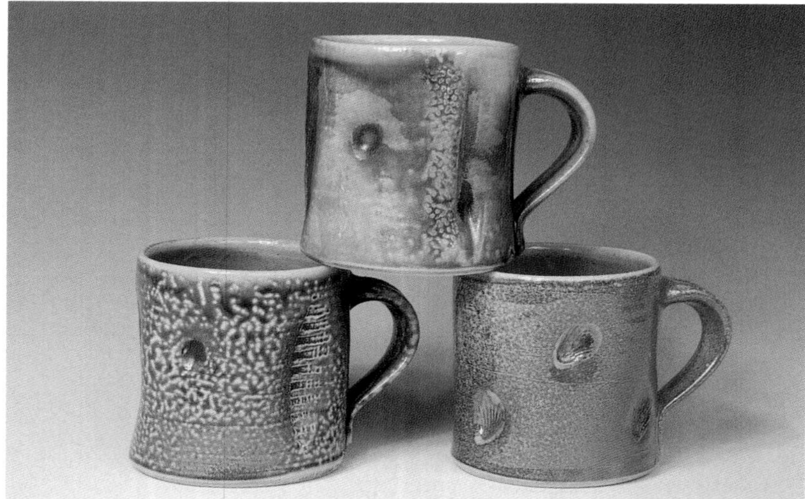

(LEFT) Cup, saucer and spoon by May Ling Beadsmoore, 2000. Soda glaze.

(CENTRE) Mugs by May Ling Beadsmoore, 2000. Soda glaze.

and interactive, and her of soda choice is partly due to her city location. But even if she did move to a rural location, she would not be tempted to change to salt firing. She finds the surface qualities of soda glaze are particularly suited to her tableware, and she is happy to continue exploring the attributes that seem particular to soda glaze. The brighter colours in the orange and turquoise ranges, and the tactile qualities of the surfaces which make handling a beaker or holding a mug a special joy, are the distinctive qualities that soda glaze gives to her pieces.

Daniel Boyle

Daniel Boyle concentrated on salt glaze and kiln development during the time he studied at Harrow College of Higher Education from 1989 to 1991. He lived and worked in London for six years before he moved to West Wales, to establish his third workshop. Concentrating on making salt-glaze ceramics, he once-fires in an 8.5cu m (30cu ft) kiln, using reclaimed wood.

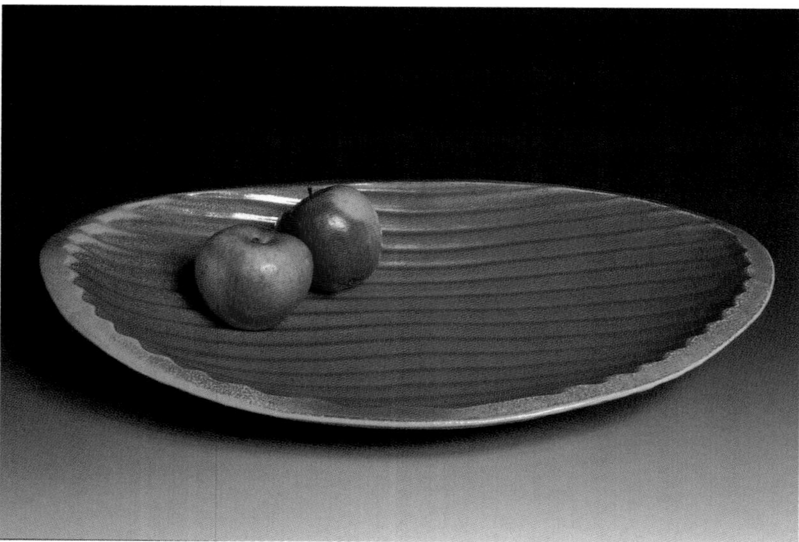

Ripple dish by May Ling Beadsmoore, 2000. 45cm wide. Soda glaze.

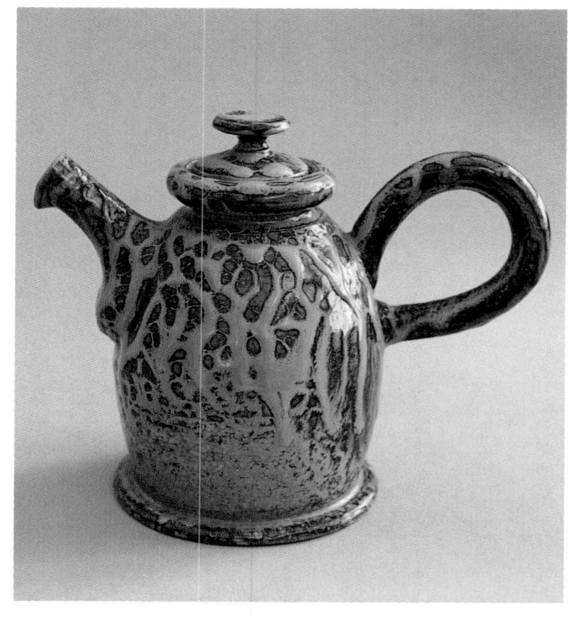

Coffee pot by Daniel Boyle. Wood-fired salt glaze.

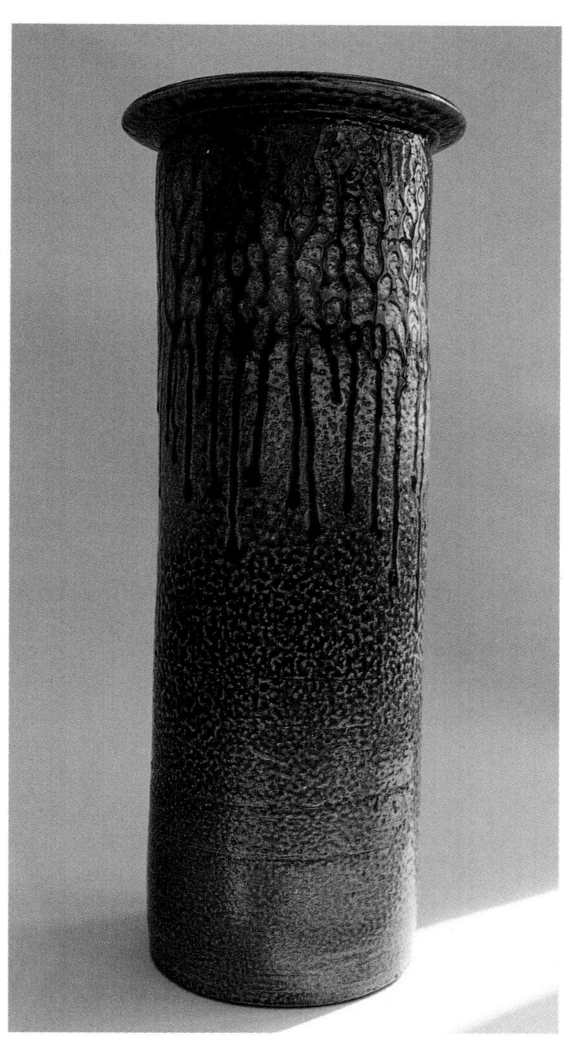

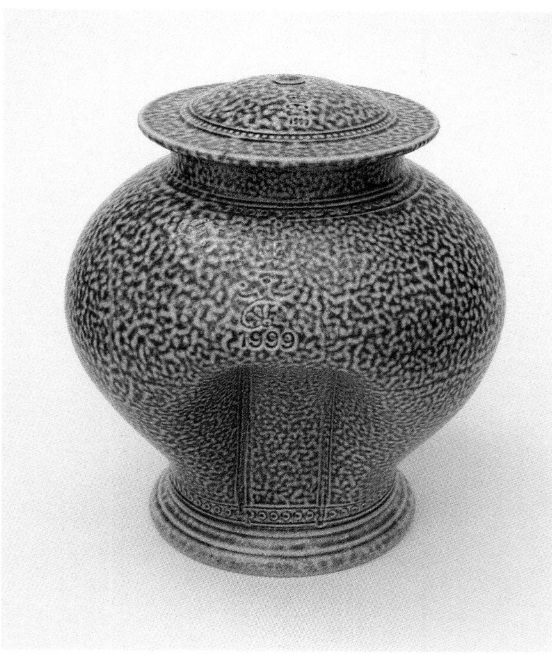

(FAR LEFT) *Vase by Daniel Boyle. Wood-fired salt glaze.*

(LEFT) *Lidded jar by Steve Harrison, 1999. Salt glaze.*

He exploits the process to create many original colours and surfaces, decorating the pots with simple slips and ash. In the firing, with the addition of the salt vapour, quite fantastic fluid surface qualities are created.

Steve Harrison

Steve Harrison made large-scale raku and reduction-fired stoneware while following the ceramics course at Middlesex University, but by the time he graduated from the Royal College of Art in 1993, he had discovered, and was producing, salt glaze. He is a potter who loves clay, and has a passion and enthusiasm for the whole process of making pots. He has built his own wheels and kilns; his salt gas kiln is in mid-Wales, away from the urban constraints of north London.

He also makes all his own tools, seeing that as part of the creative process, each one made specially to achieve one particular idea or feature. He turns the wooden handles and fashions the rollers, mouldings and stamps from brass or stainless steel. In this way he feels that the use of the tools, to finish his pieces on the wheel and to decorate the leather-hard pots, offers something extra, like a personal signature.

Harrison makes utilitarian pots that include teapots, mugs, jugs and bowls; but each one is unique and distinctly of his making. His influence comes from the eighteenth-century tin and pewter wares and their makers' methods, as well as from the lathe-turned ceramics of Wedgwood and Doulton. He has investigated the historical techniques, and has found ways to translate them to work on the potter's wheel. His work is distinctive and innovative, characterized by his own interpretation of ceramics of the past, and with contemporary application of form and detail.

The salt glaze enhances the crisp, smooth surfaces and turned and beaded details, and he has stayed with the orange-peel texture since this signifies a link with the antique and valuable. So far he has been involved in making wares that, he agrees, are like the majority of contemporary British salt glaze, in that they resemble the surfaces of the sixteenth- and seventeenth-century German salt glaze. His most recent pieces are creamware – low-fired,

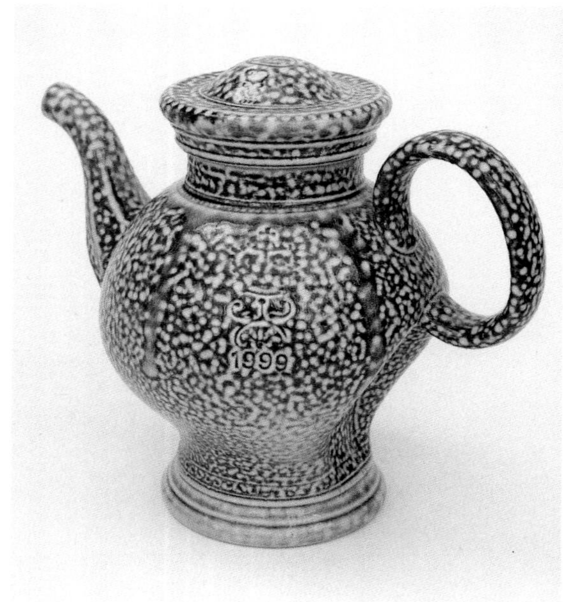

Coffee pot by Steve Harrison, 1999.

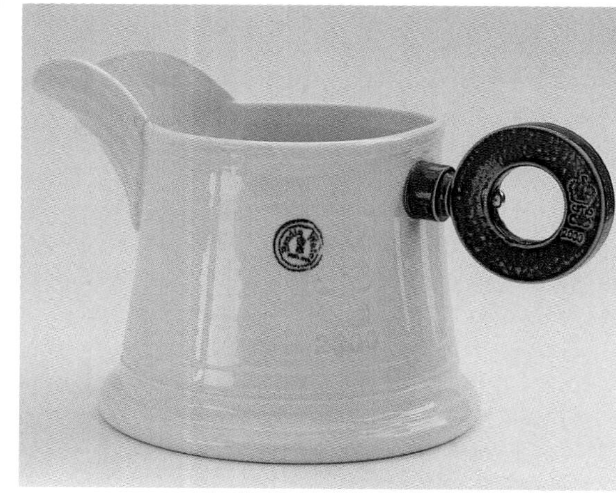

Creamware jug with salt-glaze handle by Steve Harrison, 2000

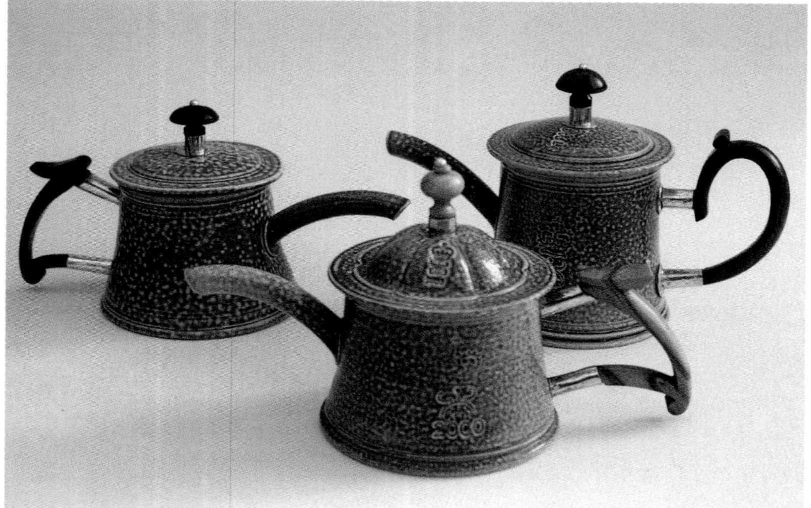

(BELOW) Teapots by Steve Harrison, 2000. With crafted hardwood handles and silver fittings.

lead-glazed earthenware: these break away from convention, with salt-glaze attachments and extra-large wing nuts. He sees them as a comment, as much as an investigation, into the possibilities of a new direction for British salt glaze.

Wobage Workshops

Petra Reynolds and Jeremy Steward

Petra Reynolds and Jeremy Steward have shared their workshop at the Wobage Farm Craft Workshops since graduating from the Cardiff Institute of Higher Education in 1995, where they had both opted to soda fire. When they arrived at Wobage they used a small Olsen fast-fire type of kiln to explore the effects of firing with wood, combined with their developing work with soda glaze. They are now using a larger kiln, experimenting with the potential of cross-draught as opposed to down-draught, and what this offers in the way of heavier fly ash, again in combination with soda vapour.

Surrounded by the experience of the other potters at Wobage, but working and firing independently, their work shows a wonderfully creative response to the physical effort and decision-making that is necessary during a wood firing. Because they are so closely involved with every firing they are able to give a special character to the final appearance of their pots. Although all their work comes from shared firings, they each produce their own distinctive styles of pot. At present they are choosing to make functional ware, thus continuing in the long tradition of British salt glaze.

Petra Reynolds

Petra Reynolds was originally attracted to soda firing when she saw the opportunity to explore a challenging firing process. She constructs her pots by folding and joining slabs of clay. She uses one of many paper-pattern templates as an outline guide to cut the slab shapes. Once these have stiffened, she is able to mitre, bend and join the clay to the desired shape. The pieces retain the freshness of a deceptively simple technique.

She decorates the leather-hard forms with simple slips and glazes, brushed or poured, occasionally using paper resist. These marks and patterns provide a canvas for more linear decoration, achieved by a form of printmaking. In this, black slip is brushed onto newspaper and left to go tacky. The slipped newspaper pieces are placed onto the pots, and the marks are drawn onto the back of the newspaper: when this is peeled away, the imprint is left on the pot. The insides of the pots are raw glazed when leather hard.

The soft edges of the forms, with their simple decoration, are bestowed with a sparkle and sheen from the lightest coating of glaze. Random variation is the nature of the process, and some pieces retain drier areas while others are given a heavier flashing from the flame and soda glaze. The qualities achieved from the wood firing and the soda glaze can be elusive, but it is clear that, from the moment the pieces are first formed, the maker is involved with visualizing the possibilities that the fire and vapour can offer each one.

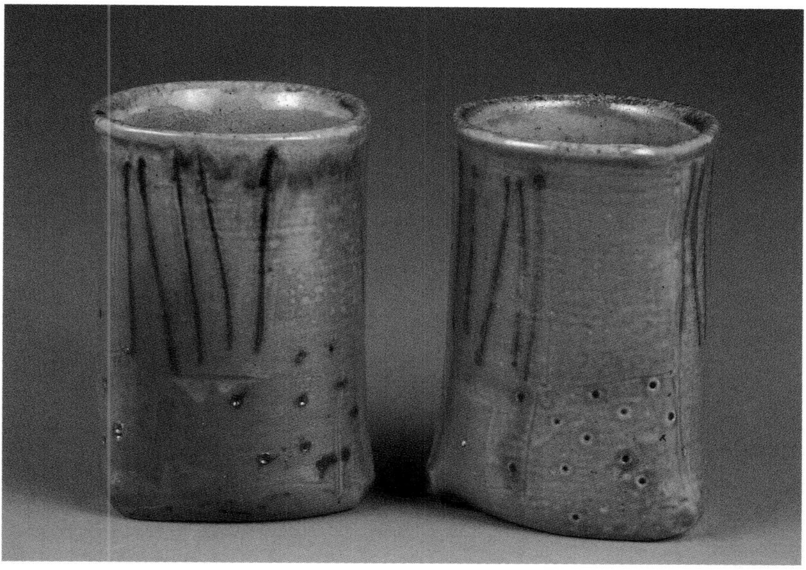

Two beakers by Petra Reynolds, 2000. 4½in high, hand-built, wood-fired soda glaze.

(BELOW LEFT) Jug by Petra Reynolds, 2000. 6in high, hand-built, wood-fired soda glaze.

(BELOW) Jar by Petra Reynolds, 2000. 7in high, hand-built, wood-fired soda glaze.

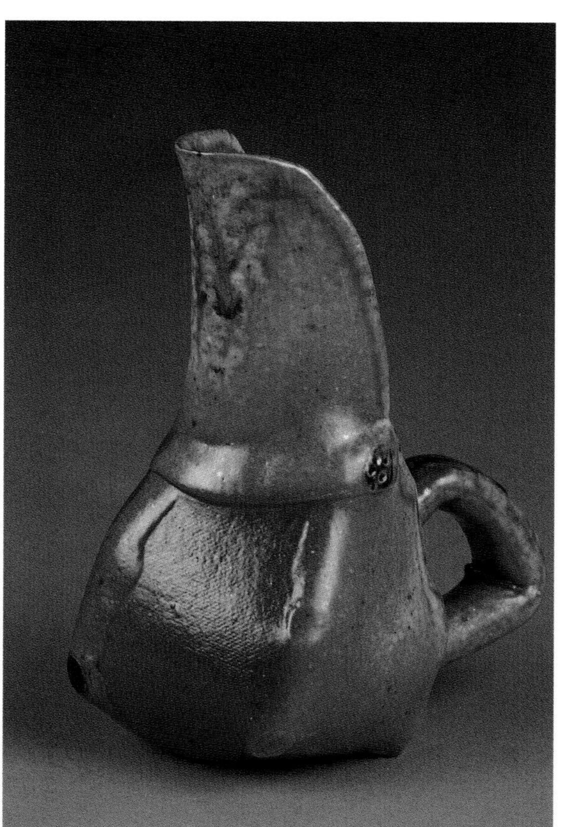

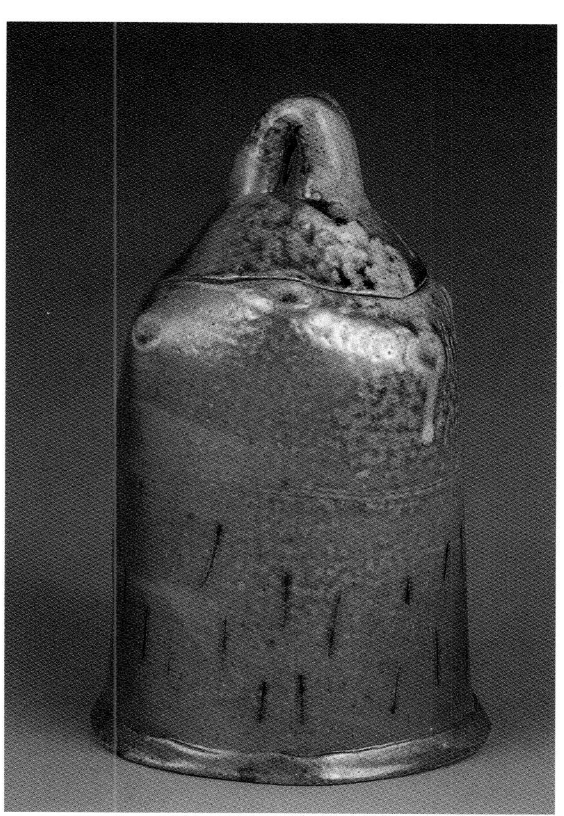

Jeremy Steward

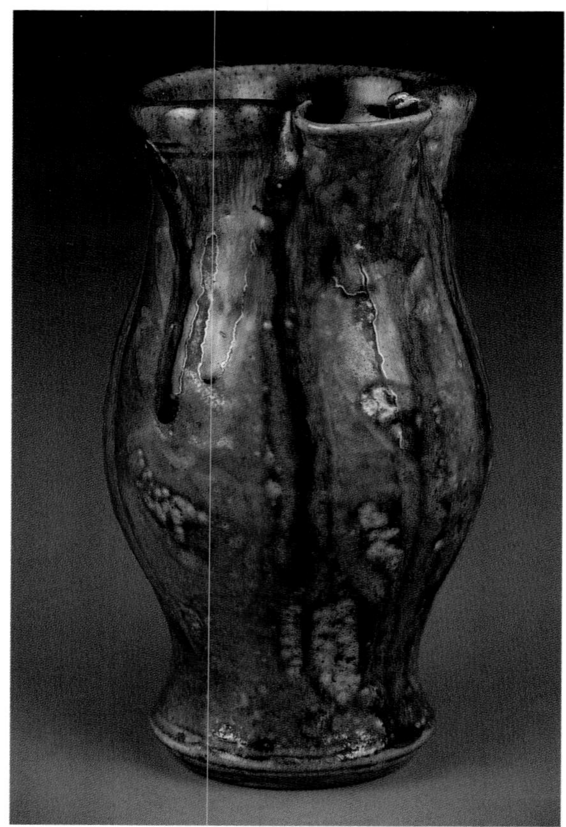

Jug by Jeremy Steward, 2000. 8in high, wood-fired soda glaze.

Jeremy Steward acknowledges that he has always found the heavily textured orange-peel of salt glaze less attractive than the qualities provided by a lighter salting. He especially favours these when they are combined with the effects of firing with wood. He describes the lighter salt or soda glaze as providing a kindness and softness to the surface, especially when it is united with a slip. He enjoys the wide range of often unpredictable variation and depth that can be created from any one glaze or slip.

He makes a range of practical pots in earthy colours. The shino-type glazes and clay slips provide the yellow creams and pinks, and the other glazes are formulated from a variety of natural materials such as granite and stone dusts, local surface clays and wood ash. He is engrossed with the process of both making and firing, and is inspired by the creative link that he perceives between the surface that he gives to his pots and the firings he has chosen. The qualities of his pots reflect this: the forms are strong and grounded, and the decoration is direct and lively, with brushed and dipped slips and runs of colour. The wood firing itself provides an inspiring random surface by creating flashes of colour and glaze melt, and often a pearly iridescence. The soda vapour adds further variation and enrichment of the glazed surface.

(BELOW) Mugs by Jeremy Steward, 2000. 4in high, wood-fired soda glaze.

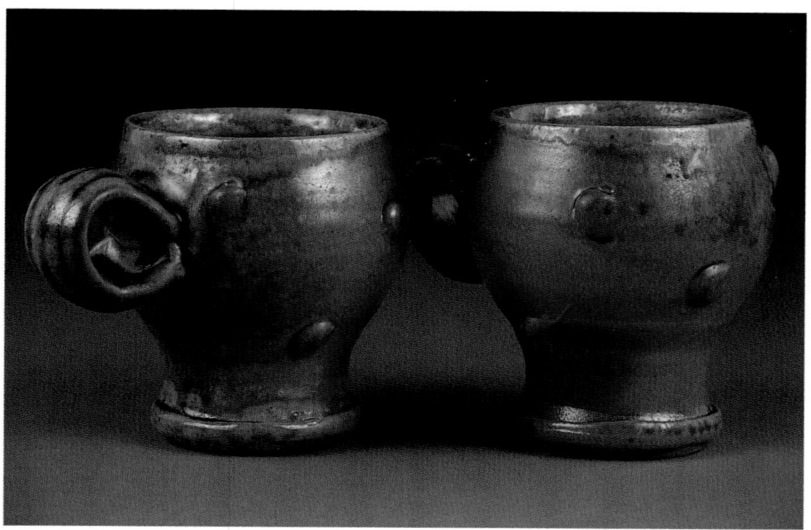

(RIGHT) Jar by Jeremy Steward, 2000. 8½in high, wood-fired soda glaze.

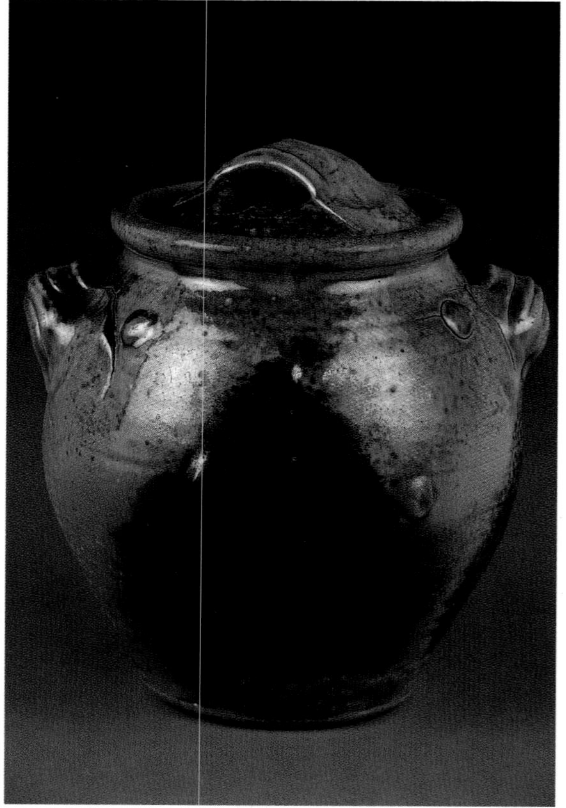

Mark Smith

Mark Smith specializes in wood-fired salt-glaze ceramics. He first became interested in salt glaze in 1991 at Derby University: like many before him, he was attracted by the unpredictable nature of the results, and drawn to the pitted orange-peel surface. He set up his own workshop and built a modified Olsen fast-fire wood kiln: in this he raw fires all his work. At the end of the firings, just after the crash-cooling period, Mark places a log of wood coated with copper oxide into each side of the kiln, before he seals it up. The copper vapour gets caught in the reduction during cooling, and creates red blushes on many of the pots.

He produces a wide range of functional pieces, all of them characterized by a great sense of movement derived from lines scored on the clay, and gestures created by the attachments. Applied handles and spouts are heavily textured, bent and manipulated, and the forms stand with humorous postures. His functional pots are for pleasurable use, but can also be seen as sculptures with attitude. Mark uses the salt glaze to coat the surface of his pieces with an overall glistening orange-peel texture that picks up every detail of the surface treatment of the clay.

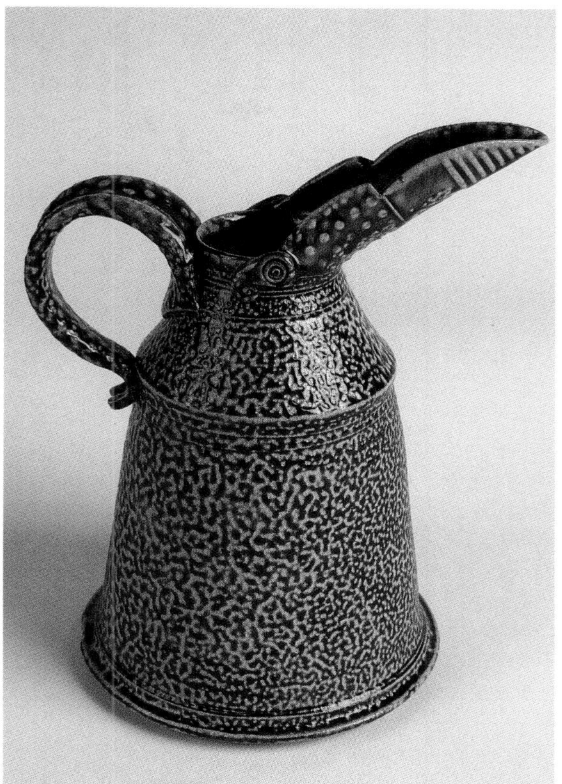

Large half-round teapot by Mark Smith. Height 7.5in, width 8in, wood-fired salt glaze.

Straight jug with collar by Mark Smith. Height 9.5in, width 5.5in, wood-fired salt glaze.

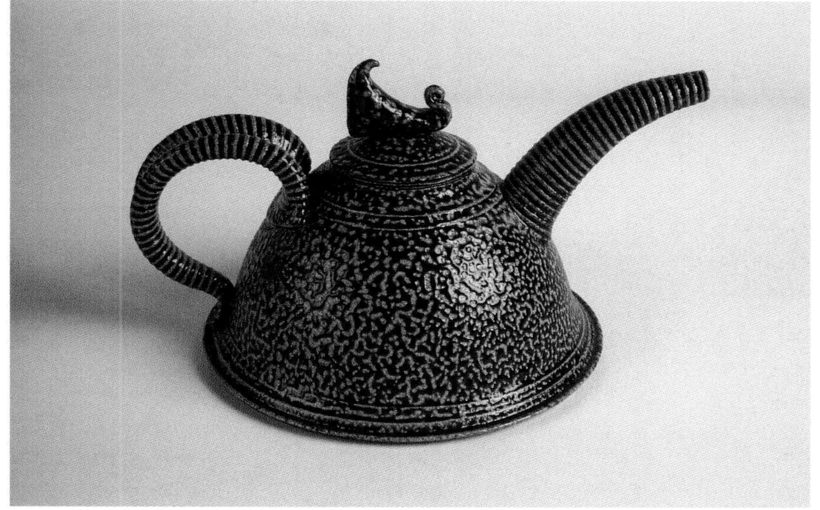

Opportunities and Exploration

Many potters choose to 'have a go' with salt by attending a short course. Others may be offered the chance to share a firing or put pieces of work into another potter's salt kiln. The Craft Potters Association and regional groups have demonstration salt firings, and the International Potters Festival, held biannually at Aberystwyth, has hosted a number of salt-glaze potters over the years. The series of Salt and Soda weekend conferences at the Royal Forest of Dean College presented another great arena for debate and practical experience. The exchange of ideas and the opportunity to see the styles that are being explored elsewhere, encourage the increased variety of work encompassed by the process of vapour glaze.

12 The International Scene

With only a few exceptions, British salt-glaze stoneware is based on function, and the twentieth-century revival in Britain has been strongly based on that tradition. The glaze surfaces are very obviously salt glaze, with all the characteristics that are recognized and appreciated as such: orange-peel texture, smooth satin coatings and fluid, bright, glassy glaze. The best makers excel in the production of forms that can carry these surfaces without any conflict, so the clay and glaze unite.

When salt glaze from elsewhere in the world is examined, a much broader view of what can be done with salt and other vaporizing sodium compounds is displayed. The American scene, built on the salt-glaze traditions brought over by the European immigrants, is as wide as the country itself and must await another book. In Germany, appropriately the place where salt glaze originated, five 'Saltzbrand' exhibitions have been held in Koblenz, since its beginning in 1983, and these invited work from around the world. The 'Westerwald' prize too, originally a German national competition, was opened to Europe in 1999. These, along with other recent exhibitions, international festivals and conferences, have opened up the opportunities to see and share the many different ideas and techniques surrounding the fullest expression of vapour surfaces.

To quote the title of an exhibition of new lines in British salt glaze held in Holland in 1997, inspirations for the future will come from the individual expression of whatever the maker feels will produce his own 'Songs in Salt'. A gallery of inspiring vapour-glaze pieces from international salt- and soda-glaze potters, some of whom have strong connections with Britain and British traditions, leads the way for the story of salt glaze to continue.

Janet Mansfield, Australia

Janet Mansfield has worked with salt glaze since the mid-1970s. After many ventures into kiln building, her favourite is now a 22.6cu m (80cu ft) trolley kiln, fuelled with fallen eucalyptus wood from her studio property in New South Wales. Her work is based on functional forms, and the salt texture is accentuated by incised decoration. She uses slips occasionally, but prefers to work on the quality of the clay body itself, testing various combinations of local clays to give richness of colour with salt.

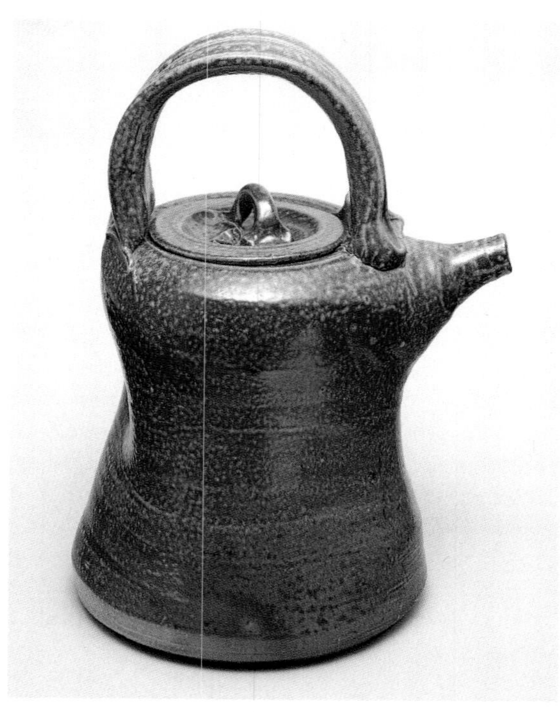

Teapot by Janet Mansfield. 20cm high, salt-glaze stoneware, wood fired. Slip and incised decoration.

Sandra Lockwood, Australia

'There's a softness and responsiveness to clay that is seductive. It holds an attraction as a very direct expression of touch and movement . . . Salt glazing hides nothing – it has a nakedness and simplicity that speaks directly to the viewer.'

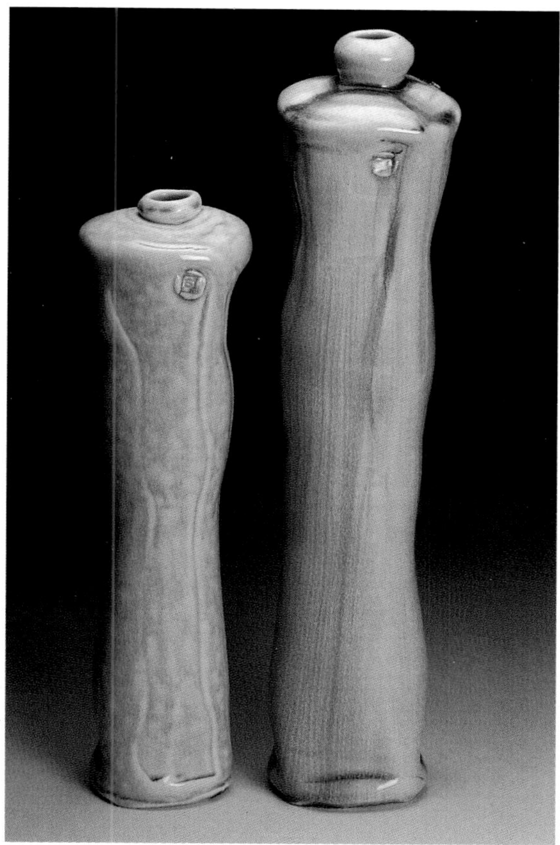

Two porcelain bottles by Sandra Lockwood. 46 × 9cm and 38 × 8cm, wood-fired salt glaze.

Cathi Jefferson, Canada

Salt firing helps to retain a thrown freshness in Cathi Jefferson's work: it produces surfaces rich in colour and texture, with each piece being directly affected by its position in the kiln. Most of her work is wheel-thrown and altered into square or geometric shapes. The intention is for each piece to be seen in its own framed window, the decorative surface reflecting the influence of the natural environment that surrounds her studio.

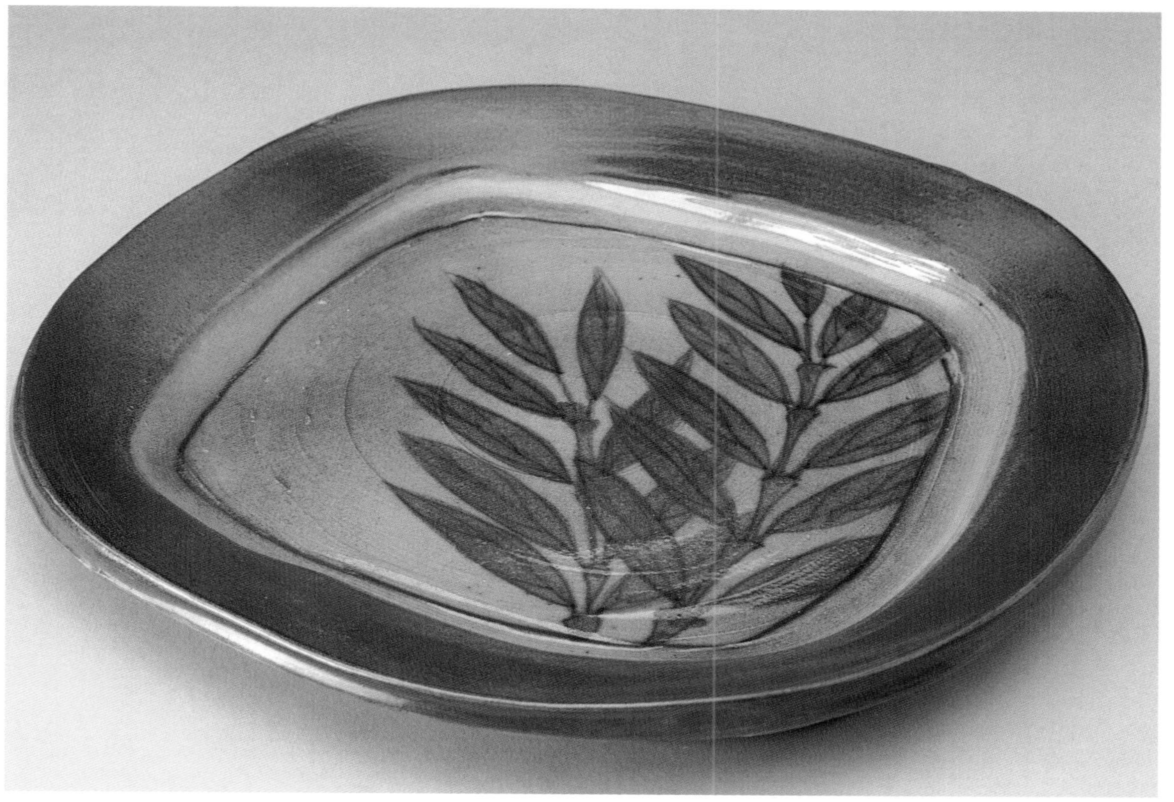

Leaf square thrown plate by Cathi Jefferson. 11 × 19in. Salt/soda stoneware.

Connie Glover, Canada

Connie Glover describes the effect of the flames on her fired pieces '. . . as if an invisible brush has passed over them.' She says: 'Soda glaze appeals to me because of its unpredictability. I like to give up control and leave part of the firing process to chance, to allow for the magical transformation that happens in the kiln.'

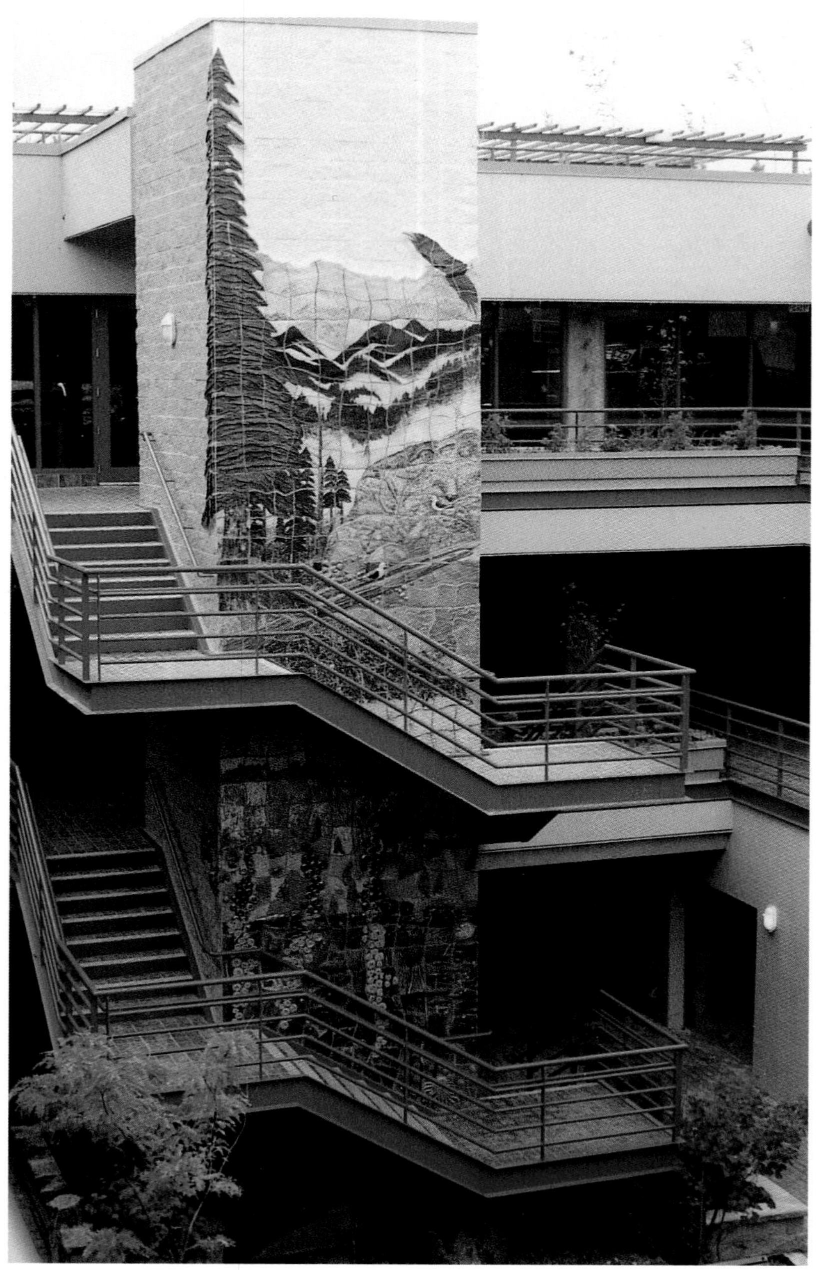

(BELOW) 'Rising Tide' mural, by Connie Glover. 250sq ft, public art project sited in Vancouver in the Cosmo Plaza.

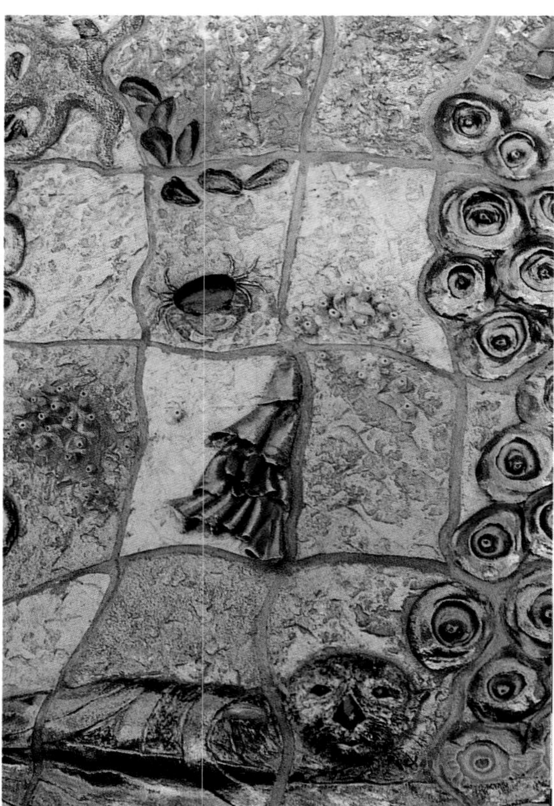

(ABOVE) Rising Tide' detail. Tile sections soda fired to 1,180°C.

Bente Hansen, Denmark

Bente Hansen's meticulously crafted vessels display a wide range of textures developed from applied slips. Subtle and tactile qualities are attained through an intimate understanding of the interaction of the materials and the firing process.

Due to the immense wear and tear on her kiln, she is developing slip glazes that require less salt and finds that, despite a layer or more of slip, the salt still merges with the clay. This makes the form 'live and breathe' in a way that is unique to this firing method.

Hans and Birgitte Borjeson, Denmark

The high-fired salt glaze used by the Borjesons has proved very useful for outdoor commissions as it resists the hard weather conditions in Scandinavia. The colour range of salt glaze blends well with both natural and man-made city environments. Commissioned work and individual pieces complement a range of thrown domestic ware.

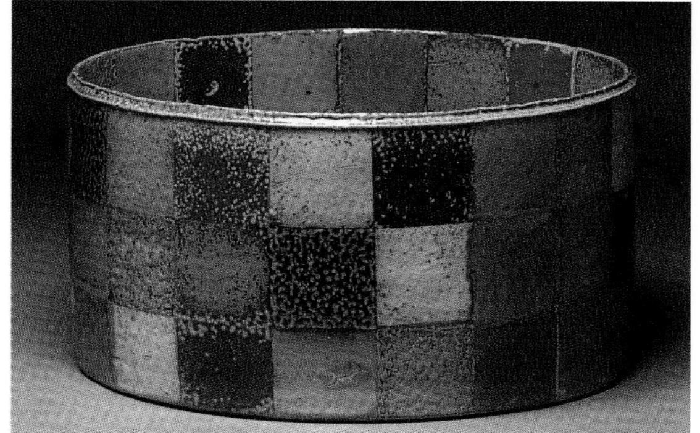

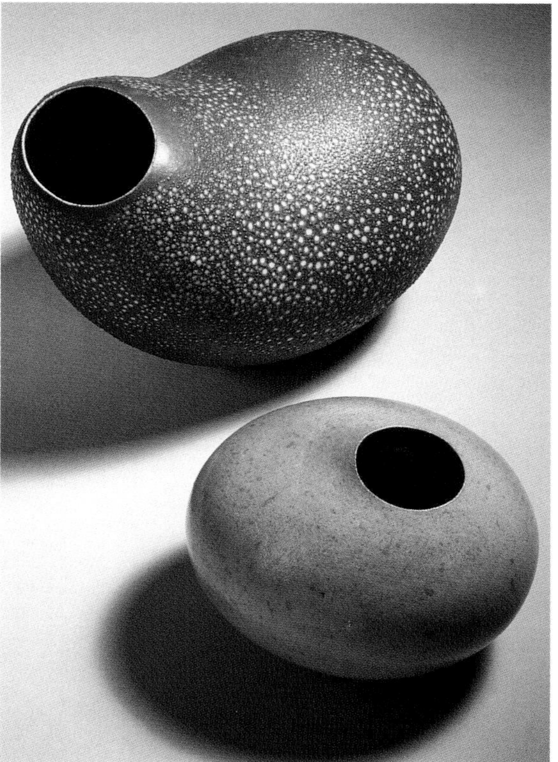

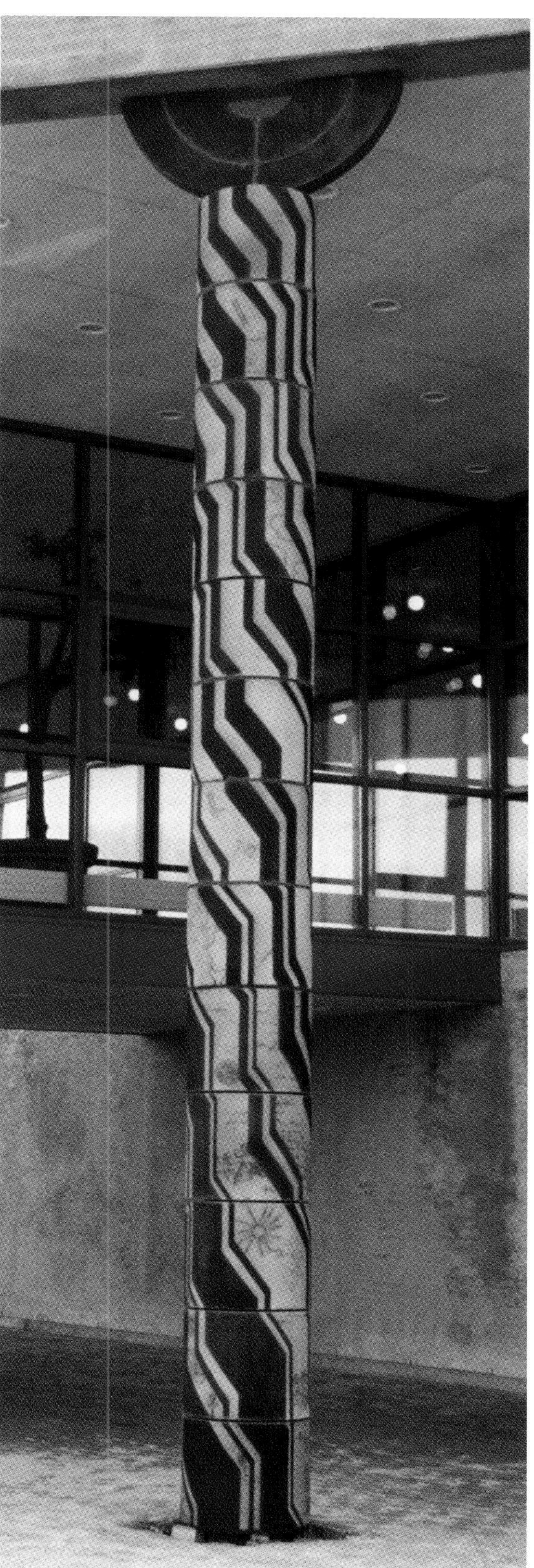

(LEFT) Column for a TV station by Hans and Birgitte Borjeson. 7.5m high, salt glaze.

(LEFT) Bowl by Hans and Birgitte Borjeson. 22cm high, salt glaze over paper resist, using a variety of matt and glossy slips.

(LEFT) Dark reclining vessel and orange tilted vessel by Bente Hansen, 2000. Salt glaze.

Richard Dewar, France

After being involved with salt glaze at Harrow School of Art in the early 1970s, Richard Dewar built his first salt kiln in 1980, after his move to France. His functional pieces are full of *joie de vivre,* with playful forms and lively decoration. He uses La Borne stoneware and Limoges porcelain clays, and experiments with various colouring stains and oxides in the slips. He salts with a coarse granular salt, rich in magnesium.

Suzy Atkins, France

Suzy Atkins continues to make functional pots that have a wonderful vitality, their colours and patterns enriched by the salt glaze. The decoration of the forms has developed to the stage where she now enjoys making pots purely for their decorative potential. She uses pure gold or platinum for the addition of sparing detail, lustre-fired to 800°C in an electric kiln.

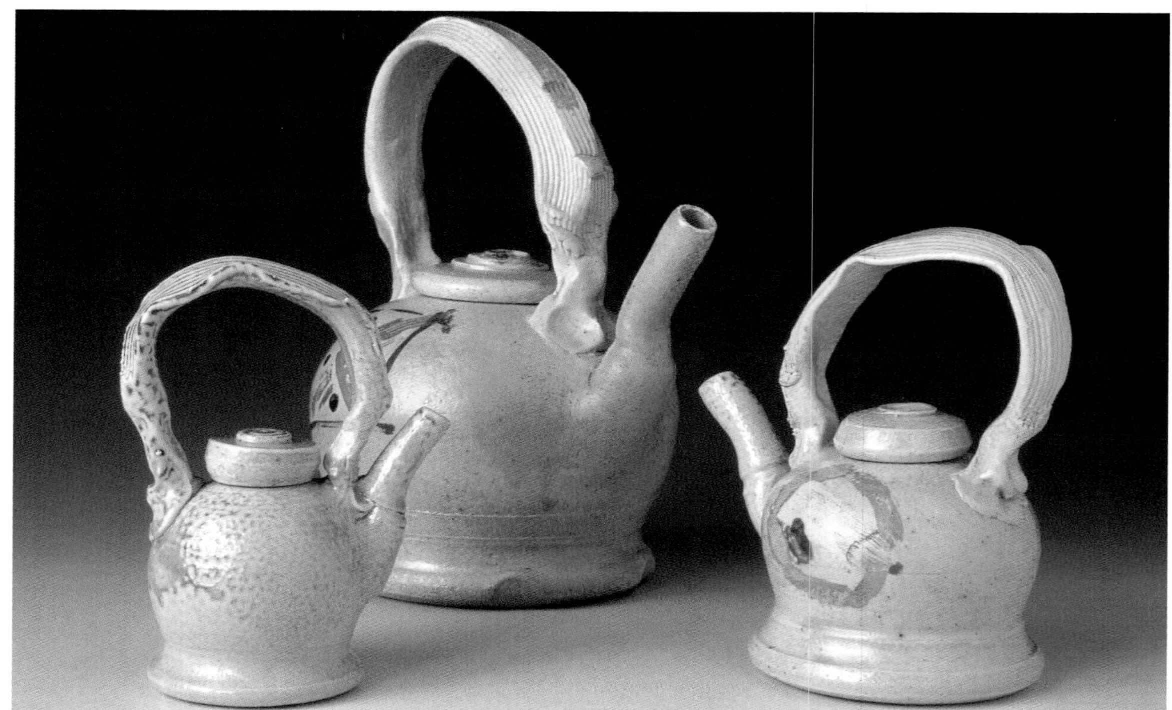

(RIGHT) Three teapots by Richard Dewar, 2000. Salt-glaze porcelain.

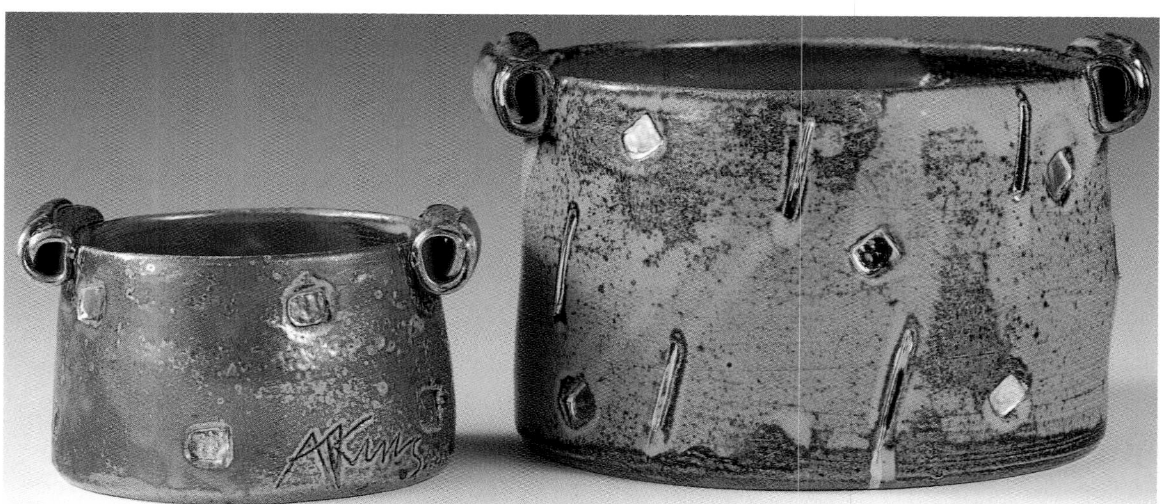

(RIGHT) Oven pots by Suzy Atkins, 2000. High-fired salt glaze, with added lustre.

Martin Goerg, Germany

Martin Goerg received a traditional pottery training in the Westerwald region of Germany, and experimented with salt glaze at a school for ceramic design. He finds this firing method ideal for his work, enjoying surface qualities that range from very dry, pale orange colour to a more heavily glazed, melted effect. He explores beyond tradition with his forms and the less usual aesthetics of vapour surfaces.

Silwia Barke and Regine Schonemann, Germany

Working under the name 'Mecklenburger Vogel', Regine and Silwia find themselves addicted to salt glazing, its enormous colour palette and its unique, often unrepeatable results. They use various Westerwald and French stoneware clays, most of which contain iron pyrites. All pieces are partly thrown, distorted, modelled, sometimes stamped, painted or finished with sgraffito. The insides are raw glazed with a shino glaze.

Stephan Bang, Germany

Stephan Bang learned the salt-glaze technique in Hohr-Grenzhausen, and is absorbed by the history of German pots for daily use. He has a particular fascination for jugs and the enormous

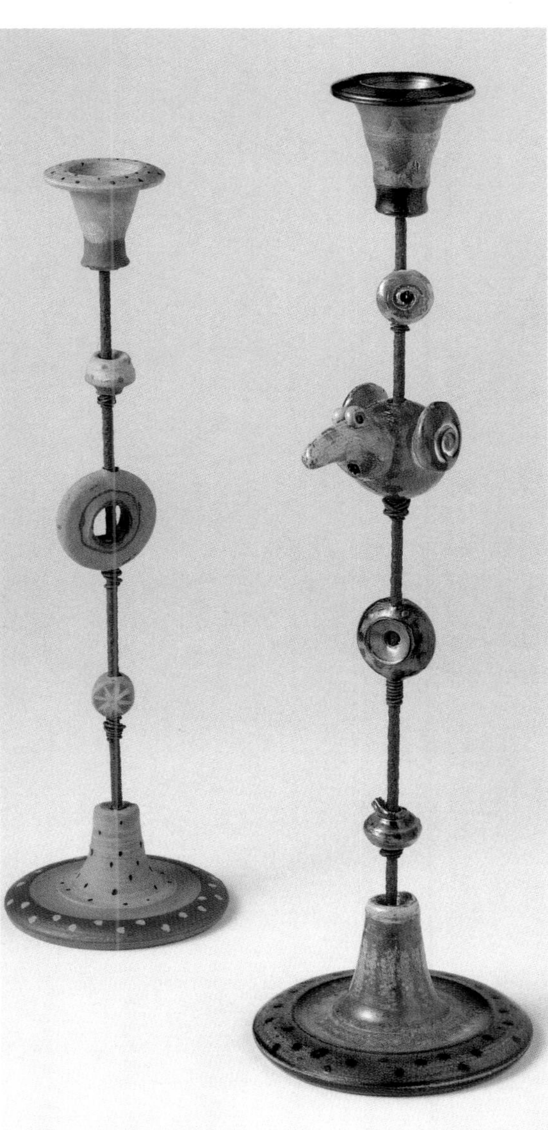

(LEFT) Threaded candlesticks with birds by Silwia Barke and Regine Schonemann. 35 and 42cm high, wood-fired salt glaze.

(FAR LEFT) Orange vessel by Martin Goerg. 85cm high, salt/soda fired.

(RIGHT) Flutes by Stephan Bang. 45cm high × 3.5cm diameter, various slips, salt glaze, fired to 1,280°C.

(FAR RIGHT) 'Ultramaros Tear II' by Maria Geszler-Garzuly, 1998. 100cm high, salt-glaze porcelain, wood fired to 1,300°C. (Private collection)

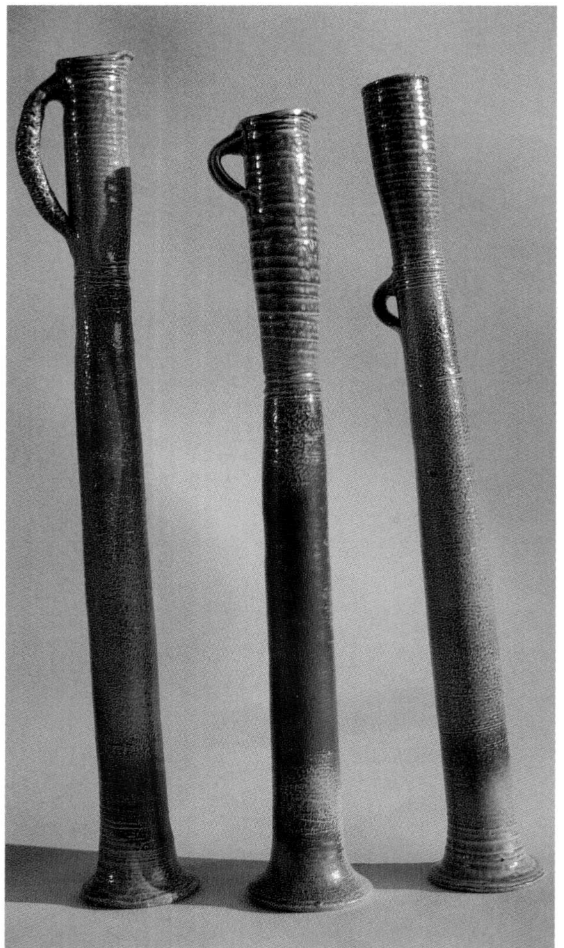

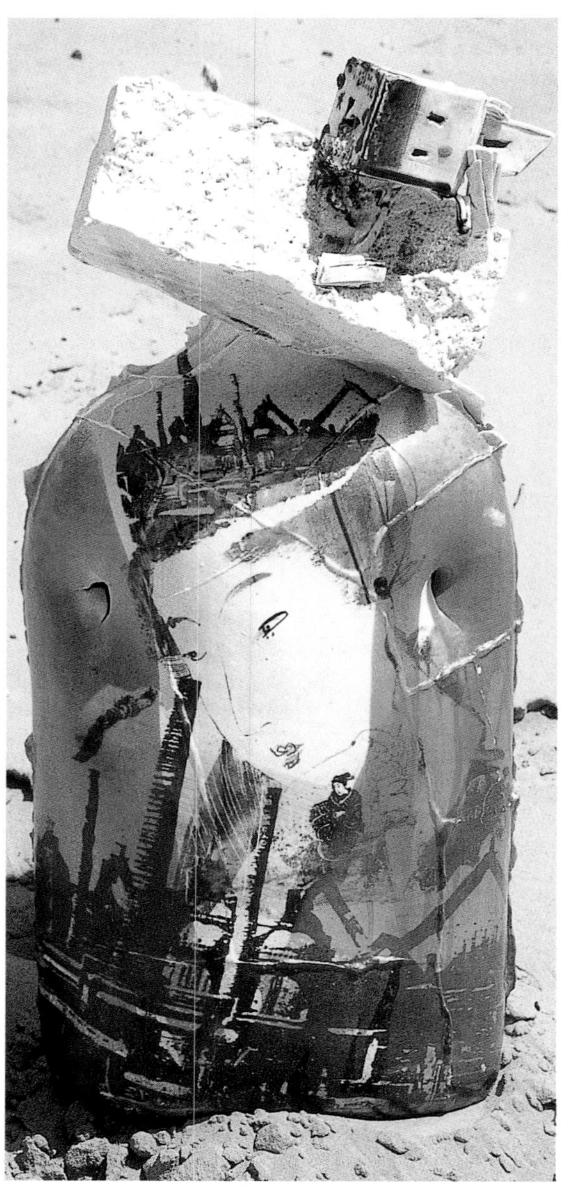

range in their regional form, typical of every age. He experiments with mixtures of clays that originate from the Westerwald region, to which he adds materials for different working and aesthetic qualities. The various slips are based on alumina and porcelain.

Maria Geszler-Garzuly, Hungary

Maria Geszler-Garzuly works in an area where there is a rich tradition of earthenware ceramics. Her interest in high-fired salt glaze arose from a visit to Germany and the Westerwald museum. She turned to wood-fired salt glaze and, using a photo silk-screen printing method, printed cobalt oxide onto a wet clay surface. In the firing the salt glaze softened the lines of colour. Her more recent large figures have a drier surface and strong colours.

Marcus O'Mahony, Ireland

Marcus O'Mahony uses throwing, with a combination of making and decorating techniques. He particularly enjoys working on the clay at the freshly thrown stage, altering, facetting, stamping and drawing onto the clay. Decorated with slips, celadons and ash glazes, the richness of the salt glaze enhances and enlivens the forms, giving warm and tactile finishes with a wide colour palette.

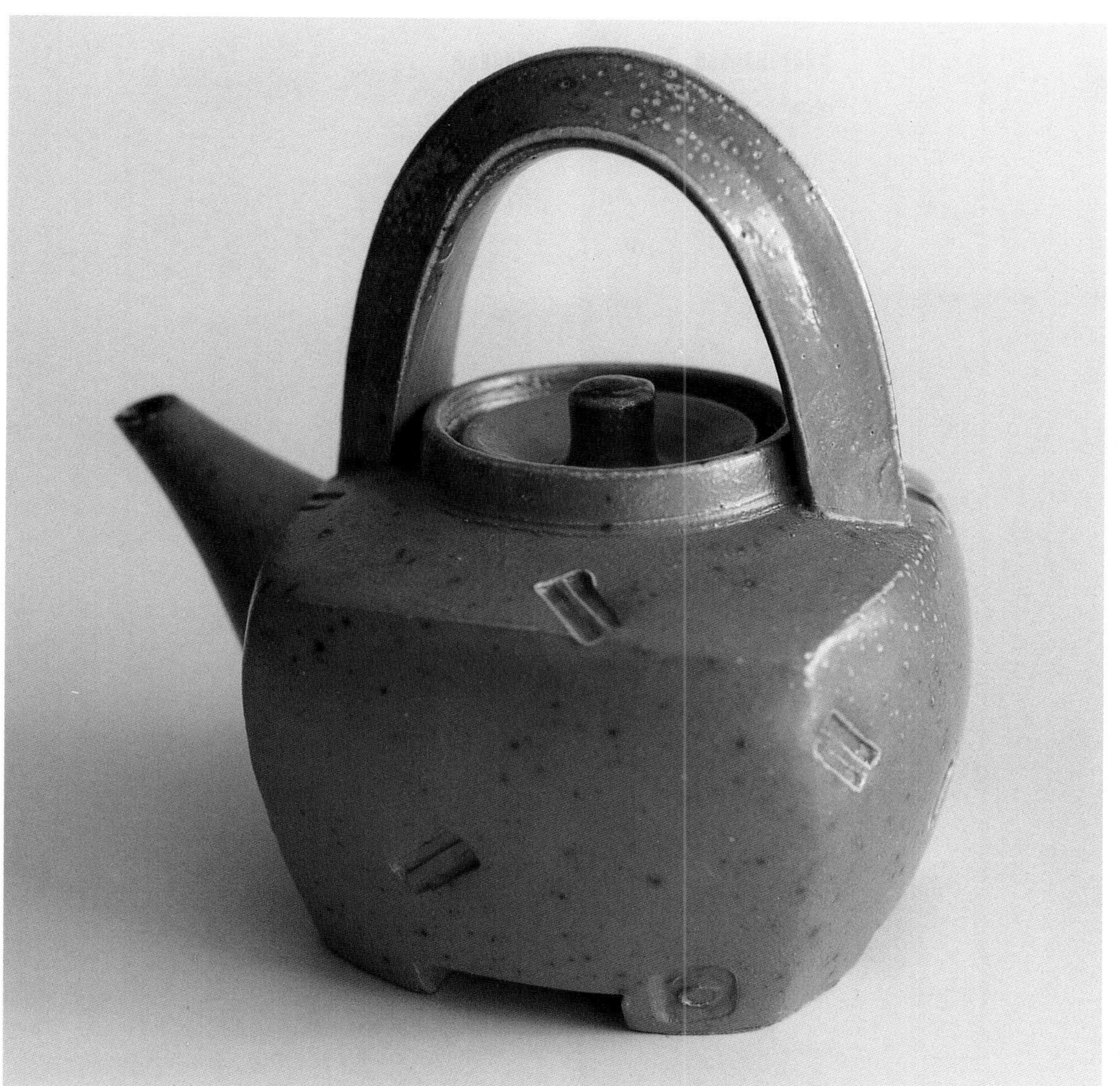

(LEFT) Teapot by Marcus O'Mahony, 2000. Thrown, altered, faceted and stamped, salt glaze.

Kristine Michael, India

Kristine Michael finds cultural connections, past and present, in her work with clay and kilns in India. She is drawn to the vessel as a metaphor for the human body, which she uses as a starting point for abstract, non-functional work. She finds that salt glaze and pit firing are techniques particularly suited to her work as they are immediate, and enhance the raw quality of the clay.

Her Comis, Netherlands

Accepting that there are limitations to his control of salt glaze, Her Comis remains fascinated by the tension between intention and coincidence of the process. The appeal lies in the surprising unity that a fired pot can attain from that combination of controlled and uncontrollable factors.

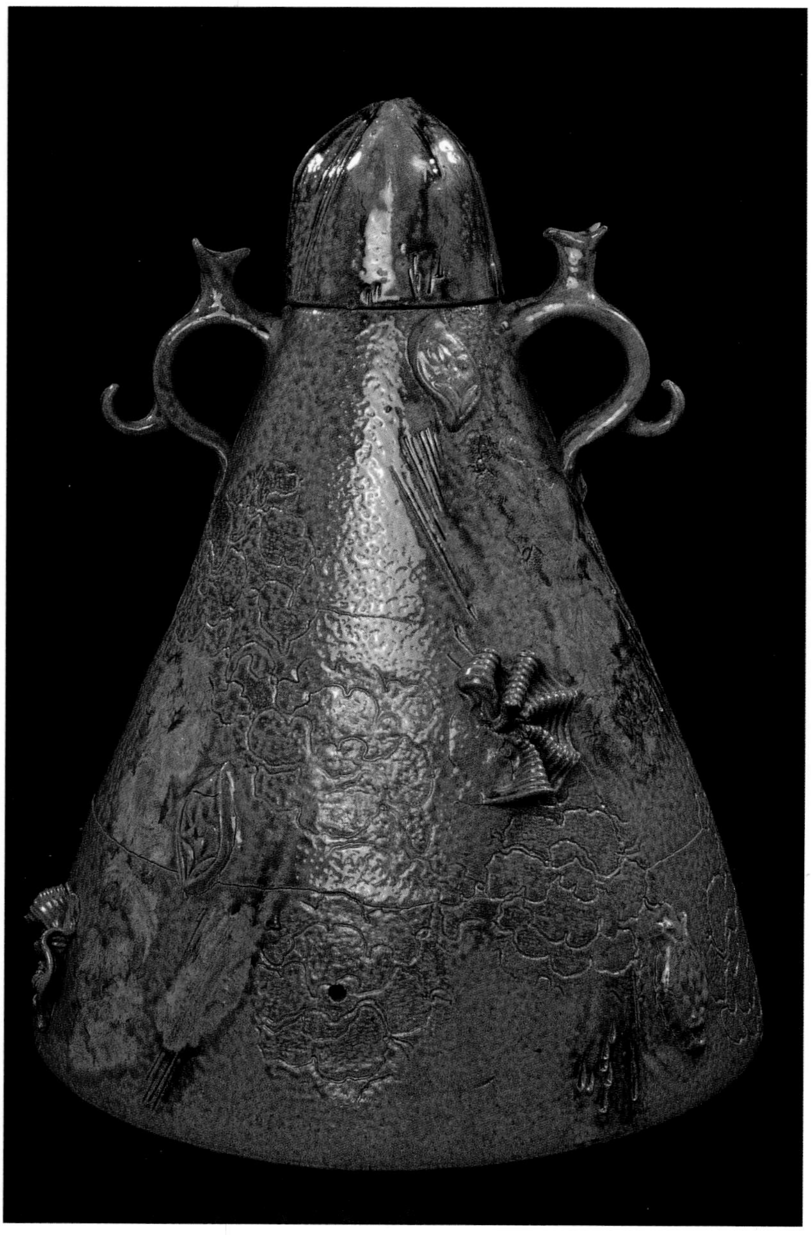

(ABOVE) 'Earth', from a series entitled 'Four sacred vessels' by Kristine Michael, 1998. 30in high, wheel thrown and modelled, wood-fired salt glaze.

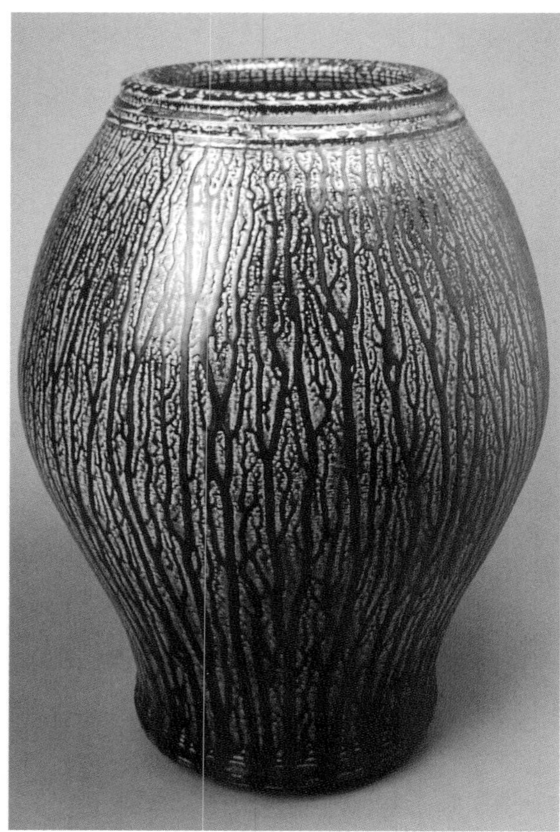

(ABOVE) 'Naga Lung' by Her Comis. 60cm high, salt glaze. Slip, cobalt oxide, black stain and ash glaze.

Pauline Ploeger, Netherlands

Pauline Ploeger makes functional ware that echoes tradition, and also individual pieces in which she explores the vocabulary of form, colour and texture. The appeal of salt glaze lies in the way that the marks of the making, and consequently the character of the maker, are revealed so clearly on the fired piece.

Rosie and Renton Murray, New Zealand

Renton and Rosie Murray met at Harrow School of Art in 1973/4. It was there that Renton first focused on salt glazing. Rosie gained some salt-glazing experience in Scotland with Zelda Mowat, before joining Renton in New Zealand. Whilst they share firings, their pots have developed in different ways. Rosie works with white clay that enhances the use of coloured glazes on her range of bowls, dishes and pourers, while Renton makes a full range of domestic pots; he has also recently started to produce large garden pots, sundials and fountains.

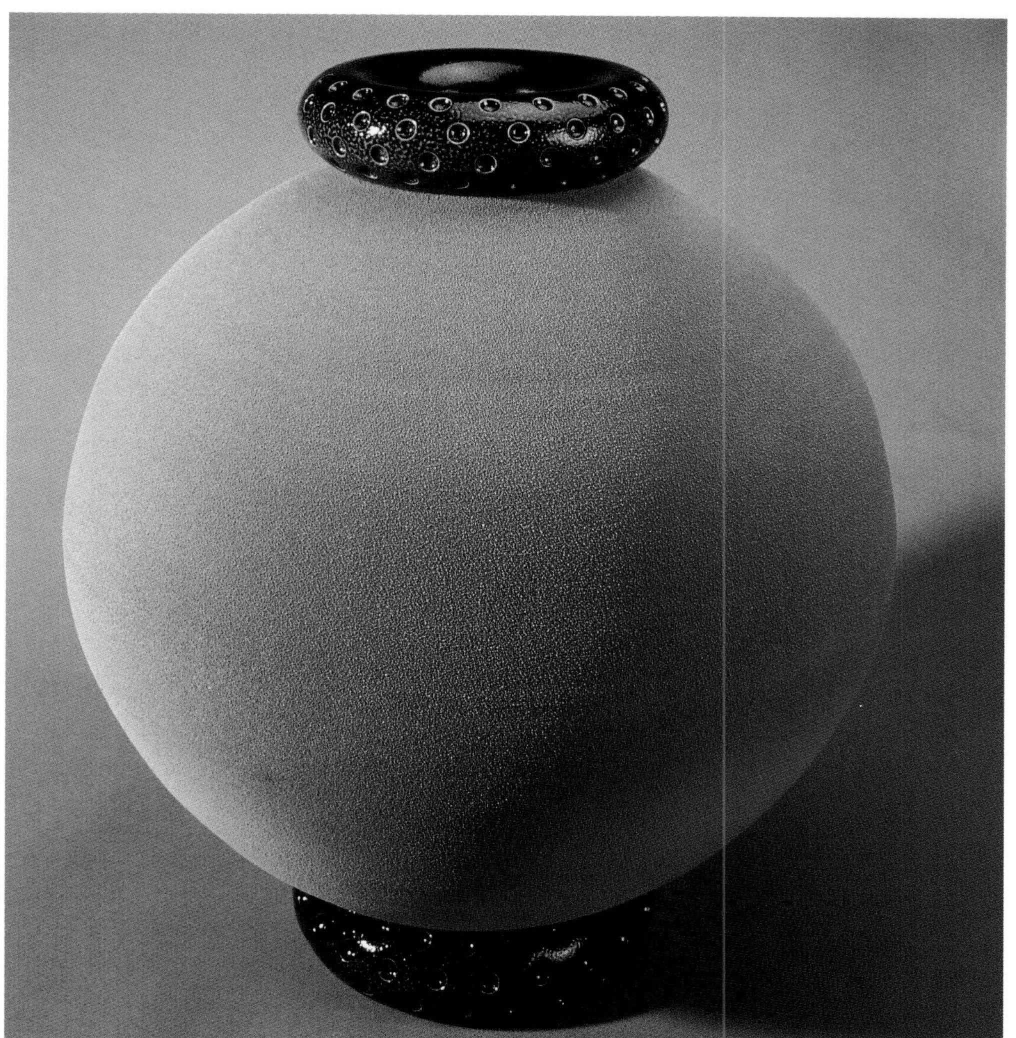

Sphere by Pauline Ploeger, 1999. 60cm, salt glaze, 1,280°C.

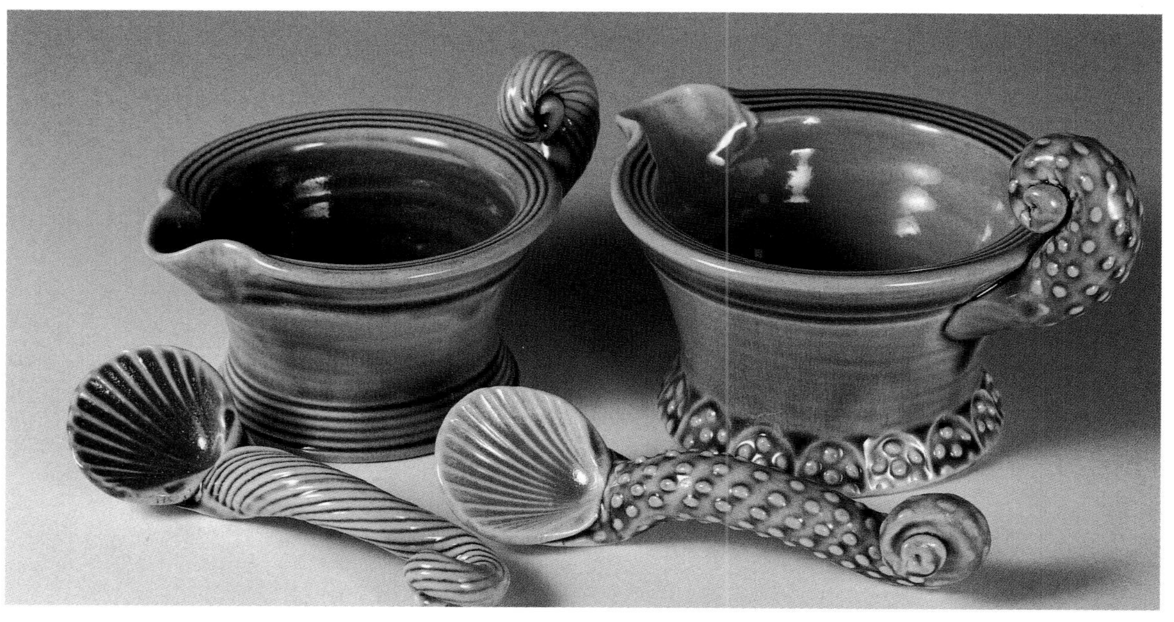

Sauce pourers and matching spoons by Rosie Murray.

John Skognes, Norway

These wheel-thrown and highly abstract forms are fired, without prior biscuit firing, in a cross-draught kiln fuelled by wood and oil. John Skognes makes use of residual salt firings to achieve a drier surface with pronounced flashing. He has recently begun firing his pots in saggars containing combustible materials. 'Salt glaze is much more than orange-peel and shiny surfaces. The options are uncountable, and the very process of packing the kiln is part of the creative process.'

Mark Hewitt, USA

Mark Hewitt lives in North Carolina, a state with a ceramic legacy of great richness and variety, including salt glaze. His work is informed by a diversity of traditions from around the world, not least from England where his pottery career began. Through an appreciation of these pots he makes connections between himself and other potters, and finds his own historical context. He fires his work in a 25cu m (90cu ft) wood-burning 'ground hog' kiln, producing localized effects of salt.

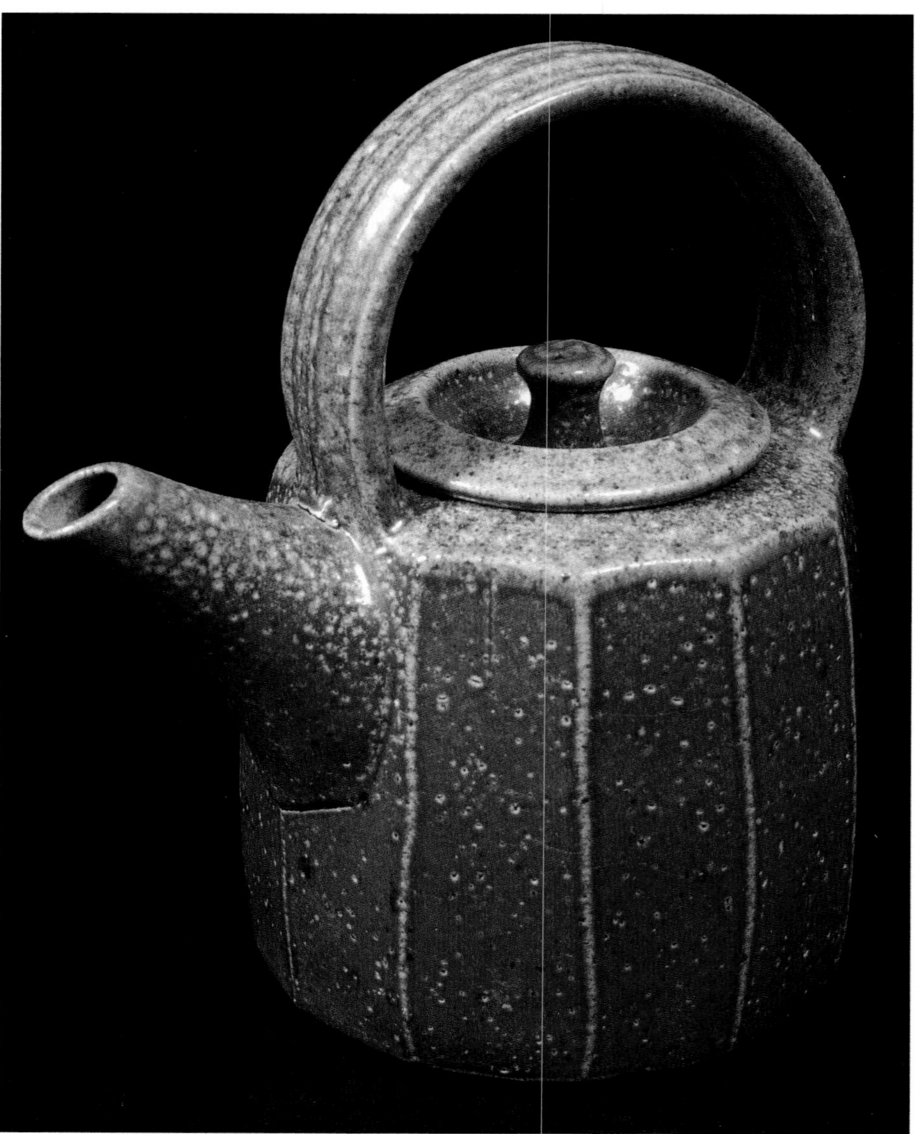

Cut-sided teapot by Renton Murray.

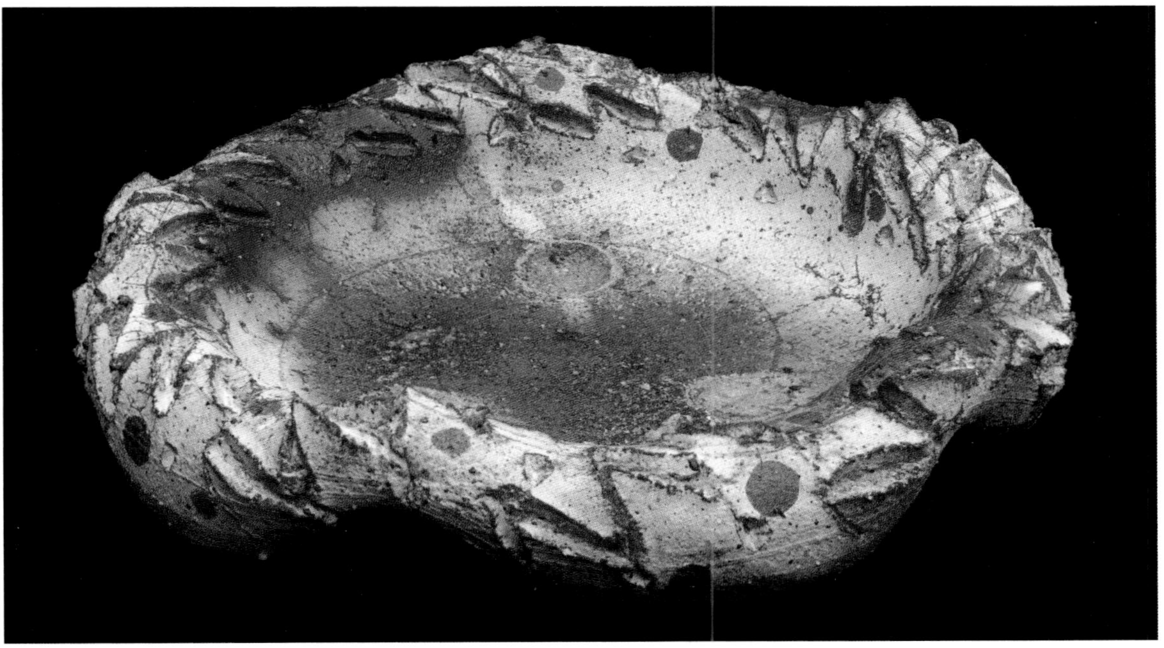

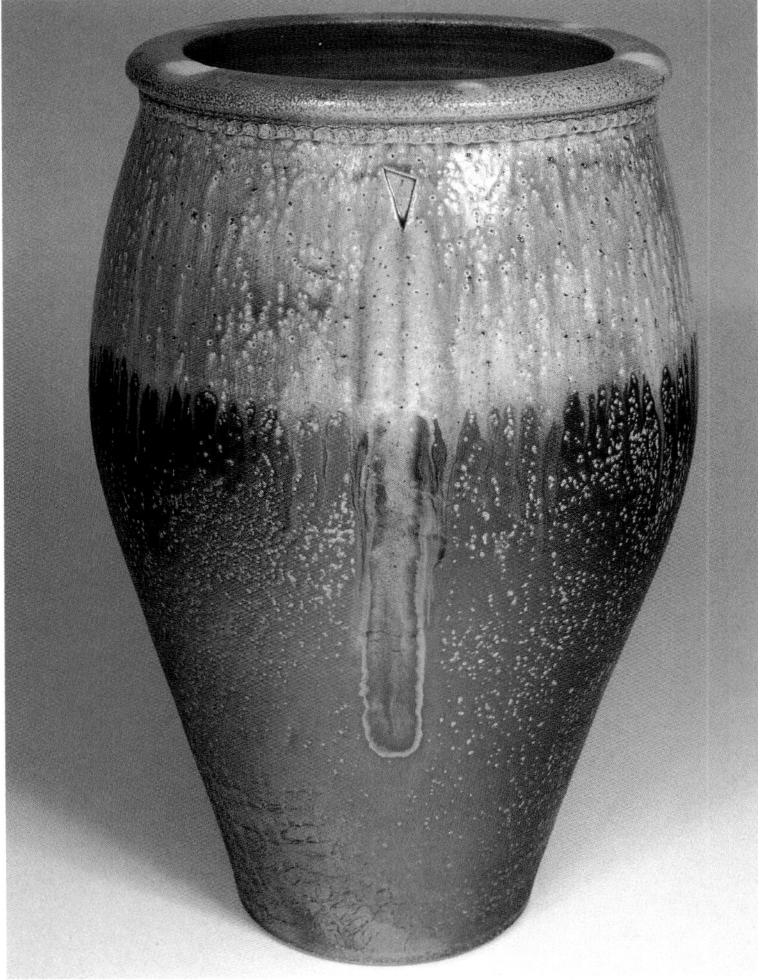

(ABOVE) 'Quetzalcoatl' by John Skognes. 35cm wide, coarse sanded body, china clay slip, incised. Saggar salt-fired with grass in salt kiln.

(LEFT) Umbrella pot by Mark Hewitt. 24in high, wood-fired salt glaze. Lower section painted manganese slip, upper part ash glaze, with large, blue-stained glass drip.

Inspirations for the Future

The vapour glaze process can capture the attention of a passer-by for just a few moments or absorb the attention of the enthusiast for a lifetime, whether it is the study of historic pots or the making, or a combination of these aspects. The traditional salt or soda firing and the more contemporary alternative ways of producing vapour effects will remain a source of delight and an inspiration for future ceramics.

Bibliography and Further Reading

History

Blacker, J.F., *The ABC of English Salt-Glaze Stone-ware, from Dwight to Doulton*, (Stanley Paul & Co., first published 1922)

Cruickshank, Graeme, *Scottish Saltglaze* (Scottish Pottery Studies Series of booklets, published by the author, 1982)

Cooper, Emanuel, *A History of World Pottery* (Batsford, first published 1972. Republished in 2000 as *Ten Thousand Years of Pottery*)

Eyles, Desmond, *The Doulton Lambeth Wares* (Hutchinson, 1975)

Eyles, Desmond, *Royal Doulton, 1815–1965* (Hutchinson, 1965)

Freestone, Ian, and Gaimster, David, (editors) *Pottery in the Making – World Ceramic Traditions* (British Museum Press, 1977)

Gaimster, David, *German Stoneware 1200–1900, Archaeology and Cultural History* (British Museum Press 1977)

Green, Chris, *John Dwight's Fulham Pottery, Excavations 1971–79* (Archaeological Report 6, English Heritage, 1999)

Honey, W.B., *English Pottery and Porcelain* (A & C Black, 1933)

McKeown, Julie, *Royal Doulton* (Shire Publications, 1998)

Mountford, Arnold R., *The Illustrated Guide to Staffordshire Salt-Glazed Stoneware* (Barrie & Jenkins, 1971)

Oswald, Adrian, R.J.C., Hildyard, and R.G. Hughes *English Brown Stoneware 1670–1900* (Faber and Faber, 1982)

Sekers, David, *The Potteries* (Shire Publications, 1994)

Shaw, Simon, *History of the Staffordshire Potteries* (originally published 1829, reprinted by David and Charles, 1970)

Wood, Karen Ann, *Tableware in Clay from Studio and Workshop* (The Crowood Press, 1999)

Wood, Pamela, *'Made at Nottm' – An Introduction to Nottingham Salt-Glazed Stoneware*, (Nottingham Castle Museum, 1980)

Journals and Other Sources

Journal of Ceramic History Supplement to Volume 11, 1992, 'John Dwight's Fulham Pottery 1672–1978' edited by Dennis Haselgrove and John Murray. Published by City Museum and Art Gallery, Stoke-on-Trent

English Ceramic Circle 'Transactions' Volume 17, 1999. Paper by Andrew Watts: 'Something Nasty in the Air: Lambeth Potters and the Archbishop of Canterbury'

Science and Archaeology, Number 18, 1976. 'Techniques of White Salt-Glaze Stoneware Manufacture in North Staffordshire around 1765'. Annotated study, by Francis Celoria, of the posthumous account by the Frenchman, Gabriel Jars

The Harrow Connection – series of essays, edited by Hazel Nicholson (Ceolfrith Press 1989)

Biographies

Haslam, Malcolm, *The Martin Brothers Potters* (Richard Dennis, 1978)

Leach, Bernard, *Hamada Potter* (Kodansha International, 1975)

Peterson, Susan, *Shoji Hamada – A Potter's Way and Work* (Weatherhill, 1995)

Sydenham, Guy, *A Potter's Life – the Island Potters of Poole* (Sansom and Company, 1999)

Wheeler, Ron, *Winchcombe Pottery – The Cardew-Finch Tradition* (White Cockade Publishing, in association with Cheltenham Art Gallery and Museum, 1998)

Kilns: Building and Firing

Gregory, Ian, *Ceramic Sculpture* (A & C Black, 1996, first published 1992)

Gregory, Ian *Kiln Building* (A & C Black, 1995)

Lou, Nils *The Art of Firing* (A & C Black, 1998)

Minogue, Col, and Sanderson, Robert, *Wood-Fired Ceramics* (A & C Black and University of Pennsylvania Press, 2000)

Olsen, Frederick L., *The Kiln Book* (second edition, A & C Black, 1983)

Technical and Techniques

Fournier, Robert, *Illustrated Dictionary of Practical Pottery* (Van Nostrand Reinhold, 1977)

Hamer, Frank and Janet, *The Potter's Dictionary of Materials and Techniques* (A & C Black, fourth edition, 1997)

Hessenberg, Karin, *Sawdust firing* (B. T. Batsford, 1994)

Lawrence, W.G., and R. R., West *Ceramic Science for the Potter* (Chilton Book Company, 1972)

Leach, Bernard, *A Potter's Book* (Faber and Faber 1976, first published 1940)

Lightwood, Anne, *Working with Paperclay and Other Additives* (The Crowood Press, 2000)

Mansfield, Janet, *Salt-Glaze Ceramics* (A & C Black, 1999)

Parks, Dennis, *A Potter's Guide to Raw Glazing and Oil Firing* (Pitman, 1980)

Scott, David, *Clay and Glazes in Studio Ceramics* (The Crowood Press, 1998)

Singer, Felix and German, W.L., *Ceramic Glazes* (Borax Consolidated Ltd, 1978, first published 1960).

Starkey, Peter, *Saltglaze* (Pitman, 1977)

Tristram, Fran, *Single Firing* (A & C Black, 1996)

Troy, Jack, *Salt-Glazed Ceramics* (Watson-Guptill, 1977; Pitman, 1977)

Tudball, Ruthanne, *Soda Glazing* (A & C Black, 1995; and University of Pennsylvania Press, 1995)

Catalogues

Atterbury, Paul, and Irvine, Louise, *The Doulton Story* (souvenir booklet for the exhibition held at the V & A Museum, published by Royal Doulton Tableware, London 1979)

The Oxshott Pottery: Denise and Henry Wren (exhibition booklet published by the Crafts Study Centre, Holburne of Menstrie Museum, University of Bath, 1984)

Hildyard, Robin, *Browne Muggs, English Brown Stoneware* (exhibition catalogue, Victoria and Albert Museum, 1985)

Saltzbrand Keramik (exhibition catalogues published by Handwerkskammer, Koblenz in 1983, 1986, 1989, 1993 and 1996)

Songs in Salt – New Lines in British Salt Glaze (exhibition catalogue, Princessehof Ceramics Museum, Leeuwarden, Netherlands 1996)

Walter, Josie, *Brampton Pots in the Kitchen* (booklet accompanying touring exhibition, University of Derby, England, 1999)

Below the Salt (catalogue of touring exhibition, University of Derby, England, 2000)

Other Useful Publications

Copeland, Alexandra, *The Ceramics Museums of Europe – an artist's travel guide* (Artists Travel Guides, 1999)

Fournier, Robert and Sheila (complied by), *A Guide to Public Collections of Studio Pottery in the British Isles* (*Ceramic Review* publication, 1994)

Yates-Owen, Eric and Fournier, Robert *British Studio Potters Marks* (A & C Black, 1999)

Potters – Illustrated Directory of Fellows and Members of the Craft Potters Association (*Ceramic Review* publication, twelfth edition 2000)

Periodicals

Pottery Quarterly/Real Pottery, published 1954 to 1991, England

Ceramic Review, 21 Carnaby Street, London W1V 1PH, England; website http://www.ceramic-review.co.uk

Ceramics in Society (previously *Studio Pottery* magazine), 2 Bartholomew Street West, Exeter, EX4 3AJ, England; website http://www.ceramic-society.co.uk

Crafts, Crafts Council, 44a Pentonville Road, London, N1 9BY;
website http://www.craftscouncil.org.uk

Ceramics: Art and Perception, 35 William Street, Paddington, Sydney NSW 2021, Australia;
website http://www.ceramicart.com.au

Ceramics Technical, address as for *Ceramics Art and Perception*

ClayTimes, 15481 Second Street, PO Box 365, Waterford, VA 20197, USA

Ceramics Monthly, PO Box 6120, 735 Ceramic Place, Westerville, Ohio 43086-6102, USA;
website http://www.ceramicsmonthly.org

The Studio Potter, Box 70, Goffstown, New Hampshire 03045, USA;
website http://www.studiopotter.org

Revue de la Ceramique et du Verre, 61 Rue Marconi, 62880, Vendin-le-Vieil, France

Neue Keramik, Unter Den Eichen 90, D-12205 Berlin, Germany

Glas & Keramiek, Postbus 14, NL-5720, A A Asten, Netherlands

Dansk Kunsthandvaerk, Herredsvejen 7, DK-8581, Nimtofte, Denmark

Many of these periodicals carry advertisements with details of suppliers of materials, and services for studio potters' requirements.

Useful Addresses

Clay Suppliers for the UK

Bath Potters' Supplies, 2 Dorset Close, Bath, BA2 3RF

Commercial Clay Ltd, Sandbach Road, Cobridge, Stoke-on-Trent, ST6 2DR

W. J. Doble, Pottery Clays, St Agnes, TR5 0ST, Cornwall

Hepworth Minerals & Chemicals Ltd., Brookside Hall, Sandbach, Cheshire, CW11 4TF

Potclays Ltd., Brickkiln Lane, Etruria, Stoke-on Trent, ST4 7BD

Potterycrafts Ltd., Campbell Road, Stoke-on-Trent, ST 4 4ET

Scarva Pottery Supplies, Unit 20, Scarva Road Industrial Estate, Banbridge, Co. Down, BT32 3QD

Solargil S. A., La Batisse, 89520 Moutiers en Puisaye, France

Spencroft Ceramics Ltd, Spencroft Road, Holditch Industrial Estate, Newcastle, Staffs

Valentine Clays, The Sliphouse, 18–20 Chell Street, Hanley, Stoke-on Trent, ST1 6BA

WBB Vingerling, 44 Provincialeweg West, PO Box 70, NL-2850 AB, Haastrecht, Netherlands

Watts Blake Bearne Devon Clays, Park House, Courtenay Park, Newton Abbot, Devon, TQ12 4PS.

Whitfields' Ceramic Materials Ltd, Alpha Whitfield Group, 10 Water Street, Newcastle-under-Lyme, Staffordshire, ST5 1HP

Refractory, Insulation and Specialist Kiln Material Suppliers

Walter Brayford, Kiln Furniture Supplies, Dyson Ceramic Systems, Scotia Road, Tunstall, Stoke-on-Trent, ST6 3HG

Jays Refractory Specialists Ltd, Callywhite Lane, Dronfield, Derbyshire, S18 2XR

Refractory and Industrial Services Ltd, 118 Longfellow Road, The Straits, Dudley, West Midlands, DY3 3EH

Saint-Gobain Industrial Ceramics Ltd, Nill Lane, Rainford, St Helens, Mersyside, WA11 8LP

Vesuvius-Premier Refractories Ltd, Sheepbridge Lane, Chesterfield, Derbyshire, S41 9BS

Polybond Ltd, 'Furnascote' Department, 42–44 Warsash Road, Warsash, Southampton, SO31 9HX.

Masks and Safety Equipment

T.A.C.S. (Metrosales), Unit 3, 46 Mill Place, Kingston-upon-Thames, Surrey, KT1 2RL

Occupational Health and Safety Products/3M, 3M House, Bracknell, Berkshire, RG12 1JU

Other UK Contacts

Health and Safety Commission, Ceramics Industry Advisory Committee, The Marches House, The Midway, Newcastle-under-Lyme, Staffs, ST5 1DT

British Ceramic Research Centre, CERAM Research Ltd, Queen's Road, Penkhull, Stoke-on-Trent, Staffordshire, ST4 7LQ

Museums and Collections

Old salt-glaze pots can be found in museums throughout Great Britain. This is a selection of some of those that have significant collections of salt glaze.

Museum of London, London Wall, London, EC2Y 5HN; website http://www.museumoflondon.org.uk

Nottingham Castle Museum, Nottingham, NG1 6EL, England; website http://www.nottinghamcity.gov.uk/watson/museums/castle.asp

British Museum, Great Russell Street, London, WC1B 3DG; website http://www.thebritishmuseum.ac.uk

Pitshanger Manor and Gallery, Walpole Park, Mattock Lane, Ealing, London, W5 5EQ; website http://www.ealing.gov.uk/pitshanger (largest UK collection of Martin Brothers ware)

Southall Library, Osterly Park Road, Southall, Middx, UB2 4BL; (exceptional collection of Martin Brothers ware)

The Potteries Museum and Art Gallery, Bethesda Street, Hanley, Stoke-on-Trent, Staffordshire, ST1 3DE, England; website http://www.stoke.gov.uk/museums/pmag

Royal Doulton Visitor Centre, Nile Street, Burslem, Stoke-on-Trent, Staffordshire, ST6 2AJ, England; website http://www.royaldoulton.co.uk

Victoria and Albert Museum, Cromwell Road, South Kensington, London, SW7 2RL; website http://www.vam.ac.uk

In Germany

Hohr-Grenzhausen, Keramikmuseum Westerwald, Germany; website http://www.keramikmuseum.de

Also of Interest in the UK

Gladstone Pottery Museum, Longton, Stoke-on-Trent, Staffordshire, England; website http://www.stoke.gov.uk/museums/gladstone (living industrial museum of the Potteries, with bottle kilns)

Lion Salt Works, Marston, Northwich, Cheshire, England; website http://www.lionsaltworktrust.co.uk (restored working museum of the last surviving open-pan salt works in Cheshire)

Index

alumina 72, 80, 82, 84–5, 104–8, 116, 120
see also clays, batt wash, wadding, slips, recipes

America 16, 44, 76, 152, 162
arch construction 105–106
ash glaze 10, 47, 54, 132
Astbury, Robert and Joshua 27
Atkins, Suzy **70,** 113, 114, **156**
atmosphere *see* oxidation, reduction, kiln
Australia 152, 153

bag wall **104**, 107, 109, 111, **113**
Ballantyne, David 49
Bang, Stephan 157, **158**
Bardon Mill 76
Barke, Silwia **157**
Barlow, Florence **37**
Barlow, Hannah **36**
'Bartmann' **11, 13,** 14–**15**, 17, 19, 44, 45 *see also* Bellarmine
batt wash 115–18
Beadsmoore, May Ling 105, 112–3, 130, **134**, 135, **145–6**
Bellarmine 14, **18, 21** *see also* 'Bartmann'
Booth, Enoch 27, 30
borax 137, 141
Borax Consolidated 45, 79
Borjeson, Hans and Birgitte **155**
bottle kiln 21, **28**
Boyle, Daniel **89, 146–7**
Brampton ware **25–26,** 48, 96
bricks 46, 103–8, 111–112, 115
bricking-up 120
Bristol 18, 22, 23
Bruegel, Pieter 15, 54
burnish 142–3
Butler, Frank **37**
Byers, William 76

Canada 153
carbon trap 128
Casson, Michael 50, 57, **65–67**, **81**, **83**, 99, 130
Casson, Shiela 65, **93**
castables 106
catenary arch 110, **111**, **122**
Chappell, John 49
Chesterfield 25–26, 48, 51
College of Art 52
'Christmas glitter' 128
ceramic fibre 106, 109
clay 79–81
deposits in Britain 23, 25, 27–29, 79
deposits in Germany 9, 12–16
modification and additions 14, 82, **118**
prepared bodies 82–83, 91
see also recipes, earthenware, stoneware, porcelain
cobalt **16**, **17**, 19, 29, **30** *see also* colour, oxides
Cochrane, Rosemary **69**, **70**, **80**, **83–84**, **93**, 111, 121–25, **126–127**
Cologne **13**–14, 20, 73
colour 86–91
colouring oxides 87–88
in clay 80–81, 87, 90–91
pigments and stains 89–90
see also oxidation, reduction
Comis, Her 159, **160**
comparisons of salt and soda **133–137**
cones **119–20**, **122**, 128, 129
Corser, Trevor 44
costs 103–5
Craft Potters Association 151
Craftsmen Potters Association 48, 50, 56
crash cooling 121, 124, 129
creamware 30, **148**
Critch pottery 25
Crouch ware 28
Cullen, Abraham 18

Dartington 43, 68, 98
Denmark 120, 154
Derbyshire 23, **25–26**, 31 *see also* Brampton, Chesterfield
deterioration of kiln 103–108
Dewar, Richard **102**, **156**
Doherty, Jack **91**, **104**
Doherty, Micki *see* Schloessingk, Micki

Doulton 33–42, 50
  Doulton, Henry 34–5
  Doulton, John 34
  individual artists 35, 41
  kilns 38, 40–41
Doulton Lambeth Studios 34–42
  artists 36–37, 41
  clays 36, 37, 42
  colour and decoration 37, 41–42
  firings 38, 41, 74
drabware 28
drainpipes 33, 42, 50, 76, 79
draw rings **119**, **120**, **124**
Dwight, John 18–22, 23, 26, 31
  patents and lawsuits 18, 21, 22, 27

earthenware 10, 21, 23, 30, 35, 59, 79, 83, 140, 141
East Anglia 18
Elers brothers 27
Elizabeth I 18
enamel painting 30
engobe 84, 85
environmental concerns 72–6
Epnor, Elenor 61
Errington Reay Pottery **76**
European tradition 9–18

Farnham College of Art 51, 52, 53, 65, 68
fast-fire kilns 110
Fieldhouse, Murray 50
Finch, Ray **94–95**
firebox **104**, **106**, 107, 111, 132, 134
fireclay 82
firing:
  cycle 103
  early salt kilns 10–11
  kiln atmosphere 121
  sawdust firing 143, 144
  schedules 121–125, 128–131
  see also kilns, gas, oil, wood
flue emissions **71**, 76–78, 124
fluxes 80–2, 84–7, 89, 106, 137, 141
form and function 93–98
France 113, 156
  La Borne 46, 53, 62, 65
  St Amand en Puisaye 54
Frechen 14
fuels 72, 74, 101–4
Fulham Pottery **19–22**, 31–32, 39
Fuller, Geoffrey 51, **52**
fumes:
  around the kiln 38–9, 78, 101, 123, 142–3
  fume washing system 46, **77–78**
  in the kiln 4, 28
  see also pollution and flue emissions
fuming 142, 143, 151
'Furnascote' 107–8, 110

Gardiner, Margaret 126
gas firings 103, 111–114, 121–24, 130
German wares **10–17**, 18
Germany 9, 152, 157
Geszler-Garzuly, Maria **158**
Gittins, Christine **143–44**
Glasgow 23
glazes 10, 90–93 *see also* recipes
Glover, Connie **154**
Goerg, Martin **157**
Golden-Hann, Mirka **86**
Gordon, William 48
'gorge' **16**, **19**, 20
Gregory, Ian **55**, 56, 137, **143**
'Greybeard' 18 *see also* Bellarmine, Bartmann

Hale, Jennie **42–43**, 98
Halliday, George 110
Hamada, Shoji 44, 47
Hamer, Frank **89**
Hamlyn, Jane 51, 57, **59–60**, 61, **80**, **88**, 116, 128–29
Hamlyn, Ted 109, 128, 129
Hammond, Lisa **104**, 137, **138–39**
Hansen, Bente 154, **155**
Hanssen Piggot, Gwyn 55, 96
Harrison, Steve **71**, 109–10, **147–48**
Harrow College of Art 50, **51**, 57, 59, 63, 65, 67, 68, 86, 94, 96, 137, 146
Harvey, Rebecca **134**
health and safety 78, 101, 103, 106, 123, 142, 143, 145
heat work 123
heavy firebrick 104, 108, 110–12
Hewitt, Mark 162, **163**
Hohr-Grenzhausen 16
Hoy, Agnete (Anita) **41**
HTI bricks 105–8, 111–12
Huggett, Barry **102**
Hungary 158
hunting jugs and mugs **31–32**
Hurn, Tim **131**

imports and exports 11, 14, 16, 17, 18, 23
India 159
industrial production 31–41
international salt glaze **152–163**
Ireland 98, 158
iron oxides 80–81, 127, 128
iron pyrites 82, 87
Ismay, W.A. (Bill) 66

Japan 44, 49, 54
Jefferson, Cathi **153**
Jenkins, Chris 126
Johnson, Robert **52**

Keeler, Walter 51, **57–59**, 96
Killigrew, Captain 18

kiln atmosphere 11–15, 17, 121 *see also* oxidation, reduction
kilns 21, **28**, 55, 101–17
  care and repair 107, 108–9
  coke-fired at Oxshott **45**, 46
  early British 19, 21
  early European 10–11
  flat-pack 143
  gas-fired 111–114
  oil-fired 110, 113, 128–29
  packing 117–120
  unpacking 127
  wood-fired 55, 110, 130–1, 148, 150–1
  see also firings, fuels
King, Ruth **88**

La Borne *see* France
Lambeth Studios 34–42
Langerwehe 12
Launder, Richard 52, **53**, **132**, 141, **142**
Leach, Bernard 44, 74
Leach, David 44
Leach, Janet 44
leaching 87, 92
legislation 73, 74, 76
Lion Salt Works **71**
Littler-Wedgwood blue 30
Liverpool 23
Lockwood, Sandra **153**
London 22, 23, 32–2, 73
loose bricks 107
low-temperature salt 53, **140–3**
Lynch, Joseph 86

Mableson, Gus 77, 78, **98**, 116
McErlain, Alex **69**, **80**, **82**, 94, **126**
McGarva, Andrew **53**, 54, 65
Mansfield, Janet 7, **152**
manufacturers:
  C.J.C. Bailey **38**
  Doulton **33–42**
  James Stiff 33
  Jones, Watts and Doulton 34
  Stephen Green 33
Margrie, Victor 50
Martin brothers 39, 44, 45
'Martinware' **39–40**
Meanley, Peter 76, **90**, 105, 108
Michael, Kristine 159, **160**
Miller, David **141**
Milway, Toff 51, 94, **96**, **97**, 111, **112**, **117**, 129
Minchin, Maureen **98**
Morley, James 23–4
Mowatt, Zelda 61
Murray, Rosie and Renton 160, **161**

Netherlands 159
New Zealand 49, 110, 160
Newcastle 18
Norway 162
Nottingham ware 23–25, 96, 98

oil firing 102–3, 110, 113, 128–9
'orange-peel' **8**, 11,**14**, 44, 82, 85, 93, 94, 119, 134, 147, 150, 151
O'Mahony, Marcus 158, **159**
Osborne, Andrew 42, **43**, 98
oxidation 11, 81, 121 *see also* kiln atmosphere
oxides 17, 20, 80–81, 87–88, 120, 127, 128, 142
Oxshott Pottery 45–48

packing 117–120
Parmalee, Cullen 75
patents 18–22, 23, 27
Pedley, Christine 54, **55**
'placing' *see* packing
Ploeger, Pauline 160, **161**
'plucking' 118
pollution 13, 45, 72–77
porcelain 20, 49, **80**, 89, **91**, 97
'Potteries' 23, 27, 29
problems 114, 128, *see also* pollution
props **115**, 116, **117**
protective coatings 107–8, 111–12, 113, 115
purge chimney 78
pyrometer 119, 123

Raeren 14–16
raku 142, 143
raw fring 122, 128, 129
raw glaze 91, 92, 93, 99, 100
recipes:
  batt wash 116
  castable 106
  clay body 86, 97, 99
  glazes 92–3, 97–9
  kiln repair 109
  kiln wash 108
  mortar 105, 120
  slips 84, 86, 88–90, 94, 97–9, 135
  wadding 116
recording results 127–8, 122
reduction 11, 81, 121, 122 *see also* kiln atmosphere
regional centres 9, 22–27
Reeve, John 51
refractory materials 103–6
research 10, 76–77, 79, 85, 89, 105, 111
residual salt 46, **47**, 49, 53, **132–133**
Reynolds, Petra 130–1, 148–**149**
Rhineland 9–17, 20
Rich, Mary **49**
rim wash 118
Rogers, Phil 93–**94**, **118**
Rous, Thomas 18
rouletting **24–6**, **30**, **147**

St Ives Pottery 44–45, 74
saggars **19**, 25, 28, 120, 143
salt:
from Spain 19
rock salt deposits 27, 71
tax 30
type 125
salt glaze:
alchemy 8, 71
chemistry and process 8, 10, 72, 79
discovery 10
see also firings, kilns
salting 45, 46, 78, 113–4, 123–7, 130–1, 134
damp salt **123**, 125
drip feed 50, 126–27
dry blown 113, 125
sprayed 127, 130–1, **138**, 139, 140
'Saltzbrand' 152
Saxony 17
Schonemann, Regine **157**
Schloessingk, Micki 51, 57, **61–63**, 67, 87, **87**, 110, **118**
'schnelle' **12**, 15
Scotland 9, 18, 52
'scratch-blue' **30**, **36**
'scrubber' system 46, **77–8**
sculpture **55**, **64**, 143, **155**
Shattuk, Ann 137
Shaw, Simeon 27, 73
shells 117, **118**, **131**
shelves 107, **115–117**
Shynkaruk, Will 76
Siegburg 12
silica 8, 10, 14, 72, 75, 80–82, 97, 104–5
Simmance, Eliza **37**
Skognes, John 162, **163**
slips 11, **83–90**, **94–100**
'smalt'and 'smaltebewurf' 17
Smith, Mark **151**
soaking 11, 13, 14, 120, 124, 129, 130, 139
soda compounds 134, 137
soda glaze:
chemistry and process 75, 137
description 8, 137–140
see also firings, kilns
sodium chloride 72
sodium bicarbonate 75
sprigging 24, **26**, **31–2**, 45
spy hole 119, 121
stacking **87**, **115**, 119–20, **139**
stacking scars **11**, 117, **118**
Staffordshire 23, 73
Staffordshire wares 26–30
Starkey, Peter 7, 51, 57, 59, **67–8**
Stengel, Gill 77
Steward, Jeremy 66, 100, **102**, 130–1, 148, **150**
stoneware 9–12, 18–21, 79, 83, 141
Stubbs, Paul 110
Swain, Helen *see* Walters-Swain, Helen
Sydenham, Guy and Russell 49, **50**, 67

Taylor, Steve 119
'terra sigillata' 142
'tiger' ware **14**, **15**, 52
Tinworth, George **35**
trial rings *see* draw rings
trials and tests:
bricks and coatings 114
comparisons **135–7**
slips 84, 85–6, 87
trolly kiln 104, **138–9**
Troy, Jack 7
Tudball, Ruthanne **139–40**
tumble stack 52, **120**
Twyford, Joshua 27

United States of America 162

vapour:
agents 101, 134
attack 103–6
distribution 118–9, 121
glaze 8, 71, 145
pressure 10, 72, 76, 113
recent research 76–7
see also firings
vitrification 10, 79–81 *see also* clay

wadding 115–8
Waldenburg 17
Walters-Swain, Helen 41, **42**
Walton, Sarah 51, 57, **63–4**, 65, 98
Wedgwood 27, 147
Westerwald **16**, **17**, 19, **20**, **33**
Whatley, Stuart **85**
whiteware **29**
wicket 105, 119–20
Winchcombe Pottery 94–5
witches bottles **21**
wood-firing 55, 102, 110, 130–1, 148, 150–1
Wooltus, Symon 18
Woolwich Ferry 18
Wren, Denise **45–8**
Wren, Rosemary **45–9**, 67